Praise for Bill Vlasic's *Once Upon a Car*

"Essential account of the United States auto industry."
                            —*New York Times Book Review,* Editor's Choice

"Compelling. . . . A human approach to an industry that couldn't be less human in scale. . . . Entertaining."   —*Wall Street Journal*

"The book is extraordinary. Vlasic offers what will probably become the definitive retelling of the crisis that nearly felled America's three car-making icons."   —*Los Angeles Times*

"With almost anthropological precision, *Once Upon a Car* is a thorough and compelling account of the collapse of the domestic auto industry."
                            —*Plain Dealer* (Cleveland)

"*Once Upon a Car* is the best book on the whole shebang that you are ever going to read. . . . A critical history."   —*Huffington Post*

"A deeply reported, full-on narrative in the style of *Barbarians at the Gate* or *Game Change.*"   —*Chicago Tribune*

"Even with all the ink spilled on Detroit lately, Vlasic's tale is as fresh as a new car. . . . Vlasic says he wanted to write a fast-paced narrative, and he's penned a page-turner in *Once Upon a Car.*"   —*Fortune.com*

"In a first-rate blend of journalism and history, *New York Times* Detroit bureau chief Vlasic rides the perfect storm that only yesterday threatened to undo America's auto industry. . . . Vlasic's tale unfolds urgently, even suspensefully, and it shows why heads had to roll in order to make the 'clean and pristine' new companies of today."
                            —*Kirkus Reviews* (starred review)

"Vlasic delivers a devastating account of auto industry arrogance, ignorance, and tragedy."   —*Publishers Weekly*

"Terrific . . . better than most novels . . . truly fascinating."
                            —*Free Lance-Star* (Virginia)

"Vlasic enriches his journalistic attention to detail with the drama and pacing of a thriller."   —800ceoRead.com

"Vlasic is a master storyteller whose prowess makes the absorption of many complex facts painless."   —strategy-business.com

ALSO BY BILL VLASIC

Taken for a Ride: How Daimler-Benz Drove Off with Chrysler

ONCE UPON A CAR

The Fall and Resurrection of America's Big Three Automakers—GM, Ford, and Chrysler

Bill Vlasic

wm

WILLIAM MORROW

An Imprint of HarperCollins*Publishers*

HarperCollins books may be purchased for educational, business, or sales promotional use. For information please write: Special Markets Department, HarperCollins Publishers, 10 East 53rd Street, New York, NY 10022.

A hardcover edition of this book was published in 2011 by William Morrow, an imprint of HarperCollins Publishers.

FIRST WILLIAM MORROW PAPERBACK EDITION PUBLISHED 2012.

———

The Library of Congress has cataloged the hardcover edition as follows:

Vlasic, Bill.
    Once upon a car : the fall and resurrection of America's big three automakers—GM, Ford, and Chrysler / Bill Vlasic. — 1st ed.
        p. cm.
    Summary: "The Detroit bureau chief for the *New York Times* takes readers inside the Big Three U.S. automakers for the rise and fall—and rise again?—of this quintessentially American industry"—Provided by publisher.
    ISBN 978-0-06-184562-8 (hardback) — ISBN 978-0-06-184563-5 (trade pb) — ISBN 978-0-06-204222-4 (e-book) 1. Automobile industry and trade—United States—History. 2. Chrysler Corporation. 3. General Motors Corporation. 4. Ford Motor Company. I. Title.
HD9710.U52V53   2011
338.4'76292220973—dc23
                                                                                    2011020572

———

12 13 14 15 16   OV/RRD   10 9 8 7 6 5 4 3 2 1

For my parents, Robert and Nancy Vlasic

[One]

Larry Buhl had been planning this rendezvous for months, and today was finally the day.

It was the second week in January, and the 2005 North American International Auto Show was in full swing in downtown Detroit. The Cobo Center convention floor, bigger than a dozen football fields, was a mass of people roaming like herds among the exhibits of the world's biggest automakers. The elaborate displays of the hometown giants, General Motors and Ford, owned one side of the hall. The German luxury brands Mercedes-Benz and BMW anchored the other end.

And somewhere in the middle was the man Buhl was looking for.

He walked along the carpeted paths between the million-dollar show stands, each one reflecting the company behind it—sleek and futuristic at Honda and Nissan, lots of chrome and bright colors at Dodge and Chrysler, stark backdrops and pretty women in slinky dresses at Ferrari and Lamborghini. Cars of every size and shape were bathed in bright spotlights, polished and posed for the hordes of journalists and camera crews and auto executives that swarmed around the hall.

Buhl felt right at home. He lived in Connecticut but had grown up just down the road in Grosse Pointe, Michigan. He had been going to the show for years. It was like an extension of the holidays in Detroit—Christmas, New Year's, auto show. It was also the perfect place to blend into a crowd and meet someone unnoticed. Buhl crossed the convention floor, took a turn behind the man-made mountain with a Jeep hanging off it, made a left at the Toyota exhibit, and spied the smallest, plainest stand in the entire place—three quirky little cars surrounded by college-age sales reps in polo shirts and khakis. And there, working by the red Scion sign, was Jim Farley.

Since last summer, Buhl had been trying to set up a meeting between Farley, a rising executive at Toyota and head of its new Scion division, and one of Buhl's oldest friends, William Clay Ford Jr., the chairman and chief executive officer of the Ford Motor Company. The idea came to Buhl during a conversation with Farley's father on a golf course in northern Michigan, where the Farley and Buhl families had owned vacation homes for years. "Something struck me when I saw Jim's dad," Buhl recalled. "I thought Ford could really use a guy like Jim."

Larry Buhl had known Bill Ford since they were kids. They went to private schools together, played the same sports, socialized throughout college, and stayed close into their mid-forties. One went on to become a successful entrepreneur buying and selling specialty metals on the East Coast. The other became the leader of the second-biggest car company in the world.

Buhl cherished their bond, but lately he had been worried about his friend. He saw what the pressure of running the Ford Motor Company, his family's business for more than a hundred years, was doing to Bill. Executives came and went at Ford headquarters, but none of them was able to help Bill stave off the flood of Toyotas, Hondas, and other foreign cars that were relentlessly beating Ford in the market. Buhl saw Bill's spirits sag when they talked about it. "It's too much for you," he kept telling him. "How can you shoulder all of this responsibility yourself?"

What Ford needed was fresh blood. Buhl would never be so presumptuous as to suggest to Bill that he hire Jim Farley. But if he could get the two of them together, who knew what might happen? When he brought it up, Bill said sure, he was open to it. It was a little trickier to convince Farley. Buhl's brother Robbie, a professional race car driver and fellow car fanatic, had been tight with Farley for years. Still, when Buhl called Farley, he was cool to the idea of sitting down with anyone at one of Toyota's biggest competitors.

"I'm not interested in going anyplace," Farley said. "I'm really happy at Toyota."

"Come on," Buhl said. "I'm just talking about introducing you to a friend of mine."

"I don't feel comfortable about this," Farley said. "Things are going so well for us, and for me."

"You have to meet him," Buhl said.

"Why?"

"Because," Buhl said, "it's good for you."

Now as he walked toward the Scion stand, Buhl still didn't know if Farley would ever consider leaving Toyota. What he did know was that Jim Farley could sell cars as well as anyone on the planet.

And he was proving it every day. In just two years, Farley had grown Toyota's new Scion brand, created specifically for younger buyers, from zero sales in the United States to 100,000 vehicles a year. His bosses in Japan and in Los Angeles had entrusted him to somehow make bland and reliable Toyota hip, and he embraced the challenge. Farley took Scion cars to rock concerts, street festivals, and college campuses—anywhere that Generation Y hung out. He was constantly on the road, setting up Scion showrooms inside existing Toyota dealerships, and making them cool, pressure-free boutiques for these interesting little Japanese cars with funky designs and small engines.

Farley inhabited the job completely—hanging out with twenty-something trendsetters on the coasts, learning why they chose their favorite products, from computers to clothes to cars. "You need to love your customer, feel their joy, understand their pain," he said. "You have to get so close to them you can smell their breath."

But as sensitive and idealistic as he sounded, Farley had an edge to him. Other automakers were the enemy vying for the same turf, and Farley would never give an inch. When he heard that Bob Lutz, the vice chairman of General Motors, had called the shoebox-shaped Scion xB "weird-looking," those were fighting words. "I could care less about Detroit," Farley said. "Give me a break. Detroit got its ass kicked trying to market to kids."

At the Scion stand, Farley was in his element—chatting up reporters, showing off the cars, greeting visitors. With a mop of brown hair flopped over his forehead and wearing a suit that looked just a size too big, Farley seemed younger than his forty-two years. He also was having way more fun than the buttoned-down, deadly serious executives holding court at the other displays. The media flocked to him, and he rarely disappointed. He was provocative, blunt, and unafraid to criticize an older generation's view of today's young consumer. "These kids are not Camaro buyers from the seventies being reincarnated," he said. "These people are sharp. They have higher expectations." He said it all with a mischievous smile that called to mind his late cousin, the comedian Chris Farley of *Saturday Night Live* fame. He even sounded like Chris, especially when he laughed.

When he saw Buhl walking up, Farley greeted him warmly, like the old family friend he was. They walked across the convention floor together and into the busy hallway dominated by a big bronze statue of the boxer Joe Louis, the embodiment of Motor City muscle. The second they entered the parking garage, Farley started shivering, the bitter chill of January in Detroit a reality check for a guy who lived and worked in Southern California. They hustled to Buhl's car and headed out onto Michigan Avenue, six lanes of blacktop bisecting some of the city's bleakest neighborhoods, and into the adjoining community of Dearborn, the home of the Ford Motor Company.

Farley was quiet as they passed the falafel joints, strip clubs, and discount stores that lined the wide avenue. In the distance he could see the belching smokestacks of Ford's famous Rouge assembly complex, stretching more than a mile long and wide, with dozens of factories, some dating back to the 1920s. The heavy gray cloud cover seemed to sit on top of the buildings, and everything looked frozen solid. *I'm from Santa Monica, I work in Torrance, I go to Toyota City in Japan,* Farley said to himself. *That's my auto industry. This is just so . . . old.*

Why would he want to meet anybody at Ford? Farley lived and breathed Toyota. He had loved the company from the day he joined it fifteen years earlier, when Toyota was an underdog fighting for respect in the American market. Farley had basically devoted his life to winning customers away from what he saw as declining, inferior carmakers such as Ford. To Farley, the car business was a highly refined arena of combat, and he had no doubt he was on the winning side. "We're the good guys, the ones wearing the white hats," he said. Farley believed that Toyota made the safest and most sensible, affordable, and fuel-efficient cars in the world. Ford was a dinosaur that lived on an unsustainable diet of gas-guzzling pickup trucks and monster SUVs. There was no question which company was growing and which one was fading. In a few days the final numbers for 2004 would make it official. Toyota had just passed Ford in global sales and was fast closing in on the number one spot, held for more than seventy years by the biggest of Detroit's Big Three, General Motors.

When he agreed to this meeting, Farley had made Buhl promise that it would be in secret, far from the auto show and certainly not at Ford's corporate headquarters. It wasn't exactly treasonous for an up-and-coming Toyota exec to get to know the major players in Detroit better, and there was no one bigger in Detroit than Bill Ford. But Farley was a little worried that someone would recognize him and that word might get back to his colleagues at Toyota.

He relaxed when they arrived at the spot for this clandestine get-together—the sprawling $35 million headquarters and training camp that Bill Ford's father, William Clay Ford Sr., had built for his beloved Detroit Lions football team in the suburban city of Allen Park. The Lions were never doing much in January. Their season had ended weeks earlier, as usual, with a losing record and another year in which they were shut out of the playoffs. The place was pretty quiet with all the players gone. At least, Farley thought, no one would see him here. They walked in the main entrance and checked in at the desk in front of a wall-size mural of great Lions players of the past. As they approached the executive offices, Buhl started getting a little nervous. This was, after all, his idea. Should he just make introductions and offer to wait outside? He suddenly realized he didn't know Farley as well as he knew Bill.

Just then, Bill Ford bounded out of his office to greet them. Farley was immediately struck by how young he was—just five years older than him—and how animated and friendly. Bill was of average height and trim like a runner, his custom-tailored blue suit accenting strikingly blue eyes. He had a way of talking fast, like he couldn't wait to share an idea or a story. The three of them sat down and, in a flash, Bill was talking about Ford—its history, its people, and how much it meant to him. "The passion I have for this company is making people's lives better," he said. "It's up to us, up to me, to look to the future."

Farley just listened as Bill went on about his family—which had absolute power over Ford through its special voting stock—and its unwavering commitment to the car business.

"We've definitely taken our lumps, but it's never been about the financial investment," Bill said. "We're in it for the long term."

Buhl kept eyeing Farley, who seemed transfixed. He could sense Farley's mind racing, waiting for the right opportunity to jump into the conversation. When Bill finally asked him about his new Scion job, Farley was a bit defensive at first.

"You know, I've been with Toyota for fifteen years," he said. "I've been in marketing and sales in Europe. I was the first product planner for Lexus. I laid out the whole product plan for Lexus with the engineering team in Japan."

Now Bill was the attentive one, nodding and asking follow-up questions and probing for more information. After a few minutes, Farley felt completely at ease. He had met a lot of auto executives in his career, but Bill was not like any of them. "It wasn't like he was happy-go-lucky, but he had a joie de vivre about him," Farley said later. "He loved certain things."

When the two of them started comparing their favorite classic cars, in particular the Ford Mustang, Buhl couldn't help but smile. *I've never seen such an instant rapport,* he thought. *It's just two guys talking about their passion for automobiles and the business.*

The discussion turned to marketing, Farley's specialty, and Bill made a joke about Ford's latest generic advertising campaign, "Built for the Road Ahead." Farley had to laugh. He and his Toyota buddies thought it was one of the lamest ad slogans they'd ever heard.

Then, out of the blue, Bill popped the question. "What would you do if you were running it?" he asked Farley.

Okay, Farley thought, *here's the sales pitch.* "Well, I'm not interested in going to Ford," he said.

Bill acted as if he hadn't heard him.

"You know, I need help," he said softly. "We're looking for someone who can help."

Farley was taken aback. He wasn't sure he'd heard him right. Bill Ford was asking for his help? There was vulnerability in his voice, a raw honesty that Farley hadn't anticipated. He wondered where the pressure was, the hard sell, the lucrative financial carrot he'd expected to be dangled to lure him to Ford. But it never came.

The hour passed quickly, and Buhl barely said a word. When they all got up and shook hands at the end, Bill held his grip with Farley a little long, then pulled a card from his pocket.

"I think there's a place for you here," he said to Farley. "Here's my number. Let's stay in touch. I want you to call me. I want you to know that I'm here whenever you need me."

Buhl did most of the talking on the drive back downtown, hardly able to contain his enthusiasm over how well it all had gone. But Farley didn't hear much of it. The words "whenever you need me" were stuck in his head.

Whenever I need him? Who, Farley wondered, *needs who here?*

[Two]

Rick Wagoner never gave a speech without checking and rechecking every word he said as the chairman and chief executive officer of the General Motors Corporation. He not only pored over speeches but scrutinized any press release, document, letter, or internal communication that his aides drafted in his name. Wagoner was particularly attentive to quotes attributed to him. "I don't want to ever say anything publicly that I might have to retract," he told his staff. He had another hard-and-fast rule, a mantra drilled into him by Jack Smith, his mentor and predecessor as the top man at the biggest car company the world had ever seen. "We don't want to ever overpromise," he said, "and underdeliver."

As Farley was heading back to the auto show after meeting Bill Ford, Wagoner was preparing to leave it. The "GM Experience" at the show was—no surprise—the grandest corporate display in the hall. More than a hundred cars, trucks, and sport-utility vehicles were decked out on the floor, and each of GM's eight North American brands, from mighty Chevrolet down to the tiny Saab division, had its own special area. In one corner was a large stage with a giant movie screen behind it for the gala press events to introduce new models. Above the stage was a full second floor that doubled as a showroom for new technology and a coffee bar or cocktail lounge, depending on the hour.

Wagoner was working in a temporary office hidden behind a thick black curtain near the stage set. Most of GM's senior executives had rooms there to do interviews, hold private meetings, and generally conduct business. General Motors hardly stopped running during the weeklong media previews. It just relocated its command center to the row of drafty cubicles that backed up against the convention center's loading docks.

The press conferences were over, but there was one last show-related duty to attend to. In midafternoon on January 13, 2005, Wagoner, along with all the other senior GM executives, marched out of the building onto Jefferson Avenue. Waiting for them at the curb was a line of very large sport-utility vehicles—Chevrolet Suburbans, GMC Yukons, and Cadillac Escalades—with their V-8 engines idling. GM sold nearly nine million vehicles each year. But these giant SUVs were the pride of the fleet—eighteen-foot-long, seven-thousand-pound, seven-passenger land yachts with every option known to man. Wagoner got in the first one, a black Escalade ESV with a GM driver behind the wheel. As always, he rode shotgun, up front in the deep leather passenger seat.

As the caravan pulled out, Wagoner reviewed the speech he was about to give. In twenty minutes he would walk into a hotel ballroom and address the Auto Analysts of New York, the watchdogs of the auto industry for the major investment banks on Wall Street. Their research reports were critical factors in daily decisions by investors to buy, sell, or hold a stock. Wagoner knew his remarks this afternoon would generate instant headlines and directly affect the value of the 564 million shares of stock that constituted ownership of General Motors.

If there was ever a time to watch his words carefully, this was it. GM had already endured a rough week in the stock market. Its share price had fallen for four straight days. The Street had not been this worried about the company's financial condition since the early

1990s, when GM came close to bankruptcy, fired its chief executive, and embarked on a seemingly endless series of restructurings. The automaker sold an average of twenty-four thousand cars each day in two hundred countries. But it was operating on razor-thin margins of profitability. Investors had a bad case of the jitters about GM. It was up to Wagoner to calm them down.

Six foot four, broad-shouldered, and wearing his usual pinstriped suit, white shirt, and solid tie, George Richard Wagoner Jr. cut an impressive figure. He had a long, serious face: high forehead, big chin, and jowly neck that looked out of place on a fit former college basketball player who would turn fifty-two years old in a month.

Wagoner stood ramrod straight and spoke in flat, even tones, with a slight southern accent from his Virginia upbringing. In public settings, he was unfailingly congenial, polite, and friendly. Most of the auto analysts had known Rick Wagoner for years. He had spent his entire working life at GM, and five years earlier had become the youngest chief executive in the company's storied history. In May 2003, the GM board of directors elected him its chairman, giving Wagoner wide authority over every facet of corporate strategy and direction. He had the perfect GM résumé—star analyst in the New York treasurer's office, head of finance in Europe, managing director in Brazil, chief financial officer, president of North American operations. By the time he reached the top, it seemed as if Wagoner had been chosen every step of the way to one day lead the world's most powerful automobile company.

Yet to many of the analysts, Wagoner was still an enigma. He was energetic, extremely smart, and clearly devoted to making GM a success. Yet the performance of GM was plodding, confusing, and generally underwhelming. Wagoner loved catchphrases—"run lean," "think global." But nobody would ever describe GM as lean or globally integrated compared to its chief rival, Toyota. Wagoner often likened GM to a premier professional athlete. "The big and the fast beat the small and fast," he said. GM was big all right—324,000 employees, assembly plants in thirty-two countries, and more models and brands than any other automaker. But whenever GM took on a new initiative, such as entering an emerging vehicle segment or downsizing its immense bureaucracy, it moved at a glacial pace.

The three dozen analysts at the Ritz-Carlton had spent most of the day hearing presentations from Ford and several of the big auto suppliers. GM was last on the list. When Wagoner stepped to the podium, he opened with a line that many in attendance swore they had heard before. "The theme of my talk today is going to be playing our own game," he said, "and playing it to win."

Nobody groaned at the analogy. They were all used to Wagoner's sports clichés. But they weren't as forgiving when Wagoner began comparing the current state of GM to when it hit bottom in 1992. "What I'm going to convince you of is that, in fact, the situation today is dramatically different and in fact dramatically better," he said.

The analysts didn't need convincing. All Wall Street wanted to know was how much money GM expected to make in the next twelve months.

GM was previously on record as predicting it could earn $10 per share in 2005, or about $5.6 billion in profits. Its 2004 numbers were well short of that. And as Wagoner went on and on about the great strides the company had made, a few analysts began to lose patience. *They deserve credit for how far they've come,* thought John Casesa of Merrill Lynch, who had been studying GM for years. *But we're trying to figure out how to value them now.*

Wagoner wasn't straying from his script. His mission was to defend GM and assure investors that it was—and always would be—a winner. "Our progress over the last decade has moved us from a company that was uncompetitive to a company that is very competitive," he said. And with that, he turned the microphone over to John Devine, GM's chief financial officer. This was the moment Wall Street was waiting for. It was getting close to 4:00 P.M., when the market closed. The meeting was being broadcast live over the Internet, so traders and investors could react immediately. With the clock ticking down, Devine broke the news. "For 2005, for earnings we're looking at a target of $4 to $5 earnings per share," he said.

Within seconds, GM's stock price started dropping. By the closing bell, it was down 3 percent for the day to a new fifty-two-week low of $37.32. The losing streak in the market was now five days and counting. By the time Devine finished talking, GM's stock was worth $21 billion in total—about $650 million less than it had been ten minutes earlier.

The meeting ran on, with multiple executives giving detailed presentations on Europe, China, employee health care costs, and new car projects. But in the question-and-answer session at the end, the focus kept circling back to the 2005 forecast. One analyst, Rod Lache of Deutsche Bank, was particularly curious about any possible shortfall in GM's all-important U.S. vehicle sales. "Are you guys anticipating any kind of volume decline?" he asked. Wagoner took the question but didn't answer it. "We don't want to go into that yet," he said. "We will give you a report on a regular basis . . . so you know what's going on."

Afterward, Wagoner couldn't hide his frustration. After taking such care to describe GM's comeback since the dark days, all Wall Street was interested in was short-term results. "I don't believe those guys," he snapped to an aide. "Don't they know how hard it is to get 75 percent of this business right?" But as quickly as he angered, he just as quickly calmed down. Getting mad or losing his cool was not Wagoner's style. He was a problem solver, a steady hand, and, above all, a true believer in the strength and purpose of General Motors. Besides, he understood the financial numbers better than anyone. And as bad as the reaction was now, Wagoner knew there was more trouble ahead.

A week later, GM announced that its corporate profits had plunged 37 percent in the final quarter of 2004. Losses were mounting in Europe, and its market share in the United States had fallen to a new low of 26 percent. Then, in mid-February, the company stunned investors when it agreed to pay $2 billion to the Italian automaker Fiat to dissolve an ill-fated joint venture overseas.

With each dose of bad news, GM's stock price sank lower. When it hit $36 a share, the telephone rang in Jerry York's condominium in a quiet suburb about forty miles north of Detroit. York had been wondering when Kirk Kerkorian would call.

"Jerry, have you been seeing what's happening with GM stock?" Kerkorian asked.

"Yeah, Kirk, it's getting hammered," York said. "I almost called you yesterday to talk about it."

The phone went silent for a moment. Kerkorian was eighty-seven years old, and his net worth was about $10 billion. He was never much of a talker. After about a minute's pause, he continued.

"How long would it take you to do a deep dive on this thing?" he said. "You know, see what you think of it?"

"Should take me a couple of weeks," York said. "I'll get right on it."

Kerkorian hung up and settled back in his office around the corner from Rodeo Drive in Beverly Hills, California.

York turned on his computer, typed in the Internet address for the General Motors corporate website, and started reading.

General Motors was running out of parking lots. Every day, unsold cars, trucks, and SUVs were piling up across the country, and there was no room left outside its assembly plants. So the company stockpiled them wherever it could find space—airports, empty shopping malls, state fairgrounds. By the end of February 2005, GM had an astonishing back inventory of 1.3 million automobiles in North America, more than double what would ever be considered normal.

The surplus didn't happen overnight. For five years, the American auto industry had been producing cars at a feverish pace. Enticed by cheap loans and fat rebates, consumers were buying seventeen million new vehicles annually. And the competition to fill their garages had never been hotter. The big Japanese companies—Toyota, Honda, and Nissan—were steadily increasing imports and expanding production in their U.S. plants. In an all-out bid to defend their market shares, the Detroit automakers churned out more and more vehicles.

But GM's sales weren't growing; they were dropping, 12 percent in February alone. And the bloated inventory was absolutely killing its cash flow. General Motors spent huge sums to buy parts for its cars and to pay the workers who made them. But it received no revenues until car dealers—its real customers—purchased the products. The obvious solution was to slow down production and bring it more in line with demand. But GM's labor contract with the United Auto Workers penalized the company if it cut a shift at a plant or temporarily sent workers home. It still had to pay idled employees nearly their full wages, even when there wasn't enough work for them to do. Moreover, GM was paying tons of money in health care benefits to hundreds of thousands of blue-collar retirees and surviving spouses of deceased autoworkers.

Decisions had to be made, and fast. In early February, the company's board of directors convened on the thirty-ninth floor of Tower 300 of the GM Renaissance Center, the company's world headquarters in downtown Detroit. All eyes in the room turned to Wagoner. He was facing the first true crisis in his five years as chief executive. He opened the meeting by outlining a critical task that would take months to complete: convincing the UAW to accept cuts in health care. All of the GM directors wholeheartedly backed that. Whatever it took, they considered reducing health care costs a crucial short- and long-term goal.

Then Wagoner laid out his action plan. First he would overhaul sales and marketing, and immediately start a new campaign to reduce inventories. Then GM would speed up the timetable for its most important new product, the T-900, which was a completely new version of GM's high-profit pickup trucks and big SUVs. Finally, Wagoner would assume daily responsibility for running the struggling North American operations.

Vice chairman Bob Lutz and group vice president Gary Cowger would be relieved of their duties as chairman and president of the unit. Neither of them had proven adept at managing the factories, suppliers, and layer upon layer of sales, marketing, and communication staffs. Moreover, they clashed on a personal level. Other GM execs were still talking about how the two had bickered over which one would take center stage at the latest auto show press events.

Lutz claimed that he didn't care and that Wagoner was welcome to take on the mundane details of supervising the legions of workers in North America. Privately he simmered, and he began sarcastically referring to Wagoner as "our commander in chief." Yet as a former Marine Corps fighter pilot, Lutz would never buck orders from above. And he totally agreed with the decision to accelerate the T-900. Pickups and SUVs made more money for GM than virtually all of its other models combined.

Early the next morning, Lutz cruised into work in his personal McDonnell Douglas MD-500 helicopter, traveling at 150 miles per hour from the airport near his house outside Ann Arbor, Michigan, to GM's immense technical center in the city of Warren, north of Detroit. His first meeting of the day was with the two dozen senior engineers and planners on the T-900 team. Lutz rarely called emergency sessions like this. Something big was up.

"Can we pull these trucks ahead by several months?" Lutz asked the group. "Tell me the reasons why it can't be done. Then tell me what it would take to make those reasons go away."

Gary White, the head of the T-900 team, swallowed hard. Accelerating a program as complex as this was rarely done. Everybody had to go faster, from the designers to the engineers, suppliers, and plants. On top of that, an intricate schedule of safety and durability tests had to be torn up and rewritten. But White knew Lutz wasn't looking to hear about the problems. "We can do it," White said. "It's like conducting the orchestra. Everybody just has to play the song a little faster."

But White was concerned about the other vehicle programs in line ahead of the T-900 in GM's research and testing labs. Lutz said he would personally make sure the trucks had top priority. "It's kind of like when you go to Disneyland in a wheelchair," he said with a grin. "You always get to go to the head of the line."

Even with a new timetable, the big trucks still wouldn't hit the market for another year, and GM was hemorrhaging cash right now.

On March 16, a press release headlined "GM Revises Earnings Outlook" went out over the newswire. "Clearly we have significant challenges in North America," said Wagoner's statement. But the bombshell was the forecast. Not only wouldn't GM earn anything close to the $4 to $5 a share in profits in 2005 that it had promised just two months earlier, but the company now expected to lose as much as $1 billion in the first quarter of the year.

"That was," said John Casesa, the veteran Merrill Lynch analyst, "the 'oh shit' moment."

GM's stock went into instant free fall. By the end of the day, it had dropped 14 percent to $29.01—its lowest level in eleven years. It was the automaker's largest single-day share loss since the stock market collapse of 1987. The pummeling by investors was so brutal it dragged the entire Dow Jones Industrial Average down 112 points.

Every analyst who had advised clients in January that GM was going to be okay felt betrayed. Casesa, who had worked at GM as a product planner in the 1980s, couldn't type fast enough to revise his analysis of the company. "We expect the company's accelerated market share decline will continue to severely impact earnings and cash flow," he wrote.

But that was the sanitized version of what Wall Street thought about Wagoner & Co. "These guys always think they are doing such a great job," Casesa said. "But institutionally they don't keep their promises, they don't follow through, they're not consistent, and they're not accountable." The market had been burned, and it was unforgiving. When Wagoner got on a conference call with the analysts, the questions came fast and furious. What about North America? How many factories did GM plan to close? How would the company reverse its slumping sales?

"North America is our eight-hundred-pound gorilla," Wagoner said calmly. "Today's announcement really shows how important it is that we get this business right."

But he refused to say how, or when, it would be fixed. That only ratcheted up the heat. What about Wagoner's job? Did the GM board still support him?

"The board is fully informed on all our strategies, and on that basis supportive," he said.

What exactly did that mean?

John Devine, the CFO, tried to make it clearer. "The board . . . it's got full confidence in Rick and the team."

No one knew it at the time, but the March 16 earnings outlook would be the last time GM would ever publicly make forecasts about its financial performance. That hardly mattered to Jerry York. He had heard enough. Since speaking to Kerkorian, York had spent hundreds of hours researching GM. He had devoured every government filing, earnings report, sales release, product review, and newspaper article, and had spoken to analysts, investors, reporters, car dealers, union leaders, and former GM executives. Then he dissected GM's balance sheet like a scientist seeking a cure for an exotic disease. York was one of the most respected financial minds in corporate America. Chrysler's legendary chairman, Lee Iacocca, had picked him to be his CFO, and Steve Jobs at Apple considered York his most valuable board member.

Kerkorian and York had changed history in Detroit once before. Together they had parlayed the big stake Kerkorian held in Chrysler in the 1990s into a $2 billion profit when the company merged with the German automotive giant Daimler-Benz in 1998. Now Kerkorian wanted York's considered opinion about buying a sizable stake in General Motors.

On April 1, York faxed Kerkorian a twelve-page analysis of GM. He prepared the document in a big, bold typeface to make it easy to read. In York's view, GM was out of shape, undisciplined, and far too full of itself. He believed there was a collection of valuable assets buried under a mountain of debt and excess brands, divisions, executives, and employees. He wasn't at all surprised that GM was losing a billion dollars a quarter. What did surprise him was that its board, its shareholders, and especially Rick Wagoner had allowed it to veer so far off track. York figured that GM had enough cash and salable parts—as much as $30 billion—to finance the most drastic restructuring in the history of the auto industry. And if it did so, the company would be a gold mine.

After reading York's bullet points, Kerkorian called him. And as usual, he got right to the point. "So, Jerry, you think we should buy?"

York didn't hesitate. "There's enough money to do the restructuring necessary to fix the company," he said. "So the $64,000 question is, do the board and the management have the fire in the belly to do it?"

Kerkorian didn't say a word. York hadn't really answered his question.

"Kirk," York said, "it's a no-brainer."

[Three]

It was 3:00 A.M., and try as he might, Bill Ford couldn't sleep. He lay awake staring at the ceiling, his mind churning thoughts he couldn't turn off. During the day, he exuded confidence and charm and lost himself in the details of running the Ford Motor Company. But at night, lying in bed, it was all questions. "What am I thinking?" he said when asked about it. "I'm thinking I need some help."

Sometimes he would flash back to the summer of 1979, just after his graduation from Princeton University. He had come home to his family's lakefront estate in Grosse Pointe Shores, a typical college grad trying to figure out his future. One evening, over a game of pool, he had a heart-to-heart talk with his father, William Clay Ford Sr.

"What do you think you'd like to do now?" his dad asked.

"I think I'd like to come and work for the company," Bill said.

His father's response was something Bill would never forget. "You know, you will have to be better than everyone else," he said, "because of who you are."

But Bill did do better than anyone expected. He never had to work a day in his life, but he harbored a sense of destiny, an idealistic spirit, and a profound appreciation of the incredible opportunity afforded him as the great-grandson of the Ford Motor Company's visionary founder, Henry Ford. Bill was determined to both fit in and excel at Ford, whether it was playing on the company hockey team or working through the night in labor talks with the UAW.

Under the watchful eye of his father and family loyalists on Ford's board of directors, Bill worked in product development and finance, did a stint in Europe, and earned his stripes in the unglamorous parts department and heavy-truck division. He joined Ford's board in 1988 at the age of thirty-one and, in 1999, with his family's backing, was elected its chairman. Two years later he grabbed the brass ring and fired Ford's chief executive, Jacques Nasser, and took the job himself.

It was his moment of triumph, and the realization of a lifelong dream. The extended Ford family—his parents, aunts and uncles, sisters, cousins, in-laws—believed in him, and the company's 320,000 employees embraced his leadership. On his first day as chief executive, hundreds of Ford workers stood and cheered as he walked onstage at the auditorium at company headquarters, some with tears streaming down their cheeks in gratitude that Bill Ford would return their company to its rightful place in the global hierarchy of automakers.

To the outside world, Bill Ford was the epitome of Motown Cool; the headline on a *Fortune* magazine cover had him looking totally hip in wraparound sunglasses. But the glossy image bore little resemblance to the harried executive clocking long hours at the Glass House, Ford's sleek rectangle of a headquarters in Dearborn. No matter how hard Bill tried to motivate and organize the vast Ford bureaucracy, it couldn't keep up with the rising tide of Japanese cars that were stealing its customers in droves. While the foreign automakers poured their resources into perfecting a select number of high-quality models, Ford squandered billions building different cars for different customers in different regions of the world.

Ford had been stuck in a dangerous, downward spiral that began long before Bill took command. It had been steadily losing ground to foreign competition for a decade. While the American auto market got bigger and bigger, Ford's share of the pie kept shrinking. Its international business wasn't much better. Ford had just introduced an amazing forty new models around the world, but it was barely making money on any of them. About 80¢ on every dollar it earned was generated by its finance company, Ford Credit, which was pushing cut-rate leases and low-interest loans to move inventory. If the economic bubble burst and consumers pulled back even slightly, Ford's finances could implode overnight. Ford's only purely profitable products were its venerable F-series pickup truck and a stable of aging sport-utilities such as the Explorer and Expedition—and even those needed thousands of dollars in rebates to attract buyers.

On April 8, three weeks after GM rattled investors with its dire profit warning, Ford issued its own disappointing forecast for 2005. It had been predicting earnings similar to the previous year's $3.5 billion. But sinking sales of its bellwether pickups and SUVs had torpedoed those estimates, and the company now said it would be lucky to earn two-thirds of that. "We are not immune to the broad economic challenges we all face in our industry," Bill Ford said in the press release. The explanation was sort of embarrassing because it came on the heels of news that his compensation package had totaled $22 million in 2004. He was the highest-paid auto executive in the business, and that revelation only added to his stress.

It was never Bill's style to rant and rave and cajole people to change. But in senior management meetings, his exasperation spilled over and the worries came cascading out. "We aren't going to get healthy until we use our economies of scale," he said. "We are way behind here. We desperately need to globalize this thing." He was particularly troubled by the passive acceptance of the notion that Ford needn't aspire to the same exacting standards as Toyota. He went so far as to formally ban the phrase "cheap and cheerful," which some jaded Ford execs used to describe their own cars. Instead, he insisted that everyone—from executives on down—adopt "back to basics" as the official Ford motto.

Ford had lost its way. It was like two totally different companies bolted together—the rich roster of European luxury brands head-lined by Jaguar, Volvo, and Land Rover, and its poor cousin, the blue-collar Ford division. None of the upscale brands made any money, yet for years they were run out of an elegant eighteenth-century mansion in London's exclusive Mayfair district. Meanwhile, Ford cranked out utilitarian SUVs and bland sedans in middle-class Dearborn.

As Ford lost more market share in the United States, the pain filtered down to the assembly lines. Plants in New Jersey, Michigan, and Ohio closed their doors. The Ford family had controlled the company for a century, and Bill had long felt connected to the men and women who punched a time clock every day. Yet when he visited the factories, design studios, and engineering labs, the pride and purpose were missing. "These people are the backbone of the company," he said. "They're terrific at what they do, but they aren't being valued."

His deeper concerns were personal ones. Did he have the intel-lect, the drive, and, above all, the experience to lead Ford out of the rut it had fallen into? He sensed doubt among his employees, and fear. "People are demoralized by our lack of focus," he said. To his closest confidants, he confessed that Ford might need a steadier hand than his. "I'm not the best person to operate this place," he told Joe Laymon, Ford's chief personnel officer. "I want to get somebody who can do it right."

Laymon was a hardened veteran in the field of human resources, having worked twenty years at Xerox and Kodak before joining Ford in 2000. He spent more time with Bill than just about anyone in the company, and he saw how the stress was suffocating his boss. But Laymon was astonished that Bill would consider giving up on being the CEO. Bill's humbling admission that he wasn't cut out for the job was a rarity in any business. "I think it's a courageous decision," Lay-mon told him. "But we can't let anyone in the company know. It would be devastating if people knew you were feeling this way."

. . . .

Nothing got under Bill's skin more than the infighting among his senior executives. Since taking over in 2001, Bill Ford had been repeatedly building and rebuilding his team in hopes of finding the right formula. But none of it worked. He compared the shifting alliances and relentless backstabbing to the *Survivor* television series.

The fighting got so bad Bill stopped chairing certain meetings, preferring to leave that duty to Nick Scheele, the affable, white-haired Brit who was Ford's president. Scheele, however, couldn't keep the peace between David Thursfield, the tough-talking head of international operations, and Jim Padilla, an old-line manufacturing veteran in charge of North and South America. Thursfield openly mocked Scheele ("The only thing he's good for is ordering the wine") and feuded incessantly with Padilla. During strategy sessions, Padilla refused to even look at Thursfield when he was talking. Younger executives didn't know what to make of it. "It's like shirts versus skins around here," said Mark Fields, who was emerging as a force in Ford's overseas divisions.

Bill bit the bullet and forced Thursfield to quit in 2004. When Scheele retired in January, Padilla became president, the number two position in the entire company. But Padilla was at best a stopgap, someone who would follow orders and keep the factories humming. He wasn't a leader. And that's what Bill Ford needed most: a leader and a partner who could help him make Ford great again.

Bill tried going outside the company. He aggressively courted Carlos Ghosn (rhymes with "cone"), an industry superstar who ran the international alliance of Nissan and the French carmaker Renault. With Laymon as his emissary, Bill made three separate offers to Ghosn to become Ford's chief executive officer. But Ghosn turned them all down, saying he would take the job as CEO only if he could be chairman of the board as well—the position Bill vowed to keep under any circumstances. Laymon described the rejection as "very, very disappointing."

When Bill approached Dieter Zetsche, the German executive who ran the Chrysler division of DaimlerChrysler, he also got nowhere. Zetsche had zero interest in jumping to Ford, and he was baffled by Bill's sales pitch. "He kept telling me how shitty his management team was," Zetsche told a Chrysler exec after his meeting with Bill Ford. "I am thinking, why would I want to take the job with this shitty management team?"

Then there was Jim Farley. Getting him to come to Ford was a long shot, and he wasn't chief executive material yet. He was too young and unproven. But he had the qualities that Bill Ford felt his company needed: a brash, take-no-prisoners attitude, an eagerness to take risks, and an intuitive feel for what consumers want and value in an automobile. He was one of Toyota's best and brightest Americans, and a key player in its drive to pass Ford and ultimately GM. And of all the worries that kept Bill awake at night, Toyota was one of the biggest.

Jim Farley felt the burn in his leg muscles as he pedaled hard down Ocean Avenue toward Venice Beach. Almost every day he biked the twenty-five miles from his home in Santa Monica to Toyota's North American headquarters in Torrance. There was no better way to start his morning than riding to work with the cool breeze off the Pacific at his back.

He had just gotten a new assignment, and it was a juicy one: vice president of U.S. marketing for the entire Toyota brand. Now he had authority over the company's strategy for selling Toyota's bread-and-butter Camrys and Corollas, as well as its breakthrough gas-electric hybrid car, the Prius. But what really made his mouth water was the upcoming introduction of the new Tundra pickup, which would take on the Ford F-series and GM's Chevrolet Silverado in the hard-fought truck segment. The year before, Ford had sold a record 939,000 F-series trucks, making it far and away the bestselling vehicle of any kind in the United States. If Toyota could crack that wall of dominance, the foundation beneath Ford would crumble. Now the company was spending billions on a new factory in Texas to produce a brawnier, more powerful version of the Tundra in hopes of driving a stake into Detroit's heart.

Farley had formed a special team to plan out every detail of the Tundra launch. They worked closely with the company's biggest dealers and met directly with the top brass at Toyota in Japan. But in mid-April of 2005, he had a short week and lots to do because of a business trip to Detroit, where he would speak at the annual conference of the Society of Automotive Engineers. The conference was the largest yearly gathering of car guys in the whole industry. Farley was really looking forward to it.

He had no plans to call Bill Ford when he was in Detroit. What was the point? Farley wasn't leaving Toyota—not now, maybe not ever. But he couldn't get the meeting with Bill out of his head. He felt for him, for the obvious burden he bore for his family and Ford. It got Farley to thinking about his own connections to Ford. He was the son of an international banking executive and had been born and raised in South America, before attending high school in Rhode Island and then college at Georgetown and UCLA. But his mother's family all lived in Michigan and had deep ties to the automobile industry.

Farley idolized his grandfather Emmett Tracy, who had gone to work on the assembly line at Ford in 1914 and later become a successful car dealer for the company. And it was his grandfather, more than anyone, who'd kindled his love of cars. Farley had been fourteen years old and working a summer job in California when he bought his first one—a jet-black 1966 Ford Mustang. At the end of the summer, he drove it cross-country to Michigan, alone, in two days, packing the car with Coke and sandwiches so he wouldn't have to stop and risk its being discovered he wasn't old enough to have a driver's license.

When Farley finished grad school, he took a job restoring classic cars in L.A., then got serious and went to work for IBM. Two years later, he received an offer from Toyota to be a product planner in its fledgling Lexus luxury car division. As excited as he was, Farley wouldn't have gone if his grandfather had a problem with his joining a Japanese car company. "Ironically, my grandfather thought it was a great idea," Farley would recall. "But then he said, 'Someday you've got to come back to Ford.'"

His grandfather had died years before. But every time he came to Detroit, Farley made a ritual of visiting his grave in Grosse Pointe. After his speech to the engineers' conference, he decided to take a detour before heading to the cemetery. It was a gorgeous spring afternoon, temperature in the mid-50s, the sky blue and crystal clear. He began driving up Woodward Avenue, the spinal column of the city that stretched from the riverfront all the way out into the leafy northern suburbs. In between was beaten-down Detroit— financially destitute, bereft of pedestrians and street life, with a museum or hospital or condo complex on one side of Woodward and acres of empty lots and abandoned structures on the other. Nothing prepared Farley for how sad and quiet and dirty it all looked. The beautiful weather only accentuated the dull palette of cement grays and dust browns, like years of ancient grit that couldn't be scrubbed out.

He took a right on Piquette Avenue and entered a no-man's-land of boarded-up buildings, barbed-wire fences, and rusted train trestles covered with graffiti. On one corner was the Abundant Faith Cathedral, a windowless, one-story bunker of a church, on another a long-deserted branch of the city recreation department. Overhead loomed the yellowed, petrified conveyor belt of an old creamery. Six blocks off the busiest street in downtown Detroit, and there wasn't a soul around. And there was Farley's first stop, a redbrick building with a freshly painted black-and-gold sign and a historical marker identifying it as the first factory built by the Ford Motor Company, 101 years before.

He wasn't quite sure why, but Farley had to see it to experience where the mighty auto industry really started, where Henry Ford began perfecting the art of mass production that would change life in America forever. Ford had partially restored the factory a few years earlier and sometimes held corporate events on the same aged wooden floors where workers once made the first Model Ts. Otherwise, it was closed up tight, there for posterity's sake on this eerie, uninhabited street that looked like an apocalypse-movie set.

"I was focused on the promise that came with that building,"

Farley said. "How many lives got picked out of nothing and were changed because of giving people better transportation?"

Farley didn't feel so philosophical after driving another couple of miles up Woodward, to the Highland Park Ford Plant. It was called the Crystal Palace when it opened because of the thousands of glass windows that let natural light into the massive factory, which was the birthplace of the modern automobile assembly line. Thirteen thousand workers, including his grandfather, made more than a quarter million Model Ts a year inside its walls. By 1921, the plant produced three out of every five cars in the United States. But most of the windows were smashed now, or blackened with grime. It was just a huge, vacant ghost of a building, several city blocks long, and littered with rubble and trash and decades of neglect. The surrounding neighborhood was a lot busier than the desolation down on Piquette and quite a bit scarier. Farley became uncomfortably aware that he was the only guy around in a suit and tie parking a new Toyota. When he got out of his car, the sheer size of the dilapidated plant took his breath away. "What a fucking mess," he said to himself.

He tried hard to imagine the open windows, the fresh air, and the feeling they had given the workers. He envisioned his grandfather seeking a better life by building cars. "I saw China and India and all the other places where the industry was vibrant and starting out," he said. But mostly he stood there and reflected on how the fabled Big Three of Detroit were losing their muscle, their innovative spirit, and their all-American stamp of excellence. Farley knew that every sale Ford lost benefitted him and Toyota. But until he laid eyes on the ruins of the Highland Park plant, he hadn't viscerally connected the domestic auto industry's decline with the gut-wrenching blight of Detroit and all the other auto towns in the industrial Midwest that had fallen by the wayside. "I was thinking, was it even possible for Detroit to come back?" he said later. "I never thought anyone lost when I was at Toyota. I never knew there were lives at the end of the market share numbers. I'm thinking, can anyone fix all this?"

[Four]

Kirk Kerkorian couldn't wait any longer. For two weeks he had been secretly buying up General Motors stock, but word was somehow leaking out. At a party in Las Vegas, an acquaintance casually asked him, "How's GM?" That was the last straw.

He called Jerry York immediately. "Let's move on this now," he said.

On May 4, Kerkorian's private investment firm, the Tracinda Corporation, filed documents with the Securities and Exchange Commission disclosing that it had bought twenty-two million shares of GM—or 3.9 percent of the company—for $579 million. And Kerkorian wasn't finished. He wanted much more. The filing said Kerkorian planned to offer $868 million to acquire an additional twenty-eight million shares from other GM stockholders for $31 a share. Once it was completed, he would own nearly 9 percent of the company, and that would give him a very big voice in its future. Kerkorian was famous for these megadeals, and other investors believed that if he saw value in lumbering old General Motors, they were going to grab his coattails. In a matter of hours, GM's stock soared 18 percent.

Kerkorian had a reputation as one of the savviest and most aggressive financiers in corporate America. He bought and sold airlines, casinos, and movie studios. His attempted takeover of Chrysler in 1995 led to its $36 billion merger with Daimler-Benz three years later. Even into his eighties, Kerkorian wasn't slowing down. Since 2000, his MGM Mirage gaming empire had bought out its two biggest competitors and owned half the hotel rooms on the Las Vegas Strip.

Right after the tender offer became public, Kerkorian's attorney, Terry Christensen, told reporters that this was only a "passive investment" in GM. "We have no plans for an acquisition and no plans to urge for strategic changes," he said.

But despite Kerkorian's assurances that he would not be aggressive, alarm bells went off inside GM. Bob Lutz and Tom Kowaleski, GM's vice president of communications, had been at Chrysler when Kerkorian went after it in the mid-nineties. He was hardly "passive," in their opinion. "This guy plays rough," said Lutz. "And you know Jerry York is lurking in the weeds somewhere."

Rick Wagoner, however, was encouraged by the rise in the stock price and seemed unconcerned about Kerkorian, an attitude that Lutz interpreted as naive. "Rick just doesn't get it," he told another GM executive. But Wagoner wasn't afraid of Kerkorian. He couldn't see GM as a takeover target. Sure, its stock was low enough to attract a hostile bidder. A buyout at current prices would cost only $18 billion or so—hardly a monumental sum for a company with $192 billion in annual revenues and more physical assets than any other industrial entity in the world. But its liabilities—corporate debt, pension obligations, and escalating health care costs—were so daunting they would scare off any buyer. GM wasn't too expensive to be bought; it was too intimidating. Besides, Wagoner believed that no outsider could comprehend GM's complexity or would willingly take on the burden of its leadership position in the domestic auto industry.

In Wagoner's view, General Motors led the American auto industry—and Ford, Chrysler, and Detroit's thousands of independent suppliers followed. As the biggest of the Big Three, GM fought the battles that ultimately benefitted its hometown rivals. Wagoner bristled at critics who sniped that GM, for example, always caved in to the United Auto Workers union on wage increases, work rules, health care, and pensions. He was quick to point out that in every decade dating back to the 1940s, GM had endured expensive strikes by the UAW over issues such as outsourcing work to nonunion suppliers or cutting excess jobs. "Let's be honest," Wagoner said. "We led, and the rest of the industry kind of drafted in our wake. We did it all, and they rode our backs."

Wagoner was fine with letting Kerkorian buy up stock if he wanted. In all likelihood, he saw the potential to make a fortune on GM when it turned the corner. For the time being, Wagoner had bigger, more immediate challenges, none more crucial than the long-awaited showdown with the UAW on health care. Publicly, he had already stated that GM could no longer keep paying the mushrooming medical bills of its 1.1 million active workers, retirees, and their dependents and continue to compete with foreign companies. In a carefully worded speech in February to the Economic Club of Chicago, he called for national health care reform to deal with the problem. "Failing to address the health care crisis would be the worst kind of procrastination," he said.

GM spent an average of $15 million a day on health care; its annual costs were nearing $6 billion. That averaged out to $1,500 for every car it sold in the United States. Even if the quality of its cars matched Toyota's—and it didn't—there was no way GM could spot its adversary that kind of cost advantage and compete.

Wagoner brought his labor negotiators together and said it was time to confront the elephant in the room. "These costs are not sustainable," he said. "Our job is to communicate with the union and convince them this has to change." The stakes were enormous. If GM was successful, it would save billions and start leveling the playing field with Toyota, Honda, and all the other foreign automakers. But if the talks failed, Detroit was destined to fall into a deeper and deeper hole.

The initial discussions with the union in the spring of 2005 focused on an incredibly sensitive area—medical benefits for retirees and their dependents. So far the talks had yielded nothing. After several closed-door meetings, the UAW's president, Ron Gettelfinger, showed little willingness to alter any health care provisions in the union's ironclad contract before it expired in 2007. "We have a negotiated agreement in place," he said after one big meeting with GM officials. "Both parties should adhere to the agreement."

This was not a promising start. Gettelfinger was a skilled and experienced negotiator, but he was barely engaging in a dialogue. Sometimes he sat in stony silence as GM officials made their case for how the health care burden was crushing profitability and ultimately jeopardizing union jobs. When Gettelfinger did respond, it was in terse bursts of thinly veiled anger. Autoworkers, he reminded the GM labor execs, sweated for decades on the assembly line with the expectation that their prescription drugs, surgeries, and dental care would be taken care of once they retired. Why, he asked, should they sacrifice that to bail out management at GM now that the company was in financial trouble? No way, Gettelfinger said. Health care for retirees was a nearly sacred trust that he would not betray.

A deal would take time. Wagoner knew it, and so did his executives and his board of directors. But he felt considerable pressure to make it happen soon. GM was at a precipice, and Kerkorian's involvement didn't help. Moreover, the GM lawyers were already preparing a legal strategy to force cuts on the union if the UAW dug in its heels. GM believed its strategy would hold up in court. But nobody really wanted to test the theory and provoke a nationwide strike. If GM was shut down, then what?

Mark LaNeve walked out of Wagoner's office and wondered what exactly had just happened.

Six months earlier, LaNeve had been promoted from head of the Cadillac division to vice president of marketing and advertising. It was a big career move for the forty-six-year-old son of a steelworker from Pennsylvania. But, with no advance notice, Wagoner had just informed LaNeve that he was now the new chief of vehicle sales, service, and marketing for all of GM North America.

"You're the best guy we've got," Wagoner said. LaNeve was shocked and almost speechless—an unusual feeling for a guy who had been selling cars for twenty years.

"Uh, thank you very much" was the best he could muster. "I'll do the best I can."

The top sales job traditionally had been held by a veteran corporate operative with a broad résumé. But GM's inventory crisis was burning up cash at a frightening rate. Someone needed to move those vehicles off the lots—fast. LaNeve had long dreamed of the great things he would do if he ever got this job, but now was not the time for grand strategies. He quickly took stock of what he was facing. "We basically had three strong truck brands—Chevy trucks, GMC trucks, and Hummer," he said. "Car brands were sick to weak to irrelevant. Chevy cars had a horrible reputation. Buick was a catastrophe. Saturn had completely lost its reputation in the market. Cadillac was improving but way behind Mercedes, BMW, and Lexus. And Pontiac was largely irrelevant."

What to do? LaNeve did not have the luxury of tailoring specific sales promotions for different brands. That might take months. He needed a one-size-fits-all sale, something so dramatic it would compel consumers to get off their couches and check out GM showrooms. He huddled with the senior marketing people on the staff. One of them, Steve Hill, had an idea. "What if we made employee pricing our cleanup program?" said Hill.

Employee discounts for everyone? It would cost thousands of dollars in incentives per vehicle. But it was worth a try. LaNeve pitched the idea to Wagoner, who told him to refine the plan and come up with a slogan. One of GM's ad agencies hit the mark with a folksy tagline that invited the average consumer to share in the special discounts reserved for the corporate family: "You pay what we pay. Not a cent more."

Next, LaNeve had to get the plan in front of the Automotive Strategy Board, GM's ultrapowerful internal conclave of senior executives from around the world. Usually it took two to three months for a decision of this magnitude to wind its way through an intricate bureaucracy of committees and memos and presentations to get in front of the ASB. Often an executive in LaNeve's position would need to make his case several times in multiple forums before he got on the fifty-page monthly agenda of the big board. But because Wagoner supported it, the employee pricing plan sailed through the process.

Bob Lutz, for one, couldn't stomach it. The seventy-three-year-old Lutz was almost universally recognized as the premier car guy in Detroit. He had been GM's top product executive for just four years, but his storied automotive career dated back to the 1960s and included successful runs at BMW, Ford, and Chrysler. Lutz was all about engines and styling, cars that handled beautifully and looked great. Wagoner had rescued him from oblivion in 2002, when he was running a battery manufacturing company after being forced into retirement at Chrysler. Since coming aboard, Lutz had pushed and prodded GM's engineers and designers to improve quality and build better-looking models that consumers would pay decent prices for. Now it was like GM was telling the world it had to pay people to buy its lousy cars.

Lutz nearly begged Wagoner to redirect the dollars spent on sales promotions to upgrade the parts and materials of the vehicles themselves. "What we've got to do is put another thousand dollars' worth of goodness into the car to give it more value," Lutz said. "You can command better prices then. We won't have to incentivize that much."

"I understand what you mean," Wagoner said. "The problem is, how are we going to live through that time when the vehicles are better but we're not commanding better prices?"

Lutz pressed his point. Adding more incentives to sell unpopular cars only reinforced the perception that GM's stuff wasn't worth top dollar.

"We've got to figure a way to back off of this," he said. "We're pouring cars out of the factory with zero margin and we're not even covering our fixed costs."

Wagoner didn't want to hear it. "We cannot back off," he said. "We've got to keep the factories running."

Lutz was getting agitated. Didn't Wagoner understand what was happening here?

"If we keep this incentive war going, we're going to give our whole margin away!" he said. "Once your margin is zero, you can multiply it all you want but it's still zero."

Wagoner looked at him hard. He trusted Lutz completely on how to build a faster, safer, better car. That wasn't Wagoner's area of expertise and never would be. But when it came to making the difficult calls on the bottom line, he had the final word. He bore the ultimate responsibility for GM's survival. He set the course for the company. Once he made his mind up, there was no changing it.

"Don't get all finance-y on me—that's my specialty, not yours," Wagoner told Lutz. "All I can tell you is I'm not going to preside over this company reducing its volume. We're trapped in this system. The only thing we can do is to move full steam ahead."

On June 1, 2005, the GM Employee Discount for Everyone program went into action. Dealers across the country reported to GM headquarters that showroom traffic increased almost immediately. For the first week, Mark LaNeve arrived at his office before dawn to check out the previous day's sales reports. He could hardly believe the numbers. "We're just blowing the doors off the industry," he said. "My God, we are just blowing them off."

GM ended up selling 550,000 vehicles in the United States during that June—a 40 percent increase from 2004 and the single best month of sales in nearly nineteen years. Inventories decreased drastically. The parking lots began to empty out. The results were spectacular, but the blowout sale didn't come cheap. Between the advertising and the cash subsidies, it cost close to a billion dollars.

For years, GM had been holding its annual shareholders meeting in the ballroom of the Hotel DuPont in Wilmington, Delaware. Usually, the room was plenty big, but on June 7, so many stockholders showed up for the 2005 meeting that another conference room was booked for the overflow crowd to watch on closed-circuit TV.

Everyone expected major moves to be announced, and Wagoner didn't disappoint them. He opened by acknowledging that GM North America, which had lost $1.3 billion in the first quarter, was in deep trouble. "Our absolute top priority is to get our largest business unit back to profitability as soon as possible," he said. GM had too many people building too many cars that consumers didn't want to buy. There was no alternative except to scale back. And for the first time, he set a target.

Wagoner pledged that GM would slash twenty-five thousand manufacturing jobs and close an unspecified number of factories by 2008. He also put the United Auto Workers on notice that it had better cooperate on reducing health care costs, saying that the costs presented "a huge risk to our collective future." GM, he said, would consider harsh actions if negotiations failed. "We have not reached an agreement at this time and, to be honest, I'm not 100 percent certain that we will," he said. "If we can't do that, we'll have to consider our other options."

Many of the shareholders stood and cheered when they heard the tough talk. But a few vented their anger at how badly GM had stumbled. "This company is sick," said Jim Dollinger, a Buick salesman from Flint, Michigan. Another shareholder, John Lauve, accused Wagoner and the GM board of steering the company into disaster. "The *Titanic* sank because the directors ignored the warnings," he said.

But there was one very interested party who liked what he had heard.

Jerry York was in his hotel room at the Bellagio, one of Kerkorian's crown jewels on the Las Vegas Strip. He watched Wagoner on an Internet hookup, and then he went downstairs to the corporate offices on the first floor to write up a report for Kerkorian.

"Kirk, this is good stuff he's announcing," York said after handing Kerkorian the report. "I don't know if it's enough. But it's a significant step in the right direction."

As usual, Kerkorian was a man of few words. "Okay," he said. "Let's see how it goes from here."

The next day, Kerkorian announced that he had successfully acquired another nineteen million shares of GM stock, giving him just over a 7 percent stake in the company. It wasn't as much as he had hoped for. But he wasn't finished yet.

[Five]

The Gulfstream V began its descent from fifty thousand feet as it crossed over Canada and into U.S. airspace, the twinkling lights of Detroit visible down below. The flight had originated in Germany on July 28, and the passengers on board were still a bit tipsy from the champagne consumed on their transatlantic journey. But the celebration was just getting started. As the sleek corporate jet got closer to the Oakland County International Airport, a familiar sight came into view—the five-pointed star logo of Chrysler atop the carmaker's headquarters tower in Auburn Hills. This was a long and emotional day, and Dieter Zetsche and his team were almost home.

Earlier that morning, Zetsche had walked into a tense boardroom in Stuttgart as the top-ranking executive of the Chrysler Group, the American division of the international auto giant DaimlerChrysler. When he came out, he was the next chief executive officer of the entire company. It was a seismic moment in the short, turbulent history of the global automaker that had been formed in 1998 when Daimler-Benz acquired Chrysler. In a surprising and unexpected move, the DaimlerChrysler supervisory board had picked Zetsche to replace Jürgen Schrempp, the mastermind behind the controversial merger.

The symbolism of the board's choice couldn't be ignored. Zetsche was German to the core, and he had a distinguished Mercedes pedigree. But since 2000 he had been The Man at Chrysler—taking charge when it was failing badly and methodically steering it back to profitability. His ascension to the top of DaimlerChrysler seemed to validate the rocky marriage of Daimler-Benz, the pride of industrial Germany, and Chrysler, the all-American maker of minivans, Jeeps, and muscle cars.

The four Chrysler executives who accompanied Zetsche to Stuttgart had known for a few days that he was in a good position for the promotion. Still, there was a chance the board would select Schrempp's protégé, Eckhard Cordes, for the job. When Zetsche emerged from the boardroom triumphant, the Chrysler guys were ecstatic. "Dieter had won," said Jason Vines, Chrysler's communications chief. "We were so freaking excited."

Right after the board meeting, Zetsche and his executives got aboard the Gulfstream, settled back into its luxurious cabin, and popped the corks on bottles of French champagne to toast his victory. They were flying back to a hero's welcome in Auburn Hills, and it promised to be a glorious event. Not only was Zetsche going to become the chief executive of DaimlerChrysler on January 1, 2006, but his successor at Chrysler would be one of the men on the jet: Tom LaSorda, a Canadian-born manufacturing expert who had joined the company five years earlier after spending twenty-three years at GM.

The next day, hundreds of employees gathered in the immense atrium at the Chrysler Technical Center for the formal announcement. As Zetsche stepped to the microphone, the crowd erupted in applause. He thanked them for their support and said he would miss them all when he moved back to Germany. "I am, and I always will be, a Chrysler man," he said. That afternoon he sent out a letter to Chrysler's eighty-three thousand workers urging them to stay the course under LaSorda's leadership. "We are a strong team," he wrote. "And my confidence in you could not be greater."

It was true. He did believe in the people at Chrysler. But his confidence in the company's future had already begun to waver.

. . . .

Rick Wagoner and Bill Ford were homegrown leaders deeply entrenched in their companies. But Dieter Zetsche was an exotic outsider in Detroit. He was tall and bald, wore little wire-rimmed glasses, and sported a bushy, walrus-style mustache. He spoke with a thick, stern-sounding German accent but had a quick wit and a jovial way. When Zetsche came over from Germany, the mood at Chrysler couldn't have been worse. Jürgen Schrempp was never trusted in Auburn Hills, especially because the employees there believed he had used Daimler-Benz to execute a blatant takeover of Chrysler under the guise of a so-called merger of equals.

Furthermore, many Mercedes executives assigned to work with Chrysler didn't bother to hide their condescending opinions of its mass-market cars and blue-collar trucks. Not Zetsche. He just rolled up his sleeves and went to work. Over time, Zetsche's warm personality slowly melted the hostility toward the Germans. "I have heard a lot about this place," he said, referring to Chrysler. "But I am a man who decides for himself."

At the same time, Zetsche didn't pull any punches. Chrysler was a perennial laggard in independent surveys on vehicle quality and reliability, and Zetsche attacked its shortcomings with a vengeance. "How shitty this quality is!" he thundered during one internal product review. "How can we do work like this?" Instead of being offended, the Chrysler engineers and designers labored hard to please him. "Dieter was one of those rare managers who could kick your ass and you didn't feel bad about it," said Vines.

With his spit-and-polish deputy, Wolfgang Bernhard, at his side, Zetsche set out to remake Chrysler's truck-heavy lineup. He added fancy station wagons and a hot little two-seat convertible, but none of them sold all that well. When Zetsche hit his home run, it was with the Chrysler 300—a muscular, statuesque rear-wheel-drive sedan with an imposing grille and a generous helping of Mercedes components.

For the merger to work in the long term, the two sides of the company needed to cooperate on products like the 300. It was never easy to get the Mercedes engineers to share anything with their

Chrysler counterparts, but Zetsche proved exceptionally skillful at advancing delicate negotiations between them. Above all, Zetsche injected a sense of discipline into Chrysler, which had long been afflicted with a boom-or-bust mentality. General Motors was always the biggest and most overbearing of the Big Three. Ford had a slightly superior attitude but too often felt stuck in GM's shadow and imitated its every move. Chrysler was the hyperactive youngest sibling of the three: scrappy and reckless, daring and creative, able to scale great heights but lacking the stability to manage its success.

And in the summer of 2005, while GM and Ford were stumbling, Chrysler was on a roll. It had just posted its eighth consecutive quarter of operating profits and was gaining market share in the United States. There was a swagger about the place that recalled its glory days of the 1980s and mid-1990s. The company had brought back its legendary chairman and pitchman, Lee Iacocca, to star in a series of television ads that paired him with celebrities such as the rapper Snoop Dogg. Auto industry analysts wondered whether Chrysler had found a winning formula that was eluding its larger rivals GM and Ford.

As the new head of the Chrysler Group, Zetsche took care to temper the enthusiasm that was building inside its headquarters. "We're doing okay, not great," he lectured his executives. "Our objective has to be to improve this performance." He confided to his inner circle that the company still relied far too heavily on the sale of pickups, sport-utility vehicles, and fast cars with big engines—all of which were distinctly vulnerable to a rise in fuel prices or changes in consumer tastes.

In 2005 Zetsche instructed LaSorda to begin quietly scouting for an Asian or European automaker to work with on smaller, more fuel-efficient cars. "We have got way too much riding on these trucks and SUVs," Zetsche warned him. LaSorda didn't need much convincing. At GM, no one ever spoke about Chrysler when it came to discussing the competition. Back then, Chrysler was too small, too restricted to the North American market, and too dependent on gas-guzzling products. LaSorda felt fortunate to have the chance to take the reins as Chrysler's chief executive. But he wasn't kidding himself about its prospects. "The only way we are going to survive is to find a partner in the small-car segments," he said. "We need somebody to help us."

But it wasn't just Chrysler's inherent weaknesses that worried Zetsche. After five years in Detroit, he still could not accept the stranglehold that the United Auto Workers had on the Big Three. Germany had its own powerful automotive labor union, IG Metall, which negotiated high wages and generous benefits from DaimlerChrysler, Volkswagen, and BMW. Yet Mercedes, for example, could charge premium prices for its luxury cars to help defray the cost. And the German health care system took care of the medical bills for the union workers. Health care was what concerned Zetsche the most. The profit margins at GM, Ford, and Chrysler were so thin, it wouldn't be long before health care bills ate them up completely. Zetsche wanted to make a stand against the UAW, but he needed to do so in a united front with GM and Ford.

He had almost succeeded once. During preparations for the 2003 contract talks between the union and the three companies, Zetsche met regularly with Rick Wagoner and Bill Ford. All three executives brought along their corporate lawyers and senior labor negotiators. The meetings moved from location to location but were always in secret. At one of the sessions, Zetsche made a stunning proposal: Why didn't they join together, he asked Wagoner and Ford, and support each other in getting relief on health care? His idea was that one of the companies would go toe-to-toe with the union and slug it out over health care. Say it was Chrysler that fought the battle. If the union went on strike in response, then GM and Ford would financially support Chrysler during its shutdown. Or if GM was the strike target, then the other two companies would support it until the union backed down.

"The question is," Zetsche said, "do you have the guts to do whatever it takes to get some relief from this structural disadvantage?"

Wagoner was intrigued. Ford was reluctant. Zetsche pushed harder. Chrysler, he said, would volunteer to wage the war. "We will be the target," he said. "I am not afraid of a strike at all."

Zetsche knew what he was proposing was provocative, even revolutionary. He went even further with his proposal, suggesting that if the union struck one company, the other two should not only financially support the third but also lock workers out of their factories. "I know this is not an easy one," he said. "You pay your competitor money when he is suffering a strike for the greater good of all of you . . . that is a big move."

At one point, the three chief executives hired an outside consulting firm to investigate the legality and financial implications of a unified confrontation. And the more Zetsche talked about it, the more he sensed that Wagoner would go for it.

But Bill Ford never got on board. It all sounded too much like union-busting, and he could never be a part of that. "Let's not go too far here," he said.

To Zetsche's disappointment, the plan was shelved before it was ever tried. He attempted to revive the strategy the following year during negotiations with the Canadian Auto Workers, but it fizzled out before it got started. "My feeling was that the other two parties were not prepared for a big fight," he said. "And this would have been the mother of all fights if something like that would have happened."

As he prepared for the transition to his new job in Germany, Zetsche felt encouraged that GM was pushing hard on health care talks with the UAW. If Wagoner could get a good deal, maybe the union would give similar concessions to the rest of the Big Three. This would help Chrysler's bottom line significantly and make Zetsche's job as DaimlerChrysler's new CEO that much easier. Once he took over responsibility for all of DaimlerChrysler, he couldn't play favorites with the American side of the company. He already was preparing to make tough moves at Mercedes, where profits were shrinking and quality was slipping. And if Chrysler hit a crisis, he would have to do the same. Zetsche was sincere when he had told the cheering workers in the tech center that he would always consider himself "a Chrysler man."

But his loyalty could go only so far.

[Six]

The summer of 2005 produced the best sales Detroit had seen in a long time. The success of the General Motors employee discount program forced Ford and then Chrysler to offer matching incentives, and suddenly consumers were splurging on new cars and trucks that just a few months earlier had been sitting unwanted on dealer lots. It was all about the deal. Once the American automakers poured on the rebates, the customers came in droves.

But the surge all came to a screeching halt in late August when Hurricane Katrina ravaged the Gulf Coast. In the areas affected by the hurricane, crude oil production shut down and gas prices soared to over $3 a gallon. Almost overnight, showroom traffic dried up and sales of sport-utilities and pickups crashed. GM's sales dropped 24 percent in September; Ford's fell 20 percent. It was scary how quickly Americans turned their backs on large trucks and SUVs.

Meanwhile, sales of fuel-sipping sedans and gas-electric hybrids from Toyota and Honda went through the roof. The gains of the summer were wiped out. Strategy sessions inside GM got ugly as executives debated the cause and effect of the losses. The product and manufacturing guys—Bob Lutz, Gary Cowger, and the new planning chief, John Smith—squared off with the finance and research staffs. Each side blamed the other for the miserable state of the business. "We told you that if gas prices got above three bucks a gallon that the SUV market would be in serious trouble," said Paul Ballew, the company's senior market analyst. "We knew this was coming."

Lutz didn't want to hear any of it. He loathed how the bean counters tried to run the company with their endless charts, graphs, and reams of data. He was trying like hell to improve GM's lackluster passenger cars, and he could do it a lot faster if the finance guys weren't constantly cutting his budgets and blowing money on expensive incentives. "You're accusing us of poor product planning?" he fired back at the finance staff. "Up until six fucking months ago, people were clamoring for more and more SUVs and we couldn't even keep up with demand!"

The only products keeping GM afloat were the big Suburbans and Escalades, Lutz said. He was already mad that one of his pet projects, a new line of rear-wheel-drive cars, had just been scrapped. Now he had to be lectured by pencil pushers who couldn't tune an engine if their lives depended on it? Nobody on the finance side had complained when GM was raking in the profits from full-size SUVs, he said. And Lutz sure didn't remember anybody predicting a hurricane.

The blowup was a revelation to a new face in the room, Steve Girsky. Girsky had been recruited over the summer by John Devine, the chief financial officer, as a "special advisor" to GM senior management, and now he was witnessing the dysfunction for the first time. He had tracked the auto industry for fourteen years as a Wall Street analyst, most recently as a managing director of Morgan Stanley. But Girsky had never been on the inside before, and he was getting quite an education.

Wagoner gave Girsky an open-ended assignment: "Go meet everyone involved in the North American turnaround plan. Then come tell me where you think it's strong and where it's weak." Girsky jumped right in, sitting in on meetings all over the company and reaching out to dozens of executives and employees. What he found was rampant frustration and a disturbing practice of keeping bad news buried and out of sight. "Nobody wanted to tell the CEO what they were telling me," Girsky said. "By the time it got up the channels to Rick, it kept getting massaged to where everything was fine."

He was particularly interested in the health care talks with the UAW. The GM negotiators told Wagoner that lots of progress was being made. Girsky wanted to see for himself. He set up a breakfast with Dick Shoemaker, the head of the union's GM division, whom he had known for years. As an analyst, Girsky had often conferred with UAW leaders and spoke at their conferences. He agreed to meet Shoemaker one morning at the Motown Coney & Grille, a squat cinder-block diner a few miles from the union's headquarters in Detroit.

It was pretty quiet when Shoemaker walked in—but not for long. Shoemaker was usually so soft-spoken that people had to strain to hear him. But the second Girsky asked him about the health care talks, he went ballistic. "He started unloading on me," Girsky said, "like there was no tomorrow." Shoemaker laid into GM on everything—its products, its people, and especially its labor relations. "You're late to the party on hybrids!" he yelled. "You're a bunch of bureaucrats. We have no relationship with you guys. You're not even talking to us!" Girsky was stunned but let him rant.

Afterward, Girsky went straight to Wagoner. "Rick, you better get engaged here, because this thing isn't going the way you think it's going," he said.

But Wagoner seemed unconcerned. He calmly told Girsky to call Gary Cowger, who was in charge of the labor talks. And when Girsky did, Cowger didn't deny that things were rough with the union. "I know there are relationship issues, but I didn't want to tell Rick," Cowger said. "I wanted to wait until they were settled."

Wait until they were settled? That seemed so typical for GM. No matter what the problem, time was always on its side. "In GM's culture, the turn is always just around the corner," Girsky said. "The product is going to be great. The market's going to get better. Just wait."

An undeniable sense of dread began to creep into General Motors and throughout the domestic industry, from the corporate offices to the union halls to the hundreds of assembly plants and parts factories and dealerships. Something ominous was unfolding. There was a pit-in-the-stomach feeling that this once-mighty juggernaut of jobs, cars, and money was cracking under its own weight—its size, ambition, and mistakes. Detroit didn't have time on its side. There was no waiting anymore.

Shoemaker's tirade at the breakfast table was symptomatic of the intense pressure building within Solidarity House, the home base for the United Auto Workers. And no one was feeling it more than Ron Gettelfinger, the sixty-one-year-old president of the UAW.

It was getting tougher for the UAW to hold on to what it had fought for in the past, and the showdown over health care was only the latest challenge to the union's tenuous grip on wages and benefits won in Detroit's better days. The latest generation of union leaders grudgingly accepted that the nonunion Japanese plants in the United States had a cost advantage over the Big Three factories. Contract negotiations had become marathon battles to maintain the status quo for workers. And the union's muscle was withering. In the 1970s, the UAW had boasted a membership of 1.5 million workers. Now that number had dwindled to 600,000 as people grew old and retired, better productivity reduced manpower, and Detroit closed plants in the United States and built new ones in lower-wage markets such as Mexico, China, and Eastern Europe.

And while the union could still cripple a company with strategic strikes, the financial state of the Big Three had become so fragile that a long walkout might topple one into bankruptcy. There was nothing the union feared more than GM, Ford, or Chrysler going Chapter 11. Once their $27-an-hour paychecks, pensions, and medical benefits were in the hands of a bankruptcy judge, they could be wiped out with the stroke of a pen.

When Ron Gettelfinger was elected president at the UAW's quadrennial convention in 2002, his acceptance speech stirred the emotions of an embattled union. "It is not enough for us to have a UAW card in our purse or our wallet," he said to thunderous applause. "We need to have union in our heart."

A lean, compact man with steel-framed glasses and a neatly trimmed gray mustache, Gettelfinger didn't fit the stereotype of a union boss. One of twelve children of a factory worker and raised on a farm in southern Indiana, he didn't drink, didn't smoke, and rarely swore or raised his voice. He'd gone to work as a repairman on a Ford assembly line in Louisville, Kentucky, when he was twenty years old, and from there he climbed up the UAW ladder—committeeman, head of the union local, regional director, vice president of the Ford division, and finally president.

Even when Gettelfinger made it to the top, his old buddies still called him "the Chaplain" because of his lifestyle and religious beliefs. He wasn't a pushover or a firebrand. His reaction to the car companies depended on how they treated his "brothers and sisters" in the union. "I can be as cooperative as they'll let you be, or as militant as they make you be," he told the *New York Times* in 2005. Above all, Gettelfinger was a shrewd negotiator who knew when to slug it out and when to cooperate. And the more he learned about GM's financial condition, the more he knew the UAW had to make drastic concessions to keep its biggest employer in business.

But Rick Wagoner was also a savvy negotiator. He had made two smart moves early in the health care talks. First, he let the union and the media know that GM would play hardball, and he suggested that GM would cut benefits if the union refused to do a deal. Behind the scenes, his lawyers were sure that the company could legally reduce health care coverage without a negotiated agreement. "The evidence is compelling it would be upheld in court," Wagoner told people in the company. "I don't think the UAW wants to test that."

But the bolder move was offering to open up GM's internal financial statements to the union. No car company had ever done that before. GM even agreed to pay for an investment banker to review the documents and counsel the union. The union chose Lazard, one of the top Wall Street investment firms. After examining the books, the bankers gave it to Gettelfinger straight: GM was slowly choking to death on health care, debt, and pensions. The next move, they said, was up to him.

By the end of September, the union's top officials were almost done wrestling with two proposals for GM. One called for retirees to pay more for medical care and prescription drugs, cutting GM's costs by 20 percent. The other was a blockbuster, and it was Gettelfinger's idea. He wanted the company to give the union a huge sum of cash—tens of billions of dollars—and from then on it would assume full responsibility for retiree health care. Wagoner's directors had basically ordered him to cut at least $1 billion a year from the annual health care bill, and he desperately needed a firm proposal from the union before the board meeting the first week in October.

Time was ticking away, and Gettelfinger would not be rushed. In between negotiating sessions, he was fielding scores of phone calls and e-mails from retired workers begging him to protect their benefits. There were people's lives at stake, he told his team, and he wouldn't be bullied into making a bad deal. The union's legal staff was convinced that GM was bluffing on its threat to cut benefits, and spelled it out in a secret internal memorandum. "The UAW doesn't believe it's legal," the memo said.

The GM side didn't know much about the two potential union proposals. But it was extremely interested in the concept of a one-time cash payout. Internally, the company estimated its future liabilities for retiree health care at a mind-boggling $77 billion. If somehow it could get rid of that burden forever, GM had to consider it—no matter what the cost.

Every day, the company's negotiators hunkered down with their union counterparts at the UAW-GM Center for Human Resources, an imposing redbrick building behind locked gates on the Detroit River. At any minute, the GM team expected Gettelfinger or Shoemaker to come into the room with a hard offer, but neither one appeared. Nerves were starting to fray. Nobody knew what to expect next. "It's like an Indiana Jones movie around here," complained one frazzled exec. If that was the case, the script was about to take a dramatic twist.

October 2 was a warm autumn day in New York, with temperatures in the mid-70s and the city bathed in brilliant sunshine. But high above Times Square, in the landmark Condé Nast skyscraper in midtown Manhattan, a grim gathering was under way in the offices of the law firm Skadden, Arps, Slate, Meagher & Flom. It was Sunday morning, and an emergency board meeting of the auto parts giant Delphi Corporation was in session. The ten Delphi directors around the table had exactly one item on their agenda: whether to pull the trigger on the biggest industrial bankruptcy in American history.

Spun off as a separate company from General Motors in 1999, Delphi was a titan in the global auto parts business, with $28 billion in annual sales and 185,000 employees around the world. It was also, by far, GM's biggest supplier and an integral provider of components from spark plugs to steering systems to sophisticated electronics. Delphi's operations were intricately woven into GM's manufacturing network, and twenty-four thousand of its American factory workers were former General Motors employees and card-carrying members of the UAW.

GM was in rough shape, but Delphi had it worse. Its longtime chief executive, J. T. Battenberg III, had retired under a cloud of federal accounting investigations, and its chief financial officer was forced to resign. As GM's market share crumbled, Delphi was dragged down along with it. The company was bleeding red ink, losing more than $700 million in the first six months of the year.

Three months earlier, the Delphi board hired a new chief executive it hoped could save the sinking ship. Robert S. "Steve" Miller didn't look like a provocateur who was about to shake Detroit to its very foundations. Tall, bald, with a monotone voice and a piercing stare, Steve Miller specialized in taking distressed industrial companies into and out of bankruptcy. He'd done it with Bethlehem Steel. He'd done it with the construction company Morrison Knudsen.

He'd done it with the auto supplier Federal-Mogul. Now he was ready to do it with Delphi.

Miller strode into the board meeting with his bankruptcy lawyer, Jack Butler, by his side, and declared Delphi too sick to fix without radical surgery. "This company," he said, "cannot compete unless we solve the current, uncompetitive labor structure we now have." For six hours he went through the litany of Delphi's woes: mounting losses, jittery suppliers, unsustainable payrolls, and the decline of its biggest customer, GM. Miller spoke in apocalyptic terms of a "tsunami sweeping through Detroit," and said if wages and pensions and health care weren't reined in, the American auto industry would collapse. "If nothing is done, it's going to take us all down," he said.

His initial meeting with the UAW to discuss wage cuts was not promising. "You do that," Gettelfinger told him, "and you can count on a strike." Now Miller saw no alternative other than to file for Chapter 11 and restructure Delphi from the bottom up. At the meeting, he told Delphi's board that changes coming in bankruptcy law necessitated a filing as soon as possible.

When the directors gave him the word, Miller said he was ready to go. "All the preparations have been taken," he said.

But then the Delphi directors blinked. They wanted more time, and instructed Miller to go back to the union and then to GM to see if something could be done short of bankruptcy. He had one week to either get big concessions from Gettelfinger or convince Rick Wagoner to throw a financial lifeline to the company. Miller nodded and closed his briefcase. He would give it a shot.

Two days later, Wagoner had to go into his own board meeting empty-handed. The union was digging in its heels, and he had no health care deal. It was too complicated and far-reaching for the company to pay off all of its retiree obligations with one big check, so they shelved the proposal. Talks with the union had shifted toward an incremental solution—higher co-pays and monthly premiums for retirees and maybe concessions from active workers as well.

But the GM directors were losing patience with Wagoner, and they let him know it. Even Wagoner's closest ally on the board, former Eastman Kodak chairman George Fisher, ripped into him. GM was scheduled to report its third-quarter earnings in two weeks, and all indications were that the numbers would be brutal. It was critical that Wagoner have a health care deal in hand by then to soften the blow of another terrible quarter.

The union was an explosive topic of discussion, but there were other threats looming. Since completing his tender offer over the summer, Kirk Kerkorian had bought another thirteen million shares of GM stock. He now owned 9.5 percent of the company—a stake worth nearly $1.8 billion—and he was itching for more. Even worse, Kerkorian indicated in a government filing that he was now interested in getting representation on the GM board.

Wagoner's office had already heard from Jerry York. He was coming in for a meeting with Wagoner on October 18—the day after the earnings announcement. What would happen with Kerkorian was anyone's guess. GM was like an empire with colonies in revolt, division in its ranks, and an unpredictable and dangerous outsider preparing a sneak attack.

In the midst of it all, Wagoner stayed stoic, organized, and deliberate. Wagoner was the protector of GM, the guardian of its power, its values, and its future. If the board needed to vent its frustration on him, so be it. If the union needed someone to attack, he could take it. All that mattered was that General Motors made it through this mess intact and able to continue its important work of building automobiles, employing people, and growing throughout the world. "We have a long-term strategy and we need to work this thing over time," he said. "Nobody ever said this would be easy."

The question was which crisis would detonate first.

[Seven]

Delphi was a powder keg ready to blow. After his board meeting in New York, Steve Miller sent a list of demands to the UAW that infuriated Ron Gettelfinger and rocked the union. Miller asked for a 60 percent reduction in wages to $10 an hour, across-the-board cuts in pensions and health care, and the right to close or sell twenty-five of its U.S. factories. Gettelfinger was so offended he refused to utter Miller's name, much less give him the satisfaction of a response.

There wasn't any help coming from General Motors either. In August, Miller told John Devine, the GM chief financial officer, that bailing out Delphi would cost the automaker as much as $12 billion. Devine turned him down flat. There was no way GM was going to cough up that kind of money—not when it was losing billions of its own and asking its retired workers to sacrifice their medical care. When Miller reiterated the request to Rick Wagoner on October 7, the answer was still an unequivocal no.

If Wagoner was the loyal defender of the status quo, Miller was the hired gun raring to blast away at its problems. "Ron Gettelfinger has a big chip on his shoulder," Miller said. "But this sense of entitlement has gone on way too long."

After GM and the union shot him down, Miller scheduled a conference call with the Delphi board. The documents for a bankruptcy filing were ready to go. But Miller had one last detail to take care of: preparing severance packages for twenty-one Delphi executives, and setting aside $88 million for bonuses for senior managers if they stayed through the restructuring. It was common for companies heading into Chapter 11 to provide financial incentives for key executives to remain on board. But Miller was tone-deaf to how the golden parachutes and fat bonuses would look at a company sharpening its axe for blue-collar jobs and middle-class paychecks.

On the morning of October 8, Delphi's directors called in to the corporate offices in Troy, Michigan. Miller and Rodney O'Neal, the chief operating officer, were on the line. Together they ran through the state of affairs. Delphi couldn't pay its suppliers, and some were refusing to ship any more parts. GM was unwilling to subsidize its labor costs. The UAW wouldn't even discuss concessions. One of the directors asked if there was any reasonable prospect of fixing the company out of court.

"No," Miller said flatly. "And we've run out of time."

After an hour they were done.

At five minutes after noon, Delphi transmitted an electronic Chapter 11 filing to the U.S. Bankruptcy Court in New York, claiming assets of $17 billion and liabilities of $22 billion. None of the company's extensive subsidiaries in Asia, South America, and Europe was included in the filing; only its American factories and personnel would bear the brunt of its collapse.

Miller had thrown down the gauntlet. The average Delphi worker made $54,000 a year—about twice what nonunion suppliers paid and many times more than the wage rate in a Chinese factory. The thousands of individual parts that make up a car could be produced far more cheaply in China, Poland, or Mexico than in Michigan, Indiana, or Ohio. The company didn't need to pay union workers to do business with General Motors or any other auto company. On the contrary, Delphi's customers demanded lower and lower prices, and those were possible only with inexpensive overseas labor.

"We all understand very well," Miller said a few hours after the filing, "that life is not going to continue the way it has been."

The bankruptcy floored Delphi workers. It was the weekend, and the plants were closed. Nevertheless, the employees gathered in union halls and taverns and coffee shops, hungry for information, wondering how the UAW would respond. They had known about Miller's draconian plans for cuts in pay and benefits, and most of them realized that this was the beginning of a long legal process. For years Delphi had been a major employer in the factory towns of the American Rust Belt, and the workers felt like their way of life was under attack.

"They just snatched the American dream from thousands of people," said Don Thomas, a machine operator with twenty-nine years at a Delphi plant in Rochester, New York. News of the filing hit Solidarity House in Detroit like a declaration of war.

Gettelfinger released a statement that said: "We will vigorously use our experience, expertise and resources to protect the interests of UAW Delphi workers and retirees." He reserved his strongest language for Miller, whom he called a "greedy pig" for lining up bonuses for executives. "Once again, we see the disgusting spectacle of the people at the top taking care of themselves at the same time they are demanding extraordinary sacrifices from their hourly workers," he said.

The union's response was predictable. But General Motors seemed confused about the bankruptcy filing. GM bought $14 billion worth of parts from Delphi every year, and every assembly plant in North America needed those components on a daily basis. Moreover, the vast majority of Delphi's union workers and retirees were former GM employees from before the spin-off six years earlier. The automaker would be responsible for at least a portion of their pensions and post-retirement benefits. GM's first public statement after the filing said it expected "no immediate effect" on its business from the bankruptcy. But by early evening, the company had revised its response dramatically: "The range of GM's exposure extends from there being potentially no material financial impact . . . to approximately $11 billion on the high end."

An $11 billion hit on the bottom line? The revelation brought an immediate reaction from Wall Street. On October 10, the first day of trading after the filing, GM's stock sank 10 percent to $25 a share. Standard & Poor's, the big credit rating agency, lowered GM's debt further into junk-bond territory. All of a sudden, some auto analysts were suggesting that GM also consider bankruptcy.

In media interviews, Steve Miller fanned the flames of a possible GM filing. "Clearly they are headed down the same Chapter 11 path as Delphi unless there is a dramatic change in their staggering legacy labor burden," he told the *Detroit News*. GM executives were furious. Through an intermediary, Wagoner told Miller to "shut the hell up." Not only was Miller stoking fear in the financial markets, he was ratcheting up the tension in GM's ongoing health care talks with the UAW.

It was up to a federal judge to restore some order. On October 11, a mob of lawyers and reporters crammed into a sixth-floor courtroom of the U.S. Bankruptcy Court in lower Manhattan for the opening hearing in the Delphi case. The space was so tight that one woman fainted and security guards had to block the door to keep more people from squeezing in. Miller arrived at the courthouse in a black limousine and was surrounded by camera crews and bombarded with questions about the executive bonuses. "Without these programs, people would simply leave us and go to our competitors," he said as he was hustled into the building by his attorneys.

There were forty motions before Judge Robert D. Drain, and he granted thirty-nine. The most critical was Delphi's request to borrow $950 million from a group of banks to pay suppliers, employees, and the other costs of running the business in Chapter 11. With that done, work in the factories could go on uninterrupted while the case wound its way through the court. But the judge postponed any decision on wage cuts or plant closings. He ordered Delphi and the UAW to start negotiating and to report back to him on December 16. It was a tight deadline, but at least the war of words could die down and real, constructive negotiations could begin.

But Miller was about to throw more gasoline on the fire.

The next day, he called a press conference at Delphi's ultramodern silver-and-black headquarters building about thirty miles north of downtown Detroit. Reporters had barely sat down before he began berating them for their coverage of the executive bonuses. "None of the changes involve me," he argued. "I could be fired tomorrow with no pension, no severance, no bonus, not even a ticket home."

Then he launched into a strange analysis of why he had to slash the paychecks of the men and women in Delphi's factories. "We are in a market for human capital," he said. "It's supply and demand. If you pay too much for a particular class of employee, you go broke." As if describing flesh-and-blood workers as "human capital" wasn't insensitive enough, Miller then made things worse. "Today we are paying double or triple more for hourly labor compared to what prevails in the marketplace," he said. "Paying $65 an hour for someone mowing the lawn at one of our plants is just not going to cut it in industrial America for too long."

It was a low blow. No factory worker at Delphi was actually paid $65 an hour. Miller's figure referred to calculations of the combined cost of wages, pensions, and medical benefits for a union member. And although there were UAW workers who did cut the grass at factories, the number was minuscule. Accurate figures or not, the damage was done. In a few minutes' time, Miller had managed to insult every blue-collar employee in his company. One Delphi worker in Ohio, Dawn Spencer, immediately fired off an e-mail to him. "You speak of us as though we were ignorant, robotic human assets that aren't worth the wages we're being paid," she wrote. "I take great offense to that."

Gettelfinger was livid when he heard about Miller's comments. "The approach he has taken has clearly angered the membership," he said. "But I can tell you one thing. He has definitely solidified the rank and file of our union."

Whether Miller had done so intentionally or not, he had hit the ultimate hot button. For every union member who reviled his attacks on the working class, there were just as many auto executives and midlevel managers cheering him on. Miller had unleashed emotions that had been simmering for decades in Detroit. Many corporate workers resented the union for strong-arming the auto companies on wages and benefits, and many factory workers hated the bosses who gave the orders and took home bigger paychecks. But the hostility was mostly vented behind closed doors, until Miller turned it into a public spectacle.

On the day after his press conference, Miller flew on a Learjet leased by Delphi to an industry conference at the posh Greenbrier resort in the mountains of West Virginia. He was scheduled as the keynote speaker for the three-day event, which was sponsored by the Detroit chapter of the Society of Automotive Engineers. And when he got up and preached how he was ready to whip bankrupt Delphi into fighting shape, the audience of auto execs and engineers gave him a standing ovation.

Meanwhile, at a Delphi plant in Lockport, New York, workers were printing up picket signs in preparation for a possible strike, wearing brand-new T-shirts that said MILLER'S LAWN CARE SERVICE: MOWING DOWN WAGES.

Rick Wagoner looked at the clock in his thirty-ninth-floor office high above the Detroit River. It was close to ten o'clock on Sunday night, October 16, and he had two different speeches in front of him. The next day, Wagoner had to announce GM's third-quarter earnings, and he still didn't know what he was going to say. One section of the speech was set and wouldn't change. As painful as it would be, Wagoner was prepared to report that General Motors had lost $1.6 billion in the quarter, the company's worst performance since the economic recession of the early 1990s. But he had no idea what he would say about a health care deal with the UAW.

At that moment, a couple of miles up the river at GM's human resources center, corporate negotiators and the union were still locked in a nerve-racking standoff after many long days and nights of bargaining. Earlier that day, it had appeared that Gettelfinger was ready to take a deal that made retirees pay monthly premiums for coverage and required active workers to give up a $1-an-hour wage increase in 2006 to help fund the coverage. But then the union backed off.

Was it simply last-minute gamesmanship to get better terms, or was it a real rejection? Wagoner didn't know, and now he had to be ready for either of two scenarios. One speech thanked the union for its amazing cooperation in reaching a landmark agreement that would benefit the entire domestic auto industry. The other said sorry, there was no deal—and GM would immediately have to cut off certain health care services for retirees and force active workers to pay more of their medical bills. One version announced a huge breakthrough. The other would set off a pitched battle with the UAW that would undoubtedly end up in federal court and quite possibly provoke a nationwide strike against GM.

Wagoner decided to go home for the night. As his driver navigated the darkened streets of the city on the way to the suburb of Birmingham, he silently reviewed his situation. No matter what happened at the bargaining table in the next few hours, there would be no turning back. His board of directors had insisted—no, demanded—that he do something substantial to curtail the so-called legacy costs that had been mounting for decades at GM. The health care costs were like a ball and chain that the Big Three dragged around the marketplace. General Motors had to compete for customers every day with extremely competent automobile manufacturers from Asia and Europe. Even if the legacy costs were reduced, GM's products still lagged behind Toyota's and Honda's in quality, resale value, and overall appeal. And the competition was relentless. It was like Detroit's market share in the United States was the feeding ground for its ravenous rivals from Japan. GM's share, which had hit 50 percent in its glory days in the 1960s, had plummeted to 25 percent. To make matters worse, the whole market was slumping. The Delphi debacle could not have come at a worse time. Miller was loudly proclaiming that GM was responsible for all of its legacy costs too. A strike at the parts plants could cripple GM's vehicle production, and there wasn't a whole lot Wagoner could do about it.

At home, Wagoner got an update from the negotiating team.

Still no deal, but Gettelfinger was in the room and that was a good sign. Then, sometime after midnight, the phone rang again. It was over. GM had prevailed. The UAW had agreed to extraordinary concessions. Retirees would pay monthly premiums for the first time and absorb more of the cost of their trips to the doctor and their prescriptions. The active workers would forgo their $1-an-hour pay increase next year—about $2,000 per employee annually—and the money instead would go toward retiree benefits. Wagoner took a deep breath, caught a couple of hours of sleep, and then headed back downtown to break the news.

He made the announcement in a closed-circuit television address to GM employees around the world. Wagoner's opening remarks set a grave tone. "We are at a critical juncture in our company's history," he said. Drastic measures were necessary. GM, he said, would accelerate a broad cost-cutting effort that included reducing jobs and closing plants. The company was also considering selling off control of its single most profitable unit—the General Motors Acceptance Corporation financing arm that made car and mortgage loans—as a way of raising desperately needed cash. But the centerpiece of the turnaround plan was the health care deal.

"We've all got bags under our eyes," Wagoner joked about the marathon talks. He praised Gettelfinger and Dick Shoemaker for their "cooperative, problem-solving spirit" but never mentioned that GM had been prepared to cut benefits unilaterally if the union hadn't stepped up. "Frankly, these are challenging times for both of us," he said wearily, "and we are both being called upon to address issues that are difficult."

Gettelfinger, however, wasn't so forgiving about the decision he had to make. Later in the day, he released a one-sentence statement. "The tentative agreement on health care matters is the result of an in-depth analysis of GM's financial situation and many weeks of intense discussion between the UAW and GM," he said. The implication was clear: GM was in such bad shape he had no choice but to make a deal.

Between the health care savings and other cutbacks, GM expected to shrink its annual operating costs in North America by $5 billion a year. This was its biggest one-time reduction ever. Reporters pressed Wagoner to go further, to predict the future. Were all these changes enough to finally fix GM?

But Wagoner wouldn't bite on that one. "We'll see," he said. "But I think for today, this is a heck of a first step."

It was indeed a big step. Outsiders had no idea how tough it had been to get the union to do a deal of this magnitude in the middle of a four-year contract. It was the first piece of positive news at GM all year.

Unfortunately, Rick Wagoner wouldn't get much time to savor it.

At eleven o'clock the next morning, Jerry York was waiting outside his office. The two men hardly knew each other except by reputation. Wagoner was very wary of York. He had been thoroughly briefed by his staff on how York had spearheaded Kirk Kerkorian's efforts to manipulate Chrysler in the 1990s. Kerkorian now owned fifty-six million shares of GM stock, which was just short of 10 percent of the whole company.

He was also in a pretty deep hole. With GM shares now trading in the low $20 range because of the company's poor earnings and the trouble at Delphi, Kerkorian had lost more than $300 million on his investment. He might have been patient with GM a few months earlier, but he wouldn't be anymore.

When York sat down across from Wagoner, he was exceedingly polite but also clear about his mission: he wanted Wagoner to meet with Kerkorian in Las Vegas. For a brief moment Wagoner seemed tongue-tied. He hemmed and hawed, but there was no polite way he could refuse a meeting with one of his biggest shareholders. Sure, he would see Kerkorian. No problem. Check the calendar and set it up, he said. Good, replied York. And then he was gone.

As he walked out of the GM Renaissance Center, York dialed Kerkorian on his cell phone. "Okay, we're on," York said. "I have to say, though, Rick didn't exude much enthusiasm."

[Eight]

In late October, Jerry York flew into McCarran International Airport in Las Vegas in his private plane for the meeting with Kerkorian and Wagoner. He brought along a ton of press clippings and GM financial statements to read on the ride. York was pleased that Wagoner had gone toe-to-toe with the UAW on health care. "A confrontation with the union was inevitable," he had told Kerkorian over the phone. "But I don't think they went far enough."

That was his general conclusion about the company's plan. "They're nibbling around the edges," he told Kerkorian. "They've got tons of middle management and too many brands and they just won't cut them."

York approved of Steve Miller's radical moves at Delphi but not his scathing attacks on the workers. He didn't, however, think GM needed Chapter 11 to restructure. What GM needed, York believed, was an alternative to Rick Wagoner—a cool and collected outsider with a point-by-point plan to streamline operations and repair the company's balance sheet. GM was so full of itself, so hierarchical and insular, that Wagoner and his deputies were incapable of admitting the ship was going down. And how could they? They had set this course. They were bred to defend its past. Without a shock to the system, Wagoner and his board would not deviate from this agonizingly slow, incremental turnaround strategy that was not producing results.

By York's calculations, General Motors was spending $24 million more every day than the company took in. That could not go on forever. GM simply had too many mouths to feed. Brands such as Saab, Hummer, and Saturn consumed mountains of cash and consistently lost money. GM employed battalions of marketing and public relations people to justify its bloated product lineup—too many plants building too many cars that too few people cared about. "I hear they have six hundred people in PR," York said to a friend in Detroit. "What the fuck do you do with six hundred PR people?" York saw waste everywhere, from the roster of seventy vice presidents to the $2 annual dividend that the company had no business paying when it was losing its shirt.

Most of all, York was turned off by Wagoner's ever-polite, gentlemanly, above-it-all leadership style. He had worked side by side with some of the most aggressive CEOs in modern American history: Lee Iacocca at Chrysler, Lou Gerstner at IBM, Steve Jobs at Apple. Those guys stepped it up in a crisis. York was convinced that GM could do better, lots better, than Rick Wagoner.

This was a delicate juncture. Kerkorian and York had to play their hand carefully. If they pushed too hard, GM would circle the wagons and fight them the way Chrysler had done ten years earlier. York needed to get on the inside, to ask the hard questions and crack the facade that Wagoner and his team had all the answers. He had the credentials: twenty-nine years of experience in the auto industry, a stellar reputation on Wall Street, and the deep respect of institutional investors. Still, he was under no illusions about the size of the task ahead.

This was GM they were taking on—the most inbred, hidebound corporate culture of them all, a virtual block of granite of tradition and resistance. With his thinning blond hair, oversize glasses, and mellow Tennessee drawl, York hardly seemed like a crusader ready to start a revolution. He was sixty-seven years old and independently wealthy, but behind the mild-mannered exterior was a fiercely competitive and astute businessman. Jerome B. York lived for big challenges, and there was none bigger than overhauling General Motors.

As he drove down the Las Vegas Strip, York passed the mammoth emerald-green MGM Grand Hotel and Casino, the cornerstone of Kerkorian's gaming empire. He never forgot the first time he'd seen it, when it was under construction in the early 1990s and he was in Vegas for a big meeting between Chrysler and the leaders of the United Auto Workers. "I was in a cab and I asked the driver, what's that big hole in the ground?" York said. "And he told me that was going to be the new MGM Grand." With the MGM as the nucleus, Kerkorian assembled the biggest casino company in the world. And ever since going to work for him a few years later, York was in awe of his boss's vision, instincts, and daring. "That fucking hole in the ground is worth $10 billion today," he said. "Kirk is a builder. He sees what's possible. He sees what others don't."

Kerkorian was dapper as usual in a checked sport coat, starched white shirt, and silk pocket square when York met him at the MGM Mirage corporate offices in the Bellagio, another one of his boss's glittering Vegas properties. About an hour later, Wagoner stepped out of one of six black Cadillac Escalades at the front of the hotel. When he came in, York, Kerkorian, and couple of other executives greeted him. They adjourned to a conference room and talked for a few minutes about the car market, the economy, and a few other safe subjects. Then Kerkorian, who had barely said a word, spoke up. "Rick. I'd like to meet with you privately," he said.

The others left, and Kerkorian cut to the chase. "Rick, I'd like to have Jerry join the GM board of directors," he said. "I think he could be really helpful to you."

Wagoner found Kerkorian polite and soft-spoken, and thought that he looked great for a man who had just turned eighty-eight years old. This wouldn't be a long conversation. Wagoner had already decided that a board seat for York was not worth fighting over with a billionaire who owned 9.9 percent of General Motors.

"It would be okay with me, but I need to put this before the rest of the board," Wagoner said. "Maybe Jerry would meet with a couple of our directors and see how that goes."

Fine, said Kerkorian, he'd like that very much. York would be a great director, he assured Wagoner.

A couple of days later, two senior GM directors, George Fisher and John Bryan, traveled to Los Angeles to discuss the terms of York's addition to the board. Bryan, the retired chief executive of the Sara Lee Corporation, had been rough on Wagoner during the health care talks. He believed GM was so vulnerable to a labor strike that management was always on the defensive with the union. Maybe York could help them figure a way to change that.

Still, Bryan was torn about giving Kerkorian an entrée into the inner circle of the boardroom. "The thought was he wants to take us over on the cheap, and that Jerry was coaxing him into buying General Motors," Bryan said. But like Wagoner, it was difficult for Fisher and Bryan to deny a huge shareholder representation on the board. It might take some time, but they were willing to do it. "The judgment was made," Bryan said, "to let the fox into the henhouse."

Delphi's first offer to the UAW was brutal—wages as low as $9.50 an hour, major cuts in health care, no profit sharing or cost-of-living raises, pensions frozen or eliminated. "There is no alternative," the company declared in its six-page proposal. "Unless Delphi can transform its U.S. operations, they will cease to exist." Miller was trying to land a knockout punch at the opening bell.

But the union had no intention of going down. "There is no way the UAW is going to accept this," said Skip Dziedzic, president of UAW Local 1866 in Oak Creek, Wisconsin. "If Mr. Miller is looking for a fight, I think he is going to get one." The Battle of Delphi had begun.

When Delphi relented slightly and raised its base wage offer to between $10 and $12 an hour, Ron Gettelfinger wouldn't respond. He flat-out refused to bring it to the union membership. "It's insulting," he said. "It's not even worthy of a vote." In his view, Miller was baiting him into rejecting everything Delphi put on the table so that the company could argue in court that the UAW was unwilling to negotiate.

This wasn't a respectful bargaining process, like the one the union went through with GM on health care. This was a bare-knuckled assault on labor, and Gettelfinger was ready to brawl. "We are on a collision course with them," he said. "This isn't just an attack on the people in this union. It's an attack on communities across this country."

Informational picket lines went up outside Delphi plants. Work-ers passed out leaflets comparing the million-dollar bonuses for exec-utives to the hardship on a family whose household income would fall to $21,000 a year under the company's hard-line offers. The fees that Delphi was paying its corporate attorneys and advisors incited the rank and file even more—$835 an hour for its lead law firm, $250,000 a month for its investment banker, $55 an hour for one consultant hired to process bankruptcy-related paperwork. "And the company is griping about paying us $26 an hour?" said Maureen Whitney, a Delphi worker on the picket line outside a plant in Flint, Michigan.

Internal company documents had begun to leak out about fac-tory closings. One document, code-named North Star, said Delphi planned to "execute ruthless portfolio management" on its U.S. facil-ities. If Miller got his way, the company's thirty-three thousand union jobs would be whittled down to ten thousand or less within three years.

When it was at the peak of its power, GM was the most vertically integrated automaker anywhere. Countless people earned a living off the production of the humble parts composed of plastic, steel, and rubber that make up a car. In the 1980s, the company woke up and realized that union labor was too expensive to sew seat covers or bundle wiring harnesses. Those tasks could be performed just as well at a fraction of the cost in Mexico and other low-wage nations.

GM got tired of fighting with the UAW over every plant it closed, and in 1999 it spun off its entire parts division to create Delphi. Now the corporate offspring had the same problems as the parent. Delphi wanted to keep its high-profit, sophisticated guidance and safety systems and electronics products. But it couldn't get rid of the low-tech stuff fast enough. One of the factories targeted for closure in Project North Star was Flint East, once the hub of a sprawling network of parts plants that employed fourteen thousand workers. Now there were only twenty-eight hundred workers left, making spark plugs, air filters, and other basic components that were already being manufactured for half the cost in China and India.

In the early days of the bankruptcy, Miller paid a surprise visit to Flint East. Clad in a blue shirt and pullover sweater, he walked the floor of the aged plant, some sections of which were a hundred years old. At one point he stopped at the workstation of Rebecca Oelfke, a thirty-two-year-old quality inspector on a line that made fuel-level monitors for GM trucks and SUVs. With her Delphi paycheck and benefits, Oelfke supported two young sons and a husband stricken with multiple sclerosis.

"This job is our livelihood," she told Miller. "I want you to know how you're affecting my family and all of us here." Miller listened intently and assured her that he would do what he could to save the plant—even though he knew there was no way Delphi was keeping Flint East.

"Parts like this are going to be made in low-wage countries and there's nothing we can do about it," he said afterward.

Union officials were irate at Miller's expressing empathy to workers when he had already made up his mind to close their plant. "He's bullshitting people, and it's sickening," said Dick Shoemaker, the UAW vice president.

Delphi was the harbinger of what the union had feared for years—a monumental restructuring of Detroit. When the Big Three dominated the U.S. market, General Motors, Ford, and Chrysler were primarily focused on gaining advantages over one another. GM's ownership of its own parts plants was considered an asset back then. Those days were long gone. GM and every other car company were constantly trying to drive costs down, to buy components from the cheapest source possible and still produce a quality vehicle. And the true commodity-type products—hoses, fasteners, wires, even spark plugs—were pouring in from Asia and the former Soviet bloc nations in Europe. Even Mexico was getting undercut on wages by the Third World.

But the more distressing trend for the American autoworker was the steady, consistent decline in U.S. sales by the Detroit companies. GM was growing in China, South America, the Middle East, and Africa. But it was losing sales every month in its home market to the Japanese and more recently the Korean carmakers. The costs associated with union labor kept rising, particularly health care for retirees. Meanwhile, the competition kept growing stronger. GM could outsell Ford all it wanted and still lose out to the high-quality Toyotas and Nissans flooding the marketplace. It wasn't a zero-sum game. The American companies were being swamped in their own backyard. And with each percentage point of market share lost, thousands of union jobs became a burden that GM, Ford, and Chrysler could no longer afford.

The rhetoric was harsher at Delphi and the confrontation uglier, but the stakes were higher at GM as Rick Wagoner and his board grappled with what to do with too many factories and too many workers. There was really only one way to go, and it would be painful.

On November 21, 2005, General Motors announced the deepest cuts in its North American workforce since the recession of the early 1990s. At a press conference at GM headquarters, Wagoner said the company would slash thirty thousand jobs and close down nine factories, including four big assembly plants located in Oklahoma, Georgia, Michigan, and Ontario, Canada. The shutdowns would eliminate a million vehicles from GM's annual production, nearly one-fifth of its total capacity in the United States, Canada, and Mexico. White-collar jobs were in jeopardy too, and as many as six thousand would be cut in the year ahead. In the most important address of his career, Wagoner said this dose of "tough medicine" would cure the ills threatening to topple the company. The only way GM could survive was by cutting loose people and plants that it could no longer support with its dwindling sales.

Still, Wagoner would not ever consider bankruptcy as an option. "We're not taking these actions to relieve pressure," he said. "We're taking these actions to get the business right."

But how would GM dump thirty thousand union workers? The UAW contract technically protected those jobs. If the workers' plants closed, they were entitled to enter the swelling ranks of the so-called jobs bank, where laid-off workers collected nearly their entire paycheck until new positions opened up elsewhere. Wagoner was deliberately vague on the details, saying the cuts would be spread over the next three years through attrition, early retirements, and possibly buyouts. "We're not going to get thirty thousand people from one day to the next," he said. "But we'll get it on a cumulative basis."

A huge buyout plan would be extraordinarily expensive and would definitely require the consent of the union. Ron Gettelfinger didn't sound like he was on board with any of it. "This is all extremely disappointing, unfair, and unfortunate," he said. He had given GM the health care concessions it demanded, and Steve Miller was sticking it to workers at Delphi. Now he was supposed to swallow Wagoner's lame explanation that GM's problems were all the union's responsibility? "GM's decline in market share is not the fault of workers or our communities," the union president said. "But it's those groups that will suffer because of the actions announced today."

Wagoner was as stoic as ever. He conceded that the epic job cuts were "very difficult" and acknowledged the devastating impact on workers and their families. But he saw no other choice. He was running out of time. GM could not delude itself that better days were just around the corner, that the market would rebound, or that the new cars that Bob Lutz and his team were developing would suddenly reverse years of crumbling sales.

With Kerkorian and York lurking in the shadows and Wall Street questioning his every move, Wagoner had to deliver results, and he needed to be tough, deliberate, and confident. Yet too often at times like this, he came across as isolated, detached, and chillingly mechanical. The men and women who worked with Wagoner every day unfailingly described him as a warm and sensitive human being in private, a "nice guy" who sent birthday e-mails to staff members and always asked about their families. Yet as the public face of GM, Wagoner never seemed to grasp the raw, emotional element of effective leadership. How could the vast number of people at GM believe in him if he never really acted like he cared about them?

Every year before the Christmas holidays, GM threw a party for the Detroit media. It was never meant to actually be fun; it was more of a quasi-social occasion that allowed reporters and editors to mingle with the top brass. The loquacious and ever-quotable Bob Lutz was usually the center of attention, holding court on any topic thrown his way. But this year, even Lutz was conscious of the stress enveloping GM. He had printed up little cards for himself and his fellow executives with tongue-in-cheek instructions on how to keep the media at bay. "If you are asked something that you should not, cannot or do not want to answer, there's nothing wrong with politely declining to discuss the subject," the card said. "The key is not to react defensively." Of course, after reading his card aloud to a group of reporters, Lutz couldn't resist talking all night long.

Wagoner didn't need any guidance to be on guard with the media. Almost always, he resolutely controlled his comments and never revealed anything beyond the carefully vetted corporate line. But on this night, something happened. One question kept coming and coming. What about the people who would suffer because of GM's woeful condition? How did he feel inside about telling thirty thousand workers they had to give up their jobs to save General Motors? For an instant, Wagoner's armor of self-restraint cracked.

"What do you expect me to say?" he snapped. "That I don't give a shit about them? That I feel like shit about closing plants? We don't do this stuff because we like it. You want me to feel bad about it? Well, I feel bad."

The GM public relations people looked stunned. Other staffers around Wagoner stared at him in disbelief. Then, as quickly as he had let loose, Wagoner pulled back. He composed himself and singled out the reporter who had broken the unwritten rule: nothing personal.

"Come on, that's not fair," he said. "You know better than to be asking me stuff like that."

It was January 10, 2006, and the ballroom at the Marriott in the GM Renaissance Center buzzed in anticipation of the guest speaker at the annual gathering of auto analysts. Usually the Detroit auto show was all about new products, and there had been plenty unveiled during the week. But this event had overshadowed everything else.

When Jerry York entered the ballroom with his wife, Eilene, at his side, a half dozen camera crews descended on them. The bright lights followed the couple, illuminating York in a white glare as he shook hands and said his hellos. Eilene York wondered when her husband had become so famous to be treated like a movie star. But this was high drama. York had come into GM's backyard and was about to go public for the first time about Kerkorian's investment. This was his one shot to tell the world that there was a better way to run GM. And when he was done, nobody in the auto industry—not even Rick Wagoner—could say they hadn't heard him.

He titled his speech "General Motors at a Fork in the Road." The crisis at Delphi, York said to the hushed room, was just the beginning. GM and the entire domestic auto industry were at a fateful crossroads. "The wrong fork," York said, "is the one that assumes that 'better products' and 'some capacity reduction' are about all that is needed—that the companies, their employees, and their unions can continue doing business in other respects pretty much as they have been."

This was not nearly enough, he said. The "right fork" required change, big change. "All of the old ways of doing business have to be scrutinized," York said, "recognizing that some aspects of the business that were affordable a decade ago are no longer economically possible." While he mentioned Wagoner by name only once or twice, his point couldn't be sharper. GM, York declared, was facing insolvency in a thousand days if management did not shift immediately into what he called "crisis mode." If it failed to do so, General Motors was headed in the same direction as the steel and railroad and airline industries: bankruptcy.

York's voice rose and fell like a preacher's giving a sermon. No more sacred cows, no more halfway measures. Sell brands such as Saab and Hummer that can't carry their own weight. Cut unneeded operations to the core. Whack the $2 annual dividend to shareholders in half. Slice the salaries of the top earners—starting with the board of directors and the senior officers of the corporation. Above all, York called for a "sense of purpose," "a degree of urgency," and an acknowledgment that "time is of the essence." He was laying down a challenge and stirring up the deep reservoir of pride and passion that had once made Detroit the most dynamic industrial engine on earth. The cynics, York said, were convinced it could never come back, that its glory days were ancient history, that the domestic auto industry was fatally wounded and headed for destruction.

"But can't we prove them wrong?" he said. "Can't we just grab hold of the steering wheel and make sure this industry gets headed down that right fork in the road? I think we can—or I wouldn't be standing up here this afternoon!"

When he finished, the applause was deafening. Even the GM executives in the front row stood and clapped. The camera crews and journalists were already lining up to get their turn for interviews. York was tingling and allowed himself a small, satisfied smile. "I knew," he told a confidant later that day, "that I would get their attention."

[Nine]

Once the conflicts were out in the open, the tension inside General Motors seemed to release like steam from a boiling kettle.

After provoking the United Auto Workers to the brink of a strike, Steve Miller abruptly retreated. Instead of petitioning the bankruptcy judge to void its union contracts, Delphi requested a six-month extension to file a reorganization plan in hopes that some compromise could be reached with the UAW.

In public appearances, Ron Gettelfinger assailed the General Motors job cuts. But behind closed doors, he quietly began negotiating with GM for an unprecedented package of cash buyouts for workers.

And shortly after Jerry York laid into GM for failing to step up and attack its problems, the company's board of directors graciously invited him to join their ranks.

General Motors ended 2005 with an $8.6 billion loss for the year, the second biggest in its ninety-eight-year history. Forty percent of the red ink was from charges taken in advance for the pending plant closures and to cover a portion of pension benefits owed to former GM workers at Delphi. At a somber press conference, Wagoner called it "one of the most difficult years" the company had ever had. He didn't even try to put a positive spin on the numbers. "It was a year," he said, "in which two significant fundamental weaknesses were fully exposed—our huge legacy cost burden and our inability to adjust structural costs in North America."

Wall Street pounded GM's stock, driving the price down to $23 a share. Analysts seemed resigned to a long, rough road ahead. "We believe things will get worse before they get better," said John Murphy of Merrill Lynch.

But at least GM's enormous issues were on the table. There was no hiding them anymore and no excuse for avoiding them. The "fundamental weaknesses" that Wagoner referred to could kill the company. Unless it succeeded in reducing its costs by billions and billions of dollars, there would never be an opportunity to prove it could still make world-class cars. GM's critics wondered whether the harsh, new reality would finally end its institutional arrogance and knock the company off the imaginary pedestal it no longer deserved.

The biggest auto company in the world was now, in terms of financial performance, the worst. Even its new chief financial officer, Fritz Henderson, conceded as much during a conference call with analysts. "It was a thoroughly forgettable year," Henderson said. "There are no highlights, really."

The implosion at GM was a loud wake-up call for the Ford Motor Company. Bill Ford knew how fortunate he was that his company was treading water while GM sank like a rock. Ford managed to earn $2 billion in 2005, despite losing another big chunk of market share in the United States. But those profits were hardly solid. The company lost nearly $4 billion on its automotive operations. All the money it made came from Ford Credit, its finance division. Financially, Ford was preparing for the worst by hoarding cash. It finished the year with $25 billion in the bank versus the $20 billion that GM had.

And even though GM's breakthrough with the UAW paved the way for Ford to have the same deal, the company was still heading in the same miserable direction as GM. For one, Ford had waited far too long to address its own overcapacity issues. It had enough factories in North America to build 4.8 million cars and trucks a year. Unfortunately, it sold only 3.3 million in the region during 2005. Though it made money in Europe, Asia, and South America, the core operations in its home market had become a black hole. Jim Padilla, Ford's president and Bill Ford's right-hand man, had not distinguished himself as anything other than what he was—an old-line manufacturing exec who rode herd on the plants, coerced suppliers into cutting their prices, and bargained hard with the UAW. The other key player in the executive suite was Don Leclair, an abrasive but brilliant number cruncher who wielded tremendous power as the chief financial officer. They were an intimidating pair, but neither one was the leader Bill Ford was desperate for.

There was one executive, however, who showed real promise, someone Bill thought he could trust to make hard, smart decisions before things really got ugly. Ford had studied dozens of executives in the company, and one stood out: Mark Fields, the forty-four-year-old head of Ford of Europe.

Born in Brooklyn, raised in New Jersey, trained at Harvard Business School, and recruited from IBM, Fields was ambitious and successful, and he worked fourteen-hour days wherever Ford put him. He had been with the company for seventeen years. His first job had been designing marketing plans for the Thunderbird, and Fields learned quickly how Ford was ruled by pay grades, status, and titles. The first time he raised his hand in a big meeting, he was shot down by his boss. "It was like, 'You said something at the meeting,'" Fields recalled. "'You never say anything until you tell your manager.'"

But Fields had good ideas and refused to keep his mouth shut. He attacked problems. Coworkers underestimated his drive and work ethic because he looked smooth in sharp suits, combed his thick black hair in a mullet, and had movie-star good looks. But Fields was a natural leader and a lot tougher than people gave him credit for. He thrived in the grind of meetings with the product planners, advertising agencies, and especially the sharp-elbowed finance guys. When

Fields was knocked down, he always got up stronger. "I have an inability to accept defeat," he said. "I really believe that no matter what, we will get it done."

He also loved the car business—the scale, the power, and especially the product. There was nothing like working on a new model from the early design stages to the day when thousands of finished vehicles rolled off the assembly line and into the showroom. "There's something intoxicating in how a car comes together and is brought to market," Fields said. "It's a male thing. We can't create life, but we can create a car."

Fields moved quickly through Ford's marketing department but was destined for bigger, operational jobs. He held several positions in North and South America before landing as the managing director of Ford Argentina. Then in 1998, he received orders from headquarters to move to Japan to become the head of sales and marketing for Mazda. Ford owned one-third of Mazda, which was losing tons of money. But this time Fields didn't want to move. He was just getting started in Argentina. "I'm not asking you to go," said Jacques Nasser, head of Ford's global auto operations. "I'm telling you." It turned out to be a career-changing assignment. Fields may have been cocky at times, but he made things happen. He took a debt-ridden Japanese automaker with dire prospects and made it profitable and exciting to be around. In two years, Fields was the president of Mazda, and an industry sensation as the first American executive to run a car company in Japan.

In return, Dearborn promoted him again—this time to take over Europe and run the luxury brands that were draining billions from Ford's bottom line.

Now he was truly in the big leagues, and he was ready to shake things up. Every country had its own management fiefdom at Ford, whether it was England, Germany, or Sweden. Then there were the brands—Volvo, Jaguar, Land Rover, and Aston Martin, each with its own vehicles, factories, offices, and chief executives. And they all had excuses for why Ford couldn't make money in Europe. Bringing order to this mess would be a huge challenge.

That was fine with Fields. He considered himself a troubleshooter of the highest order. "Every assignment the company gave me was a really shitty situation that had to be fixed," he said. "It's a great platform to get people to change." The stuffy European executives at Ford were not at all comfortable with Fields and his hyperagenda of ninety-day plans, budget reviews, and strict deadlines. He went to work in Cologne or London or wherever he was at 5:00 A.M., and was on the run until late into the night.

To drive home the message that a new sheriff was in town, Fields put Ford's four-story London town house up for sale right after it had been renovated and furnished with millions of dollars' worth of artwork and antiques. "They believed this bullshit about how you have to live in luxury to know it," he said. "I'm saying we've got to move."

Bill Ford followed closely Fields's every move. He liked the way Fields handled himself, how he wouldn't back down from the overbearing Europeans. He especially noticed how Fields stood up to David Thursfield, the burly, six-foot-four-inch Brit who had authority over international operations and global suppliers. Thursfield had a mean reputation. Some of the executives under his control were flat-out scared of him. But Fields wouldn't be bullied. "You won't be pushing me around like everybody else," Fields said when Thursfield got in his face. Bill Ford liked that a lot. He was fed up with all the confrontation and personal agendas and resistance to change. He needed someone like Fields back home in the American car market, where Ford was really struggling.

Fields was in his London office when Bill Ford called.

"I really want you to come back and run North America and figure this thing out," Ford said. "We're in big trouble if we don't do something."

Fields hadn't expected this at all. But he didn't hesitate for an instant.

"Whatever you want me to do," he said, "I'm ready to do it."

Fields hardly knew Bill Ford. Their encounters had been limited to occasional presentations he had made at Ford board meetings. But they were about the same age, and Fields felt a natural rapport between them. He sensed that Bill needed an executive who wouldn't flatter or bullshit him. "I didn't know Bill all that well, but I could see how everybody wanted a piece of him," Fields said. "He was being pulled in so many directions."

Fields made up his mind right then to be totally candid with Bill from the get-go. "I have two requests," he said at their first sit-down meeting in Dearborn. "First, what you should expect from me is a plan within ninety days for North and South America. You give me a deadline, and I'll give you a plan. The second thing is, I don't need a lot of interference from headquarters, especially from [CFO Don] Leclair. I can run this myself with your support."

By the end of his first week, Fields wondered what he had gotten himself into. He had been working overseas for ten years and wasn't at all prepared for the reality of Ford's decline in its home market. "From an operational fitness standpoint, I was shocked," he said. "It was like visiting my parents. I can see they're getting older."

He buried himself in the North American financial forecasts and realized that any money Ford was making came from shoving vehicles down the throats of the dealers. But if customers weren't buying, the dealers wouldn't keep swallowing more inventory. The raw numbers scared the Harvard grad in him. "This has the potential to be a fucking train wreck," Fields told his new executives. "We have to be ready for months and quarters where we are going to be down. It's going to take a long time for leaves to fall off the tree."

Then he went to his first weekly operating committee meeting. The discussions on product programs and marketing plans were substantial. Fields dug right in. But the agenda allowed only a few minutes for setting production schedules for all the factories. In a moment of clarity, Fields realized that the sales guys were driving the entire process. They didn't care that inventory was piling up; all they worried about was that the pipeline to the dealerships was always full. At one point in the meeting, Steve Lyons, the top sales executive, handed Fields a production order and expected him to just sign it. That was not happening.

"Excuse me?" said Fields. "I'm not signing this. In fact, I think we're going to change this whole process." He also butted heads immediately with Don Leclair. The steely chief financial officer was famous for slashing product budgets and accusing everybody of wasting money. Ford's cars were selling poorly as it was, and Fields felt that cheapening the product more would be disastrous. Meetings with Leclair and his finance wolves were always contentious and stressful. Almost everything Fields said, Leclair labeled as "stupid" or "idiotic," and then refused to talk about it more. "I don't see eye to eye on anything with this guy," Fields moaned after one session. "He just sucks the life out of the room."

But Bill Ford always had his back. Fields painstakingly put together a team of fifty people to draft a new turnaround plan for North America, and Bill vowed to support whatever they came up with. And when Fields and his people started adding up the assembly plants and said some of the company's oldest and proudest factories should be shut down forever, Bill didn't blink. As the chief executive, he couldn't let Ford slide as far as GM had. He had to move now.

The gossip around Detroit was that Bill Ford wasn't tough enough to take on the United Auto Workers, that he was too soft and sentimental to ruthlessly eliminate tens of thousands of jobs. Maybe he did need someone like Fields to carry out the dirty work. But there was no question in Bill's mind that his company had to radically shrink its operations—or suffocate from a fatal combination of higher and higher costs and weaker and weaker sales.

On January 23, 2006, Bill Ford made the announcement in one of the company's sleek design centers in Dearborn. Mark Fields, Jim Padilla, and Don Leclair were at his side. The auditorium was packed with camera crews, reporters, and Ford employees. Fields had dubbed the plan "Way Forward"—ostensibly to suggest a path to a brighter future.

But to move forward, Ford would have to leave a lot of loyal soldiers behind. Fields and his team proposed cutting thirty thousand hourly workers, four thousand salaried jobs, and fourteen factories in the United States and Canada. The numbers were stunning in their severity. One in four Ford employees in North America would be out of a job within five years. There was no gilding this message, and Bill Ford didn't even try. "These cuts are a painful last resort, and I'm deeply mindful of their impact," he said, his voice echoing through the dead-silent room. "They're going to affect many lives, many families, and many communities."

When Fields took the microphone, he didn't pull any punches. Ford was saddled with the costs, capacity, and staffing levels "of a company that is much larger than our sales and market share can support." There was no other choice than to cut and cut deeply. He paused to let the shock sink in with the audience of Ford people.

Then he did something GM hadn't when it dropped its restructuring bomb: he went out on a limb.

Ford's North American operations, Fields said, would be profitable again by 2008 at the latest. "That's not a prediction," he said. "That's a promise." It sounded brash and a little scripted. But at least Fields was willing to go on the record and make a commitment. Fields had been back in Dearborn only a few months, and not everybody in the room knew him. But his words meant something, and the Ford employees began applauding, tentatively at first, then louder and louder. Maybe there was something to be hopeful about.

Bill Ford caught the wave of emotion and rode it. He had been almost teary-eyed. But now he was feeling a surge of pride. "Today," he said, "we declare the resurgence of the Ford Motor Company."

But nobody thirty-five miles away at the hulking Ford assembly plant in Wixom, Michigan, was applauding. The plant was one of the first factories on the hit list. Built in 1957, it was among the oldest and largest automotive manufacturing sites in the country. More than six million cars had been built there over the decades, including the iconic Ford Thunderbird and Lincoln Continental. But production had been steadily dropping, and the fifteen hundred workers in Wixom had suspected the end was near.

The assembly line stopped so the workers could watch the grim news on television. While the plant wouldn't officially close for a year, their corporate lifeline had been severed. Some of the workers hung their heads when they realized that Ford Wixom had just been declared dead.

"At least we know something now," said Ron Cameron, a skilled tradesman. "We've been kind of hanging out in the wind for a while." A few workers drifted across the street on their break to commiserate at Leon's Food and Spirits, a local restaurant. One of the workers, Venessa Seldon, got a frantic phone call from her teenage daughter. "She called from school and said, 'Mom, are we broke?'" Seldon told a reporter from the *Detroit News*. "I told her that we'll be okay."

A sense of the inevitable was taking hold in Detroit. Unlike the anger and frustration detonated by the Delphi bankruptcy and the GM cuts, Ford's downsizing was accepted by workers with a measure of resignation; this had been coming, and they knew it.

Even Ron Gettelfinger's reaction was muted. "This is extremely disappointing," he said. "It's devastating news for workers and their families." But there was no talk of a fight or a strike or anything like that. The reckoning that had been predicted for years had arrived. This was the new look of twenty-first-century Detroit: plants closings, jobs lost, cities abandoned. The scary part was that no one seemed surprised anymore.

But maybe there was one ray of hope. That same afternoon, the newest Big Three chief executive made his public debut as the keynote speaker to the Detroit Economic Club. Tom LaSorda's timing could not have been better to assume the role of CEO of the Chrysler Group. The company was profitable and had already gone through a brutal round of plant closings and layoffs after Daimler-Benz acquired it in 1998. With a wealthy parent company behind it and a solid balance sheet, Chrysler now appeared to be the healthiest car company in Detroit.

Chrysler shouldn't even be lumped in with General Motors and Ford, LaSorda declared. The smallest of the Big Three had risen above its larger hometown competitors and all of their messy problems. "We are competing with Toyota and the Asian imports," La-Sorda said. He almost sounded as if he pitied poor GM and Ford. "At the Chrysler Group, we take no joy whatsoever in what's happening at our crosstown rivals," he said. "We went through similar agonies during our restructuring just a few years ago." But those days were all behind Chrysler now, he swore. Its destiny was to match the best competitors in the world—not slog along with the other two dinosaurs from Detroit.

This was heady stuff coming from a company with some of the poorest quality in the industry and a checkered past that included an unprecedented bailout by the U.S. government in 1980. But Chrysler did seem to be on a roll. During the Detroit auto show, it promised a blitz of new products: a compact Jeep, a small Dodge wagon, and a gaudy, chrome-laden, seven-passenger Chrysler SUV. It even showed off a retro-styled muscle car, the Challenger. The heavy accent on powerful engines was classic Chrysler but not exactly where the market seemed to be headed. And despite his experience in the factories, LaSorda was still decidedly unknown as a leader.

But at DaimlerChrysler headquarters in Stuttgart, Dieter Zetsche was worried. Zetsche had his hands full as the new chief executive of DaimlerChrysler, and his first order of business was to streamline the company and eliminate multiple layers of bureaucracy. On the day after Ford announced its restructuring, DaimlerChrysler said it would slash 20 percent of its administrative staff worldwide over the next three years, cutting as many as six thousand jobs. It was one of the biggest head-count reductions ever in a German corporation and served notice that Zetsche would play no favorites in whipping DaimlerChrysler into shape. Even Mercedes-Benz, the crown jewel of the company, was under intense pressure to improve its quality and defend its turf against an onslaught of new products from Toyota's Lexus luxury division.

Zetsche was also looking at Chrysler in a very different light. When he had run the American operation, he felt Chrysler had the potential to be a solid, long-term contributor to the overall success of the parent company. Now he wasn't so sure. Chrysler did have some very profitable products, particularly its pickup trucks and sport-utility vehicles. And Zetsche definitely saw opportunities for Chrysler to benefit from joint programs with Mercedes-Benz.

Most of the senior German executives had little use for Chrysler's blue-collar trucks and SUVs and its limited geographic distribution in North America. Not Zetsche. He was pushing the Mercedes engineers hard to work with Chrysler on a common chassis and components for the next generation of Jeep Grand Cherokee and Mercedes M-class sport-utilities. Zetsche had always believed that Chrysler had a promising place in the DaimlerChrysler universe—until he began seriously examining the possible downside of being forever wedded to the American auto industry.

Zetsche was a methodical man, and he spent many hours secluded in his new office in Stuttgart working his way through the finances, product programs, and organizational charts of DaimlerChrysler, an industrial behemoth with more than 380,000 employees around the world. Where were the strengths and, more important, the weaknesses?

The deeper he dug, the more he fixated on the spiraling health care costs of Chrysler's union workers and retirees and the long-term liabilities of its pension obligations. When he was working in Detroit, he'd accepted those burdens as a fact of life. After all, General Motors and Ford were stuck with them too. That's why he had lobbied Rick Wagoner and Bill Ford so vigorously to join him and take on the UAW. But now that Zetsche was responsible for the whole of DaimlerChrysler, he got a sick feeling whenever he looked at those legacy costs. His corporate attorneys confirmed what he feared most. "There are no firewalls whatsoever," he was told. "Any risk that Chrysler is facing is at the same time a risk for Daimler-Chrysler." Overall, Chrysler's health care and pension liabilities could run as high as $20 billion. Those costs weren't just Chrysler's problem—they were DaimlerChrysler's. "And there is no way to stop the liability," Zetsche concluded.

If Chrysler functioned perfectly, Zetsche figured, it could earn a reasonable return on sales and make decent profits. But if it struggled, if its sales plunged in a recession or a fuel crisis, costs would overwhelm revenues. And if that happened, Chrysler had the potential to bring down one of the greatest industrial companies in German history. Zetsche could not risk that, no matter how he felt personally about Chrysler and its people. He called in two of the key members of the DaimlerChrysler management team—Bodo Uebber, the chief financial officer, and Rüdiger Grube, the head of corporate strategy.

This would be a tight, confidential circle. Only the three of them, with a handful of trusted subordinates, would be privy to their discussions. Absolutely nothing could leak out, Zetsche warned Uebber and Grube. He wouldn't reveal their plans to Tom LaSorda for months. Even the DaimlerChrysler supervisory board wouldn't be informed until it needed to be.

Zetsche had made up his mind: Chrysler would be put up for sale. Not immediately, and not until every possible angle had been studied and every potential buyer had been scrutinized. But there was no turning back. "For me, the future is clear," he told his colleagues. "It is very clear that there is only one way to go forward. From now on, we are preparing in this direction."

[Ten]

The snow began falling just after dark on February 4, 2006, big, fluffy flakes like white frosting on the huge party that had taken over downtown Detroit. If a city ever needed a break from bad times, Super Bowl XL was the ultimate distraction. The downtown business district, so desolate on a Saturday night in the dead of winter, had been turned into a frozen Mardi Gras of nightclubs and outdoor concerts and party tents. Everything was lit up and sparkling in the frigid night air. A twenty-story-tall "XL" sign glowed from atop the GM Renaissance Center, while down below, tens of thousands of people roamed the streets drinking, eating, and celebrating on the night before the biggest sporting event in America.

It was like a slightly surreal amusement park had been set up for the weekend, with ice sculptures, food courts, and a glistening two-hundred-foot-long snow slide in the middle of it all. Crowds jammed the sidewalks and stretch limos cruised up and down Woodward Avenue, where empty storefronts had been transformed overnight into bars, restaurants, and souvenir shops.

The Super Bowl was typically played in some sun-splashed vacation spot such as Miami or New Orleans. But this year, the Big Game had landed in blue-collar, hard-knocks Detroit, home of the beleaguered Big Three automakers. The city had prepared for this moment for months, and it showed. Abandoned buildings were scrubbed clean and fixed up with new windows and fake marble siding. Streets and alleyways were miraculously rid of graffiti and garbage. Giant murals of GM cars covered the office towers overlooking party central, the Motown Winter Blast—a frosty carnival of ethnic food, live bands, and bundled-up revelers skating, snowboarding, and riding in vintage Model Ts through the fresh snow.

Nobody had done more to bring the Super Bowl to town than Bill Ford and his father, William Clay Ford Sr., the longtime owner of the Detroit Lions. Six years earlier, the National Football League had promised the Fords its championship game if a new indoor stadium was built and ready to go. Now Ford Field—a sixty-five-thousand-seat, $500 million brick-and-glass edifice in the heart of downtown—was playing host the next day to the Pittsburgh Steelers and Seattle Seahawks.

Much more than a football game was at stake. This was downtrodden Detroit's shot to shine under the brightest of lights. The high rollers, corporate sponsors, and news media had descended on one of the most economically depressed places in the country, expecting the worst. But the city and the auto industry had risen to the occasion. More than $100 million in public and private money had been raised to spruce up the aged downtown and stage hundreds of events. The biggest donations had come from the car companies, especially Ford.

It was the night before the game, and every venue in the city was jumping with concerts and high-priced parties hosted by rappers, athletes, and swimsuit models. But the hottest ticket in the car business was to Groove Detroit, the charity gala headlined by Bill Ford and his wife, Lisa. Bill's weekend was a blur of press conferences, NFL events, and last-minute preparations at Ford Field. At the Groove Detroit party at the Ford conference center in Dearborn, a crush of guests crowded around, hanging on his every word. "We should all feel incredibly proud," he told them. "This shows what we're capable of here."

Securing the Super Bowl was a personal triumph for Bill Ford as a civic leader and as a deeply loyal Detroiter. The NFL, big advertisers, and network executives had all paid homage to Detroit and its still-enormous economic impact and billion-dollar ad budgets. The only downer was the steady media coverage of the urban blight and decay, looming job cuts, and plant closings. More and more the question was, which auto giant would crash and burn first—GM or Ford?

On Super Bowl Sunday, Bill watched the Steelers defeat the Seahawks 21–10 with his dad, his wife and kids, and other Ford family members in the owners' suite high above the field. After the game, downtown was like New Year's Eve as hordes of football fans poured out of the stadium and the bars and onto the wintry streets of Detroit. Bill didn't leave until very late, soaking up the moment. He had helped pull the city out of its gloom, if only for one glorious weekend. And all he kept thinking was, could he do the same thing for the Ford Motor Company?

Ever since the Way Forward announcement two weeks earlier, he had been inundated with e-mails and calls from employees in Ford's factories, engineering labs, and design centers. Many were worried sick. Some expressed support and their confidence in him. Others raised questions he still couldn't answer: Which jobs would be cut? Was health care in jeopardy? Could he possibly keep their plant open? Was Ford going to make it?

"People are spending too much time gossiping and worrying and asking each other, 'What's going on?'" he said in meetings with his executives. "These people are the backbone of the company. They're not sure they are valued, or where they fit in."

No other auto executive had the kind of relationship Bill Ford had with the rank-and-file workers. He'd grown up in the company and personally knew hundreds of its employees, past and present; he had been through so much with these people, life-and-death moments ingrained in his psyche. Seven years earlier, on a raw and rainy Monday afternoon in February 1999, a huge explosion rocked the Rouge assembly plant, killing six Ford workers and injuring thirty others. When Bill—who was non-executive chairman at the time—got the news, his first and only instinct was to rush immediately to the plant, just a few miles from Ford headquarters.

Some panicky executives urged him to wait until the chaos subsided. When he heard somebody in the room say that "generals don't go to the front lines," he blew up. "Then bust me down to buck private, because I'm going!" he snapped, and took off.

When he got to the Rouge, the powerhouse building was engulfed in flames and billowing black smoke. Fire crews were swarming the scene, and rescue workers were already carrying badly burned workers to wailing ambulances. Bill almost lost it when he saw the horrific condition of the victims. "My God, this is so awful," he said to an aide, Niel Golightly, as he fought back tears. "What can we do to help?"

He found clusters of employees and family members in shock and stayed with them until they were evacuated. Then he went to the University of Michigan hospital in Ann Arbor, a short distance from his own home, and stood vigil for the injured workers. "You seem to be holding it together for me, and I'm trying to hold it together for you," he said to the families. That night on national television, his ashen, exhausted face brought home the sorrow and pain of the deadliest day in Ford history. "This," he said, choking up on camera, "is the worst day of my life."

The next morning, when Bill parked his car in the underground garage at the Glass House, the mechanics dropped their tools and hugged him. And as he walked through the lobby, employees applauded and cheered and cried just at the sight of him. When he turned on the computer in his office, it was flooded with e-mails expressing gratitude for his compassion and caring.

"I worked in the Rouge for forty-two years," wrote one retired worker, "and I was never more proud to have been a Ford employee than when I saw what you did."

Bill Ford was more than the chairman and chief executive of the Ford Motor Company. He was the patriarch of one of the last great industrial dynasties in America. It was his family's name inscribed on the iconic Blue Oval on the hoods of millions of Mustangs and Explorers and F-series pickups. People in the auto industry had a lot of opinions about Bill. He was too privileged, too idealistic, and too emotional to run a mega-manufacturer with hundreds of thousands of employees and $160 billion in annual revenues. Was he smart enough, talented enough, and tough enough to turn it around? Bill himself had doubts on all three counts.

Inside Ford, even some of his own executives wondered if he was in over his head. Yet what they all underestimated was his devotion to the company and its employees. Bill would never give up. Even with all its problems, Ford would be a very attractive acquisition for a foreign automaker or a big private equity fund on Wall Street. That didn't matter. He wouldn't consider selling out at any price. Ford was not just a job to him or an investment or even a birthright. It was a calling, a mission, a trust.

And he knew in his gut that the Way Forward plan was not enough to save Ford. Eliminating jobs and factories only cut costs. What Ford desperately needed was a complete makeover of its tired, uncompetitive product lineup. Its mainstream cars were safe but dull, and its fleet of big trucks and rugged SUVs had fallen out of step with the times. Ford had plenty of talented engineers and designers. But it needed more money and motivation to carry out a sweeping transition to leaner, more fuel-efficient cars that might actually excite people. Budgets were already tight. Ford was using up its cash reserves, millions of dollars a day, to fund daily operations. And the company's finance staff—particularly its hard-nosed chief, Don Leclair—was painting an increasingly grim picture for Bill Ford and the board of directors. Consumer spending was slipping, Ford's market share was shrinking, and it faced several billion dollars in charges to close unneeded plants and buy out workers. At its current rate of spending, Ford was in danger of exhausting its cash hoard within three years or less. And then what would happen?

And huge new expenses were looming. Word was that GM was deep in negotiations with the United Auto Workers about offering lucrative buyouts to every worker in the company to get them to leave voluntarily. A similar program at Ford would cost billions and further drain its dwindling bank account.

In closed-door meetings with his board of directors, Bill Ford was brutally honest. "We are up against it," he said. "We can no longer count on trucks and SUVs to carry us. The consumer is tapped out. That's what scares me the most."

In times of crisis, the inner circle tightened at Ford and secrecy became paramount. Leclair and his lieutenants prepared a confidential memorandum for Bill Ford, which he shared first with the board, a heavyweight group of outside corporate executives and policy makers led by former U.S. Treasury secretary Robert Rubin and retired Goldman Sachs chief executive John Thornton. The memo suggested a very risky option that involved borrowing an extraordinary amount of money to fund a wholesale shift from trucks to smaller, better cars. The finance team believed Ford could arrange up to $20 billion in loans from the nation's biggest banks if—and it was a big if—the company was willing to pledge everything it owned, from the factories to the brands to the Glass House itself, as collateral. No automaker in Detroit or anywhere else had ever mortgaged all of its assets, even its trademarks and patents, to raise capital. The interest payments would be enormous, enough to sink the entire business if the turnaround didn't take hold. This was a bet-the-company move—and Bill Ford was willing to do it.

Besides the Ford directors, the only other person he confided in was Ron Gettelfinger. He called the UAW president directly at Solidarity House in Detroit and invited him to coffee. When they sat down, Bill opened up.

"This is what we're going to have to do," he said. "Bear with me. I know people will say we're crazy for mortgaging the Blue Oval. But this is our best chance to get this thing turned around."

Gettelfinger just listened. He was immediately skeptical of putting Ford in hock to the Wall Street bankers. But he knew the Ford family and the board would never even consider it if the situation wasn't dire. He had eighty-seven thousand active union members at Ford, and at least one-fourth of them would be losing their jobs in the Way Forward plan. He was seething about Delphi, and in the past sixty days GM and Ford had already announced they were eliminating the jobs of sixty thousand hardworking UAW men and women. GM's new chief financial officer, Fritz Henderson, was telling Gettelfinger that buyout packages worth $100,000 per worker or more would be forthcoming if the union didn't fight the plant closings. The union chief knew that Ford would need more money if it was going to follow the same path.

This was not how the union president usually interacted with one of the Big Three, but Ford was different. Ford's top labor executives, with Bill's blessing, had just started a series of unusual meetings with union leaders, called Action America—frank talks about how Ford and the UAW could jointly come to grips with the mounting problems of the domestic auto industry. Now Bill was sharing highly sensitive, strategic information, and Gettelfinger appreciated that. He never met one-on-one like this with Rick Wagoner. Contact between the UAW and General Motors was always formal and hierarchical and charged with tension, like two superpowers negotiating treaties with dozens of people in the room. Gettelfinger didn't trust GM or the Germans overseeing Chrysler. But Ford wasn't hiding anything. On the contrary, Bill was baring his soul. He needed the union on board, to support Ford rather than fight it.

Gettelfinger didn't need much convincing. He genuinely liked Bill, and he loved the Ford Motor Company. He had also grown up with the company, but on the assembly line in Louisville. He was a good twenty years older than Bill and had been raised dirt poor on an Indiana farm, a long way from the immense wealth and power that Bill Ford was born into. But he shared a bond with Bill that he would never have with anyone at GM or Chrysler. There was a sense of kinship that transcended the strict adversarial boundaries between labor and management. And he would never, ever forget that Bill had gone to the accident scene at the Rouge, and what his presence meant to the Ford workers and their families. That act alone cemented Gettelfinger's respect for him forever. If Bill truly believed that borrowing $20 billion was going to help fix Ford, Gettelfinger wouldn't hesitate to support it.

"I believe you're going to do what's right for Ford and for the workers," he told Bill. "We're counting on you to do what's right."

It was a big relief for Bill to hear that. He valued a strong relationship with the union and the workers above almost anything. But the pressure on Bill was relentless. His insomnia got worse, and the stress started to show. When he came into work in the morning, he already had dark circles under his eyes. Bill thrived on sports and exercise—martial arts, playing hockey with his buddies at local rinks, skiing or fly-fishing at his second home out in Colorado. But he had basically given up on all of it, including much of his family time with his wife and four children.

More and more, Bill lived out of his glassed-in office at the end of a secured floor atop Ford headquarters, with two secretaries to handle his calls and a never-ending line of executives and visitors waiting to see him. The layers around him were thickening like insulation. Out of the blue, he had hired his brother-in-law and close friend, Steve Hamp, to be his chief of staff at Ford and maintain his schedule, which did not sit well with Fields, Leclair, and every other senior executive who was used to dealing with him directly.

Of all his executives, Bill was meeting most frequently in private with Joe Laymon, Ford's head of human resources. Laymon was the chess master for every personnel decision in the company, and Bill had entrusted him with the most delicate of assignments— to find his replacement as chief executive officer. After one board meeting, he called Laymon to his office to brainstorm. Laymon had been working hard for more than a year to lure a hot foreign auto exec to Ford. Carlos Ghosn of Renault-Nissan and Dieter Zetsche of DaimlerChrysler had both turned him down. He'd pursued Wolfgang Bernhard, Zetsche's right-hand man at Chrysler, but Bernhard wasn't interested either. And why would they be? Their companies were profitable and growing, while Ford was in a downward spiral. Plus, none of the foreign execs wanted to be beholden to Bill and the extended Ford family and their 40 percent voting bloc of company stock.

Unfortunately, details of the secret search were beginning to leak out. Newspapers were quoting anonymous sources that Ford had offered the CEO job to Ghosn a year earlier and been rejected. Ford's public relations staffers declined any comment and downplayed the stories. Still, the rumor in the industry was that Ford was desperate and groping for a savior, but the really successful automotive executives wanted nothing to do with it.

Bill told Laymon that they had to be extremely careful before approaching anyone else. "The chance of rejection is going to be very high," he said. "The first contact we make is so important. We can't let anybody know about it."

Then he said that John Thornton had just given him a name at the board meeting. A mutual friend of theirs, former congressman Richard Gephardt, had recently mediated an ugly labor strike by the national machinists union against Boeing, the aircraft manufacturer. Gephardt couldn't stop praising the Boeing executive who'd handled the delicate, final negotiations with the union and settled the three-week strike. Thornton wondered if this was someone whom Ford might be interested in.

Bill was shuffling through notes at his conference table when he brought it up to Laymon.

"So do you know anything about Alan Mulally at Boeing?" Bill asked him. "I'm hearing rave reviews about this guy from Thornton and Gephardt."

Laymon thought for a minute. He had an encyclopedic knowledge of potential chief executive candidates, both inside the auto industry and out. But he had to admit he was not familiar with Alan Mulally, the sixty-one-year-old president of Boeing's commercial airplanes division.

"I've heard of him," Laymon said, "but nothing about him."

Now Bill was intrigued.

"Okay, can you do some due diligence on him?" he said. "Just read everything and see what you can come up with."

[Eleven]

Steve Girsky took a deep breath and looked out at the forty General Motors executives seated in front of him. This was not going to be easy. For the past six months, Girsky had been embedded inside GM—listening, watching, and methodically analyzing the corporation. Now he was ready to unload. He had made countless presentations to investors about the automaker during his years as a Wall Street analyst. But this was a unique opportunity to critique the company directly to its senior management. Girsky was determined to lay out the cold, hard facts and to challenge the leadership team to see GM as outsiders did: a deeply flawed, failing company that needed drastic changes to survive. It took guts to lecture these people. Girsky was neither an engineer, a marketing expert, nor a manufacturing specialist. But unlike the executives, he wasn't blinded by GM's immense size, its history, or the underlying sense of entitlement that coursed through the bureaucracies of Detroit's Big Three.

Born in Queens, New York, and raised in Los Angeles, Girsky was the son of a self-made electronics wholesaler. After graduating from UCLA and Harvard Business School, he found his niche as a prolific research analyst in the investment banking world. Joining GM as an advisor was the first job he'd ever had outside Wall Street. Short and balding, with close-cropped sandy hair and wire-rimmed glasses, Girsky liked to joke that he was the only "wise-ass New York Jew" ever allowed into the inner sanctums at GM.

The talk was aptly titled "An Outside View from Inside the Company." Girsky started on a semipositive note before getting down to the ugly truth. "We are not the first car company to face an extremely difficult situation," Girsky said. "Others have successfully rebounded. But we are unlikely to rebound with a business-as-usual approach. And this is likely to make a lot of people uncomfortable."

In his estimation, General Motors was worse off in 2006 than when it had hit bottom in the early 1990s. It sold more vehicles in a much larger market, yet it was losing considerably more money. Out of 107 vehicles the company produced in North America alone, 71 were unprofitable—a staggering two-thirds of the lineup. The bond market rated GM's credit as junk, and the stock market displayed minimal confidence in the company's prospects. Wall Street, Girsky said, simply didn't trust management anymore. "They do not understand our plan, they do not believe our plan goes far enough, and they lack confidence in our ability to execute it," he said. "This suggests we have a communication problem, a strategy problem, and a management credibility problem."

Now he had the room's attention big-time. Girsky sensed the tension but plowed on. "This lack of confidence has significant negative implications for our business," he said. The big banks would never lend money to GM again without collateral or expensive covenants. Wall Street didn't believe the company could break even, much less become solidly profitable, without massive alterations. What's more, investors were paying more attention to what Jerry York and Steve Miller were saying about GM than they were to what its own senior executives were saying.

Now Girsky was really crossing the line. York and Miller were considered bomb throwers, the antithesis of the slow-but-steady, responsible GM regime. But Girsky was intent on stirring the pot. "What would Jerry do?" he said. "He'd be aggressive. He'd sell assets and reduce staff. What would Steve do? He sees bankruptcy as a way to clean out the legacy costs and the uncompetitive labor practices."

GM had run out of excuses, he said. Investors had lost all patience. The company desperately needed to "step out of the box"—to show the doubters that management appreciated how grave the situation was. What would grab their attention? They needed to focus their spending on fewer but better products. Slash more production capacity and employees. Set hard targets and be accountable for them. And above all, acknowledge that GM was in serious trouble. "Do our actions suggest we are serious?" he asked. "Are we acting like our jobs are on the line? Will we put our jobs on the line for nonperformance?"

The questions hung in the air. Nobody contradicted him or told him he was way off base. A couple of executives glared at him, as though they couldn't fathom his lack of decorum. There was an awkward silence until Wagoner thanked Girsky for his presentation and the meeting moved on to other topics. It was sort of embarrassing how little reaction he got. "What was fascinating to me was how politically incorrect it was to say these things out loud," Girsky reflected later. "I felt like a hit man, and I didn't want to be a hit man."

He didn't know it at the time, but some of the executives appreciated his candor. Wagoner, for one, recognized the value of having a respected outsider deliver a reality check. It wasn't Wagoner's style to run roughshod over people. He preferred a more collegial approach. But Wagoner was well aware that GM was suffering from a major credibility problem. And he was trying, in his own polite way, to instill a sense of urgency in the organization.

It wasn't taking hold, however. Responsibility and accountability were diffuse at GM. Rarely was anyone fired for failure. In most cases, an underperforming executive was moved to another position or gently eased into retirement. Did people act like their jobs were on the line? Not really. Girsky had found that very few senior managers at GM were held personally accountable for profits or losses in their divisions. And virtually every major decision on product programs, capital expenditures, or marketing initiatives was made by a committee. GM was a collective, where rank and power were defined by where an executive fit into its complicated hierarchy. There was no incentive to be entrepreneurial. On the contrary, managers succeeded by swimming with the current rather than against it.

It wasn't Rick Wagoner's fault; General Motors had prized conformity long before he became chief executive. For years, people inside the company referred to "the GM nod"—a reference to how a roomful of managers and executives would all nod in unison to approve a new car or a plant expansion.

Unfortunately, many executives already believed they had broken out of the old GM mold. In some ways, it was relative: compared to the past, the company was indeed moving at "lightning speed" (Wagoner's favorite expression). But the competition was blowing past GM in terms of innovation, especially on fuel economy. For example, for several years GM had had the technical capability to build gas-electric hybrids. But it was just now introducing its first model. Toyota, by contrast, would sell nearly two hundred thousand hybrids in the coming year.

When reporters questioned why GM lagged behind on hybrids, Bob Lutz argued that those vehicles would never make money. But GM's own internal research showed that consumers were growing concerned about gas prices and gravitating toward smaller, more fuel-efficient vehicles. Girsky had nailed it. General Motors, the most dominant automaker in American history, had become a puzzling underachiever. Even so, its leaders were convinced the company was on the right path and taking bold, creative steps forward. "There's no naiveté going on in this place at all," said Mark LaNeve, the top sales and marketing exec in North America. "A legitimate criticism of GM in the past was that it was not critical of itself. But now we believe in honest discussion, and I'm thrilled by the fact that we're facing the brutal facts." He went on to point out, "Don't forget that we're going to sell more than nine million vehicles this year. We must be doing something right."

Facing the facts? Maybe. But accepting that the company was teetering on disaster? GM's corporate ego could take only so much.

As work crews dismantled the temporary bars and attractions downtown after Super Bowl Sunday, Rick Wagoner called to order the monthly meeting of the GM board of directors at the Renaissance Center. The agenda was a corporate crisis in capsule form: talks with the UAW on worker buyouts and plant closings, plans to sell the giant GMAC finance division, decisions on freezing pensions and health care for thousands of salaried employees.

Wagoner presided at the head of an enormous rectangular table with a spectacular thirty-ninth-floor view of the Detroit River and the tree-lined shores of Windsor, Ontario. Seated around him were the company's outside directors—eight men and two women who probably could walk into any GM facility in the country and never be recognized. Half of them had served on the board for a decade or longer. Six were retired chief executives or chairmen of large corporations or, in one case, a major accounting firm. Both of the women, Ellen Kullman of DuPont and Karen Katen of Pfizer, were active executives of publicly traded companies. There was one private businessman, Armando Codina, who headed a big real estate development firm in Florida, and one Washington political figure, Erskine Bowles, a former chief of staff in Clinton's White House.

Today they were going to add a new member: Jerry York. Two of the senior directors, George Fisher and John Bryan, had been deputized to meet with York and negotiate the terms of how he would represent Kirk Kerkorian on the board. The discussions were amicable, given the circumstances.

Though it was not unusual for a major shareholder to seek board representation in a public company, there was no precedent for this at GM. Kerkorian had maneuvered Wagoner and the board into a very tight corner: either bring York in as a director or risk a messy confrontation with a big investor who owned 10 percent of the company. The conversations between Bryan, Fisher, and York were about ground rules and expectations, and York had played the game very professionally.

"Look, fellows, I'm a big boy," he told Bryan and Fisher. "I know as a board member I get one vote just like everybody else. I've got some things on my mind, and I'll share them just like any other board member."

Kerkorian's personal attorney, Terry Christensen, had also talked through issues related to York with the two GM directors. All sides agreed that once York became a board member, he would be prohibited from sharing any inside information with Kerkorian. But beyond that, he could be as proactive and engaged as he chose to be.

Bryan, the retired chairman of the Sara Lee food company, suspected York had one sole objective: to increase the value of Kerkorian's investment. "We thought from the beginning that his motives were nothing more than to help his buddy make money," Bryan said. "It was not the kind of thing that seemed all that attractive to folks on the board." Yet when the directors voted, York was elected without any dissent. And once they voted him in, the board validated the appointment by approving several initiatives that York had brought up in his "fork in the road" speech a month earlier.

First, the board reduced GM's quarterly dividend to shareholders from 50¢ to 25¢ per share. Then they cut Wagoner's $2.2 million annual salary—as well as their own compensations—in half. They also slashed the pay of other senior executives such as Lutz by 30 percent, and tightened the corporation's contribution to the health care plans of white-collar workers.

By all appearances, York was already making a major impact in the boardroom before he even set foot in it. While the board was meeting, York was walking the snow-covered grounds of rural Oakland Township, about sixty miles north of Detroit, supervising the construction of his new home. The project was vintage York. He was building an exact replica of his eighteenth-century Connecticut farmhouse on forty-four acres of dense woods teeming with deer and wild turkeys. Every spec was identical to his former house, from the size and cut of the virgin pine floorboards to the antique moldings adorning its seven fireplaces. York was busy making notes for his contractor when his cell phone rang. It was George Fisher, who held the title of lead director on the GM board.

"Jerry, it's George Fisher," he said. "Well, we took our vote and you're on the board."

York thought this was all very strange. Usually a prospective board member would be ready and waiting outside the room while directors voted. "If the vote was thumbs up, then the new director would be invited into the meeting and told, 'Welcome aboard, welcome to the team,'" York said later. "But I guess that's not the GM way."

"So the meeting is already over?" York asked Fisher.

"Yes, we're done," Fisher said. "We'll see you at the next meeting in March."

York thanked him and hung up. Then he dialed Kerkorian's number in L.A.

"Hey, Kirk," he said. "We're in."

Two days later, *Fortune* magazine hit the newsstands with a stark, all-black cover and a grim story titled "The Tragedy of General Motors." The lengthy article was decidedly pessimistic about GM's ultimate fate. "The company remains so central to the economy, so sprawling in its reach, that going into Chapter 11 would be ominous almost beyond contemplation," it said. "And yet the evidence points, with increasing certitude, to bankruptcy." The exposure was another blow to GM's faltering image. Mainstream newspapers had already been covering the company's troubles exhaustively. But *Fortune* was the conservative pillar of business journalism and a must-read for corporate executives and investors all over the world. GM had opened its doors to the magazine in hopes of getting a boost in public opinion. Instead, its bleak analysis read like an obituary.

Bob Lutz was one of the senior executives who had given interviews to the author, the magazine's veteran editor at large Carol Loomis. He was not pleased. "We took that kindly old lady from *Fortune* all the way through the plan, showed her all the new products, and told her why we're not going bankrupt," he complained to a visitor in his wood-paneled office at the GM Technical Center. "I honestly thought we had some impact on her, and she goes and writes that story anyway!"

To Lutz, the *Fortune* piece summed up everything that was wrong with these supposedly astute outsiders—Girsky, York, the Wall Street crowd—who were predicting doom for GM. The outsiders just did not understand how rapidly GM's products were improving, or how confident he, Wagoner, and all the other executives were that the turnaround was on track. In Lutz's mind, to suggest that GM was careening toward bankruptcy was beyond irresponsible. "We know exactly what our cash flow is, and we know exactly what vehicles we are introducing and when," he said. "We have never discussed bankruptcy. It has never been an option."

He would be seventy-four on February 12 (two years younger than "kindly old" Carol Loomis), but Lutz brimmed with energy and enthusiasm on his mission to invigorate GM's product lineup. Under his direction, GM was standardizing the basic underpinnings of its cars, allowing it to save billions while still offering distinct models tailored for different regions of the world. And outside North America, GM was growing. The company had just set sales records in Asia, Europe, and South America, and was the top automaker in China.

It was true that most of its products sold in the United States were money losers. But the tide was gradually turning. No one in Detroit knew more about creating automobiles than Bob Lutz, and he had empowered GM's designers and challenged them to take chances and be creative. He considered cars things of beauty, objects of desire, emotional expressions carved in sheet metal. He constantly fought and won internal battles for funding to upgrade the leather, plastic, and wood-grain finishes for seats, steering wheels, and instrument panels.

And he stubbornly refused to cut any corners on the engines, transmissions, and suspension systems that made driving enjoyable. A highly skilled driver himself as well as an accomplished pilot, Lutz personally tested every vehicle GM produced, from the early proto-types through the final production models. It wasn't unusual to find Lutz, in his bomber jacket and aviator shades, on the track at the GM proving grounds, putting a new car through its paces at a hundred miles per hour and then picking apart its flaws with teams of engi-neers afterward.

Lutz was proud of the newest models that GM was delivering to dealer showrooms—the sleek Buick Lucerne sedan, the European-styled Saturn Aura, the supremely rugged Hummer H3 sport-utility. Even the mundane Chevrolets and Pontiacs were improving. GM also had a huge ace in the hole: the upcoming launch in the fall of the new T-900 line of full-size pickups and SUVs. Nothing stirred Lutz's competitive juices more than the new trucks. Not only would the big vehicles make a lot of money, they would prove that GM could still dominate a key segment of the market and win head-to-head battles with Toyota and Ford. "No matter how you look at it, these full-size sport-utility vehicles and full-size pickup trucks are going to be big revenue generators," Lutz said. "And they are extremely good. People are going to say these are the best trucks ever made."

GM needed the trucks for psychological reasons as well. "At some point, we have to effect a shift in public perception," Lutz said. The unrelenting onslaught of criticism was, he believed, crippling the company's comeback before it could get started. Lutz loved to talk, and he did plenty of it at auto shows and product events. But he was not the chief executive. He pleaded with Wagoner to get out front and tell the world the truth about GM in the simplest possible terms. Lutz had worked for Lee Iacocca at Chrysler in the 1980s. Although he'd clashed personally with Iacocca, he had great respect for how the charismatic Chrysler chairman could charm and cajole people and, above all, sell cars. General Motors had become the whipping boy for the magazines, newspapers, and talking heads on cable televi-sion, and Lutz was sick and tired of it. Iacocca would have stood up and fought. Why, he asked Wagoner one day, couldn't he?

"Rick, you have got to get out there and explain our mission and the vision of the future," Lutz said.

Wagoner looked at him like he was nuts. "Well, Bob, that's really your job, to talk about the products," he said. "You do that. Everybody knows that good old Bob Lutz can say things the rest of us can't."

Lutz appreciated the compliment. But Wagoner was missing the point. "I know I do it well and I've been effective with the media for a long time," he said. "But I'm not the CEO. I'm not the number one guy. I can't be the symbol of the company out there, because I'm number two or number three. It has to come from you."

It was an argument Lutz was destined to lose every time. Wagoner was careful, organized, and thoughtful, not fiery, passionate, or combative. He had developed a stock answer whenever he was asked why General Motors didn't do something really dramatic to show it grasped the depths of its dilemma.

"We are trying to fix problems, not make headlines," he said. "And we really are trying."

[Twelve]

The first General Motors plant to shut down was Oklahoma City. Not even ninety days had passed since Rick Wagoner's promise to start cutting production. This was a stunningly swift execution. Oklahoma City had lost an internal competition with the GM assembly plant in Moraine, Ohio. Both factories made the Chevrolet Trailblazer and the GMC Envoy—sturdy but out-of-date, truck-based sport-utility vehicles that got fifteen miles to the gallon and were piling up on dealer lots. If there was one market segment in which GM was grossly overproducing, it was midsize SUVs. The company could no longer afford two assembly plants making a half million Trailblazers and Envoys a year when it could barely sell half that many.

Still, it was a tough bullet to bite. GM had made enormous profits just a few years earlier on these very same models. The Trailblazer would go down as one of GM's bestselling vehicles ever. Along with the Ford Explorer and Chrysler's Jeep Grand Cherokee, the muscular Trailblazer popularized high-riding SUVs for the masses. But its time was over. The hottest new sport-utilities were smaller, lighter, less powerful crossovers derived from passenger-car platforms and made by Toyota and Honda. They got considerably better gas mileage and looked a lot fresher than a product GM had been milking for more than a decade.

The twenty-two hundred hourly workers in Oklahoma City were stunned to learn they were the first casualties of GM's radical downsizing. There was no phone call or visit from any senior executive from Detroit. The only explanation came during a "special employee broadcast" by Rick Wagoner. "These assembly capacity reductions," he said, "were determined based on comprehensive and detailed consideration of all the relevant factors, including product life cycles, age and state of facilities, market volumes, and others." In other words, GM didn't need OKC anymore because its product was obsolete and the company had nothing new to put there.

The automaker had closed plants before, but usually it negotiated the terms and timing with the UAW. This one, however, caught the union totally off guard. "At this time, we do not have answers for all the questions that affect our future at General Motors" was the official response on the Local 1999 website. Workers were similarly blindsided. "I left on Thursday to go on vacation and my pastor called and said, 'Hey, Bobby, I'm sorry about your job,'" said Bobby Millsap, who was hired on the day the plant opened in 1979. "I thought he was messing with me. You could have knocked me over with a feather."

Oklahoma City was one of the most modern and prolific automobile assembly plants in the United States. Spread out over 430 acres, the factory had nearly 4 million square feet of manufacturing space under one roof. Over twenty-seven years, the plant had built 5.6 million cars and trucks for GM's signature brands: Chevrolet, Pontiac, Oldsmobile, Buick, and GMC. In 2001, the plant was assigned its first SUVs—the bulked-up, seven-passenger Trailblazer EXT and its upscale twin, the Envoy XL. The company invested a jaw-dropping $700 million to revamp the entire factory, including constructing a brand-new, state-of-the-art paint shop.

GM management had good reason to trust OKC with its bellwether SUVs. The workforce was among the most experienced and skilled of any in its vast manufacturing network. The plant consistently won awards for quality and productivity, and its employees were a tight-knit bunch renowned for their community spirit. When the Alfred P. Murrah Federal Building in downtown Oklahoma City was bombed in 1995, killing 168 people and wounding scores of others, an entire shift of GM workers rushed to the site to help in the rescue efforts.

The manufacturing executives back in Detroit had valued the plant highly. It was a fallacy to think of General Motors as simply a Rust Belt automaker saddled with decrepit factories in crumbling urban centers in the industrial Midwest. Few people knew that some of its best assembly plants were in Kansas, Texas, Georgia, and Oklahoma. Here, in the country's heartland, Big Three jobs were prized and consumers still embraced Detroit's products, especially its trucks.

Plants such as Oklahoma City were a big reason why GM was far and away the largest automaker in the United States. A year after the new paint shop was installed, a tornado ripped the building apart, immediately shutting down the whole factory. But GM wasn't about to let OKC miss a beat. Within days, the company brought in outdoor lighting, heavy cranes, and a battalion of contractors to work around the clock to repair the damage. In less than two months, it was running at full speed again.

No wonder employees were shocked. Their factory not only met expectations but exceeded them. Yet their jobs were being sacrificed in a "restructuring" to improve GM's sagging bottom line. The OKC workers didn't make shoddy products. They had nothing to do with consumers getting tired of Trailblazers and Envoys. But there were hundreds gathering dust outside their plant, a huge parking lot filled with just-built $30,000 SUVs that nobody wanted.

"I have a ten-year-old son," said Ray Owens, a supervisor in the plant's customer call center. "My son understands that if people don't buy cars, then Daddy doesn't have a job." Many of the workers joined GM right out of high school, when the company appeared indestructible. The Japanese were the threat back then, but now the competition seemed to spring from every corner of the globe. "We in America can no longer compete with workers in China, Thailand, even India," said Lori Darks, who fixed paint chips and scratches on vehicles at the end of the assembly line. "We try to do it with a quality performance, but it's uphill."

There was a sense of resignation when the closing was announced, like the glory days had become distant memories overnight. "We're at a crossroads right now," said Darrell Mason, who was twenty years old when he was hired in 1979, and had worked at the plant during its entire existence. "You see where the middle class is going now," he said. "You see where you may be the last of the breed. We consider ourselves very lucky. Our kids and grandkids are the ones we're worried about."

An assembly plant is like a small, self-contained city. Each factory job generates anywhere from three to five others at parts suppliers, trucking companies, and the gas stations, diners, and retail stores that cater to the workforce. Some plants have their own child care centers and exercise facilities. The extraordinary health care plans enjoyed by union workers attract doctors, chiropractors, optometrists, and dentists to nearby strip malls. The overall economic impact is substantial. In Oklahoma City's case, the plant was among the biggest corporate taxpayers in the entire state.

And whether it's on the tough streets of Flint, Michigan, or the wide-open spaces off a freeway exit in central Oklahoma, an assembly plant is a community unto itself. Working alongside another person for years—welding metal, bolting parts together, installing windshields—forms unique bonds. There's nothing easy about the job. It can be mind-numbingly repetitive, stressful on the back and shoulders and knees, an eight-hour-long daily grind. No question the work paid extremely well—$27 an hour for an assembler on up to $33 an hour for a skilled tradesman. The benefits were excellent, and after thirty years a worker could retire with a generous pension. What outsiders could not appreciate, though, were the feelings of pride and togetherness and shared history. Twenty-seven years in the OKC plant covered an awful lot of birthdays, anniversaries, high school graduations, and family funerals. And every shiny new SUV that rolled off the line was the tangible result of that spirit and collective energy.

Then, as if someone had flicked a switch in Detroit, it was all over. Despite a lobbying effort led by Oklahoma governor Brad Henry and the state's offer of a $200 million package of incentives, GM would not reconsider its decision. "I asked them if there was anything at all we could do, any discussion that we could have to keep this plant open," Henry told a local newspaper, the *Journal Record*. "And they said, unfortunately, no."

Once the shock wore off, the sorrow and frustration kicked in. "There was nothing we did to shut this plant down," said Nanette Relerford, who worked in the paint shop. "We have been through tornados. We worked the Murrah building. We fed the firefighters. We do give. It would be good if GM had a design department that would give us vehicles that sell."

Lori Darks fought back tears talking about life in the plant. "We all grew up together," she said. "We raised our families together, celebrated together, and cried together. Now we're going through the different steps of death and dying. Basically, you accept it."

To help cope, they prayed. On an overcast Saturday afternoon in mid-February, more than three hundred GM workers and their families and friends filed into the New Dimensions Ministry Church for an interfaith worship service called "Through the Pain, Change and Fear, by Faith to Hope." There wasn't an empty seat in the cavernous, cream-colored building. Clergy from five different faiths—Christian, Jewish, Muslim, Baha'i, and Unitarian—participated in the service. One of the organizers was Bobby Millsap, who, besides being an autoworker, also served as the chaplain for UAW Local 1999. A soft-spoken, forty-seven-year-old ordained minister, Millsap said employees had repeatedly reached out to him in the plant for spiritual guidance. "People asked me to pray for a new product and that GM will make the right decisions for the employees," he said. "I told them that nothing is impossible to those that believe. That's what the Bible says. You have to have hope."

There were hymns and litanies and scripture readings, and at the end the congregation stood and sang "Solidarity Forever," the traditional anthem of organized labor, set to the tune of "The Battle Hymn of the Republic." The workers seemed to sing one stanza defiantly louder, as though they were trying to be heard a thousand miles away at GM headquarters in Detroit:

They have taken untold millions that they never toiled to earn,
But without our brain and muscle not a single wheel can turn,
We can break their haughty power, gain our freedom when we
learn
That the union makes us strong.

On February 20, Oklahoma City built its last vehicle, a "summit white" Trailblazer EXT with seventeen-inch cast-aluminum wheels and a 291-horsepower, six-cylinder engine. It went straight from the assembly line to the parking lot, joining the rest of the unsold inventory. Some employees brought cameras to take sentimental photographs of their coworkers and their workstations.

"Today is a real sad day," said Bruce Arnold, another veteran of twenty-seven years on the OKC line. "All I can say is thank God for the UAW."

He wasn't kidding. Because even though the plant was about to be mothballed permanently, the workers weren't going anywhere. In a week they would all report back to the factory and clock in, just as they had for years. The difference was they wouldn't be coming to work. They would be headed to the jobs bank—and paid not to work.

If there was one single facet of Detroit's decline that totally confounded people outside the industry, it was the jobs bank. The Big Three and the union had created it in the 1984 labor contract as an "employee-development bank." Back then, it was designed as a temporary repository for laid-off workers so they could be retrained for new positions in higher-tech factories. For the UAW, the jobs bank was an ironclad means to provide security for its members when the industry hit a rough patch. What it evolved into, though, was a holding bin for excess workers.

When union workers were laid off, they first went on unemployment. The auto companies were then required by the UAW contract to sweeten the government check with payments that guaranteed employees 95 percent of their wages for forty-eight weeks. Once those benefits expired, they entered the jobs bank. In theory, they were supposed to stay in the bank—and keep getting paid—until their old plant restarted or a job became available in another factory within a fifty-mile radius.

But because positions rarely opened up in plants nearby, many remained in the bank for years. It was a weird deal all around. As part of the job bank program, workers had to fulfill obligations, and they could meet these requirements by volunteering for company-approved community service—schools, charities, homeless shelters, meals-on-wheels.

Only a small percentage chose that option. Most reported each day to some building where they punched a clock and then did nothing except pass the time. Supervisors kept a close eye on their activities. They were allowed to watch television, read, do crossword puzzles, or work on a computer. But they had to sign out to use the bathroom or go to lunch, and they were not permitted to sleep or play cards, even though workers in Michigan could leave to take classes on dealing blackjack and poker in hopes of landing jobs at one of the state's new casinos.

Detroit supported dozens of jobs banks across the country, in virtually every place where a plant had closed since the mid-1980s. Some GM workers in Van Nuys, California, had been in the program for twelve years. In Flint, laid-off Delphi workers showed up at 6:00 A.M. at an old storage shed on the city's east side. Ironically, the building was on the site of the factory where workers staged the famous 1936 sit-down strike that forced General Motors to recognize and bargain with the fledgling United Auto Workers union. Now, on the same spot seventy years later, UAW members read newspapers, played Scrabble, and watched DVDs to earn their paychecks. One laid-off worker who had been in the Flint facility for six years said the monotony was excruciating. "I feel like I'm literally in a vegetative state," Judy Rowe told a reporter from the *Chicago Tribune*. "I have nothing to think about."

Needless to say, there wasn't much sympathy for her plight outside the UAW. With the addition of the twenty-two hundred workers in Oklahoma City (who went straight to the jobs bank because their plant had no chance of reopening), GM now had nearly eight thousand people in the program. Based on the combined cost of their wages and benefits, the company was spending an estimated $1 billion a year compensating idle employees. Delphi had another four thousand people in the bank; Chrysler had twenty-five hundred; and Ford about a thousand.

Wall Street gagged at the thought of these stumbling, cash-strapped companies paying workers to watch TV all day. "They're basically spending hundreds of millions of dollars and getting nothing for it," said David Healy, an analyst with Burnham Securities. Auto executives refused to say much publicly about the jobs bank, for fear of antagonizing the union. When asked about it at a press conference, Rick Wagoner stated the obvious. "Clearly it's an area of competitive disadvantage for us," he said.

Only Steve Miller at bankrupt Delphi dared to tackle the issue head-on. In typically blunt fashion, he compared the program to welfare payments built into the cost of a new GM car. "When you buy a Hyundai, you get a satellite radio as your option, but if you buy a Chevrolet, you get social welfare as standard equipment," he said. "Long-term, the customer is going to desert you if you try to price for your social welfare costs."

No issue was more sensitive for Ron Gettelfinger than the jobs bank. The UAW president usually tried to explain its origins, and how the program was meant to offer workers a safe haven when the economy sputtered and car sales dropped. But his words rang hollow. The more money GM lost, the more the media focused on inactive workers complaining of boredom while taking home big paychecks in the jobs bank. Given the financial woes of the Big Three, the program was not only indefensible but fed the growing public perception that the union was bleeding Detroit dry. There was already enough criticism of the UAW that its members were overpaid, its health care plans were too rich, and the vehicles it built weren't as good as the Japanese imports.

What's more, Toyota, Honda, and Nissan were making first-rate cars with nonunion American workers in Kentucky, Ohio, and Tennessee. And the so-called transplant factories were thriving. Toyota was about to open a new plant in San Antonio, Texas, to make pickup trucks that would rival the market-leading Ford F-series and Chevrolet Silverado. How could Detroit compete with the juggernaut from Japan if it had to pay people who weren't even working?

The jobs bank had become, in the words of the *Wall Street Journal*, "Detroit's symbol of dysfunction." GM was choking to death on legacy costs, yet its laid-off workers were lounging around, doing nothing, and making more than $50,000 a year. Gettelfinger started losing patience with reporters who pressed him about it, and began firing questions back. Should workers just be thrown out in the street? What about the millions in bonuses the top executives took home? Were the dedicated men and women in Oklahoma City responsible for GM making too many old-model SUVs?

And the mere mention of Steve Miller and his opinions made Gettelfinger's blood boil. "He didn't come in there to run that company," he snarled. "He came in there to destroy that company. And in destroying the company he's destroying lives and destroying families." To blame Detroit's problems on the jobs bank was unfair, he argued. Those people wouldn't be without work if the companies had made smarter decisions and the federal government didn't let cars from Japan and Korea flood the marketplace. The middle-class shouldn't be penalized for the misguided policies of the power brokers in Detroit and Washington. Gettelfinger vowed that he would not be bullied into giving up a program that autoworkers needed now more than ever. "That jobs bank," he said on a Detroit radio program, "is not going to go away."

Gettelfinger had more immediate concerns anyway. For weeks he had been in secret negotiations with GM about the buyout packages it would offer workers to leave the company. The offers had to be lucrative enough to entice employees to walk away from the automaker and their health care benefits forever (and stop filling up the jobs bank). And the numbers were staggering. Wagoner had set a target of eliminating thirty thousand jobs, and the only way that could happen was if GM opened the vault.

One proposal on the table was a lump-sum offer of $140,000 to any worker with ten years or more of service. In exchange for the cash, an employee would have to leave GM immediately and waive his or her right to future medical coverage—not an easy choice by any means. The company also wanted to rid itself of workers who already had thirty years of service and were eligible to retire but were still hanging on to their jobs. GM was prepared to give them $35,000 to nudge them out the door with their health care and pensions intact. Half of the company's 113,000 hourly workers in the United States were retirement-eligible or very close to it. The big money being waved in front of them might just be too attractive to pass up. The rumor mill was already churning in the plants. "I've got a thousand guys ready to go," said Chris "Tiny" Sherwood, president of UAW Local 652 in Lansing, Michigan.

A few days after production ceased in Oklahoma City, rows of tables and chairs were set up inside for the jobs bank. Some workers scrambled to line up volunteer opportunities so they wouldn't have to sit all day in the eerily quiet factory. Nobody was sure what to expect next. "It could be pretty solemn around here for a while," said Bobby Millsap. Union officials were besieged with questions about the future. Nanette Relerford summed up what was on most people's minds. "A buyout?" she said. "I'll take it."

So far, the buyout talks in Detroit had been surprisingly smooth. One reason was the involvement of Frederick "Fritz" Henderson, who was leading the GM bargaining team. Henderson had been on the job as chief financial officer for less than three months but had quickly become the company's ace troubleshooter. His plate was very full. Wagoner had deputized him to find a buyer for the GMAC financial services division, a supremely delicate task given the size of the business and the potential cash that its sale could generate. Henderson also inherited a mess of accounting problems that were under investigation by the U.S. Securities and Exchange Commission. And he was now GM's point man on Delphi, which by itself could be a full-time responsibility.

But Henderson was handling everything thrown his way. He was forty-seven years old and had been with GM since 1984, rising through the ranks rapidly in North America before making his mark overseas—first as managing director in Brazil, then as president of Latin American operations, head of the Asia-Pacific region, and finally chairman of GM Europe. Henderson was in a business meeting in Amsterdam in December 2005 when Wagoner called and said he wanted him to replace the retiring John Devine as CFO.

"We need you to do this," Wagoner said. At first Henderson protested. He loved running his own operation, and GM Europe was in the middle of a gigantic restructuring of its own. "In the end, what he kept saying was, 'We need you,'" Henderson said. "And so I came back." And once he returned, Henderson was thrust into the middle of GM's biggest challenges. "There was no doubt in my mind," he said, "that this company was in a five-alarm crisis."

In short order, Henderson brought a steady hand to some chaotic situations. He had a different, more informal style than Wagoner. He had been born in Detroit into a GM family, the son of a career sales executive in the Buick division. Short and compact, prematurely bald with a jaunty salt-and-pepper mustache, Henderson displayed a common touch that belied his pinstriped suits and Harvard Business School pedigree. "Fritz always went the extra mile to get everyone engaged," said Tony Cervone, Henderson's top communications executive in Europe. "Even if he already knew the solution, he would go around the table and make sure each person had a chance to contribute."

Henderson had an easy smile and a sense of humor, and clearly didn't take himself too seriously. When he was in Brazil, he danced on the GM float in the raucous Carnival street festival in Rio de Janeiro. During his constant business trips throughout Asia, Europe, and South America, Henderson regularly traveled alone and carried his own bags. He also had a legendary capacity for work, the kind of guy who brought briefcases full of documents home at night after spending twelve-hour days in the office. "I'm a realistic guy," he said. "There was a lot of stuff that needed to get done around here. And I liked that. I enjoyed it. I was invigorated by it." To some people inside GM, Henderson came across as cocky or too sure of himself. He talked very fast, had an amazing recall of facts and figures, and seemed blessed with inexhaustible energy. "Look, I'm 100 percent focused, and I'm not interested in getting off track," he said. "People appreciate decisiveness. That's why you get the job—to decide."

Henderson was determined to work with Gettelfinger, not fight him. The UAW president didn't much trust GM, and Wagoner did not interact well with the union at all. But the stakes were too high for the mutual animosity to continue. "The relationship with Ron was not good," Henderson said. "Somebody had to build a relationship with him. It ended up being me. I liked Ron. I ended up spending a lot of time with him."

Gettelfinger respected Henderson too—possibly because he wasn't Steve Miller or Rick Wagoner. Whatever the reason, they got down to business on the buyouts. Maybe the union and GM could navigate these troubled waters together and both survive.

[Thirteen]

W here are the market share numbers?"

Jerry York stared across the boardroom at Rick Wagoner. It was his first meeting as a GM director, and already he was putting Wagoner on the spot.

"We can get those for you," Wagoner said.

The other board members just watched. Suddenly the table seemed to have tilted in York's direction. Confronting Wagoner was not typical boardroom behavior. But York was not interested in business as usual.

"My understanding is our market share is down 1.6 percent from a year ago," York said. "I want to know what the numbers are—without the rental sales."

Wagoner nodded and made a note. York took his own notes. The meeting continued. Fritz Henderson gave updates on GMAC, Delphi, and the union buyouts. As he began going over the proposals under discussion with the UAW, York stopped him.

"What's the cash effect of this?" he asked.

That couldn't be calculated until the deal was done, Henderson said. York made another note. As if on cue, other directors did the same. The meeting went on. But the tenor had changed, and nothing in the General Motors boardroom would ever be quite the same again. At one point, Wagoner was asked to leave the room so the outside directors could meet in executive session.

Now York really opened up. He proposed that the board draft hard targets for the management team, paying specific attention to how much cash GM was burning and whether its new products could stem its chronic slide in market share. "The key part here is stabilizing market share," York said. "I want to see a five-year forecast for market share."

George Fisher couldn't argue with York. But the former Motorola and Kodak chief executive officer—Wagoner's staunchest ally on the board—was visibly uncomfortable with how York was setting the agenda. Fisher had the title of lead director and usually ran the executive sessions. But York was taking a backseat to no one. He was going to ask pointed questions and demand answers. Some of the other directors liked that immediately.

"There were a lot of board members who were really concerned about cash and cash flow," said John Bryan, a board member for thirteen years. "And one thing about Jerry was he had a lot of knowledge. He knew more about the auto business than the rest of us."

Wagoner commanded a lot of respect in the boardroom. But York firmly believed the chief executive worked for the board, which represented the shareholders, who owned the company. "Jerry was very polite, very cordial," said Bryan. "But it was written all over him that he thought this was a poorly managed company."

After the March 6 meeting ended, York took stock of what he had seen and heard.

"What is missing in this equation is planning," he told a friend in Detroit. "Why did they have to wait until three-quarters of the damage was done to figure out they had to restructure the company?"

He hadn't formed opinions yet about all the other board members. "Looks like there may be five good directors," he said. "But it doesn't look like they have enough information. I was shocked they didn't know what is going on with market share."

York was scrutinizing Wagoner's every move but was withholding judgment on him for now. He suspected that management was doing everything it could to boost revenues and bring down inventory levels, including selling excess production to car rental companies at a discount. That was a bad sign, in his view. He hated the idea that GM was putting a Band-Aid on a fatal wound. "What makes Rick Wagoner tick?" he wondered. "No one knows. It looks like he's pulling out all the stops to make the first-quarter numbers. They haven't pulled back on rentals, and that's one of the big reasons the shit has hit the fan. You can only play that game for so long."

York was just beginning to put GM under the microscope. His boss, Kirk Kerkorian, considered himself a long-term investor. But he had zero tolerance for underperformance. If changes were necessary at GM, he expected York to push hard to make them happen as soon as possible. And the quickest way to light a fire under management was by bringing in a new chief executive. "I don't give a fuck how GM gets fixed," York said. "If Rick Wagoner can do it, fine. If not . . ."

He didn't bother to finish his own sentence.

Wagoner wasn't ruffled by York's aggressive approach. He enjoyed a good working relationship with most of the board. He knew some directors were impatient with GM's progress and were upset by the constant criticism from Wall Street and the media. But he felt they understood the enormity of the task at hand. General Motors was no ordinary company; it was an essential institution, a national asset, the backbone of American manufacturing. When terrorists struck the World Trade Center on 9/11, the White House turned to GM to stabilize the economy. And it was Rick Wagoner who stood front and center, launching the "Keep America Rolling" program that offered free financing to car buyers for up to five years. When the country needed help, GM was there.

Now the company was hurting, but Wagoner was convinced it was on the right path. GM would not turn around overnight. It required patience and persistence—something York just did not appear to have. "Jerry would come in and ask for all this data, but never offer a single idea," Wagoner said. "I mean, he's out there telling everybody else all his great ideas, but he won't discuss them with me?"

Above all, Wagoner believed in The Plan. The best and brightest at GM crafted it, and he would not deviate from their course of action. Shrinking North American operations was critical; so was improving and diversifying the product lineup. GM had taken a big step forward on reducing legacy costs with the previous year's health care deal, and Wagoner expected the 2007 labor talks to finish that job. He had an experienced team in place: Bob Lutz was fixing the product, Fritz Henderson was tackling finance and labor issues, Gary Cowger was running manufacturing, and so on down the organization chart.

Best of all, there was huge opportunity to grow overseas. Like his predecessor Jack Smith, Wagoner was certain that the future lay in China, India, Brazil, and all the other exploding markets where General Motors was gaining, not losing, market share. The problems at home made international expansion even more essential. Wagoner relished the competition in the emerging markets, where GM was not hamstrung by health care costs, pensions, and legions of entrenched workers. On the morning of March 15, Wagoner boarded a company Gulfstream for a long-planned trip to China and Korea. It turned out to be an inopportune time to leave town.

GM was racing to file its 2005 annual report that night with the Securities and Exchange Commission. This was hardly a routine filing. Mistakes had been made in the previously reported $8.6 billion loss for the year. Because it underestimated the cost of Delphi and the North American restructuring, GM had to swallow the embarrassment of amending the loss to $10.6 billion. But there was more. The SEC was cracking down on how the company accounted for payments to suppliers, forcing it to restate results for the five previous years. The changes weren't substantial. But taken all together, the revisions looked pretty bad. With Henderson's supervision, a team of auditors had combed through millions of documents to check for any errors that could taint the annual report. The SEC was digging through GM's books, and the final paperwork had to be perfect.

Then, just hours before the filing, a bombshell landed on Henderson's desk. Somehow cash flow numbers from the GMAC mortgage business had been misclassified. The auditors were in a panic. "Tell me more," Henderson said sternly. There wasn't time to change the numbers; the entire document needed revisions. GM was facing a midnight deadline, and filing a flawed annual report—on top of the restated losses—would be a disaster. Henderson had to make a decision. He called Wagoner, who had just landed in Korea. "Hey, we can't file today," he told him. "We have to get an extension."

A press release was hastily written. When it went out the next morning, GM's stock dropped like a rock. Wall Street came down hard on Wagoner & Co. "This is likely to take a toll on management's already embattled credibility," said an instant report from Lehman Brothers. But investors' reactions were mild compared to those of the GM board. A number of directors got on a conference call with Wagoner and unloaded. One of the angriest was Phil Laskawy, the retired chief executive of the accounting giant Ernst & Young and chairman of the board's audit committee.

But even George Fisher ripped into Wagoner. GM looked ridiculous, he said, like it couldn't even manage to get a simple annual report in on time. York took the high road. Rather than bash management, he called for an internal investigation. The other directors wholeheartedly agreed.

All Wagoner could do was listen and take it. He left it to Henderson to explain the situation and issue a public defense of GM's integrity. Inside corporate headquarters, people tried to assess the damage done to the CEO. At best, Wagoner appeared out of touch for going out of the country under the circumstances. Momentum had suddenly shifted to his critics, particularly York. "The perception of Jerry [had] changed from a guy who wants to raid the GM treasury to a sharp-minded source of accountability," said Steve Girsky.

The next day, Wagoner cut short his trip to Asia and flew back to Detroit. He returned to a rash of media coverage attacking him and praising York as a driving force for change. This was a turning point. Until now, the criticisms of GM had centered on its strategy, focus, and sense of urgency. But the accounting mess triggered questions about competence and responsibility, the very qualities Wagoner's defenders often cited about him. The GM directors were burning up the phone lines talking to each other, worrying about damage control, and reaching out to York for direction. Management desperately needed some positive news.

Thankfully, Fritz Henderson and the labor team delivered. On March 22, GM announced a deal with the UAW to offer buyouts to all of the company's 113,000 union members as well as 13,000 Delphi workers. The agreement would go a long way toward cutting the U.S. workforce down to size. But it wouldn't come cheap. GM would offer $35,000 to retirement-eligible employees to leave and up to $140,000 for some workers to cut all their ties, including health benefits. The program represented one of the biggest employee buyouts ever made by an American corporation. All told, GM estimated the buyouts would cost between $2 billion and $4.6 billion—an astonishing amount for a public corporation to downsize blue-collar workers.

It also marked a symbolic break with GM's storied past. Thousands of employees who joined the company at its peak in the 1970s were expected to move on. Thinning the ranks was also intended to take some of the sting out of future plant closings and stop the flow of laid-off workers into the jobs bank. Overall, the buyouts would mark a pivotal step forward in the long-overdue restructuring of GM. Wagoner's quotes led the press release, even though he had not spent a single day in the labor talks. "We are pleased that this agreement will help fulfill an important objective," he said.

The buyout deal was followed in rapid succession by other moves, including plans to slash hundreds of white-collar jobs and the sale of GMAC's commercial real estate unit. The sales executive Mark LaNeve called an unusual press conference to say GM was now backing away from unprofitable sales to rental fleets. "We are taking some pretty painful and necessary steps to run this business the right way," LaNeve said. He added, almost apologetically, that the company was also weaning itself off big discounts to move inventory. "We have learned our lesson," he said.

York was watching it all carefully. He had begun holding deep-dive meetings all over town as he dug into GM's operations. He sat down with Ron Gettelfinger one day, then the GM labor negotiators the next. He had a long one-on-one with Bob Lutz, whom he knew well from their days together at Chrysler in the 1980s. Lutz didn't trust York and definitely didn't want him meddling in product development. But he couldn't hide his own frustrations with GM's rigid culture and bureaucracy. He described Wagoner as a good guy who sweated the details but too often missed the big picture. "It's basically what's been wrong with GM for the past thirty years," Lutz said. "It's all analytical, businesslike and risk avoidance—keep everything on an even keel at all costs."

One afternoon York drove out to the tech center to look over new vehicles. He wasn't pleased with what he found. "It was like two separate companies," he said. "They had these terrific trucks and SUVs, and these cars that made you want to throw up, with all these chintzy materials and ugly plastic parts." Then he talked with a half dozen senior people overseeing engines and transmissions. York loved getting under the hood of an automobile. He had actually started in the industry at GM in the 1960s, working on Pontiac muscle cars. And he was very impressed when he saw all the new technology in the engineering labs. But the tone of the presentation was strangely flat. There was all this great hardware, but nobody in the room seemed very enthusiastic about it. York pulled aside Tom Stephens, the head of the global power train division. "Tom," York said, "can you come outside with me for a minute while I have a cigarette?"

Once they were alone, York shared his observations.

"What I'm finding are very intelligent, educated, knowledgeable people who know what they're doing," York said. "But I'm not seeing the fire in the belly."

Stephens, a tall, burly engineer with a reddish beard, didn't mince words. "If you could work in this place for one fucking day, you would understand," he said. "It is so bureaucratic, no decisions ever get made."

York was beginning to build arguments for a change at the top. He sensed Wagoner had never been more vulnerable, and he stoked the growing concerns about his leadership. He quietly confided his doubts about Wagoner to influential journalists, stock analysts, institutional investors, and the board members he thought shared his views—John Bryan, Phil Laskawy, Erskine Bowles, Kent Kresa.

When it came to assessing Wagoner, York could be very convincing. "Let's say Rick had the same track record at Ford over the past six years as he's had at GM," he said. "Would he be a candidate to run GM? I don't think so." York was a bit of a chameleon. With his blue blazers and turtleneck sweaters, he came across as an intellectual with business acumen, someone who did his homework and thought matters all the way through. But there was an earthy side to the thrice-married, chain-smoking, martini-drinking southerner who kept a .357 Magnum under the front seat of his SUV ("Just in case," he explained, "somebody wants to fuck with me"). That Jerry York could be pretty blunt about General Motors and Rick Wagoner, its courtly chairman and chief executive officer. "GM executives are smart, pleasant, well-dressed, well-groomed," he said. "But there's not one ounce of killer instinct." No one would ever accuse York of lacking a killer instinct. He smelled blood and was ready to make his move.

The GM board was meeting more frequently than usual, mostly to consider a massive deal to sell a majority interest in the GMAC finance unit to the private equity firm Cerberus Capital Management. At a meeting in New York in late March, the directors asked Wagoner to excuse himself early on. He wound up waiting two hours without ever being called back in. Wagoner didn't know that behind closed doors, the directors weren't discussing GMAC; they were talking about him.

"The board was trying to figure out what to do, in terms of Rick's tenure," said Bryan. "Jerry was pumping for having a role of some sort . . . CEO or chairman. There was no question he was itching to try."

The conversation among the directors got heated, and opinions were split on whether GM was better off with or without Wagoner. Several ideas were thrown around, including installing York as chairman and Fritz Henderson as chief executive. But George Fisher had a scheduling conflict and was not present. Another board member had to leave early. It was decided that the topic was too important to proceed without all the directors in the room. Some who were there—especially York—wanted to continue the discussion to its conclusion. So they agreed to hold a special meeting on April 9 to debate whether Wagoner should keep his job.

When Fisher learned what had gone on, he privately told Wagoner about it. The message was clear: GM's chief executive was in some serious trouble.

Wagoner's inner circle gathered on March 30 around the conference table in his Renaissance Center office in Detroit. His two most influential advisors on hand were Steve Harris, the veteran public relations executive who had just come out of retirement to rejoin GM, and Thomas Gottschalk, the automaker's top corporate lawyer. Both men were close to Wagoner, and both told him point blank he had better fight for his job. "You can't afford to be stoic at this point," Gottschalk said.

Harris was even more forthright. "You have become the story of this company," he told Wagoner. "Perception has become reality." Harris knew how uncomfortable Wagoner was with talking about himself, much less defending his accomplishments as CEO. That didn't matter anymore. "Rick, you have got to confront this now," Harris said.

Harris and an outside consultant, Dan McGinn, had come up with a strategy. One part was called the Detroit Project, which consisted of Wagoner personally defending GM and himself in interviews with major newspapers, magazines, and television networks. The second was dubbed the Arlington Project (which would operate from the city in Virginia where McGinn's company was based). This was a broader effort involving dozens of GM executives touting the company in sixteen key markets across the United States. "We aren't telling our story consistently," Harris said. "We need consistent messaging."

GM dealers would be involved as well, trying to build grassroots support for the company and its beleaguered leader. It all sounded distasteful to Wagoner, who felt that GM was obviously making all the right moves as fast as it could. And he really didn't want more of the spotlight on him. "I hate the idea of going out and talking about me," he said. But he knew his career at GM was at a dangerous crossroads. Wagoner was competitive and would not go down easily. He agreed to do whatever interviews Harris set up.

The tougher issue was with the board. If Wagoner was losing support among the directors, it was only a matter of time before York got him fired. He needed to act before the special meeting convened on April 9.

The board was holding a conference call on April 2 to approve the GMAC sale, which at any other time would have been a seismic event. It gave Wagoner an opening to do something he had never imagined doing—asking for a vote of confidence. If he didn't get it, he saw no alternative but to resign.

In his darkest hour, Wagoner sought advice from Jack Smith, his friend and predecessor as chairman and CEO, and George Fisher, whom he had worked so closely with as lead director. Smith urged Wagoner to take a stand. "You have got to assert yourself," he said.

Fisher wholeheartedly agreed. He was aghast that York had stirred up the board to the point where it would consider replacing Wagoner. "There's nobody better in the industry than you, Rick," Fisher said. "You're our guy." He offered to draft a statement of support and then try to convince the other directors to go along with it.

Wagoner still wasn't sure. It just wasn't his style to make himself the issue. He was a team player, a loyal soldier who consistently tried to keep his ego out of the equation. If the board really thought someone else could do a better job, maybe it was right.

Finally Wagoner went to Bob Lutz. They were as different as any two auto executives could ever be: the self-effacing, by-the-book chief executive officer and his mercurial, outspoken deputy. It gratified Lutz immensely that Wagoner was turning to him. He had been begging his boss for months to stand up for what was right at GM and to put all these annoying critics in their place. Lutz didn't want York turning GM upside down any more than Wagoner did. And one thing Lutz knew was how to wield power. Sure, there was some risk in asking for a vote of confidence. But winners stick their neck out for what they believe in. "Under the circumstances, it's what you have to do," Lutz said. "You have got to get out there and take it on."

On Sunday, April 2, the GM board members dialed into a conference call from their homes in Miami, Chicago, Phoenix, and as far away as Sweden. York was in his condo in suburban Detroit. Wagoner was in his office. Fisher had already told the other directors that the embattled CEO planned to make a personal plea for their support. He also had forwarded drafts of press releases that affirmed the board's confidence in management, noting that the GMAC sale underscored the positive direction GM was heading in. With those releases on the table, Wagoner made his pitch.

The agenda of the upcoming April 9 board meeting, Wagoner said, put him in an "untenable situation" and compromised his authority to run General Motors. They had made great strides, but he couldn't keep doing his job without knowing whether the board was behind him. "The plan is in place," he said. "The plan is working. But I cannot operate without the strong support of the board." He wasn't going to belabor the point. He simply needed their complete confidence to execute the turnaround all of them had worked so hard for. "You all have received the draft press release," he said. "If GM can't put out this press release Monday morning, I'm going to have to resign." Then he thanked them and left the call.

Threatening to resign was an unexpected and powerful move. Wagoner had raised the stakes big-time. If he didn't get what he wanted, the board would have a five-alarm crisis on its hands. At Fisher's suggestion, the directors responded in alphabetical order. Some expressed reservations about publicly issuing a show of support that might not hold up down the road. Most of them, though, were more worried about the fallout if Wagoner abruptly resigned before they could decide on a permanent replacement. A few defended him outright, citing the progress made with the UAW buyouts and health care deal. As expected, Fisher argued forcefully that keeping Wagoner was in the company's immediate best interest.

York was the last to speak. After hearing everyone else, he knew where this discussion was headed. Wagoner wasn't going anywhere—for now. "You know how I feel," he said cryptically. "There has got to be some accountability here." Fisher then called for a consensus about putting out a vote of confidence, and a majority concurred. But York and at least three others were adamant that the press release could not describe it as a "unanimous" vote.

Almost as an afterthought, the directors approved the sale of a 51 percent stake in GMAC to Cerberus—a monumental deal that could net GM about $14 billion in badly needed cash over the next three years. Then, as if to slam the door shut on the Wagoner discussion, Fisher officially canceled the April 9 board meeting.

The next day, GM announced its epic agreement to sell a controlling stake in its finance division. It was hardly a victory; GMAC had been one of the company's few reliable sources of earnings for years. But selling it would help pay for the buyouts, fund new products, and shore up an increasingly weak balance sheet. In the press release, Wagoner hailed the move as a "milestone" and another in a series of "bold initiatives" that positioned the automaker for "long-term success."

Buried in the fifth paragraph was a seemingly innocuous quote from Fisher: "While there is much work to be done, the GM Board has great confidence in Rick Wagoner, his management team and the plan they are implementing to restore the company to profitability." The world had no way of knowing that single sentence was the only reason Wagoner was still in charge at General Motors. At the media briefing afterward, Wagoner was asked about the statement. "I appreciate the support from the board, our employees, my wife—anybody I can get it from these days," he said with a weary smile.

Over the next week, the Detroit Project cranked up. Wagoner did a ton of interviews, and the theme of his remarks was remarkably consistent: GM had big challenges ahead, and he was the best man to lead it through them.

"I'm doing what I'm doing because I love General Motors," he told the *Detroit News*. "I think it's very important what we're doing as a company, and I think I'm by far the most qualified person to do it." He expressed gratitude that the directors, employees, and executives were standing behind him. "Some days you feel better than others," he said to *Newsweek*. "But people count on me every day to be out there and drive the business and be positive." And when he was asked on the CBS News program *Face the Nation* if he had any plans to resign, he didn't blink, even though just twenty-four hours earlier he had been ready to walk out the door.

"I have no plans at all," Wagoner said. "I wouldn't be in this job if I didn't think I was the right guy to do it."

[Fourteen]

Rick Wagoner cared about his job. And tens of thousands of autoworkers across the United States cared about theirs. The difference was that the GM chief executive saw his talents as essential to the company, while the men and women in the factories were considered expendable.

That view wasn't unique to GM. The management of Ford and Delphi were also building their comebacks on the oldest restructuring formula in America—eliminating jobs and shutting factories. Chrysler had already led the way by downsizing drastically. There was no question Detroit had too many workers and factories. In the first half of 2006, foreign brands accounted for 53 percent of all retail vehicle sales in the country, marking the first time that the Big Three's combined share fell to less than half. Their immense size was once an advantage. But it had become a slow-acting poison. The companies just couldn't sell enough cars to support the generations of people who built their products. Detroit was suffocating under the weight of its own history. And the emergency surgery to save it would be traumatic, painful, and expensive.

While the power struggle at GM went on behind the scenes,

Detroit's foundation continued to crumble. Once again it was Steve Miller wielding the sledgehammer. On March 31, 2006, Delphi asked the bankruptcy court to allow it to close twenty-one of its twenty-nine U.S. factories, freeze pensions, cut a quarter of its salaried workers, and void all its labor agreements. It also wanted to cancel $5 billion in contracts to sell parts to GM. Altogether it was a blueprint for gutting the largest parts-making operation in America and wiping out thirty thousand union and white-collar jobs.

In the court filing, Miller said that Delphi's future was primarily in China, India, Mexico, and other low-wage nations. "Emergence from the Chapter 11 process in the U.S.," he said, "requires us to make difficult, but necessary decisions."

The news hit Ron Gettelfinger like a kick in the teeth. "This is a travesty, and a concern for every American," he said. It didn't take long for the UAW to threaten a counterattack. If its labor contract was canceled, the union said it would be "impossible to avoid a long strike." Within days, local union officials at targeted plants were talking about unauthorized wildcat strikes that would not only hurt Delphi but cripple General Motors. Analysts estimated that GM stood to lose up to $8 billion during a sixty-day strike (although some added that a shutdown would have a silver lining of reducing its bulging backlog of unsold cars).

A ruling by a bankruptcy judge on the Delphi plan could take months. Miller claimed he'd rather negotiate the radical reorganization with the union and GM than rely on a judge's order. But this was a test of wills, and it was unlikely the UAW would go down without a fight.

Fritz Henderson was the man in the middle. Gettelfinger refused to talk to Miller and vice versa, so Henderson shuttled back and forth between the two sides. Both Delphi and the union wanted GM to absorb all the costs of worker buyouts, pensions, and health care. It had been seven years since GM spun off the sprawling parts business so it wouldn't have to pay big wages for commodity components. Now Delphi had come back to haunt the automaker when it could least afford it.

The UAW had an amazing track record over the years of leveraging wage hikes and benefits out of GM, Ford, and Chrysler by pitting one company against the others. If the union negotiated a sweet deal with Ford, the other two would be forced to match it or suffer a costly and debilitating strike. The root of the union's power was always a strike. Used strategically, it was the ultimate weapon. The last major one had occurred in 1998, when workers at two GM parts plants in Flint, Michigan, walked off the job for fifty-four days to protest outsourcing. The break in the supply chain shut down almost every GM assembly plant in the nation. The strike ended up costing the company more than $2 billion, and the workers got what they wanted—guarantees of jobs and investment. A year later, GM spun off all its parts operations into newly formed Delphi. And now one of the plants on the bankruptcy closing list was Flint East—the site of the 1998 strike.

But strikes didn't empower the UAW anymore. A walkout at Delphi could push GM itself into bankruptcy. As Detroit got weaker, the union's muscle withered along with it. The best Gettelfinger could do was extract as much money as possible from the companies to buy out some workers so that jobs would be left for others. The union's historic swagger was fading fast, and reality was setting in. For decades the union won higher pay and benefits because it was a tough, powerful opponent. But those days were over.

"The global economy has turned a blowtorch on Detroit," said Harley Shaiken, a University of California at Berkeley labor professor who worked closely with the UAW. "Delphi is the watershed event that pushed the union into uncharted territory." More and more, the midwestern towns and cities that were bastions of union jobs had been hollowed out. The struggles of Detroit and Flint were obvious—soaring unemployment rates, waves of home foreclosures, empty downtowns that looked like sculpture gardens of abandoned buildings. But it wasn't just old urban areas in Michigan that had hit bottom.

One of the hardest-hit places was Anderson, Indiana, home to twenty-two thousand GM jobs in the 1970s and now down to twenty-five hundred autoworkers. A dozen factories had systematically been closed and boarded up. One last Delphi plant remained, and its future looked bleak. Yet Anderson was still dependent on GM and the pension checks and medical care it provided for thousands of retirees and their family members. How long the corporation could keep paying its bills was anyone's guess. "You just take it day by day," John Lollar, a seventy-four-year-old retiree, told the *New York Times*. "I just hope my benefits last longer than I do."

At Delphi plants across the country, vague worries had turned to fear and anger. "I'm afraid the union has sort of become a toothless dog," said Jim Grego, a twenty-five-year UAW worker at a fuel injector plant in the pristine little city of Coopersville in western Michigan. The factory had been a cornerstone of the local economy since it opened in 1981. Now Delphi wanted to shut it down and consolidate production at other facilities in Michigan and New York.

It was hard to argue with the business logic. But how could the UAW allow Coopersville's 560 jobs to be eliminated, just like that? The president of Local 2151, Robert Betts, said this would ultimately deepen the union's resolve and bind its members closer together. "It's like the Romans," said Betts. "The more they persecuted the Christians, the more the faith grew."

Workers whose jobs were on the line weren't so sure. They were too concerned about their mortgages, car payments, and doctor bills. If the UAW was going to let Delphi close their factories without resistance, what good was a union? "I think Gettelfinger has pussyfooted around the issues," said Dan Lamb, a machinist at Delphi's endangered brake plant in Dayton, Ohio. "It's time to go back to our roots, when the union was militant."

Gettelfinger was fighting battles on multiple fronts—Delphi, buyouts, plant closings, health care. He was both an idealist and a pragmatist, a true believer waging a holy war and a hardheaded negotiator determined to cut the best deals possible. But it was getting harder to keep his emotions in check. The executives with the big paychecks were cutting jobs and shutting plants like it was just another day at the office. "This slash-and-burn crap is beyond irresponsible," he railed to one of the Big Three's negotiators. "It's simply a matter of greed now. What are we, in a race to the bottom? You have a great workforce here and you want to walk away to Mexico where they're paying $10 a day?"

Gettelfinger never gave an inch in negotiations until he had to. The buyout deals were unavoidable; GM and Ford had to reduce their employment rolls to survive. The union's only option was to make it palatable and get workers enough cash to cushion the blow. But Gettelfinger tried to draw the line when he could, and he was doing it at Chrysler. Unlike GM and Ford, DaimlerChrysler was making money. Gettelfinger saw no reason to give the German powerhouse the same break on health care as the other two Detroit automakers.

It was a provocative stance. The bedrock principle of all Big Three labor contracts was parity. Whatever one company negotiated with the UAW, the other two had to follow suit. But health care discussions with the new head of the Chrysler division, Tom LaSorda, were going nowhere. As a longtime manufacturing executive, LaSorda was supposedly adept at the bargaining table. But he couldn't get Gettelfinger to budge. Every time he argued that Chrysler deserved the same adjustments as GM and Ford, the union boss stubbornly pointed to the bottom line. "Your company is in a different situation than them," he said.

At one point Dieter Zetsche stepped in. He was already deeply distressed over Chrysler's legacy costs, and he had instructed his top German executives to investigate dumping the American division. It was still a well-kept secret, known only to his inner circle. Even Tom LaSorda didn't know that Zetsche was considering a sale of Chrysler. But the plan was gaining momentum in Stuttgart in the spring of 2006 when Zetsche sat down with Gettelfinger in Detroit.

Zetsche was baffled that Gettelfinger was so obstinate about not giving Chrysler concessions on health care. This was no small matter; the automaker stood to save hundreds of millions of dollars with the same deal as its two Detroit rivals. And the union wouldn't do it because DaimlerChrysler was earning a profit? "I was totally convinced it would only be a question of time that we would get a comparable deal," Zetsche said. "I couldn't believe it."

When Gettelfinger told him the union wouldn't bend, Zetsche looked at him hard. He wanted the UAW to know it should not count on the rich German parent sticking with Chrysler indefinitely. "The assumption that there will always be big coffers behind Chrysler could be the wrong assumption," he said.

Gettelfinger didn't get the hint. So Zetsche spelled it out. "You know, the status quo might not necessarily be the situation forever," he said.

Whatever Zetsche was saying, Gettelfinger wasn't buying it. Chrysler retirees, he said, should not have to sacrifice health care at a company that was earning big profits—end of story.

That attitude was exactly why Zetsche was losing sleep over Detroit. These union guys didn't get it. This was business, and he could play hardball too. He had one last warning.

"You might make a major mistake," Zetsche said, "if that is your final position."

The General Motors board convened on May 2 for its regular monthly meeting, the first since the showdown on Wagoner. The storm had passed, but the tension was still palpable. Wagoner clearly was wary of York. "Rick didn't have to say anything," Fritz Henderson said. "You could see it in his body language." The Detroit Project media blitz had spread the word that the GM chief executive was firmly in command. When the company reported its first-quarter results—a $323 million loss—Wagoner hailed the numbers on live television as evidence of progress. "Clearly we're moving in the right direction," he said on CNBC. (GM would later get a ruling from the SEC that allowed it to restate the quarter as a $445 million profit.)

But all was not well inside the Renaissance Center. In a rare bloodletting, two senior executives—Paul Schmidt, the corporate controller, and Peter Bible, the chief accounting officer—were forced to resign because of the accounting blunders. Steve Girsky was also leaving, by his own choice. He said he was anxious to return home to his family in New York. But privately Girsky sounded dispirited by his lack of influence on management and concerned that GM was doing too little too late to turn itself around. "Time is the big enemy," he said. "Does GM have enough time to do what it needs to do?"

The most intriguing item on the board's agenda was the presentation that Jerry York had asked for on U.S. market share projections. Paul Ballew, GM's top market analyst, concluded that GM's current 24 percent share would fall to 20 percent within five years. It was a disturbing decline considering the company had lots of new products coming. Some of the loss was the result of fewer factories, less production, and a conscious effort to pull back on fleet sales and cheap leases. But the bigger factor was more competition from new models planned by Toyota, Honda, and the other Asian automakers. This was not news to anyone. But to see it in such stark terms was unsettling. York looked over to gauge Wagoner's reaction. "He could hardly bring himself to talk about it," York said. "How can you stand there and accept that you are going to keep losing share?"

Right then, York vowed to get rid of Wagoner. Instead of wasting time trying to sway the board, York had a better idea. He would match Wagoner up with a rival, someone who would show the GM directors what a truly dynamic CEO looked like. And he knew exactly who he wanted.

Carlos Ghosn got the call in his office in Paris.

"Hello, Carlos, this is Jerry York," York said on the phone. "I'm calling on behalf of Kirk Kerkorian."

Ghosn had never met York or Kerkorian. But he knew of their dealings with Chrysler and their role in its 1998 merger with Daimler-Benz. They were working on GM now, York said, and they were very interested in what Ghosn had accomplished with the alliance of the French carmaker Renault and Nissan Motor of Japan.

"Is there anything we can do together?" York said. "I'd like to talk to you about your strategy, how you see GM and the industry."

It was not unusual for Ghosn to get inquiries about the alliance from other automakers. But this sounded different, almost urgent. Of course, he said, he would be delighted to meet with York.

On May 8, York walked into a private dining room at the elegant

Dorchester Hotel in London and introduced himself to Ghosn, the fifty-two-year-old chief executive of Renault and Nissan and one of the auto world's brightest stars. Over the previous seven years, Ghosn had resurrected debt-ridden Nissan, streamlined stodgy Renault, and fashioned a groundbreaking alliance between the two. While the corporations were independent, each owned a large stake in the other, and they collaborated closely on purchasing parts and developing products. The arrangement had been a smashing success. Both companies were solidly profitable and growing steadily. Together, the Renault-Nissan alliance ranked as the world's fourth-largest automaker, behind GM, Toyota, and Ford. And Ghosn made no secret that he would like to add a third, North American–based automaker to their international coalition.

Bill Ford had already tried to lure Ghosn to Ford but to no avail. Why work for the Ford family when he had freedom to run both Renault and Nissan as he pleased? Ghosn had created something unique in the auto industry. Running two carmakers simultaneously was no small feat. In the process, he had earned a reputation as both a cost-cutter and an inspired manager. Investors revered him for publicly setting targets and delivering results; the stock prices of both companies had gained substantially under his leadership. He was skilled (two engineering degrees), exotic (born in Brazil to a Lebanese father and a French mother), and terribly charismatic (hero of a Japanese comic book, *The True Story of Carlos Ghosn*). Short in stature, with an oval face, jet-black hair, and piercing dark eyes, Ghosn captivated York from the moment they sat down to lunch.

Ghosn was candid, confident, and brimming with ideas. In French-accented English, he explained how the alliance not only had saved Renault and Nissan billions but also blended their respective strengths in engineering and design. He impressed York with how he supervised early decisions on vehicle styling. "For our large-volume products, I'm looking at clay models before they're even finished," he said.

He also believed strongly in building cars with specific consumers in mind. "You try to put yourself in the situation of the buyer," he said. "I'm not looking at it as Carlos Ghosn. I'm looking at it as a thirty-five-year-old male with a high income." And he was convinced that with a strong third partner in the alliance—General Motors or Ford, for example—the combination would be a leading force in the global auto industry for decades to come.

York asked him straight out: "Would you consider adding GM as a partner?"

Absolutely, Ghosn replied. There were huge potential synergies that could benefit GM as well as Renault and Nissan. Then he made a point that York couldn't have said better himself. "Jerry, I call Toyota the beast," he said. "The beast just keeps getting stronger and stronger. And the source of the beast's food is General Motors and Ford. The most important issue in the worldwide auto industry is for the beast to run out of food."

York was blown away. He couldn't remember the last time he had agreed so completely with someone. He wanted Ghosn to meet Kerkorian as soon as possible. When they finished lunch, York called his boss in Los Angeles. "Kirk, you've got to meet this guy," York said over the phone. "He's a product maniac. Compared to him, Rick Wagoner is pathetic."

The lights dimmed in the big hall at the MGM Grand Hotel and Casino in Las Vegas as Ron Gettelfinger took the stage on June 12 to open the thirty-fourth Constitutional Convention of the United Auto Workers union. Thirteen hundred delegates from across the UAW quieted down and took their seats. Over the next four days, the union would assess its challenges, plan strategy, and reelect Gettelfinger to a second four-year term as president. The straitlaced union leader had tried to move the convention from its traditional location in Vegas to Detroit. But too many union officials had their heart set on meeting in Sin City, where coincidentally the UAW was trying to organize casino employees to replace the thinning ranks of autoworkers.

For his state-of-the-union speech, Gettelfinger changed from his usual open-collared work shirt and slacks into a dark suit and blue necktie. He had a heavy message to deliver not only to the delegates but also to the TV crews and reporters covering the convention. The Big Three were telling workers to give up their hard-earned paychecks and benefits for the good of the corporations. Now it was his turn to tell the world what the men and women on the assembly line believed in, and what they would fight for.

"What's at stake," he said to the hushed crowd, "is more than our paychecks and benefits. What's at stake is our shared vision of an America that lives up to its promise of freedom, opportunity, dignity, and social and economic justice for all. That's our American dream. Now, we know that many of those who measure their lives by the value of their stock portfolios, the square footage of their homes in gated communities, and their exotic vacation homes think our vision belongs to a fading past that has no place in today's global economy. In fact, whether they say it publicly or not, they wholeheartedly agree with Delphi CEO Steve Miller that American workers need to get over the idea of having a middle-class lifestyle and resign themselves to barely scraping by."

He paused for a second and then went on, his soft southern drawl the only sound in the room: "Well, we've got news for them!" he said, pounding the lectern. "We're not going to surrender. We're not going to lower our sights, give up our dreams, or give up the fight for a better world for our children and grandchildren. We're going to keep fighting for what we believe in!"

The place erupted. Delegates jumped to their feet and cheered. Gettelfinger had hit a nerve and unleashed the anger, frustration, hope, and spirit of a union tired of being on the ropes. The rest of the speech was like a revival meeting; by the end everybody was standing. As the hall rang with applause, Gettelfinger locked arms onstage with other union leaders. Loudspeakers blared out the song "No Surrender" by Bruce Springsteen, the rock-and-roll poet of the working class. Together, the entire assembly marched out of the hotel and onto the street, waving signs and shouting slogans in the brutal heat of the Las Vegas summer.

The rest of the convention was anticlimactic. Gettelfinger's reelection was basically unopposed. On the final day, he named the officials who would lead the bargaining for new contracts with the Detroit automakers in 2007. "We have to roll up our sleeves," he said, "and get to work." His last order of business was to meet with reporters. He shared one bit of news with them: with a week to go in the buyout program, twenty-five thousand GM workers and more than eight thousand Delphi employees had so far accepted cash offers to leave their jobs.

That same day, Ghosn arrived in Nashville, Tennessee, to unveil plans for Nissan's new U.S. headquarters. This was a big step for the Japanese automaker. Its main office had been in California along with all the other Asian car companies. But now its American executives would be working just down the highway from Nissan's assembly plant in the town of Smyrna. "This is a good opportunity to make some changes in the organization and get more efficiency," Ghosn said. After the event, he went to his suite at the Vanderbilt Hotel, where Jerry York, Kirk Kerkorian, and Terry Christensen, Kerkorian's attorney, joined him for dinner.

Ghosn was no innocent. He knew these men had grave concerns about where GM was heading. They wanted an alternative strategy and an aggressive one at that. Kerkorian didn't say much during dinner, but when he did, Ghosn noticed how York and Christensen immediately deferred to their billionaire boss. "Nothing is happening with GM and the stock price," Kerkorian said. "I'm afraid they're going nowhere with the people they've got." Ghosn described how the Renault-Nissan combination worked. He said he welcomed General Motors as a third partner, but only if it entered the alliance willingly. Renault and Nissan worked so well together because their managements totally embraced the process.

Another critical factor in the Renault-Nissan combination's success was the cross-shareholding arrangement. Ghosn suggested that Renault-Nissan buy a 20 percent stake in GM to cement the alliance.

If that could happen, he envisioned great success for all three companies. He had studied how GM would fit into the picture, describing in detail how Nissan could seamlessly build its models in one of the Detroit automaker's underutilized truck plants.

Then York threw out what was uppermost in his mind. Assuming GM could be brought into the alliance, he eventually wanted Ghosn to take over as its chief executive. What did he think about that possibility?

That discussion, Ghosn said, was premature. "I cannot run three companies at the same time," he said. "The only thing we can do is select a CEO for General Motors that we all agree on."

His answer seemed to satisfy York and Kerkorian for the time being. The next move was up to them. They left in high spirits and went to the airport. Before they split up, they agreed that York would put their cards on the table with Wagoner and see how he reacted. And they came up with a code name for their grand plan: "Project Supercar."

Three days later, York laid the situation out to Wagoner on the phone. "Kirk and I met with Carlos Ghosn," he said. "Carlos is interested in expanding the alliance with GM. I'd like you to call Kirk and get his thoughts on this."

Wagoner was shocked. They had met with Carlos Ghosn, the chief executive of two rival auto companies, without telling him or the board? He didn't know what to say. Now he was supposed to call Kerkorian? What was going on here? After an awkward silence, he agreed to make the call, then hung up.

The next day, June 20, Kerkorian waited for the phone call that never came. He was not happy. He owned almost 10 percent of GM and Wagoner was ignoring him. When the GM chief executive finally did call the following day, the conversation was hardly satisfactory. Once it was over Kerkorian called York, who later described his boss as "pissed beyond belief."

"Wagoner called me, Jerry, and he didn't want to talk about any of the business arguments," Kerkorian said. "He just goddamned wanted to know who was in the meeting and why he didn't know about it. He didn't even care about the business arguments. Well, fuck him! We'll do a fucking 13D filing."

York tried to calm him down. This wasn't the time to go public with an SEC filing that detailed their plans to seek an alliance with Renault-Nissan. "Let me talk to him, Kirk," he said.

On June 22, York met with Wagoner in his office. He brought along a spreadsheet to show exactly how Renault-Nissan and GM could pool their resources to purchase parts, share engines and vehicle platforms, grow in overseas markets, and keep all their plants running at full capacity. York found himself getting really excited describing it. "Rick, this could be the King Kong company in the industry, way larger than Toyota," he said. "My God, there are opportunities to generate huge efficiencies."

Wagoner just looked at him. Did Kerkorian and York really believe they could muscle GM into an alliance? These guys were dangerous. Wagoner had to be careful not to start a war on the spot. "Okay," he said stiffly. "I'll call Carlos."

That afternoon he made a brief, cordial phone call to Ghosn. They agreed to meet in mid-July, on a day Ghosn was already scheduled to be in Detroit. When he relayed the information back to York, Wagoner thought for sure this would placate Kerkorian.

But it didn't. A few more days went by, and the elderly financier started getting antsy, calling York and peppering him with questions. Why wasn't the GM board meeting on this? What was taking so long? This was a great idea. Why didn't Wagoner move on this now? Finally, on June 30, Kerkorian couldn't wait any longer. "Jerry," he said, "put out that 13D."

"Okay," York said. "But now the shit is really going to hit the fan."

The 13D filing with the SEC consisted of a letter written by the Tracinda Corporation (Kerkorian's investment firm) to Wagoner and the GM board of directors. It was brief and to the point: Renault-Nissan was interested in bringing GM into their alliance and buying a big chunk of General Motors stock. "We urge the Board of Directors to form a committee to immediately and fully explore this opportunity together with management," the letter said.

As soon as the filing hit the newswires, GM's stock shot up 9 percent. The GM board called an emergency meeting by phone. Afterward it issued a statement saying it would take Kerkorian's proposal "under advisement."

Ghosn was as surprised as anybody that Kerkorian and York had gone public. In response, Renault-Nissan put out a carefully worded statement emphasizing that the alliance would pursue a deal only if GM wanted it. "It is necessary that the GM Board and top management fully support this project in order to start the study of this opportunity," it said.

The media jumped all over the news with banner headlines and breathless coverage. This was potentially the biggest deal in automotive history, a shocking development that riveted the entire industry. It was so epic that it completely overshadowed the final tally of blue-collar buyouts: thirty-five thousand GM workers and another twelve thousand at Delphi.

The GM board met in person a week later. In his opening remarks, Wagoner said management was "uncomfortable" with how GM had been thrust into this situation but was willing to investigate the merits of the alliance. Some directors vented their anger at York for meeting with Ghosn behind their backs. But the board had to be careful. The GM attorneys warned that rejecting the alliance idea outright could spark shareholder lawsuits.

Instead, George Fisher and others proposed that the board authorize Wagoner—and not a committee of directors that might include York—to lead "exploratory talks" with Renault and Nissan. That would give Wagoner the power to set the agenda going forward.

"We are committed to an objective and thorough review," Wagoner said in a statement. But in interviews after the meeting, he barely hid his exasperation with Kerkorian and York. "It's not the way I would have done this," he said. "And I don't think it's particularly helpful."

Ghosn flew into Detroit on July 14 for internal meetings at Nissan's technical center outside the city. He met with reporters afterward, and they bombarded him with questions about GM. Ghosn played it cool and said he was keen to have a constructive dialogue with Wagoner. "I'm not interested in his job," he said matter-of-factly. That night he had dinner with Wagoner at the Renaissance Center. The GM chief executive seemed uncomfortable and extremely cautious. There was no general discussion about the alliance or even a hint that GM's management wanted any part of it. Instead, Wagoner proposed a formal ninety-day study period, with Fritz Henderson leading the GM team. Ghosn agreed and promised to put his own top executives on the project. Before parting, they decided on a joint public statement. "We are looking forward to having our teams work together to explore our ideas," the statement said.

This is going to be interesting, Ghosn thought on his way out. He had already concluded that there was very little chance that General Motors would join the alliance under pressure from Kerkorian. But he sure could learn a lot about GM in the next ninety days.

[Fifteen]

The drama at General Motors had all the twists and turns of a Hollywood cliffhanger. At Ford, the descent was more of a slow, torturous slide into mediocrity. Sales dropped consistently, month after month, to the point where Toyota passed it in July as number two in the U.S. market. The red ink kept flowing too—not as fast as at GM, but just as predictably and with no end in sight. In the first half of 2006, Ford had lost $1.4 billion. Its plans to shed workers and factories seemed like déjà vu; whatever buyouts GM offered, Ford was destined to follow.

Inside Ford headquarters, a revolving cast of inbred executives kept churning out the same lackluster results. Even Bill Ford had lost some of his aura. Hailed as the one Detroit exec with an environmental consciousness, he had to back off his pledge that Ford would build a quarter million hybrid vehicles a year by the end of the decade. Now he was embarrassed to admit it wouldn't even sell twenty-five thousand in 2006.

The famous Blue Oval had come to define bland, predictable, and slightly above- or below-average vehicles. Ford had two popular passenger cars on the market: the iconic Mustang and the new midsize Fusion sedan. But besides those, its only reliable sellers were the venerable F-series pickup and an over-the-hill lineup of boxy, low-mileage sport-utility vehicles. The company's high-priced foreign brands—Jaguar, Volvo, Land Rover, and Aston Martin—could barely dent the dominance of Lexus, Mercedes-Benz, and BMW. "Is Ford Running on Empty?" asked a headline in the *New York Times*. There was no reason to believe otherwise.

Bill Ford's burden grew by the day. His president and chief operating officer, Jim Padilla, had proven ineffective and was forced into retirement on July 1. Bill was left with a thin roster of promising but inexperienced executives. To harness their talent, he formed an operating committee that he had to chair himself (in addition to his duties as chairman of the board and chief executive officer). He tried to pump up his people, organizing offsite retreats to build camaraderie and generate new ideas. But he couldn't defuse the escalating conflict between two of his key players: Mark Fields, the hard-driving head of the Americas division, and Don Leclair, the ultraintense chief financial officer.

The Fields-Leclair feud was dividing the leadership team. They fought incessantly over money and control. At one strategy session, Leclair tore into Fields for overspending on new vehicle programs. "You have got to cut the product plan!" Leclair snapped. "We're going out of business here. Don't you understand we're going to go bankrupt if we don't do this?"

Fields barked right back at him. Didn't Leclair understand that Ford had to pour all the money it could into new models to have any chance of recovering? The two were yelling nose to nose, and for a moment Fields thought they were going to fight. "I went fucking bananas," he said later. "Don and I almost literally went at each other's throats."

Bill Ford couldn't believe it. These were the guys who were supposed to be leading the turnaround, not brawling in front of their fellow executives.

Fields could be a hothead at times, and he had made enemies in the UAW with his blunt negotiating style. He also raised eyebrows in the Glass House by taking a starring role in a quasi documentary about the turnaround that was broadcast on the company's website. (His most memorable line: "Change or die, baby, that's what it's all about.") But Fields was trying his best to rally the troops. Leclair was needlessly provoking him, and Bill Ford was losing patience with his sharp-tongued CFO. The situation got so bad that the board of directors had to step in. Irv Hockaday, one of the senior outside directors, sat down with Fields and Leclair. "You guys better get on the same page," he warned.

Ford was perilously close to unraveling. The Ford family was growing restive with the mounting losses and sinking stock price, and they were starting to bicker among themselves. Edsel Ford II, Bill's older cousin and a longtime Ford director, in particular chafed at the expanding influence of Steve Hamp, Bill's brother-in-law and chief of staff. At family meetings, there was talk about possibly taking the company private in a leveraged buyout or even selling it. That was a long shot and couldn't happen unless the biggest of the family stock-holders—including Bill Ford and his father—supported it.

Bill was spending a lot of his time and energy calming the waters and reassuring his sisters, cousins, aunts, and uncles that the turn-around was on track. "We had some pretty lengthy family meetings where there were lots of questions and a lot of different scenarios were played out," Bill said. "But thankfully there was a collective resolve in the family to see this thing through."

On July 12—two days before the Ghosn-Wagoner dinner—the Ford board met on the top floor of company headquarters in Dear-born. The agenda was packed with pressing issues, none bigger than the plan to mortgage Ford's North American assets to borrow bil-lions of dollars for the restructuring. There was also discussion about General Motors and whether Ford should consider pursuing an alli-ance with Renault-Nissan if GM rejected it. But everything else was pushed aside when Bill Ford made his plea for help. "I am really struggling to keep all these balls in the air," he said. "I want to get somebody in here."

Joe Laymon, the Ford personnel chief, had kept a running list of potential CEO candidates. One name continued to stand out: Alan Mulally, the executive vice president at Boeing. Bill Ford had asked months earlier for a dossier on him, and Laymon was impressed with what he found. Mulally had all the skills needed in the auto industry—an engineering background, lots of manufacturing experience, success in labor relations, and the ability to manage thousands of employees and develop extremely sophisticated products.

John Thornton, the director from Goldman Sachs, had first suggested Mulally, and Bill asked him to make the initial contact. "Can you call him and feel him out?" Bill said.

Thornton reached Mulally at his home in the Seattle suburb of Mercer Island, Washington. The Goldman Sachs director identified himself and briefly described the need for a top-flight chief executive at the auto company. "Would you be at all interested in coming to Ford?" Thornton said.

Mulally was about to turn sixty-one and had worked for Boeing for thirty-seven years; he lived and breathed airplanes the way Bill Ford did cars. He had been passed over twice for the chief executive position at Boeing, so it was not unusual for large corporations to contact him about CEO openings elsewhere.

Mulally said he was flattered to be considered but wasn't looking to make a change. He was, however, willing to talk more. A few days later, Laymon flew to Seattle and met with him at the Four Seasons Hotel. When he got back, he went straight to Bill Ford's corner office. "I think I've just met," he said, "the most remarkable operating executive in the country."

Laymon couldn't get over how refreshing Mulally was—his sunny disposition, his rapid-fire mind, and especially his infectious enthusiasm. Alan Mulally had one of those old-fashioned, all-American life stories. He grew up in Lawrence, Kansas, the son of a postal worker, with dreams of becoming an astronaut until he learned he was color-blind and couldn't qualify. Instead, he studied aeronautical engineering and joined Boeing fresh out of the University of Kansas.

He still choked up talking about it. "I remember driving along the airport in Seattle and there were all these Boeing hangars and the doors were open and there were all these planes," Mulally said. "Here were these 737s and 747s, and it was like, 'My God, this is what I want to do, to build the best airplanes in the world.'" He climbed the corporate ladder to vice president of engineering, then head of airplane development, and finally to president and chief executive of the entire commercial aircraft division. (Boeing had moved its corporate headquarters to Chicago a few years earlier, but Mulally's division remained based near Seattle.)

Mulally's job was extraordinarily complex, even by auto industry standards. He commanded small armies of engineers, designers, and suppliers, and he shepherded new planes from the blueprint stage all the way through the assembly of million of parts, past the rigors of testing, and ultimately onto the runway for the maiden flight.

He was also intimately involved in the business side, responsible for sales and marketing, labor contracts, and government relations. Mulally had a great résumé, but what captivated Laymon was his personality, the twinkle in his eyes, and the toothy smile that lit up a room. He wore a blue blazer, pressed khakis, and penny loafers, and went on and on about how "neat" it was to work for an American icon like Boeing. Lean and athletic, with short auburn hair and fair skin, Mulally seemed uncommonly youthful for his age and infused with a rare, lofty spirit. "I've always wanted to contribute to a compelling vision, something big, something important," he said. "It's all about service, what I can do to help and contribute."

Laymon had worked with many executives in his twenty-seven years in corporate human resources, but he had never encountered anyone quite like Mulally. Laymon was a tough labor negotiator and definitely not a pushover. And he had done his homework. He knew Mulally wasn't a saint. He had a reputation as being intensely demanding of people, to the point where Boeing sent him to a career coach to polish away his rough edges. But right now the guy was achieving results at Boeing that nobody at Ford was capable of. And the best part was that he seemed keenly interested in Ford and asked lots and lots of questions: What kind of guy is Bill Ford? Why did he want to step aside as chief executive? How involved was his family? Where does the company need to go? Was Ford looking for a leader?

Bill stopped Laymon right there. "I've heard enough," he said. "I want to meet him."

Mulally wanted to meet him too. He had not seriously considered leaving Boeing until he really started thinking about Ford. He secluded himself in the den of his home and read everything he could find about the company: its history, its brands, its financial results, its international presence, the industry, the competition.

"All I know is they're looking for a leader, and I'm a leader," Mulally said. "So if I'm going to lead, where does it need to go? Where's it been? Seeing these numbers and these losses and market share going down and cash going out, I'm in the mode of 'What needs to happen here? What should the plan be?'" Mulally had enjoyed an extraordinary career with Boeing. But both times he had competed for the CEO position, the board had chosen someone else. The chances of getting a third shot were slim. He could visualize himself starting over at Ford. The more he studied the company, the more it felt right, like destiny.

When Laymon called again, Mulally was primed to see Bill. But he was hypersensitive about secrecy. He didn't want anyone at Boeing to know. Neither did Laymon. "We thought if they got wind of it, they'd throw a shitload of money at him to stay," he said.

The plan was to send a Ford corporate jet to pick up Mulally in Seattle and fly him to Michigan. Bill suggested they hold the meeting at his home in Ann Arbor, which was a surprise to Laymon: "Bill had never taken any job candidates to his house before."

July 29 was a hot, steamy Saturday afternoon, with temperatures in the 90s. A Ford security officer met Mulally at the Willow Run Airport west of Detroit and drove him to Bill's house. As the car pulled into the driveway, Bill, wearing shorts and a polo shirt, came outside with his wife, Lisa. Mulally popped out of the car and sort of ran toward them. When he got to Bill, he threw his arms out and hugged him. It caught Bill off guard. Lisa's eyes got big. Then Mulally smiled and hugged her too, like they were the oldest of friends. Bill had met an awful lot of job candidates at Ford in his time. But no one had ever done that before.

"I thought it was kind of cool," he said.

They went inside and sat down, and Bill opened up immediately. "I have a very young management team, and I need someone to help us," he said. "I'm pretty fearful of what I sense is coming at us, and it would be so much better if I had an executive who had been through what we're about to go through."

"Tell me," Mulally said, "what you think you're about to go through."

Bill laid it all out—the global competition, the need to integrate the company, shifting from trucks to greener cars, downsizing the North American operations, borrowing billions to pay for it all. Bill was baring his soul, and Mulally sat on the edge of his seat, taking it all in. Bill found himself thinking about how relaxed he was in Mulally's presence. Then it was Mulally's turn to talk.

"I think you need clarity," Mulally said. "You need real clarity of the plan, clarity of communication. Let me ask you, why do you have so many brands? Why do you have different cars in different regions? If the Ford brand doesn't shine brightly, why do you have all the rest?"

Good question, Bill thought. He explained that the other brands were meant to do what the Blue Oval couldn't—attract upscale buyers, broaden the company's appeal, and bring some European cachet and know-how to a blue-collar American company.

Mulally didn't get it. At Boeing, the company and the brand were synonymous, and everybody pulled together in the same direction. Why couldn't it be done at Ford? "Remember, I'm an engineer," he said. "I solve problems, and I create things. If you're going to turn this around, you need a plan." When he began describing how he would refocus the company, it suddenly dawned on Bill that this stranger who'd hugged him at the front door knew more about Ford than any outsider he'd ever met. "It was disarming how extremely well prepared he was," he said.

When Bill brought up fuel economy, hybrid cars, and protecting the environment, Mulally almost leapt out of his chair. "God, I have your green vision too!" he chirped. "I have to make that happen!" They had been chattering on for two hours without a break when Bill suddenly got up and went into the kitchen. He came back with two sheets of paper. On one he had outlined the duties of the chairman's job at Ford; on the other, the corresponding responsibilities of a chief executive officer. It struck Mulally that Bill had already mapped out how they would work together at Ford. "What do you think?" Bill said. "Would this possibly work for you?"

Mulally didn't answer him directly. He couldn't tell if this was a job offer or what. All he knew was Bill Ford liked him, they got along very well, and this had the potential to be an amazing opportunity. "One thing I knew is I could work with this guy," he said. "Because he had clearly decided he could work with me."

The afternoon wore on into the early evening, and Bill and Lisa took Mulally to dinner at their favorite Italian restaurant in the Kerrytown section of Ann Arbor, near the University of Michigan. The conversation kept rolling over red wine and pasta, and got more personal. Mulally talked about his wife, Nikki, their five grown children, and their great life in Seattle, and how he loved golf and tennis and the beautiful country in the Pacific Northwest. "The last thing on our minds is to pack up and move," he said.

Uh-oh, Bill thought. He was so impressed with Mulally, his skills and ideas, and the chemistry between the two of them. "He was exactly who I was looking for," Bill said. "At dinner, we were almost finishing each other's sentences." But every time it seemed that Mulally was falling for Ford, he'd bring up how much he loved Boeing and Seattle. After coffee, Bill and Lisa drove Mulally to his hotel. He would be flying home on the Ford plane in the morning and promised to get back in touch soon. On the drive to their house, Lisa read her husband's mind. "He seems almost too good to be true," she said.

Bill wondered the same thing. "Is it too perfect?" he said.

Back in the office, Bill called in Laymon and gushed about Mulally. "On a scale of one to ten, he's an eleven," Bill said. "We need to put the hard sell on him." Laymon's job was to craft a compensation package of salary, bonuses, and stock options that Mulally couldn't refuse. And they needed to get the Ford board on the case. Bill called Mulally and gently asked him what he was thinking.

"I'm really intrigued by Ford," Mulally said. "It's such an iconic company, and it means so much to America. I really think there are a lot of things I can bring to the table." But Bill wasn't getting the answer he wanted.

"Alan was kind of cagey," he said. "He never said yes, but he never said no. I could tell he was just torn between us and Boeing." Bill suggested that he send the Ford plane to pick him up the next weekend and fly Mulally to Aspen, Colorado, to meet with Irv Hockaday and John Thornton, the two directors overseeing the CEO search. They could answer any other questions he might have about Ford, the board, the executive team, whatever he wanted to know. Mulally said okay, he could do that.

While the recruitment effort swung into high gear, other wheels began to turn in the Glass House. The Ford board brought in a former Wall Street investment banker, Ken Leet, to begin a strategic review to decide which of the ailing luxury brands to sell and to start assessing the market for potential buyers. Aston Martin and Jaguar were at the top of the list.

Leet was also weighing the future of the huge Ford Credit finance arm. With GM selling off control of its credit company, maybe Ford should do the same to raise cash for the turnaround. On top of that, Mark Fields was pushing for big production cuts in the North American factories. Ford's unsold inventory levels were growing dangerously high, and Fields wanted to idle the plants for several weeks to bring the numbers down.

Ford was also squarely in the media crosshairs. The hiring of Leet sparked speculation about big changes coming as well as dissension in the executive ranks and the Ford family. To make matters worse, the company was gearing up buyout offers, and union officials were slamming management for scaring workers into giving up their jobs. "I don't call them buyouts," Mark Guerreso, head of a union local in Dearborn, told the *Detroit Free Press*. "I call them sellouts."

Fields, to his credit, took it upon himself to fight back. In an appearance at an industry conference in northern Michigan, he lashed out at the media for its constant attacks on the American carmakers. "This dismissive portrayal of Detroit and the cynicism we sometimes have for the home team is like nothing I've ever seen before," Fields said. "It's time to believe in ourselves again, so that consumers around us can do the same." It was an inspired speech, but unfortunately, within a few days, reporters were only interested in the 21 percent production cuts planned for the fourth quarter—the biggest at Ford since the early 1980s.

Bill Ford was keeping his fingers crossed about Mulally. He was delighted to hear that Mulally had had a positive five-hour meeting with the Ford directors in Aspen. Soon after, Laymon went to Seattle to present Mulally with a formal offer sheet. The numbers were impressive: a $2 million annual salary, a $7.5 million signing bonus, at least $10 million to cover his potential future earnings at Boeing, and a boatload of Ford stock options down the road. Laymon figured that would clinch the deal and told Mulally to call when he was ready to sign it.

But what he didn't know was that Mulally had developed reservations. He was in the middle of assembling the team and designs for Boeing's next jetliner, which would be a magnificent way to cap his career. And he was so close to his people, so proud of what they had done together, that he couldn't bear the thought of leaving them. "I know every person here. . . . I loved them. . . . I grew up with them," he said. "We had been in the depths of despair together after 9/11. I never felt more loved and appreciated." He broke his silence and talked about the Ford offer with his boss, Boeing chief executive Jim McNerney.

"I've been approached by Ford, and I'm thinking about it," Mulally told him.

McNerney couldn't believe he was even considering it. "You've got to be kidding me," he said. "You have a great job here at Boeing. You know, the automobile business is really tough."

Mulally was torn up inside, trying to decide. He huddled with his wife and his children. He weighed the pros and cons, the excitement of starting fresh at Ford versus his heartfelt affection for Boeing. Finally he called Bill Ford on a Friday night.

"Bill, I regret I'm going to have to pass on this fabulous opportunity," he said. "I really love you. I really love Ford. But I just can't do it. I've decided to stay." When he stopped talking, he didn't hear anything. He thought the phone had gone dead. "Bill?" he said.

"I'm here," Bill Ford said softly. He felt a distinct pain in his gut. It took him a minute to gain his composure before he could speak.

"Alan, I respect you so much and your decision so much," he said. "I'm deeply disappointed. But I respect your decision. I just want you to know that if there is anything else you can think of that I can do, we can do, or anything you need that in any way might change your mind . . . that I'm here. I know you're the right person for Ford."

After they hung up, Bill called Laymon on his cell phone, getting him in the middle of dinner with his wife. "We just lost Alan," he said. "The deal's off."

At first Laymon laughed. "I thought he was bullshitting me," he said.

But Bill was in no mood to go into details. He hung up and got on a conference call to tell the Ford directors.

Thornton was stunned and promised to call Mulally as soon as he could. "Let me take a crack at him," he said.

Meanwhile, Laymon frantically dialed Mulally's home over and over. Finally his wife, Nikki, answered. "Alan isn't taking any calls," she told him. Laymon was so upset he was ready to drive to the airport and get on a plane to Seattle that night.

But Mulally went underground and couldn't be reached all weekend. He told McNerney that he had turned Ford down. But he felt terribly conflicted. "I knew this wasn't about Bill," he said. "It was about me. I had to decide what I was going to do."

Thornton reached him a couple of days later and put on the full-court press. "Alan, you've done everything you can for Boeing, and you should feel good about it," he said. "But a great American company needs you. This is about America and our competitiveness." Mulally was taken aback by the emotional appeal and wondered aloud whether he had made the right decision.

Thornton sensed he had left the door open a crack. He immediately called Bill Ford. "It's not over," he said.

When Bill heard that, he felt a surge of energy and summoned Laymon. "I want you to go to Seattle and don't come back until you have him," Bill said. "I mean it. Do not bring your ass back to Detroit without Mulally. And if you don't come back with Mulally, don't come back. I don't care if you have to buy a house out there. Get him."

The next day, as soon as he checked into the Four Seasons in Seattle, Laymon called Mulally, who was plainly irritated with him.

"Why are you here?" he said.

"Because I'm not giving up on you," Laymon answered.

They met at the hotel, and Laymon pitched Ford as hard as he ever had in his life. Over the next few days, they talked and ate together and took long walks along the shore of Puget Sound. In the end, after a lot of soul-searching, Mulally arrived at the moment of truth. What it finally came down to was simple. Boeing could go on without him. Laymon could tell that Mulally was disappointed that the Boeing board had never made a substantial counteroffer, such as promoting him to chief operating officer. The fact was, Ford needed Mulally, and he needed Ford. "I was just so excited about that," he said. "The more I kept thinking about it, the more I thought I could serve another American global icon. I can take Ford flying again."

He called Bill, and this time gave him the answer he was praying for. "This is just so compelling," Mulally said. "I want to turn around this great company with you."

"Oh my God," Bill said. "How soon can you get here?"

On August 31, Mulally flew to Chicago—where Boeing had its corporate offices—to tell McNerney that he was going to leave the aerospace giant after thirty-seven years to become the new president and chief executive officer of the Ford Motor Company. Laymon flew separately and waited nervously in a conference room at Midway Airport. The Ford personnel chief was petrified that Boeing would make a last-ditch effort to keep Mulally. But when Mulally walked into that conference room, he had a big grin on his face. He reread the employment contract Laymon had with him, then signed it. And for the first time in as long as he could remember, he didn't scribble a little cartoon airplane next to his signature.

Mulally wouldn't officially start at Ford until October, but Bill and the board were anxious to make a public announcement. On the evening of September 4, Mulally sat alone in his suite at the Ritz-Carlton Hotel in Dearborn. For the longest time, he stared out the window at the illuminated Blue Oval sign, just across the highway, on top of Ford's world headquarters. "I kept thinking: a compelling vision, a comprehensive strategy, and then relentless implementation," he said. "That's our plan."

Early the next morning, a driver took him to the Glass House. He mentally cataloged all the vehicles he saw parked in the underground executive garage—Jaguars, Volvos, Land Rovers. Not a single Ford model in sight. That, he said to himself, was going to change.

He met with Bill, whose eyes were puffy and red-rimmed after a sleepless night worrying that the news would leak out before the press release. Together they entered a first-floor auditorium filled with employees and executives, journalists, and camera crews. Bill spoke first. He promised that even though he was giving up the CEO job, he would stay on as executive chairman of the company his great-grandfather had founded 103 years before. "I'll be here every day, and I will not rest until a prosperous future for this company is secured," he said. "I have been part of this company since I was born, and I will be part of it for the rest of my life."

Then he turned it over to Mulally, who blinked into the banks of TV lights and said he had come to Ford to prove something. "Some people think the United States can't compete in the design and production of sophisticated products," he said. "I personally think we can."

[Sixteen]

An enormous stage and tiers of bleachers were set up in a grassy field at the four-thousand-acre GM proving grounds in Milford, Michigan, about fifty miles northwest of Detroit. Buses shuttled hundreds of journalists to the site, where a dozen immaculately restored, vintage pickup trucks, including a century-old Chevy, sparkled under the hot August sun.

It was a debut worthy of GM's most anticipated new products in years. The homage to the past was almost reverent. But the real guests of honor were GM's billion-dollar bets on the future—the all-new, 2007-model Chevrolet Silverado and GMC Sierra full-size pickups. If there was any question about how critical these vehicles were to GM's comeback, Rick Wagoner answered it as soon as he stepped to the microphone. "They are the most important component," Wagoner said, "of the most important part of our turnaround."

GM had spared no expense developing what it believed were the finest new products in the most profitable segment of the U.S. market. Americans loved their pickup trucks, and they bought an average of 2.7 million a year. The Asian manufacturers may have dominated the passenger car market, but Detroit still owned the truck business. The market was a gold mine for the Big Three, who held an amazing 92 percent share of the truck segment and were committing vast resources to keep it that way. And no wonder: each truck earned an estimated $10,000 in profits.

Wagoner had pushed up the timetable for the new models in early 2005, just when the automaker was beginning its financial free fall. His decision had only added to an already huge budget. All told, it had cost more than $2 billion to design and engineer the pickups and their sister products, the hulking Escalade, Suburban, and Yukon sport-utilities.

But GM was determined to raise the bar with its new trucks. They came with options galore: eight different engine configurations, three cab styles, three cargo box lengths, five suspension packages, and all the creature comforts of a luxury sedan, from the plush leather seats and heated steering wheel to the touch-screen navigation systems and flip-down DVD displays in the roof. These trucks were like rolling living rooms that could climb a mountain, ford a river, tow a horse trailer, and carry a ton—literally—of stuff.

The GM project team was swarming all over the event, eager to explain every last detail of the new Silverado and Sierra. GM sold more than a million of these big rigs each year, and it wanted to sell even more. Getting good reviews from the media was the first element of a marketing blitz built around a monster advertising campaign that featured roots rocker John Mellencamp and his new song, "Our Country."

After the speeches and the unveiling of the trucks onstage, a horde of reporters gathered around Bob Lutz. Wearing a blue denim GM shirt and aviator sunglasses and smoking a long cigar, Lutz puffed with pride as he described just how awesome these pickups were. "There is no other truck that can touch us," he said. "It's not even close." He scoffed at concerns about fuel economy. These pickups could get twenty miles to the gallon, and GM wasn't at all worried that rising gas prices might diminish their appeal. "The effect will decrease over time as people adjust to the thought of $3 a gallon, just as they did when it was $2 a gallon and just as they did when it was $1 a gallon," he said.

Lutz saved his most pointed comments for Toyota. The Japanese automaker was putting the finishing touches on a new $1.3 billion assembly plant in San Antonio, Texas, where it would build the latest generation of its Tundra pickup. Toyota had been trying to crack Detroit's stranglehold on the full-size pickup market for years. But its first two models weren't muscular enough to stack up with the Silverado, the Ford F-series, or Chrysler's Dodge Ram. "Toyota has had three tries to get it right, and Toyota usually gets things right on the third try," Lutz said. "But they will not be able to take over our trucks."

No matter how much money or market share GM lost, its sense of superiority never seemed to waver. The new pickups were the first wave of an armada of new vehicles that GM management was sure would turn the company's fortunes around. But only two days after the truck rollout, GM reported that it lost $3.2 billion in the second quarter of the year. A big chunk of the loss was the cost of buying out thirty-four thousand workers. Apparently that was the price of progress at the world's largest auto company. Yet somehow it didn't add up. How could GM justify giving people billions of dollars to leave when it wasn't earning enough money to pay the employees it still had? No problem. GM was going to spend its way out of trouble, whether it was cutting jobs or expanding its product lineup. Most companies couldn't live that way. But the conceit of GM was that it was too big to fail and didn't need to play by conventional rules.

Wagoner never pretended to be a car guy, but he still got chills over a gorgeous new automobile. On August 18, he drove the sleek Chevrolet Camaro concept car down Woodward Avenue in the Dream Cruise, an annual celebration of Motor City history that drew tens of thousands of classic-car lovers from across the nation to the streets of suburban Detroit. With a police escort leading the way, Wagoner made a dramatic entrance at the event, and it felt good to hear the cheers and honking horns saluting the latest incarnation of one of GM's legendary muscle cars. "This car is kind of an exclamation point," said a beaming Wagoner. "It shows that people have a connection to our history and that we still have the ability to do great cars and trucks."

Call it confidence or a bad case of denial, but GM management felt it was on a righteous mission. And no one had any desire to change course and join forces with Carlos Ghosn and Renault-Nissan. "It's just an all-around bad idea," Lutz said. "Everything about it tilts in their favor."

But Wagoner couldn't afford to take the alliance talks lightly. Kirk Kerkorian wasn't the only shareholder growing impatient with management. Other large investors were intensely interested in what Ghosn might bring to the table. Fritz Henderson's first face-to-face meetings with Ghosn's team—Patrick Pélata of Renault and Carlos Tavares from Nissan—happened in late August in Detroit. Henderson set strict parameters from the start. He proposed that the two sides limit the study to potential savings on six different vehicles, three dozen parts systems, and two hundred individual components. His rationale was that they could identify specific savings by looking at individual models and comparable parts. But that was like studying a map with a microscope. There was no way to extrapolate how three companies building millions of vehicles could work together to design, engineer, buy parts, and ultimately build products.

"They want to do the bare minimum," Ghosn said. "I think from the beginning they are not interested in the alliance."

He was right. Wagoner, Lutz, and a majority of the GM board viewed the deal as a thinly veiled attempt by Kerkorian and Jerry York to take over General Motors. If Renault-Nissan bought 20 percent of GM, their stake combined with Kerkorian's stock would effectively give them control. "It was a way to get ahold of General Motors and turn it over to Carlos Ghosn," said John Bryan, the GM director.

Publicly, GM promised to investigate the merits of a possible partnership. But as soon as the talks got under way, GM's communications staffers began pushing stories that raised questions about Ghosn's leadership and the effectiveness of the Renault-Nissan alliance. In briefings with other GM executives, Henderson mocked the alliance's reputation as a model of industrial cooperation. "Some of these Renault and Nissan people haven't even met each other before," he said. "I mean, they've been together for eight years, and they're finally getting ready to roll out their first joint engine program. It only took them eight years!"

Ghosn wasn't deterred by the trash talk. He was committed to finding out what could be done in a three-way alliance, even if it was just an academic exercise. "Sharing platforms, sharing engines, buying parts together . . . at the end of the day there is huge potential for savings," he said. And he wasn't bashful about putting numbers out in public. He told analysts in Paris that, at a minimum, he envisioned the companies saving $3 billion to $5 billion a year by purchasing parts together. Privately, he wondered whether the GM executives even realized how uncompetitive their company was. "Even the kind of organization they had was a complete mess," he said. After the first few weeks of talks, Ghosn sensed that GM was just going through the motions. "Very courteous, very polite, very nice people," he said. "But in a certain way, they don't listen. They already have their conclusion."

While GM reluctantly explored an unwanted alliance, the biggest international auto merger of them all was coming apart at the seams.

The DaimlerChrysler merger was nearing a breaking point. On September 7, Ron Gettelfinger formally rejected a health care deal that would have saved Chrysler more than $300 million a year. When he heard that, Dieter Zetsche went ballistic. "I do not fucking believe this!" he said to Jason Vines, the head of Chrysler communications. "What do we have to do to get what GM and Ford got? Lose $10 billion?"

Chrysler was already spiraling down under the leadership of Tom LaSorda, and whatever market momentum it had came to a screeching halt over the summer. Just like GM and Ford, Chrysler was also overrun with inventories of unsold vehicles, mostly big SUVs such as the new seven-passenger Jeep Commander. And its management team seemed incapable of steering it out of trouble. Dealers across the country were in open revolt against Joe Eberhardt, the German executive who headed its sales and marketing department. Eberhardt had been relentlessly pushing dealers to accept more products from the factories, but the dealers finally balked and refused to take any more cars. "We voiced our complaints over and over and nothing changed," said Carl Galeana, a big dealer in Michigan and Florida. "It's just an ugly, ugly situation."

Chrysler's senior executives appeared to be in over their heads. Eric Ridenour, Chrysler's chief operating officer, had done nothing to adjust the overheated production levels, and a sense of panic was sweeping through the headquarters tower at the Chrysler Technical Center in Auburn Hills, Michigan. In desperation, Eberhardt started offering costly "employee-pricing" discounts to lure consumers into Chrysler showrooms. And Zetsche agreed to appear in an offbeat ad campaign, taking on the wry persona of "Dr. Z," sort of a German version of the legendary Chrysler pitchman Lee Iacocca.

But none of it was working. On September 15, Chrysler announced that after twelve consecutive profitable quarters, the company had imploded; its third-quarter losses were forecast at $1.5 billion.

Two days later, Zetsche flew from Stuttgart to Auburn Hills for an emergency meeting with LaSorda and his team. When the door was shut in the fifteenth-floor conference room, Zetsche unloaded. "This is unacceptable!" he shouted. "This cannot continue. There are no more chances." Contrite and defensive, LaSorda promised to slash production immediately to bring down inventories. "We know what we have to do," he said. "And we'll do it." When the meeting broke up, the chastened execs knew that Zetsche had run out of patience. "I've never seen Dieter that angry before," said Vines. "We are all in trouble."

He had no idea how shaky Chrysler's future had become. The next day, LaSorda announced a deep round of production cuts and ordered an analysis of more permanent restructuring moves, including plant closings. He also stepped forward and took the heat personally. "The decision for what's going on at the Chrysler Group sits right on my lap," he said in a conference call with reporters. "I take full responsibility."

LaSorda still didn't know that high-level executives in Stuttgart were already secretly preparing for a sale of Chrysler. But seemingly overnight, Chrysler was on the firing line. And his boss wasn't hiding his frustrations anymore. For the first time, Zetsche—Chrysler's most steadfast defender in Stuttgart—went public with his concerns about Daimler's Detroit partner. "I myself am more than dissatisfied with the situation," he told analysts on September 19. "It's not acceptable."

GM's talks with Renault-Nissan didn't even make it to ninety days. Renault's lead negotiator, Patrick Pélata, pressed Fritz Henderson to see the bigger picture and emphasized how an alliance would help GM close the cost gap with Toyota. But the GM side increasingly viewed Renault and Nissan as smaller, less accomplished automakers trying to piggyback on the Detroit giant's immense size and global muscle. "The analysis is quite clear that there are substantial synergies," Henderson said. "But what is even more abundantly clear is that the synergies inure hugely to the benefit of Nissan and Renault, and not so much to General Motors."

Lutz wasn't actively involved in the talks, but he made his opinion known to Wagoner and his fellow execs. "You cannot say yes to an alliance that tips completely in favor of the other guy," Lutz said. "We're going to make Nissan and Renault rich and there's nothing in it for us."

Ghosn was offended by the tone of the criticism. After all, Renault and Nissan were profitable and GM was losing its shirt. "They're trashing everything we say and everything we've done, even our recovery," he said. "Well, you can't deny the facts."

Then Henderson dropped a bomb in the negotiations. GM, he said, was getting the short end of the savings in the deal. So to even things up, he proposed that Renault-Nissan pay GM more than $2 billion in cash as an "equalizing contribution" to join their alliance. "We're entitled to some compensation to make it more equitable," Henderson said.

The demand infuriated Ghosn, according to his associates. The idea that Renault-Nissan should pay GM to become their partner was an insult. Still, Ghosn didn't want to be the one to prematurely end the talks. He was convinced that a three-party alliance could be worth as much as $10 billion a year in cost savings and value created by combining resources. How could GM walk away from that kind of deal? Was Wagoner so paranoid about his job that he would turn down a working relationship with two successful companies? Why wouldn't he want Nissan to build its products in GM's underused plants?

Something had to give soon. If this was all a charade, it could not go on much longer. Wagoner was scheduled to have a status conference with Ghosn at Renault headquarters during the Paris auto show in late September. "We'll see in Paris if GM is serious about this or not," Ghosn told his team.

Jerry York was stuck in an uncomfortable position. He had been outmaneuvered by Wagoner, George Fisher, and the management loyalists on the GM board. Once the board turned the alliance talks over to Wagoner, York lost his influence. Kerkorian had asked that a committee of directors study the deal. But in the heat of the moment, York couldn't deliver. And it was eating him up. By pushing so hard to get Ghosn in the picture, York burned the trust he had been gradually earning with some board members. Now he was shut out. He sure couldn't expect Wagoner or Henderson to keep him in the loop on the talks. So he tried frantically to find out what was going on through Ghosn and his sources within GM. "I just want this thing to get a fair shake," he complained. "What's the alternative? Plan A is to go it alone. And Plan B is to enter an alliance. This would turn GM into a truly international company." The most disturbing thing he heard was that GM kept changing the numbers, that one day Henderson said General Motors could save $6 billion in an alliance, and the next it was $2 billion. "What the fuck is the real number?" York wondered to a friend.

On September 27, Wagoner and Ghosn met for three hours at Renault's headquarters in the Paris suburb of Boulogne-Billancourt. Their teams took turns explaining their findings, but the two CEOs couldn't find any common ground. Wagoner held fast to the notion that GM needed compensation to cut a deal. Ghosn wasn't buying it. Neither side would budge. But neither Wagoner nor Ghosn wanted to be the one to shut down the talks. They agreed to keep the discussions going until the October 15 deadline. After the sit-down, Wagoner went to the Paris auto show. He told reporters that he would not make any deal that jeopardized GM's budding turnaround. "Our primary focus has to be doing what's right for General Motors," he said. "We've made it very clear we have a detailed turnaround plan and growth strategy that's working very well. That's going to be what saves the company."

Ghosn let Wagoner flex his muscles. He would take the high road. "I'm not going to force anyone to act against their interests," he said. "This is going to be a friendly cooperation or not at all." But he could not let GM's demand for compensation pass without comment: "It's nonsense," Ghosn said. "It's against the spirit of an alliance." If Wagoner truly felt GM was better off going it alone, Ghosn sure wasn't going to beg him to join Renault-Nissan.

Kirk Kerkorian was not going to sit back and let Wagoner call all the shots. A day later, he raised the stakes again. In an SEC filing by his investment firm, Kerkorian indicated he wanted to buy as many as twelve million more GM shares, on top of the fifty-six million he already owned. And he made it clear he was not about to let the alliance talks die at the bargaining table. This deal, he said in the document, was too important to let GM management decide on its own. "Tracinda continues to believe that a strong opportunity exists in a potential alliance between General Motors, Renault and Nissan and there should be strong General Motors Board involvement in the analysis of such a potential alliance, including the utilization of independent advisors," said the filing.

In typical Kerkorian fashion, he was itching for a showdown. So was Wagoner. On the night of October 2, the GM chief executive and Fritz Henderson had dinner with their board of directors at the Renaissance Center. Together they walked the board through the alliance discussions, claiming that Renault-Nissan would get at least triple the savings because GM accounted for the lion's share of all the parts they would purchase together. The only equitable solution, Henderson said, was for GM to be paid a fee to join up. But that wasn't all. The executives also said that Renault and Nissan should be forced to pay a premium on the GM stock price if they wanted to acquire a 20 percent stake. "They want to buy 20 percent and have supermajority rights to make certain calls in what we do in the alliance activities," Henderson said. "But they don't want to pay a premium."

When the board convened the next morning, Wagoner played his final card. If Ghosn wasn't willing to pay up front to equalize the deal, he saw no choice but to recommend that GM walk away from the alliance. Maybe Renault-Nissan would consider doing a few joint projects together, but otherwise there was no need to keep talking. He never mentioned Kerkorian or his insistence that a board committee and outside advisors study the deal. Then the discussion went around the table, with each director getting a chance to weigh in. A few of them vented, saying the whole thing had been a big waste of time. But when York's turn came, he didn't say a word.

Then Wagoner called for a voice vote. There was a resounding chorus of ayes in favor of management's recommendation to end the talks, but there wasn't a single nay heard in opposition. Again York just sat there, like he was frozen. After a break for lunch, GM's corporate lawyer asked Wagoner to call the vote again, to make sure that any director who didn't agree had a chance to speak up.

"Anyone who does not agree, please say so now," Wagoner said.

Everyone looked at York, who kept silent.

"So it's unanimous?" Wagoner asked.

York just stared straight ahead.

"Okay," Wagoner said, looking at the lawyers. "Yes, it's unanimous."

Afterward, the outside directors went into executive session without Wagoner present. Fisher made a point to ask York what was on his mind.

"You're as welcome as any other director to say your piece," Fisher said.

"No, I'm not," York said.

The next morning, Wagoner called Ghosn in Paris. He said the two sides were just too far apart and the GM board had voted to cancel the alliance talks. When he offered that GM might be interested in doing an individual project or two with Renault-Nissan, Ghosn cut him off.

"Let's just end it," he said.

A joint statement from the three companies was released. It said that GM, Renault, and Nissan had "agreed to terminate discussions" and that "the parties did not agree on either the total amount of aggregate synergies or the distribution of those benefits."

A short time later, Wagoner held a press conference at the Renaissance Center. He said that ending the discussions was the board's call, not his alone. "This follows a unanimous decision by our board of directors that the structure of the proposed alliance would not be in the best interests of GM and its shareholders," he said. After thanking Renault-Nissan for its "great spirit of cooperation," Wagoner reminded the media that GM was making substantial progress on its own.

The question came up whether the alliance might have helped in those efforts. Wagoner didn't think so. "It would have potentially been a distraction," he said.

That afternoon, Kerkorian's investment firm put out its own statement. "We regret that the [GM] board did not obtain its own independent evaluation of the alliance," it said.

York was furious. He was particularly upset that GM kept saying the board voted unanimously to end the talks. Just because he didn't vote nay didn't mean he supported it. "This is such typical GM shit," he said. "But it doesn't make much difference whether it's twelve to nothing or eleven to one." Why hadn't he argued his case in front of the room when he had the chance? "It's like having an argument with your wife," he said. "You can't win, so you shut up."

After discussing it with Kerkorian, York decided to resign from the board immediately. Whatever they did next, York would feel freer to operate from the outside. He sat down and wrote a letter of resignation to Fisher. In the letter, York said that while he believed GM had made "excellent progress" in some areas of the business, it wasn't enough. "I have grave reservations concerning the ability of the company's current business model to successfully compete in the marketplace with those of the Asian producers," he wrote.

His reservations, however, weren't the reason why he was quitting. The GM board, York concluded, was weak and unwilling to act independently. "I have not found an environment in the boardroom that is very receptive to probing much beyond the materials provided by management," he said. And given that environment, there was "little point in my remaining on the board."

York wasn't sure where he and Kerkorian would go from here. They needed to regroup, survey the possibilities, and talk it over. York had been on the GM board for eight eventful months. That chapter, he said, was over. "My understanding is that Rick feels like he's won," York said. "At the end of the day, we'll find out."

Carlos Ghosn surfaced in public a few days later in Asia. At a media briefing in Jakarta, he said that Renault-Nissan wouldn't be initiating alliance talks with any other automakers soon. "We are not impatient," he said. "We will continue with our life."

The GM negotiating team disbanded and went back to their old jobs. On the night of York's resignation, Fritz Henderson treated himself to a ticket to the Detroit Tigers–New York Yankees playoff game at Comerica Park in downtown Detroit. Henderson had been a pitcher in college at the University of Michigan, and he cheered like a rabid fan throughout the tense contest. And when the Tigers prevailed, 6–0, he let loose, dancing in his seat and high-fiving people around him in the stands.

It must have felt good to win a big one.

[Seventeen]

Ford crashed soon after Alan Mulally was hired, when the company announced huge layoffs on September 16, 2006. The newspapers in Detroit called it "Blue Friday"—the day that Ford's storied oval emblem crumbled.

Mark Fields delivered the news. Ford was cutting ten thousand salaried jobs on top of the four thousand already cut. Every one of the company's seventy-five thousand UAW workers would be offered a buyout or early retirement package. The company said it would begin plant closings in 2008, four years earlier than projected in the Way Forward plan. And Fields had to back off his promise that North American operations would turn a profit in two years; now it would take at least three. Financially, Ford was a basket case. An internal report prepared by Don Leclair predicted it could lose as much as $9 billion in 2006.

Despite the extraordinary cuts and losses, management refused to scale back its product plans. Fields pledged that nearly three-quarters of Ford's cars, trucks, and SUVs for the U.S. market would be replaced or upgraded over the next two years. Still, the extent of the downsizing raised questions about whether Ford had waited too long to retrench. Its U.S. market share had now dwindled to 16 percent and still hadn't hit bottom. The company was burning through $1 billion in cash a month, and that was before the huge costs of buying out workers.

Ron Gettelfinger had little choice but to go along with the bloodletting. "The UAW agreed to amputate an arm and a leg to save the body," said Sean McAlinden, an economist at the Center for Automotive Research.

Mulally stayed in the background on Blue Friday; technically he wouldn't be a Ford employee until October 1. But he was already showing up at his new office before dawn, studying organization charts, factory schedules, product plans, sales reports, global market trends. He didn't anticipate bringing in outside help or firing a lot of executives. What he wanted to see was who was ready to follow his lead. "Some people can't adapt to me, but that's okay," he told Bill Ford. "People will self-select around me. Either they're going to make it and be part of the team, or they'll know it before I say it."

A few senior executives left on their own, starting with Anne Stevens, second in command in the Americas division. On her way out, she took a parting shot. "The company is too bureaucratic, and it takes too long to get things done," she said in an interview with the *Detroit Free Press*. Steve Hamp, Bill Ford's brother-in-law, was shown the door by Joe Laymon, who said there was no room for a chief of staff in the new regime.

Turning Ford around was going to be a long, uphill struggle. Mulally wanted to change the mind-set of those who were there, the true-blue loyalists who were sick and tired of losing. He had a way of asking seemingly innocent questions that provoked tough, introspective answers. In one of his first meetings with the executive team, Mulally pulled out a historical chart of the world auto industry twenty years earlier, when Ford had had a 13 percent share and Toyota 9 percent. Now the numbers were flipped. Toyota had 13 percent, and Ford had 9. "How's that going, guys?" Mulally asked. "Does that work for you?"

He seemed to have a chart for everything—the growth in Asia versus that in North America, the steady rise in small car sales and decline in truck and SUV sales, the costly complexity of Ford's brands compared to Toyota's. And with every chart, he tossed out a challenge: Why was Ford doing things this way? What's the reason? Could they change it?

At one meeting, someone suggested that the auto industry was pretty complicated and plans weren't rewritten overnight. Mulally wasn't buying that. "I've been with a global company for thirty-seven years that uses a lot more technology than an automobile," he said. "Airplanes have four million parts, and a car has ten thousand. So I feel pretty comfortable with this."

Despite his smile and sunny disposition, Mulally was a hard, battle-tested executive with no patience for long-winded explanations. He purposely didn't criticize Ford or its history. That would alienate people. But he had a crystal-clear view of Detroit's decline. "These three companies have been slowly going out of business for eighty years," he said. "They were insulated and had great success early on with 70, 80 percent of the market. But they were arrogant. They made fun of the Japanese. And then they made shoddy products, all of a sudden they had some competition, and their arrogance caught up with them."

Mulally saw no reason to keep doing business the way Ford had done it for decades. He was intent on remolding the organization one step at a time. A lot of the way it operated just didn't make sense to him. He couldn't fathom the proliferation of brands or why it built unique cars for every region. Even the most basic parts were different from one model to the next. Executives would find him in his big corner office with door handles and switches laid out on a table, trying to understand the endless variations that cost money to design, engineer, and produce.

He left his wife and family back in Seattle and devoted every moment to Ford, from five in the morning until late at night. He read every book he could find about the auto industry and blocked out an hour each afternoon to clear his head, think, and reflect. Every breakfast, lunch, and dinner was part of his ongoing education—meeting dealers, getting to know his executives, reaching out to anyone who could teach him the intricacies of Ford and the culture of Detroit.

Each day he drove a different Ford, taking notes on why dashboards and controls varied from car to car. "Why is everything so inconsistent?" he kept asking product execs. "World-class companies don't do things this way." He wasn't trying to be politically incorrect; he simply didn't care if the truth stung a bit. "If you look at Ford, it's the antithesis of Toyota—we've got different Fords all over the world," he said, fully aware that praising the Japanese automaker was not popular in the Glass House. But when Mulally said it, somehow it sounded okay.

Mulally quickly learned how bureaucratic Ford was, but he felt in no way bound to convention. His first week on the job he slashed his meeting schedule in favor of informal one-on-ones, field trips to the design centers and engineering labs, and long conversations with Bill Ford. It had been hard for him to leave his cocoon at Boeing. But in a few weeks' time, he bonded hard with his new home. "I have never seen the depth of feeling for a company as these people have for Ford," he said. "Everybody has this pent-up feeling, and they want to tell me everything they can to make Ford successful." People warmed to Mulally and confided in him. In turn, he made them feel important, valued, needed. "Alan has a way of making it safe to speak up," said Laymon.

Admitting a shortcoming, in Mulally-speak, was a "gem." Coming back after a failure was a sign of "emotional resilience." Owning up to problems was "liberating." He had a knack for making people feel wanted and respected, whether in the employee cafeteria or in a dealer showroom, around the boardroom or on the factory floor.

He knew people were dispirited, worried about their jobs, and fearful instead of confident. "Competitors may try to divide and conquer us," he said in a companywide e-mail addressed to "the Ford Team." "I'm determined we are not going to do that to ourselves." He preached a message of hope and promised a light at the end of the tunnel. "As demoralizing as a slide down may be," he wrote, "the ride back up is infinitely more exhilarating."

But Ford's downward spiral had cemented some bad habits. Several executives didn't talk to one another (there was a long tradition of that). Others kept information secret, not wanting to share their own internal issues. Divisions were self-contained companies within a company, with their own budgets, finance staffs, and public relations people. Even product teams operated independently of one another.

Way too often, senior managers took their issues or disputes to the CEO. Early on, a number of execs tried to circumvent Mulally and appeal directly to Bill Ford. How could they do their jobs if the new guy kept questioning everything they did? Bill stopped them in their tracks. "If you have an issue, take it up with Alan," he said. "I agree with everything he is doing."

It wasn't easy for Bill to give Mulally so much latitude. He was used to being the boss. But he knew that without autonomy and authority, Mulally didn't stand a chance of taming the corporation.

Mulally's Thursday-morning business-plan reviews became the epicenter of Ford's transformation. All the division chiefs and department heads (Fields, Leclair, Laymon, product chief Derrick Kuzak, and on down the line) were required to attend. There was a strict code of conduct. No cell phones, BlackBerry devices, or encyclopedic briefing books allowed. No assistants or aides in the room. No jokes about another person, no side conversations at the table. And above all, no opinions—just facts. "Data will set you free," Mulally said with a smile.

One day someone in the meeting made a wisecrack about the "ladies' section" because three women were sitting together. When Mulally stared him down, so did the rest of the room. "I can't stand jokes at anybody's expense," he said sternly. He called his rules "working-together behaviors" and said he understood if some people couldn't adapt. "If you can't do it or don't want to do it or it's too hard, that's okay," he said. "You'll just have to work somewhere else." It was tough love with a hug, a smile, and a zero-tolerance policy. "The important thing is we're all accountable to each other," he said. "You are accountable to the team, and the rest of the team is here to help you."

During the weekly reviews, Mulally and his top fifteen executives systematically deconstructed, questioned, debated, updated, and refocused every aspect of the business—product cycles, market conditions, investment plans, sales performance, factory schedules, productivity rates, and cost improvements. And each business unit had its own defined space on the walls of the windowless Thunderbird Room for the reams of graphs and charts that marked their progress—all beneath a photograph of the executive responsible.

For so long, Ford's leaders had hunkered down in their own departments, huddled with their people, crafted plans on their own, and presented them at formal strategy sessions with the CEO and his coterie of advisors. Now the nexus of all decisions was the big circular table in the Thunderbird Room. Mulally showed the executives how to color-code their status reports: green (on target), yellow (somewhat short), or red (in trouble). Everybody talked about everyone's plan, no exceptions allowed. "What is the real situation?" Mulally would ask them repeatedly. "And what do we need to do to change it?"

First and foremost, Ford had to cut costs, standardize processes and parts, and reduce the number of models and brands. That focus would improve quality and create an identity around the Blue Oval. And Mulally absolutely loved that little badge with the Ford name written out in script. "Gosh, it must be so cool to have your name on all these millions of cars!" he said to Bill Ford. As far as product, he wanted more cars, less trucks, and a relentless drive to improve fuel economy in every segment. The balance sheet obviously needed immediate help, and he constantly prepared for the big pitch to the banks to borrow billions of dollars. And the foundation of the comeback would be two words that were stuck in his head: "one Ford." Not a Ford in Asia and a Ford in North America and a Ford in Europe—one Ford, with one mission, one goal, and one singular purpose. "I had a point of view of where we wanted to go," he said. "And every week it got clearer and clearer because they were all talking about it."

On October 24, less than a month into the job, Mulally stood front and center to report Ford's worst quarter in fourteen years—a

$5.8 billion loss, including $2 billion in red ink in North America. Wall Street gasped, driving the stock down below $8 a share. Auto analyst David Healy said, "It's difficult to tell if they are getting out of the woods, or just getting into the woods." If Mulally needed a stick to prod Ford to change, the third quarter numbers provided it. "These business results are clearly unacceptable," he said. "This is not a viable business model going forward." Plant closings and job cuts would not be enough. Fixing Ford required new behaviors and the humility to admit that the old ways had failed. "This is a critical time," Mulally said. "It absolutely demands decisive action and a clear focus."

A day later, Bill Ford left Dearborn for a trip to China, where Ford was lagging behind its rivals in establishing a manufacturing foothold. The trip had been long in the works, but symbolically it couldn't have come at a better time. He'd be seven thousand miles away from the Glass House. And Mulally was now on his own.

Oh, shit, thought Mark Fields. *Why me?*

He had just received a report from Ford's assembly plant in Oakville, Ontario, and it couldn't have been worse. The first two thousand Ford Edge crossovers off the line had a problem with their hydraulic lift gates, and production had to be stopped. The Edge was Ford's single most important vehicle launch of the year—it was its first fuel-efficient, high-tech SUV replacement and a cornerstone of the Way Forward product offensive. To make matters worse, dealers had already ordered thousands of Edges, and customers were waiting.

Fields had two choices, neither one of them good. He could ship the Edges that worked, restart production, and hope the glitch could be found and fixed on the fly. Or he could delay the launch and be the first executive to go into Mulally's Thursday-morning meeting with a big fat red dot on his weekly progress sheet. He sat down with his team in Dearborn and made the call. "We are not going to ship a vehicle before it is ready," he said. "We just can't. We have to delay it.

I'm going to have to call it a red." His staff members looked at him. He could almost feel their pity.

At the next business review, Fields took his seat, right next to Mulally. As luck would have it, he was the first executive to present. His mind raced. *I'm going to get killed here,* he thought. Then he took a deep breath and showed everyone the launch page with a large red dot on it. "The Edge launch is red," he said. "And we're delaying it."

Fields thought he felt people moving their chairs away from the table, away from him. Bringing bad news to senior management at Ford was typically avoided at all costs. Nobody wanted to even be near the culprit. The Thunderbird Room got very quiet. Everyone looked at Mulally, waiting for his reaction. A few seconds passed. Then Mulally turned toward Fields, stood up, and started clapping. Fields was momentarily stunned. Then Mulally really started clapping, as though Fields had just hit a home run. "Thank you, Mark," he said, "for the transparency." At that moment, the atmosphere in the review room changed for good. Someone had had the guts to put a red out there—and survived. Not only that, Mulally liked it!

"Mark, that is great visibility," Mulally said. "Now, is there any help you need from any member of the team?" All of a sudden, people started to speak up. Bennie Fowler, head of the quality department, said he'd seen that type of problem before and had some ideas. The head of procurement weighed in about the parts on the Edge. The manufacturing exec promised to send some extra engineers to the plant. Fields couldn't believe it. A crucial launch was delayed, and somehow he was a hero. "A picture was worth a thousand words," he said. "And that picture was Alan clapping." Within two weeks, the red had turned to yellow. Three weeks later, the Edge launch was green to go.

It was fitting that Fields broke the ice and showed the courage to admit a problem. He had been doing the heavy lifting on the Way Forward restructuring and had drawn the ire of the UAW in the process. He also had been a lightning rod in the Glass House, viewed by some other executives as Bill Ford's favorite and a little too cocky for his own good. But Fields had nothing to apologize for. He worked extremely hard, stuck his neck out, and fought for what he believed in.

Some people thought Fields would leave Ford after it brought in a new CEO. His star was on the rise, and he always had job offers. But right before Mulally's hiring was announced, Bill called Fields into his office, brewed him an espresso, and prepared him for getting a new boss. "There's going to be a management change," Bill said. "I'd really like you to support and work for this new CEO, Alan Mulally."

At first Fields was crestfallen. If Bill was giving up the chief executive job, why wasn't he considered? But very quickly Fields took stock of the situation. Bill had shown a lot of faith in him and had given him an enormous amount of responsibility at a critical time. There was no way he would walk out on him. "Bill, whatever you want me to do, I'll do it," Fields said.

And after the Edge episode, he was glad he'd stayed. "I am very loyal to this company that gave me this opportunity," he said. "And I've grown a lot and learned a lot just by observing Alan. He's taught me how to participate."

So far, Mulally had sold his principles and methods successfully to the organization. People were responding, coming up to him in the hallways and thanking him for injecting new spirit into the place.

But now he had a much tougher sales pitch to make.

Despite its troubles, Ford had been extremely frugal with its cash hoard. Thanks to Leclair's tight hold on the purse strings, the company had $23 billion in reserve at the end of the third quarter. But with business worsening and buyouts looming, its bank account was shrinking fast. At best, there would be $20 billion left at year's end. And it already had $17 billion in debt.

In normal times, that type of spread might work. But the plant closings and new products would be very expensive. "We are going to have a big liquidity problem," Leclair had told the board in the early spring. Since then, he and his team had been working out the details of a plan to borrow a huge amount of money. For decades, Ford's credit was so good it could easily get loans without pledging assets. But times had changed. To get the big banks to lend now, Ford had to put up nearly everything it owned in America as collateral—its factories, office buildings, stock in Ford Credit, and all of its patents and trademarks, including the rights to the Blue Oval itself.

At a board meeting, one of the directors asked, "Does that mean we're hocking the Ford brand?"

Yes, said Bill Ford. They were, in fact, ready to bet the house.

Mulally was totally on board. He saw no other choice. There was only one opportunity to fix Ford. They might as well get as much money as possible. If the turnaround didn't work, it wouldn't matter whether Ford had mortgaged the Blue Oval or the Glass House because the company would be heading into bankruptcy. Ford had hired the biggest and the best investment firms to arrange the debt package—JPMorgan Chase, Goldman Sachs, and Citigroup. Their working goals for the borrowing were to raise $15 billion in loans secured by collateral and another $3 billion in unsecured financing backed by notes or bonds that could be converted into company stock.

But it would be up to Mulally to sell the loan package to all the banks that would lend money into the deal. He had to convince them that Ford had a bright future and that he had a strategy to get the company there.

On November 29, he walked onto the stage of the Grand Ballroom in the Marriott Marquis in midtown Manhattan. There were four hundred bankers in the room, representing some of the largest financial institutions in the country. It was at moments like this that Mulally shone. When the pressure was the hottest, he brought his best game. And today he would lay it all on the line for Ford.

"We face an industry that is increasingly competitive," he said, as slides flashed on a screen behind him. "Consumer preferences are changing, particularly in North America, where higher fuel prices are shifting demand from trucks—our strength—to cars. And excess capacity continues to add downward pressure on our prices. Our cost structure is not competitive, and our business units are not well integrated."

But, he said, Ford has a plan.

"The number one thing we need to do is deal with reality and tackle those issues head on," Mulally said. "A key opportunity going forward is to operate as one company."

He went through every last detail: what new products were coming, how the company was downsizing its workforce and operations, when it would pull its far-flung divisions together, and how he would change the corporate culture that drove it into the ditch in the first place. He even ad-libbed a little, calling the financing the "world's largest home improvement loan," which drew a few laughs from the buttoned-down crowd. Then he hammered home the message: *Please trust us. We will get this right.*

"This liquidity," Mulally said, "is needed to execute the plan I have highlighted to transform the company and provide a cushion to protect for a recession or other unexpected event." Later, he called the speech a "defining moment" and proof that Ford was on a new and different path.

That same day, he got some unexpected positive news. Thirty-eight thousand UAW workers had accepted buyouts to leave Ford—half of the company's U.S. workforce. And a week later, the returns came in from the banks. The demand to participate in the financing package was way bigger than anyone hoped for. All told, the banks were willing to lend Ford as much as $23.5 billion to turn itself around.

When he heard that, Mulally didn't hesitate. He recommended to the board that Ford go for it all and borrow the maximum. "We're going to need it," he said.

[Eighteen]

It was the most famous sight in Stuttgart: an immense silver three-pointed star inside a perfect circle, shining atop the headquarters of DaimlerChrysler AG. But it wasn't the corporate logo of the transatlantic auto giant created in the 1998 merger of Daimler-Benz and Chrysler. The star was the universally recognized emblem of Mercedes-Benz, the pride of industrial Germany and the gold standard for luxury cars around the world. Ever since Daimler-Benz and Chrysler joined forces, there was never a doubt which of their brands was the foundation of the new company. It wasn't an American-made Chrysler minivan or Jeep sport-utility or Dodge truck. The heart and soul of DaimlerChrysler was, and always would be, Mercedes-Benz.

The financial crisis unfolding at Chrysler in the United States had unleashed a groundswell in Stuttgart to dump the faltering American division and save the cherished three-pointed star from being dragged down with the disaster in Detroit. A few weeks earlier, Dieter Zetsche had told Tom LaSorda and his senior executives that their jobs were on the line: they had to fix this business or else. But it was too late—Chrysler was as good as gone.

In early October, three hundred DaimlerChrysler communications staffers gathered in Stuttgart for their annual global leadership conference. They came from all over the world, including a contingent from Auburn Hills, Michigan. The American staffers could sense the tension directed toward them as soon as they entered the meeting hall. Several senior company executives, including Zetsche and LaSorda, made presentations over an interactive satellite hookup. When LaSorda's face appeared on the large video screen, some of the Germans in attendance started booing and making rude remarks.

LaSorda methodically went through the challenges Chrysler faced. After his speech, people fired pointed questions at him about how poorly the American division was performing. LaSorda promised to stop the bleeding. "This happened on my watch," he said. "And I'm going to fix it."

Zetsche, however, had been planning in secret for months to sell off Chrysler. The process kicked into higher gear after the UAW rejected health care concessions. During the Paris auto show, Zetsche had met with Carlos Ghosn to gauge any interest the Renault-Nissan alliance might have in Chrysler. Ghosn was intrigued but had not yet completed discussions with General Motors. "Let me finalize everything," he had said. "And then we can talk." But Zetsche was not waiting. Even as LaSorda and his team prepared their survival strategy, DaimlerChrysler had engaged investment banker JPMorgan Chase to quietly scout for potential buyers for Chrysler.

Chrysler's fall from grace was sudden and swift—particularly because it came on the heels of a remarkable comeback.

During the five years that Dieter Zetsche was Chrysler's chief executive, the company had risen from the chaos of the ugly transition period following the 1998 merger with Daimler. The combination of the two companies was never the merger of equals it was supposed to be. Daimler's CEO, Jürgen Schrempp, had executed a takeover in disguise, stacking all of the authority and power at newly formed DaimlerChrysler in Germany.

The first two American executives to run Chrysler after the so-called merger were fired, and emotions ran high in Auburn Hills when employees realized their fate was in German hands. But in early 2000, Zetsche and his swashbuckling deputy, Wolfgang Bernhard, arrived from the Mercedes division with a plan to bring order and restore morale at Chrysler. It was tough going at first; Zetsche was vilified for closing plants and cutting jobs to streamline the organization. But then he and Bernhard set out to improve Chrysler's quality and invigorate its product lineup. And they hit the jackpot with the first flagship car they turned out—the audaciously statuesque, unashamedly powerful, in-your-face Chrysler 300.

It quickly became the hottest car Detroit had made in years. With its striking rectangular grille, glitzy interior, and high-revving Hemi V-8 engine, the 300 was a pseudo-luxury car with an attitude. Cheaper than the big European sedans but way cooler than bland Japanese models, the 300 was the ride of choice for rappers, athletes, and Hollywood hipsters. One of the first 300s off the line was specially requested by Snoop Dogg, the hugely popular star of the L.A. rap scene. Snoop later became an unlikely spokesman for the company by starring in a TV commercial with none other than Lee Iacocca.

Snoop and Iacocca's ad was funny and timely. It was staged on a golf course in Southern California, where the lanky, diamond-studded Snoop teed off with the gray-haired, eighty-year-old Iacocca. When Iacocca said that "everybody gets a great deal" on a new Chrysler, the goateed Snoop agreed in his unique street lingo. "Fo-shizzle," he replied, "Ica-zizzle."

The 300 was an overnight sensation. Its annual sales exceeded those of GM's entire stable of Cadillac cars. The results gave Chrysler a halo of style and urban buzz that GM and Ford sorely lacked. And the expressive, mustachioed Zetsche became a star in the Motor City, outshining charisma-challenged Rick Wagoner and old-money Bill Ford. Unfortunately, the magic of the 300 didn't rub off on Chrysler's other new models. Its bread-and-butter minivans, Ram pickups, and Jeeps still sold well, but a new line of sporty wagons flopped, and its midsize cars were woefully uncompetitive with the high-quality Toyotas and Hondas on the market.

Zetsche's biggest mistake was expanding the Jeep lineup to smaller, less robust SUVs that got better gas mileage but seemed wimpy compared to the rugged Wranglers and Grand Cherokees the brand was known for. By the time Zetsche moved back to Germany to succeed Schrempp at the end of 2005, Chrysler's resurgence was beginning to fade. Its factories were cranking out too many models with paper-thin profit margins. Tom LaSorda—low-key, industrious, and uncomfortably stiff in public settings—didn't have the product savvy to come up with another hit like the 300. And in the summer of 2006, the market turned on Chrysler with a vengeance. Rising gas prices crippled sales of its stalwart trucks and sport-utilities, inventories skyrocketed, and, like at General Motors and Ford, the losses started piling up.

Now the situation had turned dire. The German side of DaimlerChrysler was fed up, from the top-level management board on down to the Mercedes engineers and managers. LaSorda, a nuts-and-bolts manufacturing veteran who had spent most of his career at GM, was ill-equipped to turn Chrysler around quickly, even though he had to give it his best shot. On October 16, LaSorda and his top sales executive, Joe Eberhardt, met with Chrysler dealers and virtually begged them to put in orders for the tens of thousands of older-model cars and trucks sitting in storage lots all over Detroit. To entice them to play ball, Chrysler offered $1,500 in cash per vehicle to close deals with customers. But even the new rebates didn't help sales.

More heat came from Stuttgart when teams of Germans from the Mercedes division began arriving in Auburn Hills to assist in Project Refocus—an efficiency drive intended to cut a thousand dollars in costs out of each car Chrysler made. There was irony in the fact that executives from Mercedes, one of the highest-cost producers among all the auto brands in the world, were supposed to help Chrysler find ways to save money. Employees at the Chrysler Technical Center wondered why Germany was suddenly taking such a keen interest in its mass-market cars and trucks. They got more suspicious when they learned that Rainer Schmückle, the powerful chief operating officer of Mercedes-Benz, was leading the effort. Rumors swirled that Schmückle was standing by to replace LaSorda if Chrysler's tailspin got worse.

On the morning of October 25, the depths of the troubles were made public. Chrysler announced that it had lost $1.5 billion in the third quarter, driving down the entire corporation's profits by 37 percent from a year earlier. DaimlerChrysler's chief financial officer, Bodo Uebber had flown to Auburn Hills to oversee the earnings release. That was unusual; he had rarely done so before. After the announcement, Uebber, LaSorda, and several staffers gathered around a table on the fifteenth floor of the Chrysler headquarters tower to field questions on a conference call with analysts and the media. When one analyst asked whether there was any possibility of Chrysler being jettisoned, Uebber spoke up. "We don't exclude anything here," he said.

Jason Vines, Chrysler's chief of communications, noticed that the Germans in the room all nodded in approval. "I'm looking at LaSorda, going, 'What the fuck?'" Vines said.

LaSorda appeared baffled. When Uebber was pressed to explain further, he said the Chrysler situation was under study and no conclusions had been reached. "We don't exclude anything," he said again. "We need to safeguard sustained profitability for the Chrysler group and for DaimlerChrysler."

When Vines heard Uebber say that, he bolted from the room to his office. His frazzled secretary said he had gotten fifteen phone calls from journalists within five minutes. All of them had asked if Chrysler was on the auction block. It took hours before the overall head of DaimlerChrysler communications, Hartmut Schick, issued a statement saying, "There are no plans to sell Chrysler."

But the word was now out, and it marked a huge turning point. Never in DaimlerChrysler's eight years of existence had a senior executive even remotely suggested in public that Chrysler might be sold. Uebber was arguably the second-most-powerful official in the company after Zetsche, and investors knew he was not a man who made casual remarks. "It wasn't a slip by Bodo Uebber," said Willi Diez, head of the Auto Industry Institute in Germany. "Those remarks were placed to open the discussion."

The reaction was instantaneous, triggering a 5 percent surge in DaimlerChrysler's stock over the course of the day. Apparently the company was worth more to investors without a struggling Detroit carmaker wrecking its profits. In interviews afterward, Zetsche was strangely vague when asked how much time Chrysler had to get back on track. "Sometime toward the end of the year we should start to get a clear picture," he said. "And sometime in the beginning of next year we should be at a point where we can inform the public about what we will be doing."

Soon after the press conference, Zetsche finally took LaSorda into his confidence. "Chrysler needs another partner," he said. "That's the only way it will survive." LaSorda was stunned. He knew about the overtures to Ghosn in Paris, and he had been very involved in joint-venture talks with a Chinese automaker to provide a small car for the U.S. market. But he had no clue that Chrysler was at such a precipice.

Zetsche told him that Rüdiger Grube, the company's top corporate strategist, was involved in the plans and might need his input if a deal was going down. But otherwise, Zetsche told LaSorda to keep his mouth shut, pretend nothing was amiss, and stay focused on the business. "Keep the blinders on," Zetsche said. It would be hard enough to find a buyer for Chrysler and a lot more difficult if it deteriorated further.

There's an old saying in Detroit: "It's your turn in the barrel." The point is that at least one of the Big Three is always hurting and drawing negative attention, while another is on the rise. Chrysler and Ford were tumbling down, but in late 2006 General Motors was surprisingly on the rebound. GM's third-quarter loss had narrowed to just $115 million, which was a significant improvement over the billions it had been losing. The company also had promising new products coming, including its first salvo of more fuel-efficient crossovers. "We need to show that when we launch a vehicle—whether it's a car or a truck—that we can have a smash hit," said Fritz Henderson. Even though GM was looking good compared to Ford and Chrysler, Henderson cautioned that the turnaround wasn't solid yet. "We're a long way from finished here," he said. But with Jerry York now off the board and Renault-Nissan out of the picture, GM had reassumed its customary spot atop Detroit's hierarchy.

GM's return to dominance was clear when the Big Three chief executives went to Washington on November 14 for a long-anticipated meeting with President George W. Bush. Rick Wagoner had been pushing the hardest for the sit-down in the White House, and he pretty much set the agenda with his public comments about health care reform and trade policy. Alan Mulally and Tom LaSorda were new at their jobs, so they didn't carry nearly the weight that Wagoner did.

The White House meeting was a seminal event. President Bush had been critical of Detroit's products and reputation in the past, but he showed some empathy and support after talking with the CEOs. "These leaders have been making difficult decisions, tough choices to make sure their companies are competitive in a global economy," Bush said. "And I'm confident that they are making the right decisions, and that's good news for the American people." Vice President Dick Cheney and Treasury Secretary Henry Paulson also attended. Paulson was the first administration official to emerge from the White House after the session. His only comment: "Interesting meeting."

After a tumultuous year, Wagoner was once again the leader of the American auto industry. Now that the buyouts were taken care of, his next major hurdle was getting retiree health care completely off the books. Wagoner agreed with Dieter Zetsche that the three companies had to stand firm together to relieve themselves of their crushing legacy costs. He knew he could count on Chrysler in that regard, but he wasn't so sure about Ford.

Wagoner felt a little sorry for LaSorda because Chrysler was obviously a mess. He also considered Zetsche a friend and missed their give-and-take about the industry, the union, and the future. He could kick back with his German counterpart and talk man-to-man about the challenges of running a car company in Detroit. One time, when Zetsche was venting his frustrations about the Big Three's reliance on expensive cash incentives to move vehicles, Wagoner jokingly said he had a lot to learn. "Stop whining, Dieter," he said. "You don't understand." On the other hand, Wagoner was just getting to know Mulally. Joe Laymon had brought Ford's new chief executive over to meet him, and Mulally asked a ton of questions about how GM was organized and managed. Wagoner wished him well and hoped he would be a positive influence at Ford when the 2007 labor talks got under way.

But Wagoner didn't have time to worry about the other guys. It was, as they say, their turn in the barrel. He had held tight onto the reins at GM during a difficult stretch. Though he would never admit it in public, the pressure in the boardroom and constant criticism in the media had taken a personal toll. He was stressed about how it affected his wife and three sons. At one point, his sister started hiding negative articles about him from their elderly mother.

"Rick went through a lot," said Steve Harris, his communications chief and good friend. "But he never complained." Henderson marveled at Wagoner's self-control when Jerry York was trying to get him fired. "He was too much of a gentleman to say anything," Henderson said. "That's just the way Rick is."

And after standing tall during the storm, Wagoner's fortitude paid off when Kerkorian bailed out on GM. On November 22, the Tracinda Corporation announced that it had sold fourteen million shares of GM stock for $462 million, cutting Kerkorian's stake in the company to below 8 percent. After York quit the board, Kerkorian had considered a counterattack on GM, possibly in the form of a proxy battle to elect a slate of directors and challenge for control. But the billionaire financier didn't care to wage a long, protracted battle with slim odds of winning. That wasn't his style. Kerkorian operated on instinct, nerve, and an uncanny sense of timing. That's how he rose from a penniless high school dropout to one of the richest men in America. Kerkorian wasn't interested in wasting time on a management team that didn't see things his way. "I want to be with a winner," he said to a friend. "Wagoner has never accomplished anything. They're not going to make it—not if they keep going like this."

GM's stock fell 5 percent on the news that Kerkorian was divesting his shares. But when the price stabilized a few days later, Kerkorian called York. "Let's get out of it," Kerkorian said. On November 30, he sold off his remaining forty-two million shares in two large transactions. It was an unusually quiet and peaceful retreat for such an aggressive investor.

He ended up making about $100 million overall on his eighteen-month bet on GM, which was not the big payoff he was hoping for, but he told York he was "happy with it" and it was time to move on.

GM watchers said Kerkorian's departure had to be a relief for Wagoner and the board, even though there was no guarantee he wouldn't take another run at the company. But for now, the danger had passed. "It was the shootout at the O.K. Corral that never happened," said David Cole, the chairman of the Center for Automotive Research.

York wasn't second-guessing himself. He would have relished a proxy fight for control of the GM board. But dumping the stock was Kerkorian's call. York saw more trouble coming for GM anyway. "I don't think Rick Wagoner has it," he said. "There are terrific peacetime officers who can't operate in wartime, and there are wartime generals who can't deal with the politics in peacetime. Rick Wagoner is not a wartime general. And GM is fighting a war."

The day of reckoning was drawing near at Chrysler. Eberhardt was finally relieved of his duties as head of sales and marketing on December 5, 2006. He was let go right after Chrysler mailed coupons to three million consumers worth a thousand dollars toward the purchase of a new Dodge, Jeep, or Chrysler vehicle. Even in rebate-crazy Detroit, that was a sign of desperation.

LaSorda took over Eberhardt's responsibilities. "I'm your new sales and marketing guy," he told six hundred slightly bewildered staffers at a town hall meeting. LaSorda's words hardly inspired confidence in a comeback. Chrysler was clearly groping for answers. The inventory glut had gotten so bad the company shut down six of its big assembly plants for a month. And on December 20, LaSorda made a tense presentation to the DaimlerChrysler management board in Stuttgart that recommended permanent plant closings and job cuts to save Chrysler. Even Ron Gettelfinger woke up and, realizing that Auburn Hills was in deep trouble, offered to reconsider the union's rejection of health care relief. But that was hardly enough to change Zetsche's mind. Chrysler had to go, and the sooner the better.

Zetsche reached out to the one auto executive who he thought could make good use of Chrysler—Rick Wagoner. They met in secret in New York, and Zetsche made his pitch. Chrysler was available for sale immediately, and it wouldn't cost much. The bottom line was for the German side to get out from under the UAW pensions and health care obligations. And he made compelling arguments for General Motors to buy Chrysler. "There are plenty of synergies if we put the two together," Zetsche said. The Jeep brand was still strong in SUVs, and adding the Ram pickup would give GM an incredibly dominant position in the truck market. Chrysler also had some very capable engineers and designers, modern plants, and successful dealers. It would be relatively simple, he told Wagoner, for GM to absorb Chrysler's capacity, its best products such as the 300 sedan, and its state-of-the-art technical center without taking on the baggage of its administrative staff and executives.

Zetsche couldn't tell what Wagoner was thinking by looking at him; he never could. And the GM chief executive rarely made decisions on the spot. But he surprised Zetsche when he said the plan had merit and promised to take the proposal to his board. A few days later, Zetsche got the response he was hoping for when Wagoner called and said the GM directors had authorized him to enter into formal discussions about buying Chrysler. Zetsche could hardly believe his ears. This could solve all his problems. Beyond that, if General Motors bought Chrysler, it would be a blockbuster deal, a game-changing event in the history of the American auto industry. The idea that Detroit's Big Three could become the Big Two was now a distinct possibility.

But just when Zetsche was approaching GM, another attractive option had come up from an unexpected source—Jürgen Hubbert, the distinguished retired head of Mercedes-Benz. Zetsche nad Hubbert were old friends and colleagues. In fact, Zetsche had worked for Hubbert for several years before and after the Chrysler merger. In the midst of the Chrysler crisis, Hubbert came to see Zetsche in Stuttgart.

"Would you be willing to have a meeting with some of the European guys from Cerberus to talk about our company?" Hubbert asked.

"That sounds fine," Zetsche said.

Zetsche had no idea how Hubbert became the messenger, or that the German office of JPMorgan Chase had established close contact with Cerberus Capital Management, one of the hottest private equity buyout firms on Wall Street. Cerberus had just completed its acquisition of a majority interest in GMAC, the giant financing arm of General Motors. That deal made it a major player in the automotive world overnight. Zetsche was more than willing to hear what they had to say. And at the first meeting, the Cerberus executives wanted to open talks about buying Chrysler. What did Zetsche think of that?

He could barely suppress a smile under his walrus mustache. As Zetsche would recall later with a touch of sarcasm, the timing could not have been better. "As I was already pretty far along in my process," he said, "I was not terribly disappointed by this offer."

[Nineteen]

Hope springs eternal at the Detroit auto show, and the 2007 event was no exception. Sixty new vehicles from around the world made their debut, including the show's first-ever models from China—five odd-looking trucks and cars produced by the obscure Changfeng Group, run by a Communist Party official in Hunan province. Its small display was lost among the Big Three's huge exhibits, and the company's plans to sell products in the United States seemed like a pipe dream. But its very presence underscored the new reality in the global auto industry.

Change was constant. Cars could be built anywhere by anybody and sold wherever people could afford them. No nation had an insurmountable edge anymore. An American, German, or Japanese autoworker wasn't intrinsically superior to a Chinese, Russian, or Indian. Rather, they were just more experienced, better-paid, and blessed with safer, cleaner, and more advanced factories.

But the gap was shrinking. The advantages enjoyed by workers in the developed countries were fast becoming a ball and chain of extra costs, wages, and benefits. The underdog nations were hungry, and the traditional powers such as General Motors, Volkswagen, and

Toyota were investing in them to gain a foothold where the hottest growth was coming. It was only a matter of time before upstarts such as Changfeng showed up in the United States and Europe, looking for a piece of the action.

The show floor at the Cobo Center was a mosaic of intriguing story lines. How would Ford fare under new management? Was Chrysler falling apart? What did Renault-Nissan do next? Were the Korean twins, Hyundai and Kia, ready to make their big move in the United States?

But the bulk of the attention centered on the heavyweight match between General Motors and Toyota for the title of world's biggest auto company. The Japanese goliath brought some powerful products to Detroit, including a four-door version of the new Tundra pickup and two high-performance models from its Lexus luxury division. Although company officials weren't confirming it yet, Toyota was also preparing to announce its eighth assembly plant in the United States.

GM had its own product offensive to brag about: a new midsize, mainstream Malibu, the sharp-edged Cadillac CTS sedan, and a bright orange, seriously sexy Camaro convertible. But its surprise star was a concept car called the Chevrolet Volt—a four-door hatchback that ran on electricity from a lithium-ion battery but could be recharged by a small gasoline engine.

The Volt's unlikely champion inside GM was Bob Lutz, who was determined to prove the company could make more than just gas-guzzling trucks and fast cars. The white-haired former U.S. marine couldn't resist poking fun at environmentalists who blamed Detroit for global warming in the documentary *An Inconvenient Truth*. Lutz cited the film when he unveiled the Volt at a packed press conference. "A GM electrical vehicle is an inconvenient truth," he said with a wry smile.

But he wasn't joking about the company's commitment to claiming the leadership position in new technology. "We have the talent," he said. "And we have the will." They also had a new goal—to get the American public to care about GM, even root for its success.

Internal research showed that many consumers viewed the company as stodgy, slow, and out of touch. During the Detroit show, GM executives tried hard to dispel its ultracorporate, conservative image. Executives had already been crisscrossing the country touting its progressive side as part of the Arlington Project, hatched a year earlier. "There is this perception that we just don't get it, that we're this midwestern, bureaucratic, smokestack kind of company," said Mark LaNeve, the North American sales chief. "That couldn't be further from the truth."

It was a mixed message at best. General Motors wanted to be embraced as an all-American success story, even as it was closing factories across the country and racing to build new ones overseas. And it was hard to generate warm feelings for a gigantic company with a king-of-the-hill mentality. Rick Wagoner made clear that "The General" wanted to stay number one ahead of Toyota. And behind closed doors, Wagoner, Lutz, and Fritz Henderson were studying a move that could keep GM on top for a long time to come: buying Chrysler.

The discussions were just under way and limited to an airtight circle at GM. The same was true on the German side. And at Chrysler, only Tom LaSorda knew what was brewing. Nobody was more under a microscope at the Detroit show than LaSorda. At Chrysler's press conference, he wore an apron in a skit with celebrity chef Bobby Flay to introduce the company's new minivan. LaSorda and Flay were supposed to be cooking up a spicier and bolder version of the ubiquitous soccer-mom van. LaSorda played his role and got some laughs after Flay said the Chrysler chief executive had been spending "a lot of time in a hot kitchen."

"Thank you for bringing it up," LaSorda deadpanned. "I've got enough press about it already." LaSorda was in a very tough position; he was working on a restructuring plan code-named Project X with executives at Chrysler and Mercedes, while at the same time secretly working with Zetsche to sell the business. The two duties were interrelated. DaimlerChrysler needed a blueprint to cut costs and straighten out its American division fast, whether it was sold or not. And if they did find a possible buyer, the company would be more attractive with a leaner cost structure and better balance sheet. Either way, LaSorda was in the middle of a historic juncture in the American auto industry.

It had been a long time since one of the Big Three was this vulnerable, maybe not since Lee Iacocca went to Washington in 1979 to ask the federal government to guarantee loans to save Chrysler from bankruptcy. General Motors had its extraordinary resources to draw on. Ford was getting money from the banks to fund a turnaround. But Chrysler was stuck in limbo with a parent company that wanted to sell it, a business model that was falling apart, and an uncertain market of potential buyers willing to take a chance on saving it.

On February 13, DaimlerChrysler's supervisory board (the equivalent of a U.S. board of directors) and its senior management landed in Detroit for a critical meeting scheduled the next day. Dieter Zetsche would be announcing the details of Project X: Chrysler was cutting thirteen thousand jobs, closing one assembly plant, cutting shifts at two others, and reducing the workforce at several other factories. In addition, he would pledge a closer working relationship between Mercedes and Chrysler and promise more fuel-efficient cars and fewer trucks for the U.S. market. The more significant part of the meeting would be a formal vote by the supervisory board to pursue other, unspecified options for Chrysler, including an outright sale.

But the plans went awry at 2:30 A.M. on February 14, when the phone rang in Zetsche's room at the Royal Park Hotel in suburban Detroit. Corporate lawyers were on the line from Stuttgart. A German newspaper had reported that DaimlerChrysler was exploring a possible sale of its struggling American division. The lawyers urged Zetsche to put out a statement immediately, even though the supervisory board was not meeting for hours. Reluctantly he agreed.

Just before dawn, a press release went out. It first quoted Zetsche as saying the company was "looking into strategic options" regarding Chrysler. Then the big news: "In this regard, we do not exclude any option in order to find the best solution for both the Chrysler Group and DaimlerChrysler."

By the time employees plowed through a heavy snowstorm to get to work at 8:00 A.M. in Auburn Hills, the news had gone global. Chrysler was, in effect, officially up for sale. There was no turning back. Zetsche was still furious that the news had leaked in Germany, but that hardly mattered now. During a tense press conference at Chrysler headquarters, he and LaSorda tried to dodge direct answers to the barrage of questions: What were the criteria for a sale? Could it possibly be avoided? Had talks already begun with potential buyers? Zetsche kept repeating the same words from the press release over and over. "Our thinking does not exclude any options," he said in his heavy German accent. "That means all options are on the table."

LaSorda sat stone-faced next to him, trying to show solidarity with his boss about the "options" for Chrysler. "It is something that he and I are teaming up on and we fully endorse," LaSorda said. But that was it. The reporters couldn't pry any real details out of them, and not even a hint about General Motors, the investment bankers, or the overtures from Cerberus.

The news rocked Detroit. Nine years before, the Big Three's fraternal circle had cracked when Chrysler hooked up with Daimler-Benz. Now the biggest automotive marriage in history seemed to be heading toward a messy divorce. Employees in Auburn Hills were dumbfounded, huddling in their office cubicles, design studios, and product labs, trying to make sense of it.

"It's pretty solemn in there," Joe Kubina, a Chrysler engineer for twenty-four years, told the *Detroit News*. "I don't know what to think. I'm still confused by it all."

Not only was DaimlerChrysler on the verge of splitting up, but thousands of workers were on the firing line in yet another brutal restructuring in the Motor City. "Disregard the numbers—real people and real communities are suffering here," said an angry John Dingell, the powerful U.S. representative from southeastern Michigan. After the massive cutbacks at GM and Ford, the crisis at Chrysler seemed like a final sucker punch to an industry on the ropes. "We're starting to enter the darkest part of the tunnel," said Sean McAlinden, a labor economist at the Center for Automotive Research.

No one was more irate than Ron Gettelfinger. The union leader felt blindsided and betrayed. He was, in fact, a member of the DaimlerChrysler supervisory board. Under German law, half of a company's governing body represents shareholders and half represents employees. As president of the UAW, Gettelfinger was awarded one of the labor seats. The decision to dump Chrysler had not even been brought before the board until the day of the announcement. In Gettelfinger's view, management was unfairly punishing American workers for the 1998 merger's failure. And the German labor unions, which held several board seats, were throwing the United Auto Workers under the bus too.

Gettelfinger vowed to fight to keep Daimler and Chrysler together. "Today's action by DaimlerChrysler is devastating news for thousands of workers, their families, and their communities," he said. "We will do everything in our power to hold the company to its commitment to grow the business by developing new products with Mercedes-Benz."

But he received no sympathy from his counterpart in Germany, Erich Klemm, a senior official of the IG Metall autoworkers union and the top employee representative on the supervisory board. "We want to ensure that the core of Daimler can be protected from a possible financial downward spiral at Chrysler," Klemm said. "It's clear that the synergy potential between Mercedes-Benz and Chrysler is limited."

DaimlerChrysler shareholders endorsed the possible breakup of the company by bidding up the stock price by 8 percent. "Investors are sick of the losses and the problems," said Jürgen Pieper, an analyst with Metzler Bank in Germany. "They have been pressing for an end."

Almost immediately, industry experts speculated on suitors for Chrysler: Renault-Nissan, Hyundai, perhaps an ambitious Chinese carmaker. But no one could seem to agree on what Chrysler might be worth to another auto company. And what if nobody stepped forward? Could Chrysler be spun off and survive as a stand-alone business? No matter what happened, the organization had to keep moving, building vehicles, and selling them while a sword hung over Auburn Hills.

The day after the "all options" announcement, a grim LaSorda addressed his top two hundred executives in a darkened auditorium at Chrysler headquarters. "If we don't deliver," he said, "all bets are off." At least people in the community were pulling for the Chrysler team. The Germans, especially Zetsche, were being viewed as turncoats and traitors, ready to kick Chrysler to the curb when the going got rough. A big headline on the front page of the *Detroit News* said it all: "Dr. Z: Hero to Zero? Zetsche's About-Face Feels Like Betrayal in Detroit."

General Motors and DaimlerChrysler had already met three times before the February 14 supervisory board event (dubbed the "St. Valentine's Day Massacre" by one Michigan politician). Zetsche had turned over the GM talks to Rüdiger Grube, DaimlerChrysler's dapper, fast-talking chief of corporate strategy. There was a weird symmetry to that. Grube had been one of Jürgen Schrempp's key operatives during the merger negotiations with Chrysler in 1998. Meanwhile, Fritz Henderson, Grube's counterpart on the GM side, approached his task with the same determination he brought to the Renault-Nissan discussions. But in this case, he didn't have a strong opinion about a GM-Chrysler deal.

The biggest proponent at GM for a Chrysler deal was Bob Lutz. He knew Chrysler better than anyone at GM, having been president and vice chairman before being pushed out during the Daimler merger. Lutz had fond feelings for Chrysler, mostly because he was responsible for some of its best-known products: the sleek LH sedans and funky PT Cruiser, the muscular Ram pickup and go-anywhere Jeep Grand Cherokee, and most of all, the 400-horsepower, superfast Dodge Viper sports car.

Lutz believed that bigger was better for GM and that the market could no longer support three independent Detroit carmakers. "The consolidation of the U.S. industry is absolutely mandatory," he said. "Somebody has got to die." He argued that buying Chrysler would allow GM to spread its fixed costs over a larger volume of products and dominate certain segments. "Chrysler as a corporation would go away," he said. "You would consolidate everything. You could keep the brands and get rid of everything else and fold it into the global GM organization—finance, legal, government relations, manufacturing."

Lutz had told Wagoner, Henderson, and the GM board that this type of opportunity wouldn't come along often and should be seized. "Obviously it's got to be ultra-affordable," he said. "But I think Daimler would do anything to get rid of it." Lutz could be very persuasive. And he drooled at the idea of putting GM's Hummer brand side by side with Jeep to form a killer SUV lineup, or adding Ram's market share to the Chevy Silverado and GMC Sierra. Besides, he was sure GM could get Chrysler dirt cheap.

But Wagoner and the GM board members weren't so convinced. Zetsche wanted to sell Chrysler to get rid of the billions in pensions and health care benefits owed to union workers. GM already had that problem. The more the directors debated it, the less they liked the idea of taking on more UAW baggage. "So you want to combine two businesses that have unsolvable problems with unions and legacy costs?" asked John Bryan, the GM director. The only way the board would consider buying Chrysler was if the union agreed to health care cuts and plant closings beforehand. In other words, Zetsche had to convince Ron Gettelfinger to make major concessions at Chrysler to allow GM to swallow it up.

Henderson took the outlines of an offer to Grube. Instead of any cash changing hands, General Motors proposed giving a 10 percent stake in its stock to DaimlerChrysler in exchange for Chrysler. Then the two companies would collaborate to fund Chrysler's legacy costs, with the German side kicking in at least $1 billion. But the main condition was the most controversial: the UAW had to agree to a health care deal and other concessions, and give its blessing to the entire transaction before it could occur.

Zetsche rejected those terms immediately. "We have to first negotiate a deal with the union to change the contract before changing ownership?" he said. "No way—then the union is totally in the driver's seat and can blackmail us. I'm not going to do that. We could be in a position to do that afterward, but not before."

When GM basically said take it or leave it, Zetsche decided it was time to move on. "It's a no-go for me," he said. "I prefer to decide my own destiny and not give it to the hands of the union."

GM's low-ball offer crystallized Zetsche's dilemma. On the surface, Chrysler was a powerful industrial machine that built and sold more than 2.6 million vehicles a year. It had a storied history, established brands, a good workforce, and excellent facilities. But 90 percent of its sales were in the intensely competitive North American market. A new owner could theoretically revamp its truck-heavy product lineup and expand into international markets. But the big burden was the legacy costs, an estimated $19 billion in long-term health care obligations to union workers and retirees. Chrysler was like a fine-looking house with a monster mortgage. Another auto company could not justify adding Chrysler's assets if it came with the crushing costs of its union workforce. Soon after GM's bid was turned down, Renault-Nissan said it wasn't interested in acquiring Chrysler or bringing it into their alliance. Hyundai didn't want it either. And there was no Chinese player on the horizon.

The potential buyer would have to be a very prosperous corporation—industrial or financial—that had a burning ambition to manufacture automobiles. Despite the risks, it was still a glamorous business with a huge potential for profits in a strong market. Zetsche realized that the most promising arena to pitch Chrysler in was the private equity sector. On February 22, DaimlerChrysler authorized its investment banker to release confidential financial data about Chrysler to four large private equity buyout firms: Cerberus Capital Management, the Blackstone Group, Apollo Management, and the Carlyle Group. GM was also on the list, just in case it was willing to improve on its first offer. But it wasn't long before the choices narrowed to the two most interested parties—Blackstone and Cerberus.

The Blackstone Group was one of the largest and richest investment funds on Wall Street. Led by its high-flying chairman, Stephen Schwarzman, the company had amassed a war chest of $125 billion. Firms such as Blackstone raised money from big private investors, acquired distressed businesses on the cheap, and then stripped them down and rebuilt operations under new, handpicked management. The trick was to fix acquisitions quickly, run them hard, and then sell out or do a public stock offering within five to ten years, generating big returns for the investors and extraordinary fees for the buyout firms.

Schwarzman was the envy of the private equity world—a high-society billionaire who lived in a $37 million Manhattan apartment and had recently graced the cover of *Fortune* magazine as "the new king of Wall Street." He was eager to do a deal and very solicitous of Zetsche at a meeting in Germany. "We want to make the deal work," he told Zetsche. "We'll fit it for you like a tailored suit." Blackstone had a glittering record of success buying hotel chains, food companies, real estate developers, and auto suppliers. And despite his flamboyant lifestyle—he rented out the Seventh Regiment Armory on Park Avenue for his sixtieth birthday and hired Rod Stewart to perform—Schwarzman and his partners excelled at fixing nuts-and-bolts industrial companies. Blackstone already owned a majority stake in the TRW automotive unit, a huge maker of air bags and seat belts, and backed the spin-off of GM's former American Axle division.

It also brought a savvy partner to the Chrysler bidding: Steve Girsky, the ex-analyst who had made such an impression during his stint as an advisor at GM. Girsky's firm, Centerbridge Partners, was hungry for automotive opportunities and could be a big asset because of Girsky's relationship with the UAW. Girsky believed that Zetsche was more interested in finding a stable home for Chrysler than in getting a good price. "The best sale is not how much money Daimler gets but what lowers its risks and improves the odds of success," Girsky said.

Blackstone had the reputation, experience, skill, and financial resources to buy Chrysler. But Cerberus had an edge—and it was named Stephen Feinberg. Cerberus was the anti-Blackstone: secretive rather than celebrated, bare-bones offices instead of fancy furnishings and museum-quality art, an underdog attitude versus Wall Street royalty.

Its very name conjured up a ferocious image: Cerberus was the three-headed hound that guarded the gates of the underworld in Greek mythology. And the man behind the mean dog was Feinberg, the Bronx-born, forty-seven-year-old son of a steel salesman, who never gave an interview or agreed to be photographed, much less featured on magazine covers. With his short, reddish hair and wispy mustache, Feinberg didn't look like a multimillionaire mogul. He didn't act like one either. A Princeton graduate and star tennis player, he was also a former U.S. Army reservist who loved to hunt, wore cowboy boots with his dark suits, and drove a Ford pickup. In fifteen years, he had taken a $10 million investment and built a private equity powerhouse that owned dozens of companies with combined annual sales of $60 billion. No deal was bigger for Cerberus than its acquisition of a 51 percent stake in GMAC. Fritz Henderson had led the negotiations for GM and marveled at the energy the Cerberus execs brought to the table. "They were like random atoms bouncing off the walls," he said. "They are really tough to deal with, but when they give you their word, they're good for it."

Feinberg wanted Chrysler badly, and Zetsche knew it. "I got the feeling early on that Feinberg was very emotional about the deal," he said. "This patriotic element of buying an American icon and saving it was a strong motivation for him." As professional as Blackstone's people were, the Cerberus officials seemed to operate in a higher gear, plying Grube with hundreds of questions and requests for data.

Feinberg also sensed quickly the pressure that Zetsche was under to make a deal. He figured the German's job was in jeopardy if he couldn't cut Chrysler loose quickly. "He was in a sell mode," Feinberg said. "He wanted to sell the company and sell it fast. And we were willing to do it in an expedited time frame."

From the moment he began studying it, Feinberg was confident Cerberus could make Chrysler work. "We can run this better than them," he said. "And what could be a better opportunity than an orphan in an industry that's at the bottom?" He thought the Germans had mismanaged the company by loading it down with bureaucracy and too much production for its natural market share. He saw a plethora of opportunities to cut costs and do joint ventures with other automakers for engines, small cars, and overseas distribution. And he relished the chance to connect with the blue-collar guys at the UAW and show them that not everyone in private equity was a rich snob driving around in a Mercedes-Benz.

Grube and the investment bankers set up camp in New York, meeting with Blackstone one day and Cerberus the next. A third, unexpected bidder, a big auto parts maker named Magna International, had elbowed its way into the process. But Magna was only in the mix if Daimler needed an alternative to the private equity players.

In early March, the bidders traveled to Detroit for their first inside look at Chrysler. LaSorda told his top executives to approach the meetings "as the most important job interview you've ever had." Secrecy was paramount. While the bidding teams were in Detroit, they traveled in Ford-made Lincoln Town Cars rather than Chryslers. At the Chrysler Tech Center, their movements were choreographed to avoid any contact with rank-and-file employees. On the morning of March 5, Cerberus senior executive Lenard Tessler and his aides arrived at the Walter P. Chrysler Museum on the tech center campus. From there, they were shuttled to the cavernous "design dome" to meet LaSorda and his execs.

The dome had been transformed into a showroom: trophies and product awards were on display along with several future models, including the top-secret, next-generation Ram pickup. For several hours, LaSorda and his team outlined Chrysler's product plans, finances, labor costs, and competitive pressures. At 5:30 P.M. everyone headed back to the museum for a white-tablecloth dinner of filet mignon and lobster. Chrysler repeated the show a few days later for Blackstone and Centerbridge officials, and then again for Magna.

Several of the visitors were familiar to the Chrysler executives. Cerberus had hired Robert Rewey, the retired head of sales at Ford, as an advisor. Magna's contingent included Mark Hogan, a former GM executive and colleague of LaSorda's. And of course everyone knew Steve Girsky.

But the most valuable player was still hidden in the background— Wolfgang Bernhard, Chrysler's former chief operating officer and Zetsche's right-hand man during its revival. Cerberus hired Bernhard as a potential chairman of Chrysler, but he would also be a valuable asset during the due diligence process. "Let's get this guy on our team," Feinberg said. "He used to run Chrysler. He knows where the bodies are buried."

In late March, each of the three suitors made opening offers, with Cerberus definitely the leader. Its biggest hurdle was the UAW. Gettelfinger still hoped that a sale could be avoided. And he went public with concerns about private equity ownership, criticizing the buyout firms as "strip-and-flip" operations that might carve up Chrysler and sell it off in pieces. The sale process, however, was gaining momentum by the day.

A pivotal moment came on April 4, when hundreds of Daimler-Chrysler shareholders gathered in Stuttgart for the company's annual meeting. Zetsche told the investors what they wanted to hear: a Chrysler deal was happening. "Everything is going according to plan," he said. Some of the shareholders weren't satisfied. "You've been sitting on this scrap heap called Chrysler for nine years!" said one named Ekkehard Wenger. "You are now analyzing all the options?"

People could complain all they wanted, but Zetsche was not about to alter his carefully plotted course. Then suddenly he drew the ultimate wild card: Kirk Kerkorian. On the day after the annual meeting, Kerkorian—with Jerry York assisting—announced an unsolicited $4.5 billion cash offer for Chrysler. It was almost twelve years to the day since Kerkorian had launched a surprise takeover attempt of the company in the middle of the 1995 New York auto show. That scheme had failed, and this one was destined to as well.

York had been trying to get Kerkorian into the Chrysler talks for weeks, but he had been rebuffed repeatedly by the investment bankers. The German executives in Stuttgart wanted nothing to do with Kerkorian, primarily because he had sued DaimlerChrysler (unsuccessfully) over the price he and other Chrysler shareholders received for their stock in the original merger. But Kerkorian was determined to be heard. "If they won't work with us, we'll go public," he told York. Unfortunately, it was too late, and Kerkorian was frozen out. This was a closed auction, and Cerberus was in the lead.

By early May, Feinberg had a hundred people working on the deal day and night. Speed was now Zetsche's top priority, and Cerberus was ready to make it happen. The transaction finally fell into place during marathon negotiations in New York: Cerberus would acquire 80.1 percent ownership in Chrysler for $7.4 billion; Daimler would retain a 19.9 percent interest after kicking in $650 million and would walk away from Chrysler's health care and pension liabilities forever. Tom LaSorda would stay on as Chrysler chief executive, with Wolfgang Bernhard playing an active role as a special advisor to management.

On May 12, LaSorda and Gettelfinger flew to Germany to meet with Zetsche, who told the union boss point-blank that this was not a negotiation. Cerberus was buying Chrysler and Gettelfinger could either support the deal or oppose it. There was no middle ground. Without allies on the supervisory board, Gettelfinger didn't have the muscle to block the deal. He decided to go along and hope for the best. "You have to play the cards you are dealt," he said.

Two days later, Zetsche, LaSorda, and John Snow, Cerberus's non-executive chairman, stood together at a packed press conference in Stuttgart to announce the breakup of the DaimlerChrysler merger. After nine tumultuous years, the great German-American automotive experiment was over. "We're confident that we have found the solution that will create the greatest overall value—both for Daimler and Chrysler," Zetsche said.

Immediately after the announcement, Zetsche flew to Auburn Hills for one last town hall meeting with Chrysler executives and employees. His heart began pounding as he walked into the auditorium. He had no idea what to expect. Selling Chrysler was the most emotional experience of his career. These were his colleagues, his friends. How could he look them in the eye now? Would they call him a traitor? "Of course, I felt like shit," he said. "But I knew it was the only decision I could make." But instead of shunning him, people smiled and shook his hand. Some even hugged him. "It is important to me," he whispered to one former aide, "that you know I did not want to do this." And when he addressed the crowd, Zetsche spoke from the heart. This was, for him, good-bye. "The five years I spent here in Auburn Hills were professionally and personally the most satisfying years I spent anywhere," he said. Now Chrysler was getting a fresh start. And he had no doubt the man they were about to meet would restore it to its former glory.

Then he introduced Steve Feinberg. The room got totally quiet. Feinberg rarely made public appearances. He spoke in a soft voice, but his intensity was obvious. He told them how proud he was to buy Chrysler and to make it an American-owned company once again. "I want to take care of it," he said. "This is a once-in-a-lifetime chance." He took a few questions, and then tried to slip out of the building unnoticed. But when he saw the photographers and reporters stationed in the lobby, he rushed back inside. He wasn't talking to them. That wasn't part of the deal.

[Twenty]

The hour was late and the black-tie crowd a bit tipsy at the afterglow party following the big charity gala at the auto show. The setting was one of those only-in-Detroit institutions: a shuttered car dealership that had been converted into a new Museum of Contemporary Art. Bud Liebler had been attending these auto show bashes forever—as an advertising executive, a Ford marketing guy, and then for twenty years at Chrysler, where he ran public relations for his close friend Lee Iacocca. He knew everybody who was anybody in Detroit—except Alan Mulally. And all of a sudden the new Ford chief executive walked in the door. "I saw Alan walk in alone," Liebler said. "There were these two cleaning ladies, and he goes right up and starts talking to them."

The night before, Liebler had heard Mulally speak at another function and was very impressed. "He seemed so sincere and genuine, and talked about how thrilled he was to be in Detroit," Liebler said. Now there was Mulally, chatting up the cleanup crew while the party people boogied around him. Liebler walked up and extended his hand. "Alan, I'm Bud Liebler," he said. "I saw you speak last night, and I wanted to say it's exciting to have you here. What you were saying is exactly what this town needs to hear."

Mulally looked at him and smiled. "Really?" he said. "You couldn't tell that I was scared shitless?"

It was a joke—and it wasn't. For five months Mulally had been the bright new face of Ford, telling anyone who'd listen that this iconic American company was going to become great again. He never varied from his script. The Blue Oval was special, he said, and Ford had a unique place in automotive history. But it needed to change its ways to survive. Mulally was always so disciplined, so positive, so relentlessly optimistic in public. But Ford had fallen to scary depths. It was sinking faster than even GM or Chrysler, burning through money and losing market share by the day. Mulally could not afford to look back. His stellar career at Boeing was in the books, over, done. He had made his decision. And the reality he faced now was pretty harsh.

The comeback had better start soon. Ford had ended 2006 with a thud, losing a total of $12.6 billion, the worst results in its 103-year history. "We are," Mulally said, "at the bottom." Those gigantic bank loans could not come quickly enough. Just closing plants and buying out workers cost the company nearly $5 billion.

And then there was the product. "The customer gets to decide," he said. No more telling consumers what they wanted. Ford would respond to what the American public demanded—safety, fuel economy, quality, styling, value. If that's what made Toyota the best, then Ford would respect that, emulate it, and hopefully improve upon it.

He put up a chart in his office that compared Ford and Toyota, product by product. "I don't want anybody coming in here and not knowing what the competition is," he said. Slowly but surely, Ford's executives began to move to Mulally's rhythm, absorb his message, and believe in what he preached. "Before, this was a culture of always trying to explain why we were off plan," said Don Leclair, the chief financial officer. "The difference now is we're actually committed to staying on the plan."

So far the plan had brought a lot of pain. Tens of thousands of Ford workers, both salaried and hourly, took buyouts or early retirement packages to start their lives over outside the auto industry. One hard-hit department made going-away T-shirts—FORD RETIREE: CLASS OF 2007. People wept openly as they carried their belongings out of world headquarters on their last day of work. "It seems kind of unreal," said Diane Faught, who left Ford after a thirty-year career that took her from mailroom clerk to supervisor's job. "Tomorrow I wake up and start my to-do list." White-collar workers who were lucky enough to stay saw their medical insurance payments increase 30 percent overnight. All merit pay raises were canceled. Ford even closed the day care centers for the children of its employees. "The business realities that we are working through forced us to make this difficult decision," the company said in a statement.

It wasn't just Ford. The struggles of the Big Three impacted every aspect of life in metropolitan Detroit. Nearly one hundred homes a day were being foreclosed upon. An estimated two thousand people packed up and moved away each month. On more than one occasion, police were called to break up unruly crowds that couldn't get into overflowing job fairs at Cobo Center. When one of the city's casinos advertised for new workers, ten thousand people lined up on the first day. The skeleton of the domestic auto industry seemed racked by some infectious disease. The biggest parts suppliers tumbled one after another into bankruptcy: Delphi, Dana, Collins & Aikman, Federal Mogul, Dura, Tower Automotive. The trickle-down depression had become a flood, washing away decades of prosperity. There was no quick fix, not like in the 1990s when cheap gasoline fueled the SUV boom and pumped up profits. Detroit couldn't rely on new trucks to pull it out of the abyss this time. It had to get lean, hard, and hungry again and fight its way back, one round at a time. Even then, it might be too late.

Mulally had one advantage over every other auto exec in town: He hadn't lived through the good times. He had no memories of how business was done for decades or hardened notions of what was and wasn't possible. So Ford was at the bottom? Accept it—but don't keep staring at the hole it fell into. "Expect the unexpected and deal with it," he said. "It can't be 'I think' or 'I wish' or 'I hope it could be.' We're in tough shape. But what's the plan?" Mulally was determined to make Ford smaller and more streamlined, and to learn from past mistakes and not repeat them. After Ford's products took a beating from the magazine *Consumer Reports*, Mulally flew out to Connecticut and listened for hours as the publication's staff critiqued every model. To understand the challenges at the retail level, he spent part of a day as a salesman at a dealership in Dearborn.

He always liked to ask the obvious questions. In one of his first reviews of new vehicles, he couldn't put his finger on what was missing. Finally, he asked, "Where's the Taurus?" Someone said the Taurus name had been dropped and replaced by the Five Hundred. Mulally couldn't believe it. The Taurus was one of the few Ford cars he'd ever heard of. It had been a major player in the midsize segment for years. And now they changed the name? "You have until tomorrow to find a vehicle to put the Taurus name on," he told the product team. "Then you have two years to make the coolest vehicle you can possibly make."

He drew his team together and urged them to act confidently and think outside the box. When the press began speculating about Mark Fields's job security, Mulally put his arm around Fields in public. "Mark is a terrific leader," he said. "I have the utmost confidence in him." He knew Leclair had a prickly reputation, but that didn't stop him from challenging the finance exec to work more closely with his peers and straighten out Ford's convoluted accounting. Mulally liked what he saw in Derrick Kuzak, the new global product boss who had developed some excellent small cars in Europe. Mulally told him not to be bashful about bringing cars like that to the United States. And he took a special interest in his young head of North American manufacturing, Joe Hinrichs, a thirty-nine-year-old Harvard Business School graduate and former plant manager.

Mulally pushed Hinrichs to broaden Ford's dialogue with local union leaders and get factory-by-factory commitments to reduce absenteeism and improve teamwork. The one gaping hole in the lineup was in sales and marketing. Mulally wanted someone with fresh ideas in that job and authorized an outside search firm to identify potential candidates.

The more Mulally settled in, the less he relied on Bill Ford. Bill tried to stay in the background as much as possible. But he continued to come to his office almost every day as he had done for years. One time, Mulally asked Joe Laymon what was up with that. "Is he always going to be there, right next door?" he said.

Laymon had anticipated this. Mulally was a thoroughbred executive and accomplished leader. Naturally he was antsy having the former CEO (and current executive chairman) around all the time. Laymon gently brought the topic up with Bill. "Maybe you might want to leave the office once in a while," Laymon said. "You know, don't come in so frequently."

But Bill made it clear he wasn't going anywhere. "That shit will happen," he snapped, "when my name is not on the building." Laymon backed off and never brought it up again. He knew that even with Mulally on board, Bill Ford still felt big pressure. The historic losses, mortgaging the Blue Oval, going outside the industry for a CEO—the responsibility still fell on him. He heard the snide comments from GM executives about how desperate Ford must be. "It was like, 'Ha-ha, hope that works for you,'" Bill said. "'Now we're going to really kick Ford's ass.'"

Private equity's courtship of Chrysler also cast an unwanted spotlight on Ford. The company's sunken stock prices and myriad salable parts (particularly the foreign brands) made it very attractive to the buyout boys on Wall Street. But the shield protecting Ford from an unwanted takeover was always the special class B stock owned by the heirs of Henry Ford. The shares were a fraction of the overall common stock. But collectively, they gave the family an iron-clad 40 percent voting stake.

The problem was that the Ford family was growing, and the value of their shares was shrinking fast. In 1999, when Bill Ford took over as chairman of the board, the seventy million special shares had a market value of $2.2 billion. Now that figure had dwindled to about $580 million. And when Ford negotiated its big loan package, the banks demanded that the company suspend its quarterly stock dividends to shareholders. Eight years earlier, those dividends amounted to $130 million in annual income for the Ford family members. But since the deal, they hadn't received a penny.

The Ford family tree was broad and eclectic. At the top were the two surviving grandchildren of the original Henry Ford: William Clay Ford Sr., Bill's father, and Josephine Ford, Bill's aunt. Both were in their eighties. Then there were the thirteen members of the fourth generation—Bill Ford, his three sisters, and their nine cousins, including Edsel Ford II, an influential company director and the only son of Henry Ford II (who had dominated Ford as president and chairman from the mid-1940s until 1980, and remained its commanding figure until his death in 1987).

Other than Bill and Edsel, none of the fourth-generation Fords worked for the company. One of their cousins was a prominent devotee of the Hare Krishna religious sect. Another cousin owned a winery in upstate New York, and another raised purebred hunting dogs on a seven-thousand-acre farm in Georgia. A few lived in Michigan, but most were scattered around the country. And each member of the fourth generation had his or her own growing family; the sprawling fifth generation already numbered more than thirty members, several of whom were adults with their own children.

Although Bill and Edsel were the only Fords with any visibility, they were still considered Detroit's royal family. No name defined the city the way Ford did. It graced hospitals and schools, libraries, highways, parks and recreation centers. Pro football was played at Ford Field and high school graduations held at Ford Auditorium. Even the gleaming, glass-sheathed Renaissance Center, home of General Motors and the tallest structure in the state, was conceived by Henry Ford II and financed primarily by Ford Motor to help downtown Detroit recover from the devastating race riots of the 1960s.

A few times each year, the extended family gathered in Dearborn to discuss finances, legal matters, and the source of their great wealth—the Ford Motor Company. On a sunny, warm Saturday in late April 2007, the family convened for a crucial meeting that was noteworthy because of two invited guests: Wall Street investment bankers Joseph Perella and Peter Weinberg.

These weren't just any outsiders. Joe Perella had been a star on Wall Street for thirty years and was a veteran of landmark deals including the leveraged buyout of RJR Nabisco. Peter Weinberg was the grandson of Goldman Sachs legend Sidney Weinberg, a confidant of the original Henry Ford and the architect of Ford's first public stock offering in 1956. Together, they specialized in advising corporations and institutions confronted with enormous, turning-point decisions, such as whether or not this family should sell Ford and end one of the great industrial dynasties in U.S. history.

The Fords were at a serious crossroads. If Ford went bankrupt, the family's stock was worthless. The critical issue before them was whether to hire the bankers to investigate all available options, including a potential sale. Bill Ford and his father wanted no part of it and argued vigorously against retaining the two financiers. Edsel Ford was traveling in Australia but sent a long letter in support of Bill's position. Elena Ford, Edsel's niece and a junior executive at the company, also spoke out against hiring Perella and Weinberg and offered to personally buy out the shares of any Ford who wanted to sell.

But what really squelched the dissent was Mulally. He addressed the family face-to-face and gave a spirited, point-by-point synopsis of how he and his management team were going to fix Ford. His pitch to the banks had been a dress rehearsal compared to this performance. The family's fortunes rested on his shoulders. Mulally had to convince them he would deliver the turnaround—and he did. He so impressed the group that he got an ovation after his presentation.

At the end of the meeting, the family voted not to hire Perella Weinberg Partners. The dissident relatives were not only neutralized but firmly back in the fold. Even Steve Hamp, the former Ford chief of staff who had been let go, sounded like a cheerleader afterward. "The notion that there's a revolution going on, or that there is in any way a lack of confidence in what Alan is doing, is categorically wrong," he said in an interview. "He was applauded by every single person in the room—not only for what he said, but [for] what he's doing and what he represents."

It was only a statistic, a number in an industry that churned out reams of facts and figures. But when Toyota announced on April 24 that it had sold 2.35 million automobiles around the world in the first quarter of 2007, the auto industry knew something monumental had finally happened. General Motors had sold almost as many vehicles, 2.26 million, but still came up short. For the first time in more than seventy years, GM wasn't number one anymore. Detroit's pride was hurt. But more important, Toyota's results proved that it had gained the upper hand and taken the high ground. It was growing while the Big Three were declining; it was winning customers whom Detroit was losing. While the American carmakers were posting huge losses, Toyota earned a record $13.6 billion in its latest fiscal year. That meant more cash to fund new products, build new factories, and develop new technology. Toyota was rich and getting richer. And Detroit had hit the wall.

The Big Three were all counting on upcoming contract talks with the United Auto Workers to help them fight back. The union's four-year deal expired in September, and formal discussions would not kick off until the summer. But GM, Ford, and Chrysler were already laying the groundwork to reduce what everybody in Detroit called "the gap," the difference in labor costs between the Big Three's unionized workforce and the nonunion Japanese factories in the United States. The number was a complicated calculation that took into account the wages and benefits of active workers, but also added the cost of supporting legions of retirees who didn't build cars anymore. The Big Three said the cumulative hourly cost of a union worker was between $70 and $75 an hour, versus $40 to $45 for an employee at plants owned by Toyota, Honda, and Nissan. The UAW disputed the number, saying it was unfair to add in medical care and pensions to retirees and their family members. But the fact was

Detroit spent way more on labor per car than the Asians did. And it was losing tons of money doing so.

Ron Gettelfinger hated the media's fixation on "the gap." He believed that the Big Three wasted a lot of cash on bureaucrats, PR people, and advertising that didn't sell vehicles. Was it the workers' fault that the companies kept cranking out old-style SUVs long after the public got tired of them? And he absolutely boiled over at the paychecks of the executives who were responsible for driving Detroit into the ditch. Even though GM lost almost $2 billion in 2006 (a big improvement over the $10.4 billion loss the year before), Rick Wagoner took home $10 million in compensation, Bob Lutz got $8 million, and Fritz Henderson earned $5 million.

And Delphi was the worst. Gettelfinger vowed again that the union would strike the bankrupt parts supplier if it canceled its labor agreement, especially after Steve Miller arranged for its executives to get nearly $400 million in retention bonuses. "If they void the contracts, we are going to shut them down," he warned. "They're a bunch of hogs slopping at the trough that's full of money and they can't get enough."

But the strike talk was just that: talk. The UAW was in no position to shut down Delphi, which would cripple GM's assembly plants. The union had lost about eighty thousand members in less than two years through buyouts and early retirements, with several thousand more on the way at Chrysler. Its total membership was down to about a half million people—the lowest since World War II—and fewer than half of its members were employed by the Big Three.

Despite Gettelfinger's anger, his members were receiving extraordinary packages to give up their blue-collar jobs. At Delphi, workers would get up to $105,000 over three years in exchange for a 30 percent wage cut. Where else in the United States was a factory worker going to get that kind of soft landing in an industry losing billions? The fortunes of the UAW and Detroit were completely intertwined. If the Big Three needed to close "the gap" to survive, how could the union fight them?

But Gettelfinger had to talk tough. No union leader wanted to go into negotiations admitting that concessions were inevitable. "Collective bargaining is not collective begging," he thundered at the UAW's bargaining convention in Detroit. "It would be a grave mistake to equate our actions with capitulation."

But the auto executives were already unusually plainspoken in public about these talks. "If we don't nail these negotiations," said Joe Laymon, "we might not be a viable company anymore." The discussions among the Big Three were even franker behind closed doors. For several months, the top execs at GM, Ford, and Chrysler had met in secret to plot strategy. And the idea that Dieter Zetsche proposed during the last labor talks was coming to fruition. The companies had retained an outside advisor, the heavyweight investment firm Evercore Partners, to draft plans for the three-way mutual-aid pact that Zetsche had wanted four years earlier. It wasn't a complicated arrangement. All three automakers would pursue the same principal objectives in the new contract: off-loading retiree health care to union-run trusts, instituting a two-tier wage system that paid new hires significantly less than $27 an hour, and abolishing the dreaded jobs bank that kept laid-off workers on the payroll indefinitely.

Then if the union went out on strike and shut down one of the companies, the other two would give it money to weather the storm. It was an unprecedented move in the history of Detroit labor relations. GM, Ford, and Chrysler would stand together, no matter which one took on the UAW.

The plan was called Project Compass. And if it worked and "the gap" was closed, Detroit might turn around—and start heading north again.

[Twenty-One]

How can I trust what you guys are doing?"

Ron Gettelfinger wanted straight answers from Steve Feinberg. The UAW president was deeply suspicious of what private ownership would mean for Chrysler. He had once trusted the Germans, and that sure hadn't worked out. So why should he believe Cerberus would fix Chrysler without whacking more union jobs?

They met at Solidarity House, the union's gated headquarters on the Detroit River. Feinberg could see that Gettelfinger was worried. *This guy really cares about his people,* he thought. Feinberg may have been a millionaire many times over, but he cherished his own middle-class roots and was fiercely patriotic. These were hardworking Americans making cars and trucks at Chrysler, and Feinberg believed that Daimler had hurt the company badly. He had no doubt his people could do better. It was all about superior management, attention to detail, and aggressive moves. "We won't bring the company back by pounding on labor," he told Gettelfinger. "That's not our way. I promise you, we're going to make it here. We've got a shot at this."

Cerberus had outhustled its competition to buy Chrysler, but it still had to close on the deal. Its consortium of banks was already having trouble convincing investors to purchase the $20 billion in loans needed to fund Chrysler's auto operations and finance unit going forward. The market for corporate debt—the nuclear fuel of the private equity boom—was drying up. And a flailing automaker from Detroit was hardly a promising opportunity. No one was more concerned than Dieter Zetsche; he couldn't rest until the sale was final in August. Until then, Chrysler was still technically under his watch. But for all practical purposes, Cerberus was in charge.

The private equity model was based on quick decisions and intensive restructuring. Chrysler was still losing big money, almost $2 billion in the first quarter of the year. Tom LaSorda was too invested in Chrysler's existing blueprint to oversee the delicate task of retooling the company. Feinberg wanted him to focus on union negotiations and finding overseas manufacturing partners. And as much as he respected Wolfgang Bernhard's automotive skills, there was no way Feinberg was making him chairman or chief executive. "We have to have an American CEO," he said. "Wolfgang wanted the chairman role. But we had no intention of making him top dog."

Cerberus was famous for paying top dollar to hire experienced operating execs from blue-chip companies, then dispatching them to overhaul the businesses it bought. It was akin to a pro sports team spending heavily on free-agent players to build a winner. In Chrysler's case, Feinberg had two potential chief executives in mind: Jim Press and Bob Nardelli.

Jim Press was Toyota's top U.S. sales executive, and hiring him would be a coup. He was also definitely interested in the job. But Feinberg was a big believer in Nardelli, a fifty-nine-year-old acolyte of General Electric's legendary chairman, Jack Welch, who rose to become head of GE's huge Power Systems division. Nardelli abruptly left GE after he lost a three-way race to succeed Welch and landed at Atlanta-based Home Depot.

Nardelli was intense, methodical, military-minded, and painstakingly devoted to the bottom line. In six years as Home Depot's chief executive, he doubled sales, streamlined operations, and boosted profits. But his blunt, my-way-or-the-highway style alienated those executives and store managers who were used to a decentralized, entrepreneurial culture. When the company's stock languished and expansion leveled off, shareholders got restive. Nardelli did not react well to criticism and was roasted in the media for wielding a digital timer to limit disgruntled investors to one minute at the microphone during the company's tense 2006 annual meeting. He left Home Depot in early 2007 with a severance package estimated at $210 million (much of it compensation for leaving benefits behind at GE) and a badly bruised reputation. But Feinberg wasn't fazed by his flame-out and figured Nardelli could whip Chrysler into shape. "This guy will run through walls for us," he said.

In early July, LaSorda was on his way to New York for a weekend with his wife when Feinberg called him. "Tom, I'd like to bring in a new CEO," he said. "His name is Bob Nardelli."

LaSorda was expecting this. "I'll be quite honest with you," he said. "I've done a lot of research on private equity, and you guys always bring in a new CEO."

"But I want you to stay too," Feinberg said.

"I'll make it real simple for you," LaSorda said. "If I like Nardelli, I'll stay. If I don't, I'll walk."

That night, LaSorda and his wife, Doreen, met Nardelli for cocktails at the Waldorf-Astoria. They clicked immediately. One thing about LaSorda: He was flexible. He had to be when he worked for the Germans. And he liked that Nardelli was direct, uncomplicated, and seemingly without a hidden agenda.

"Tom, this isn't Cerberus talking, it's me," Nardelli said. "I'd like you to be part of my team."

They talked for four hours and closed down the bar. After that, it wasn't hard for LaSorda to make up his mind. He had earned more than $3 million the year before at Chrysler and was due a big bonus once the sale was final. Sticking around was the smart move. The next morning, he called Feinberg. "I'm still in, if you want me," he said.

Feinberg wasn't so lucky with Wolfgang Bernhard. After spending several weeks inside Chrysler reconnecting with the troops,

Bernhard was chagrined to learn he would have to take a backseat to Nardelli. He felt Cerberus had reneged on a promise to give him the leadership role and quit in a huff. His departure would raise a lot of questions both inside and outside the company.

But Feinberg still had Jim Press waiting in the wings, which gave him the makings of an all-star lineup: Nardelli as the boss and efficiency expert, flanked by LaSorda as point man for manufacturing and labor, and Press running sales and marketing with a Toyota-like consumer focus. All that was left was to close the deal.

But by late July, the market for Chrysler's debt offering had totally evaporated. Investors had barely nibbled on the $20 billion package of loans, and the offering was postponed indefinitely. Instead, the deal's underwriters, including JPMorgan Chase, Citigroup, and Goldman Sachs, were forced to come up with $10 billion of their own cash to lend to the automaker. Zetsche personally had to call each of the banks' CEOs to pressure them to honor their commitments. Additionally, Daimler had to kick in an additional $1.5 billion and Cerberus $500 million to get the newly independent Chrysler off and running.

It was the first major glitch in the private equity game plan. Selling the debt to investors would have established parameters for Chrysler's recovery by allowing the company to pay interest out of its earnings, and the principal when it blossomed and sold stock in a public offering. Cerberus would be accountable for the loans, but a broad pool of investors would not have had much of a collective voice in what was happening inside Chrysler. Now the biggest banks on Wall Street were stuck with very large outstanding loans to a shaky car company in Detroit. That would become a problem down the road.

In early August, a giant banner was hung from the side of the Chrysler headquarters building that read GET READY. It was as if a surprise was coming. But get ready for what? An auto company's reputation, for better or worse, is built on what it delivered in the past, and Chrysler was all about innovation, flair, and unique products: the first family-hauling minivan, Jeeps that handled any terrain and weather condition, fresh, eye-catching packages such as the PT

Cruiser and the 300 sedan. But the "new" Chrysler was shaping up as a completely unknown quantity.

The sale was set to close on August 3, with a big celebration planned at the tech center three days later. Chrysler's employees were a resilient bunch. The shock of the Daimler divorce had worn off, and people were getting swept up in the excitement of American ownership again. The name Cerberus had meant little to them a few months before. Now the three-headed dog from Wall Street was their designated savior.

But Chrysler's new absentee owner operated in the shadows. Besides LaSorda, no one at Chrysler knew anything about Bob Nardelli coming in as its new chairman and chief executive officer. In fact, press releases had already been written in Auburn Hills announcing Bernhard as the chairman and LaSorda as the chief executive. Because Nardelli was Feinberg's big secret, Chrysler's PR staff couldn't caution the media against prematurely reporting the Bernhard-LaSorda leadership team. Virtually everyone inside thought it was a done deal—until the Sunday night before the announcement, when Nardelli's appointment leaked out.

Instead of a rush of positive publicity heralding the dawn of Chrysler's new era, every newspaper and television station ran with the bolt-from-the-blue choice of this unexpected CEO. They focused predictably on Nardelli's messy exit from Home Depot, his gigantic severance package, and his shot for a comeback in Detroit. Cerberus's secrecy had backfired badly. Chrysler's resurrection wasn't the first-day story. It was all about Nardelli. The *New York Times* put him on the front page under the provocative headline "Once Tainted, Now Handed Chrysler Keys."

The postsale celebration was a choreographed extravaganza. Just after noon on August 6, thousands of employees were ferried by buses to the front lawn of Chrysler's fifteen-story headquarters tower. There was a concert-style stage and a big video screen that beamed out congratulatory messages for the "New Chrysler" from celebrities such as NASCAR legend Richard Petty. When LaSorda came out to speak, acrobats rappelled down from the top of the tower, doing flips and dancing along the side of the structure. "This is the day we've all been waiting for," LaSorda said, "the first day in the life of our incredible new company!" On cue, loud fireworks and colored streamers exploded from the rooftop, eliciting wild cheers from the throng of workers down below. It was a hearty party in the hot summer sun, with free ice cream and rock music and the ceremonial replacement of the DaimlerChrysler signs with Chrysler's traditional bright-blue, five-pointed-star logo of old.

But the crowd didn't quite know how to react when their new leader appeared for the first time. A smattering of polite applause greeted Nardelli, who wore a crisp white shirt and dark suit as he stepped onstage. Stocky and of medium height, with a high, broad forehead, square jaw, and deep-set blue eyes, Nardelli came off pretty stiff addressing the troops, like he was reading from a script. "As a private independent company, we'll move forward with speed and a renewed focus on meeting the needs of our customers," he said.

He wasn't much looser in the press conference afterward. Nardelli made a point to put his hand on LaSorda's shoulder and deferred to him on specific questions. When pressed on what Cerberus had in store for Chrysler, the new chief executive refused to open up. "I come here today, my first day, with a fresh approach," Nardelli said. "I don't come with mandates." He emphasized, however, that any changes would happen quickly. "We have the ability to move with speed," he said. And when the topic turned to Home Depot and his big severance deal, he said he hoped that controversy would fade away as soon as possible. "The last thing I would want to be," he said, "is a distraction."

Contract talks between the Big Three and the United Auto Workers open with a ritual. The chief executive and his labor negotiators meet the union president and his bargainers in some drab, windowless room at corporate headquarters. Then as photographers aim their cameras, the CEO reaches across the long table and shakes hands with Ron Gettelfinger. The ceremony dates back decades, and the forced smiles in the photos always look the same. It's the Detroit equivalent of two boxers touching gloves at the start of a fight. Shake hands—then come out swinging.

It seemed that every four years a new contract was called a watershed moment for the industry. But these negotiations could not be overhyped. Detroit had undergone its deepest restructuring in twenty-five years. Yet the companies were still losing enormous sums of money. The so-called legacy costs had outstripped the Big Three's ability to pay them. Even after the landmark health care deal, GM was still spending $4.8 billion a year on medical coverage for more than a million employees, retirees, and dependents—an average of $9,000 every minute of every day. Every two seconds, GM paid for a prescription somewhere in the United States; every second it paid for some medical procedure. And there was no end in sight. Its health care obligations going forward for retired union workers and their spouses were estimated at $47 billion. No matter how much GM improved its products, it could never sell enough cars and trucks to cover those costs.

All three companies went into the 2007 negotiations with the shared goal of getting retiree health care off the books once and for all. It would be incredibly expensive to do so. The idea was to create trusts, fund them with colossal amounts of cash and stock, and let the UAW administer its own medical coverage to retirees. The term for the trusts was "voluntary employee beneficiary association"—VEBA for short. During the 2005 health care talks, GM had balked at going for a full-scale VEBA because it was too complicated and Wagoner was under pressure to deliver savings quickly. But now it was paramount. Without a health care deal, the chances that GM would be forced to go bankrupt increased exponentially. As GM's labor team girded for the challenge ahead, Wagoner laid out the stakes. "We need to do this on our own," he told his executives. "We don't need the courts. We don't need outsiders. We can figure this out."

Once again, Fritz Henderson would play a key role. Troy Clarke, the new head of North American operations, would lead the bargaining team on a broad range of issues. There were other big goals, including lower pay for new hires and doing away with the jobs bank. But it would be up to Henderson to craft the VEBA and sell Gettelfinger on it.

Henderson did a simple calculation that he would often use to dramatize GM's predicament. "One hundred and three," he said. "We have spent $103 billion since 1993 on post-retirement health care and pension contributions. That's $7 billion a year. We spent $7 billion on capital spending globally. So for every $1 on capital spending we spent $1 on legacy costs. It's not the people's fault. It's not the union's fault. But the business cannot withstand it any longer."

He wasn't the only CFO in Detroit who lost sleep over it. He had a close ally at Ford in Don Leclair. The two chief financial officers had developed a strong working relationship. They had discussed potential joint ventures and even brainstormed about how GM and Ford could fit together if they ever had to merge to stay competitive. Leclair supported the Project Compass mutual-aid pact in case of a strike. Mulally wasn't completely sold but was willing to keep the option open. Bill Ford was the wild card. Would he stick it to the union by backing GM or Chrysler in a strike? Wagoner and Henderson didn't think Bill would play that kind of hardball. The GM executives knew they could count on Chrysler. But would Ford back them up? "I'm not sure about them," Henderson said. "Don says they'll do it. But I don't see it in their DNA."

Gettelfinger went on offense in the days before the opening handshakes in late July. "We addressed health care in '05," he told reporters. "You don't get two bites at the apple, do you?" But he was posturing. His Wall Street advisors had already studied how much cash and stock the union would need to make VEBAs work. But Gettelfinger knew he couldn't give an inch publicly before negotiations started. Selling the previous health care deal to the union membership had been very, very difficult. At some plants, the concessions passed by the slimmest of margins. Gettelfinger had to manage expectations. There were a lot of volatile union locals out there, where plants were closing. Even as he took a hard line, he had to be straight with them. "The kinds of challenges we face aren't the kind that can be ridden out," he told his bargaining teams. "They're structural challenges, and we need new solutions."

The truth was, a UAW member was the most expensive autoworker to support in the world. Something had to give. But if Gettelfinger made concessions, he absolutely needed to get a return. And more than anything he wanted real guarantees to retain real jobs, with commitments to assign specific products to specific plants. He'd agree to lower wages for new hires if it meant more jobs. He'd even dump the jobs bank if he had to. The union was shrinking and he had to preserve the core. The sale of Chrysler was the latest shock to the system. Private equity firms were circling the industry. Who was to say Ford and GM wouldn't be next? Then there was the biggest nightmare of them all: bankruptcy. And if it could happen to Delphi, it could happen to GM.

They shook hands in late July, and for the first six weeks the union moved slowly and deliberately. Each UAW bargaining team had fifteen negotiators, and they faced off day after day with their counterparts from the companies, plowing their way through the existing four-hundred-page contracts, talking about wages, health and safety issues, absentee rates, job classifications, and work rules. But the hard bargaining wouldn't begin until Labor Day, when Gettelfinger would pick one automaker to take on seriously.

GM badly wanted to go first. But it was Gettelfinger's call. He picked the target. Historically, the union chose Ford first because it was the easiest to deal with. But this time around General Motors— hard to believe—was in the best financial shape of the Big Three and therefore the most opportune target for the UAW. Meanwhile, the management of GM, Ford, and Chrysler strategized in conference calls. A sense of collective confidence built among the execs with each discussion. The union was in a tight corner. Refuse a health care deal and possibly drive the companies into bankruptcy? The threat alone was a powerful weapon for the Big Three. And what would be the UAW's answer to that—a strike? Wagoner believed the union wouldn't risk a walkout. Public opinion would turn quickly against the UAW if it shut down Detroit and deprived Americans of their new pickups and SUVs. Still, it was a high-risk bet. GM was using up $1 billion in cash a month. If the UAW walked out, the burn rate would triple. That's where Project Compass came in. The final figure hadn't been decided yet, but the working agreement was that the other two Detroit automakers would help the company that was stuck with millions of dollars a day to defray its costs.

The key to negotiating a contract is who blinks first. Neither side wants a concession without getting a commitment in return. But by the end of August, nothing had happened on any of the major issues. Labor Day came and went, and the VEBA had barely been talked about. The union was stalling. Gettelfinger was hardly even present at the table. The GM executives were getting rattled by the silence. "What's going on over there?" Wagoner asked Henderson. "What are they waiting for?" Then suddenly, on September 13—the day before the contract would expire—a message was conveyed to the Renaissance Center: Gettelfinger was ready to talk.

Troy Clarke, who ran all of GM's plants in North America, was the first to face off with the union president. As soon as Gettelfinger came into the main bargaining room, he immediately tried to intimidate Clarke. "Do you realize how hard we're going to negotiate?" he said, inching close to Clarke's face. "Do you understand we're not going to bend over backward for you?"

Clarke didn't flinch. "We've got this problem we have to solve," he said. "We have to close this cost gap."

"Do you understand we are not afraid to strike you?" Gettelfinger fired back.

Clarke showed no emotion. He wouldn't raise his voice or react. "Like I said, we have this problem we have to fix," he replied.

That afternoon, Gettelfinger announced the union would focus all its resources on getting a contract first with GM. Within an hour, the talks were going full force. The VEBA was on the table. GM made its initial offer, proposing to fund 50 percent—about $24 billion—of future retiree health care obligations. The union trust would have to invest that amount wisely and make it last.

No good, Gettelfinger said. The union wanted GM to fund the trust by 110 percent—more than $50 billion. That was quite a spread. And the sheer size of the health care obligations created infinitesimal calculations to fight over—inflation rates for hospital stays, actuarial tables for retiree life spans, forecasts for prescription drug costs, flow charts on cancer rates. But the only real question involved the percentage of the total bill that GM was willing to pay. And what would the union decide was enough? Every time the union negotiators— primarily UAW vice president Cal Rapson—pushed for higher VEBA funding, Clarke pulled back on possible job guarantees. It went like that, back and forth, day after day, like a tug-of-war.

Fritz Henderson was now fully engaged. He spent most of his time with the union's Lazard advisors, hashing out how the trust could invest GM's billions to keep retiree medical coverage coming for the next thirty years. "I was always ready on a moment's notice to see Ron when he wanted to talk," said Henderson. "No matter where I was, I would be there in ten minutes."

But Gettelfinger was totally unpredictable. Some days he'd sit in an office down the hall from the bargainers, with the blinds pulled and the lights off, glued to his computer, reading and writing e-mails. Then, without warning, he'd burst into the negotiations and threaten to pull the VEBA off the table if GM didn't give in to the union demands. "You know we're not afraid to strike on this," he said repeatedly. Gettelfinger's behavior confused the GM team. Sometimes he'd blow into the room and tell his negotiators to go home immediately. Then he'd sleep overnight in the office down the hall, using a clear plastic bag stuffed with shredded documents as a pillow.

At the end of each day, the existing contract was formally extended for another twenty-four hours. Meanwhile, GM plants around the country were on red alert. With the contract technically expired, a strike could be called at any time. "We've got our picket signs all made up and ready to go," said Tiny Sherwood, president of Local 652 in Lansing, Michigan. "We're just waiting for the word and we're out the door."

Even Gettelfinger's own people didn't know what he would do next. One morning, Rapson came in and sat down across from Clarke. "I'm supposed to be mad at you today," he said with a straight face. "Ron wants me to be angry with you." Little was getting accomplished. The two sides kept arguing and debating over job guarantees at a plant in Wisconsin, the cost of emergency room visits for retirees in fifteen years, the rate of inflation for drug prescriptions. But it was all minutiae. The VEBA was at a stalemate. GM had drawn a line at 65 percent funding. When would Gettelfinger compromise? Nobody knew but him.

Then on the sixth day of the contract extension, September 20, the union boss threw a hand grenade into the talks. He called for Henderson to come to the bargaining room. "The VEBA is off the table," Gettelfinger said angrily. "We're going to negotiate without it—no VEBA." Then he said the talks were done for the day.

"Hey, we've got a lot to do here," Henderson protested. "We can't go home now."

But Gettelfinger wouldn't budge. "We're done," he told his team. "Go home."

The GM bargainers came back the next morning with an explosive counterdemand. No VEBA? Then the automaker had no choice but to propose what it called Plan B—a series of draconian economic changes including pay cuts of up to $10 an hour, a fourfold increase in health care premiums for active workers, and multiple additional plant closings. It was a Delphi-like package of hurt. Rapson groaned out loud when he heard it. "This isn't going to fly," he said. But the point was crystal clear. Without a health care deal, GM was going to close "the gap" with a wholesale assault on wages, benefits, and jobs. The UAW bargainers huddled. If they walked out en masse, that meant a strike was imminent. Instead, the VEBA was put back on the table immediately. GM folded up Plan B. It was never discussed again. There were no more games to be played.

By evening, the hard outline of a VEBA was in place. And with health care getting close, GM started giving on the jobs issue. Plant by plant, the automaker made commitments for new models—the

Chevy Volt in Michigan, a new truck in Wisconsin, a small car in Ohio, another SUV in Tennessee. It was like a dam had broken. The union even agreed to limit the time idled workers could stay in the jobs bank and accepted a lower starting wage for new hires, $14 an hour.

Henderson was meeting with the union's VEBA team in one room when he heard about the progress being made at the main table. By Saturday night, September 23, he had been negotiating for thirty-six straight hours, running on adrenaline and optimism. This was the most important labor deal in Detroit history, and GM was almost there. The contract was in sight.

Then, at about ten minutes to midnight, Gettelfinger barged into the conference room, grabbed Henderson by the arm, and pulled him out. "What are you doing, man?" he said with a wild look in his eye. "We've got to get a deal done here! I've got all these people in this room."

He dragged Henderson to the main room and opened the door. It was jammed with GM and union bargainers. The noise level was off the charts. Henderson thought this was a great sign. But then Gettelfinger started ranting and swearing.

"Goddamn it, we have got to go in there, and we've got to get a deal done!" he yelled. "Where are we? Where are we, damn it? What are we going to do? What are you going to do?" He was jumping up and down, cussing in Henderson's face.

The union guys didn't know what was going on. Their president seemed to have snapped. "What are we going to do?" Gettelfinger shouted at Henderson. "We've got to get a deal here!"

Henderson took a deep breath. "What," he said, "in the next ten minutes?"

That broke the tension. One of the union bargainers started laughing. Gettelfinger glared at Henderson and then stormed into the conference room, slamming the door behind him. Henderson took a moment to clear his head. *Ron must be under a ton of pressure,* he thought.

But the VEBA was really close. GM had agreed to a 63 percent funding commitment. Only a few more big items were on the table, including the all-important cash bonus to entice members to vote for the agreement. The negotiations seemed to be in the home stretch.

Then on Sunday night, Gettelfinger came back into the room, visibly agitated. "I don't think we're getting a final agreement," he said. "You guys think you're making so much progress, but you're not. We're setting a strike deadline." Then he walked out.

When Henderson heard about it, he called Wagoner. "They set a deadline," he said. "Eleven o'clock tomorrow morning." He also made sure calls were made to the senior labor execs at Ford and Chrysler. He wanted them ready in case of a strike. The Project Compass papers had to be signed fast if it happened. The whole plan was predicated on GM standing its ground and the other companies backing it up.

At 10:15 A.M. on Monday, September 24, there was still no final agreement. The union negotiators picked up and left the bargaining room. The GM team—Fritz Henderson, Troy Clarke, and lead negotiator Diana Tremblay—weren't sure what would happen next. They found out at eleven o'clock when they learned that the United Auto Workers had just gone out on strike against General Motors.

Tens of thousands of employees began streaming out of GM plants across the country, the first nationwide walkout during contract talks in more than thirty years. Within minutes, picket lines formed outside factories. At the company's assembly plant in the Detroit enclave of Hamtramck, workers wielded UAW ON STRIKE signs as they marched in the street. All of the defiance, frustration, and anger of the last three tough years came pouring out in a swell of emotion. "It's about time the union stood up against the company and stood for the people!" one of the workers, Sylvia Hill, told reporters.

At Solidarity House, Gettelfinger and his entire bargaining team assembled for a dramatic press conference on live television. It was like the calendar had been turned back decades to the days when the union flexed its muscles and brought Detroit to its knees. "Nobody wants a strike," Gettelfinger said to the cameras. "But there comes a time when somebody pushes you off a cliff. And that's exactly what has happened."

Henderson and the GM labor execs were down the hall from a now-empty bargaining room while they watched on television. Pushed off a cliff? What the hell did that mean?

"Oh my God," Henderson moaned. "This is the theater of the absurd." Then, all of a sudden, he heard Gettelfinger change his tone on TV. "If they want to sit down," the union chief said, "we're ready to go." The GM executives looked at one another for a moment. *They want to come back to the table?*

Henderson gathered himself. "Okay, if they come back, we're going to pick it back up like nothing happened," he said. "And we'll get this thing done and done quickly." But before anything else, he had to make two phone calls. It was time to reach out to Ford and Chrysler. Henderson had no idea how long this strike would last. The Project Compass documents had to be signed immediately. His first call was to Joe Laymon at Ford.

"Okay, Joe," he said. "We've got to sign these things."

There was silence on the line for a second, and then Laymon spoke up. "We're not going to do it," he said.

Henderson was speechless. He was so mad he could feel the blood rushing to his head. After all the meetings and strategy sessions, Ford was going to screw GM and back out? He had suspected it all along. But to wait until now, when the union was out walking the picket line?

Laymon spoke again before Henderson could react. "I thought you would have known we weren't going to sign," he said.

That put Henderson over the edge.

"You should have told me!" he shouted back. "You could have at least called me before we were on strike!"

He slammed down the phone. He wasn't even going to bother calling Chrysler. There was too much to do.

But then, just like that, the whole situation turned. At 2:00 P.M. the entire UAW team, including Gettelfinger, returned to the bargaining table. They were ready to talk.

Henderson and his labor execs didn't even mention the word

"strike." They acted like it was business as usual and began negotiating. While the nation watched striking workers parading around GM plants on live TV, the talks resumed at a feverish pace. Henderson and Gettelfinger sat across from each other, surrounded by their teams, and went through the deal line by line.

They nailed down the VEBA. GM committed to put nearly $30 billion in cash and stock into the new health care trust—an astonishing number given its precarious financial condition. The union, in turn, agreed to its first two-tier wage system in history. Gettelfinger got his job guarantees when the company pledged to assign new products to at least fourteen of its U.S. assembly plants. And to clinch the whole deal, GM would give each of its seventy-three thousand active workers a $3,000 signing bonus, then lump-sum payments in the second, third, and fourth years of the deal.

At 3:05 A.M. on Wednesday, September 26, the union and GM announced a tentative agreement on a new four-year contract. The strike was officially over, forty hours and five minutes after it started. General Motors immediately put out a statement by Rick Wagoner: "This agreement helps us close the fundamental competitive gaps that exist in our business," he said.

Then the news media filed into Solidarity House early in the morning to hear what Gettelfinger had to say. His negotiators looked haggard and sleep-deprived, but he seemed full of energy. "We feel very good about this tentative agreement," he said. "I think the strike helped our side more than theirs."

That was about it. He was moving on—to Chrysler and Ford.

[Twenty-Two]

Gettelfinger had to call the strike to seal the agreement. The UAW had cut a phenomenal deal. General Motors agreed to pay $5 billion for retiree health care until the new trust kicked in, and almost $30 billion in two years to fund it. On paper, the fund amounted to a $90,000 contribution to the medical plans of each of 340,000 retired workers and their surviving loved ones. How GM would come up with that kind of money was another question.

It was the single most expensive retiree program in American corporate history. And despite GM's dire financial straits, active workers kept everything—their health care, pensions, and full wages. They didn't care that new hires would earn $14 an hour when their $28-an-hour paychecks were safe. But the big "get" for the union was the product commitments. The contract saved fourteen GM assembly plants, with two others kept open temporarily. After the deluge of buyouts, the heart of the union's largest employer was still intact.

Chrysler would be tougher. The plants and the local union officials were more urban and militant, and the company had the greatest concentration of big assembly plants in and around Detroit—Jefferson North, Sterling Heights Assembly, Dodge Truck, Jeep down in Toledo.

Gettelfinger had stiffed Dieter Zetsche and Chrysler on health care before because he couldn't get his members to vote for it. There were only forty-nine thousand UAW workers left at Chrysler—about half what it had had when Daimler took over nine years earlier. The workforce had endured a miserable, prolonged downsizing and was deeply suspicious of management.

The feeling was mutual. After the union rejected their plea for relief on health care, Chrysler execs had given the UAW president a new nickname—Ron "Middlefinger." These talks could get ugly. At least Gettelfinger had had a relationship with Zetsche. He didn't know Bob Nardelli, and he didn't trust Cerberus, which had owned Chrysler for only two months.

Bargaining started right after Gettelfinger walked into the soaring lobby at Auburn Hills on October 5. The table was set. Nardelli, Tom LaSorda, and their people sat on one side, with Gettelfinger and his wingman, General Holiefield, the UAW vice president in charge of Chrysler, on the other. They were an interesting pair— Gettelfinger with his southern drawl, white mustache, and wire-rimmed glasses, and Holiefield, the union's highest-ranking African American, a three-hundred-pound former assembly-line worker from the east side of Detroit. The first session was rough. Gettelfinger was dead-set on "pattern" bargaining: Chrysler had to match everything GM gave the union. That meant the VEBA, the job commitments, the bonuses, the works. Besides that, there wasn't much to talk about.

Nardelli tried to give a "we're all in this together" speech. "Cerberus wants to restore Chrysler to its rightful place as an American icon," he said. "And we respect collective bargaining as part of that."

That was fine, Gettelfinger replied. But he wanted the same deal as GM, nothing more or less. Was Chrysler prepared to do that?

Nardelli said he didn't think that would be possible. There couldn't be any job guarantees, he said, at the "new Chrysler."

Things deteriorated pretty quickly from there. Holiefield got into a shouting match with John Franciosi, the wily old head of labor relations at Chrysler. After a few minutes, they started yelling and swearing at each other. Gettelfinger just sat there. Holiefield was his battering ram. And LaSorda didn't bat an eye. He had seen these two veteran negotiators go at it many times before and considered it healthy to get the venom out early. He expected these meetings to be extremely hostile at the start.

But Nardelli looked spooked when the insults started flying. He left in the middle of the meeting, making a show of turning things over to LaSorda, and went up to his new office on the fifteenth floor. He had decisions to make. And the first ones involved eliminating thousands of jobs—not negotiating to save them.

For nine years, every major decision at Chrysler had to go through Stuttgart. For most of that time, Zetsche had called the shots, and protected the interests of Auburn Hills. It would be hard to overstate how closely supervised Chrysler was; even mundane press releases were translated into German for approval before they were released in English. But the breakup was complete. Chrysler was on its own, left to drift away from its former owner. The Germans couldn't change their company's name back to Daimler fast enough. Chrysler was a bad memory, and the automotive merger of the century a regrettable failure.

Now instead of the Germans, Chrysler was overrun by Cerberus's SWAT team of specialists—lawyers, accountants, purchasing experts, human resource types. Nardelli brought in his own sidekicks, including his favorite PR man from New York, Bob Marston, and the flamboyant marketing consultant Peter Arnell, who had worked with Chrysler a few years before on a terribly expensive and ineffective ad campaign for minivans featuring the singer Céline Dion.

Feinberg had also hired Jim Press from Toyota. Press had been with Toyota for thirty-seven years and was known for his steady, cerebral approach to selling cars and nurturing the brand's impeccable image of safety, value, and reliability. But when executives in Japan began making more decisions in the United States, Press's career had stalled. He made his availability known to GM and

Ford, but was lured to Chrysler by Feinberg to be the co-president with LaSorda and a possible CEO down the road. "The way we talked about it was that when Chrysler got back on its feet, Bob would probably move to another of Cerberus's operations," Press said. "He was not here for the long term, and I was sort of his understudy."

But Nardelli didn't want or need Press around. When the two of them first sat down together, Nardelli didn't talk about cars or dealers or consumers. He walked over to a board in his office and taped up a single dollar bill.

"I have only one request, and it's very simple," Nardelli said, looking hard at Press. "I just want to make a dollar. Just make a dollar. Is that unreasonable? We're a $60 billion company, and we sell all these products. Shouldn't we at least make a dollar?"

Press didn't know what to say. How could he disagree with that? But the dramatics didn't seem necessary. It was pretty obvious that Chrysler was bleeding cash. And when Press dug into the company's weaknesses in its model lineup, the festering inventory issues, and the painfully dysfunctional dealer relations, he came to an unsettling conclusion. "I went from the best-managed company in the world to the worst in one day," he said. "And my instruction was, very simply, to help Chrysler make money."

That was Nardelli's mission—to get Chrysler to make money. He was a meticulous, disciplined, and obsessively organized individual, impeccably groomed from his razor-cut hair to his polished nails. Nardelli was totally focused on making sustained, sequential, incremental improvements in every corner of the business. He completely bought into Feinberg's patriotic pitch about saving the soul of American manufacturing. "I desperately want Chrysler to be successful," Nardelli said. "We don't need another strategy. What we need is execution."

He held a two-day workshop, dubbed "Recovery and Transformation," for the top three hundred executives and brought in consultants to teach statistics-driven management processes he had learned at GE. He was always intense and serious, and prone to taking off on intellectual tangents that were tough to follow. His first speech in Detroit left people shaking their heads at his sheer verbiage. "I am blessed to have individuals with me who can take responsibility," he said, "and do vertical dives to really get the granularity and make sure that we're coupling horizontally across functions so that we have a pure line of sight to the customer."

Inside Chrysler, the engineers and designers were a bit stunned by how Nardelli gave orders. In one week, he came up with two hundred specific improvements he wanted made to the interiors of its cars and trucks. He was all about decisions, lots of them, as if he were in a tremendous hurry to change everything he thought was wrong with Chrysler. And he was. Chrysler was essentially living on borrowed time and money. Cerberus paid less than $2 billion to Daimler, some of which the Germans put back into Chrysler as a contribution toward legacy costs. Cerberus had also invested $5 billion in Chrysler's operations and another chunk of money into its finance arm. That budget, along with the $10 billion in bank loans and another $2 billion in borrowed cash from Daimler and Cerberus, was what Nardelli had to work with.

That nest egg wasn't going to go very far if the business kept losing more than $100 million a month. So Nardelli and the Cerberus efficiency experts started cutting. Chrysler's U.S. market share had shrunk to 12 percent? Then eliminate shifts at five assembly plants. Poorly selling products were history—four models would be dumped, including the Pacifica and Magnum sport wagons that were centerpieces of the Zetsche era. And even though Chrysler had barely completed its Project X restructuring that cut thirteen thousand jobs, Nardelli was raring to do more. The next round would be just as deep. Another twelve thousand workers were about to be chopped.

With Nardelli scouring Chrysler for factory shifts to cut and jobs to eliminate, there was no way he could give the union the GM pattern agreement. And it didn't take long for Gettelfinger to figure that out. "The company has failed to make an offer that addresses the needs of our membership," he said in an e-mail to union locals. On

October 7, he set a strike deadline. Chrysler had three days to give the UAW the same deal as General Motors or the union would shut it down.

This time Gettelfinger didn't want a strike. He took a more conciliatory approach with LaSorda than he had during the first health care talks. Management and labor at Chrysler had something in common: Daimler had broken promises to both of them.

LaSorda, whose grandfather was once president of a union local in Windsor, Canada, very effectively used the German merger mess to extract concessions on health care. First, Gettelfinger agreed to the $300 million savings on retiree benefits that the union had balked at in 2006. Then he gave Chrysler a better deal than GM on the VEBA by allowing it to use more stock and less cash to fund the $10 billion trust. But when it came to job guarantees, LaSorda was under strict orders from Cerberus not to give any.

"I can't do it, Ron," he told Gettelfinger. "We need the flexibility."

But Gettelfinger and Holiefield needed assurances on jobs. Otherwise, they couldn't sell the contract to the UAW members. While the talks ground on, the GM workers were approving their deal by a two-thirds margin. It would not be that easy in the Chrysler plants. People were still steaming about Daimler, and the picket signs were all printed up and ready to go.

As the hours ticked by in the basement of Chrysler headquarters, Gettelfinger was feeling the most pressure. He pushed LaSorda hard to give him something positive in the deal, some kind of a commitment. Nardelli's mush about the "new Chrysler" wasn't going to placate workers if they didn't get any job guarantees.

Finally, late in the evening on October 9, LaSorda met the union halfway. First, Chrysler would back off from selling its parts centers, saving union jobs in the process. Second, he could pledge to keep 80 percent of Chrysler's fifty-three U.S. factories running for the full four-year contract. That was it. He wouldn't agree to specific products in specific plants, and no commitments at all beyond 2011.

Just after ten in the morning on October 10, Gettelfinger and Holiefield gave a summary to the nine senior members of the national negotiating team. The two union bosses had been bargaining for sixty straight hours; they were exhausted. After the presentation, they left the room for a few minutes. And when Gettelfinger walked back in, he got the shock of his career.

"We can't accept this," said Bill Parker, the president of Local 1700 at the Sterling Heights assembly plant and chairman of the negotiating committee. "We voted to reject it."

A proposed agreement recommended by the UAW president had never been turned down by a bargaining team before. But a deadline is a deadline. And at exactly eleven o'clock the union went on strike against Chrysler. Workers dropped what they were doing, walked out of the plants, grabbed their picket signs, and started marching outside factories across the country. At the sprawling car plant in Sterling Heights just north of Detroit, workers had no idea what was happening with the negotiating team. They just knew it was time for a show of force. "They say strike, so we strike," said Reggie Redding, a thirteen-year veteran at the plant. But unlike the spirited crowds outside the GM plants in September, the Chrysler picketers seemed pretty subdued. "I'm not angry," said Joseph Badalamenti, who worked in the paint shop in Sterling Heights. "I'm just worried about what's going on."

The Chrysler executives didn't know what was going on either. Nardelli was dumbfounded. "I thought we had a deal," he kept saying. LaSorda was just as confused. Gettelfinger had agreed to the terms, but something crazy must have happened with the committee.

Down in Chrysler's basement, Holiefield was trying to sway opinion on the bargaining team. He told them this was the best they were going to get. They had to back the leadership—it was the way the union worked. He begged them to vote again.

They did, and they rejected the contract again. This was becoming big trouble. It felt like a mutiny was taking place. Gettelfinger and LaSorda needed to huddle and fast. The union needed more, another promise, anything that would stop this insurrection.

Couldn't Cerberus at least take outsourcing out of the equation? After talking it over with Nardelli, LaSorda agreed to the change.

Gettelfinger and Holiefield rushed the new deal through for a third vote, and they finally got their approval, by a margin of eight to one. Bill Parker was the lone dissenter. The news went out through the union grapevine, and at 5:22 P.M. the strike was over. The pattern agreement had held on wages, bonuses, and health care, but it fell short of GM on the all-important job guarantees.

Workers putting down their picket signs weren't sure what they had achieved by walking out. "I think the whole strike was a lot of hype," said Bill Gresham, a tool-and-die maker at a Chrysler engine plant in Detroit. "We're the losers here, not Cerberus."

Five days later, Chrysler union leaders from across the country met in Detroit to discuss the deal. It was a raucous, contentious session. The details of the tentative agreement upset some of them. Parker, the dissenting voice in the committee vote, argued that the contract fell too far short of what GM workers had gotten. "This is a devastating break from the pattern," he said.

Some plants, such as the minivan factory in St. Louis, were protected only if sales volumes stayed at a certain level. And other plants were labeled "non-core" assets that might be closed. Holiefield tried to calm down the dissenters. "We did our very best," he said. "I believe once the members view it, they will support it."

Voting began on October 20, and three of the first six plants turned down the deal. Then Jefferson North, the big Detroit factory where Holiefield hailed from, overwhelmingly rejected it. A Big Three contract backed by the union leadership hadn't been rejected by the members in twenty-five years. The last time was in 1982, also at Chrysler.

No way could Gettelfinger afford to let the vote fail. He still had to go to Ford, and a rejection at Chrysler would throw off the timetable completely. He began lobbying hard, calling the local unions and pumping them up to get a positive vote. When two big plants in Indiana voted against the deal, the overall national tally was almost dead even: half the members were for it and half against. It was all coming down to four union locals outside Detroit—Sterling Heights assembly and stamping, and the Dodge Truck assembly and stamping plants in Warren.

And on October 24, the agreement passed in all four plants. In the end, workers couldn't handle the uncertainty anymore. They just wanted some security. "Right now is a bad time to strike," said Melro Brooks, a thirty-four-year Chrysler worker. "Twenty years ago, sure, we were the Big Three then. But we're not so big anymore."

On November 1, Gettelfinger was ready for Ford. But just as he was heading over to Dearborn, Chrysler announced it was slashing twelve thousand jobs, including as many as ten thousand union positions. That wasn't all. Five plants were losing shifts, including Sterling Heights and Jefferson North. Chrysler would still keep 80 percent of its union workers through the contract—as promised. But the other 20 percent were history.

"It's pretty shady to have layoffs right after the contract is ratified," Anthony Majka, a worker in Sterling Heights, told the *Detroit News*. Lydia Johnson, another worker at the plant, just shook her head. "It's sad," she said. "I guess promises don't mean that much."

At Ford, Gettelfinger pulled aside one of the company's senior negotiators. "Do you know anything," he asked him, "about Project Compass?"

The Ford executive was taken aback. How had Gettelfinger found out about that? He mumbled something about it being a mutual-aid pact and then shut up.

"Well, one thing I know about you," Gettelfinger said, "is that you don't lie."

The union president had known all about Project Compass and that Ford had backed away from it at the last minute. One of his bankers at Lazard had been tipped off to it. Gettelfinger was impressed that Ford had refused to come to General Motors' aid in the strike. He figured that was Bill Ford's decision, and he was right. "The UAW is Bill's ace in the hole," Joe Laymon said. "He wouldn't do anything to screw that up."

The atmosphere at Ford was more positive than at either GM or Chrysler. Bill Ford and Alan Mulally were both at the table. Gettelfinger was willing to give more too. He would allow Ford to use mostly stock for its $13 billion VEBA, and he let Ford hire more lower-wage workers than at the other two companies.

Ford gave concessions as well, promising to take two assembly plants off the Way Forward closing list for the time being. The negotiations were moving like a freight train headed downhill. Different bargaining groups were meeting simultaneously on the second, sixth, and eleventh floors of Ford headquarters. By eight o'clock on Friday night, November 2, several dead-tired members of the Ford and union teams went home for the night. They were close to a deal and figured a good night's rest would have everyone fresh to wrap it up over the weekend.

But Gettelfinger wasn't ready to stop. He prowled the darkened halls of the Glass House, looking in offices and wondering where the bargainers had gone. He ended up at Laymon's door. Where, he asked, was everybody?

They had quit for the night, Laymon said, and would resume first thing in the morning.

"Get their asses back in here!" Gettelfinger said. "Let's finish the deal."

Laymon got on the phone and within an hour the teams had reassembled. Even Mulally—unlike Wagoner or Nardelli—was present at the main table for the last stages of the talks. At 3:20 A.M. they were finished. Ford and the union had reached an agreement without a hint of a strike.

On November 14, Ford workers overwhelmingly ratified the deal. "New Era Begins for Big 3" was the front-page headline in the *Detroit News*. Wall Street and industry analysts overwhelmingly endorsed the unprecedented accomplishments at the bargaining table: health care trusts, two-tier wages, scaled-back jobs bank, bonuses instead of pay hikes.

. . . .

The day that GM workers approved their new contract, the company's stock price soared to $42—its highest point in more than three years. But for all the talk of a new era, the fundamentals hadn't changed much. The Big Three's car sales were still weak, and trucks were slipping. The health care deals wouldn't impact actual spending for another two years, the buyouts had drained mountains of cash from the balance sheets, and still there were no profits in North America.

The perception of Detroit was positive, but the reality was as fragile as ever. On November 6, the illusion of progress was shattered when GM reported a record quarterly loss of $39 billion. Its actual operating loss was only $1.6 billion, but it had taken a massive, unexpected accounting charge. Tax credits it had built up over years of losses had to be wiped off the books because there was no foreseeable income to apply them to. Bottom line: GM didn't know when it would start making money again. But it wouldn't be anytime soon.

By mid-November, the optimism surrounding GM began to evaporate. The stock price dropped to $26. The housing market was faltering, gas prices were climbing, and showroom traffic was drying up. And the road ahead was looking rough. "We do have concerns," said Fritz Henderson, "over near-term economic conditions."

[Twenty-Three]

It was one of those moments, when months of soul-searching suddenly sparked a decision. It came to Jim Farley while he was driving on the 405 freeway through Los Angeles. He punched a number into his cell phone, and a few seconds later he was talking to Bill Ford.

"I think it's time," Farley said. "I'd be interested in talking if that North American job is open."

"That's great," Bill said. "But you've got to meet Alan. You've got to talk to Alan. I'll set it up."

Farley couldn't believe he had finally made the call. In the two years since he met Bill at the Detroit auto show, Farley's career at Toyota had been on a steep upward trajectory. He excelled as the U.S. marketing chief for the Toyota brand, successfully launched the new Tundra pickup, and earned a promotion to group vice president in charge of the Lexus luxury division. While the Big Three muddled along, Toyota was smashing sales records and making more money than any car company in the world. Farley was a star player on a winning team with a bright future.

So why was he on his way to a clandestine meeting with Alan Mulally at the L.A. airport?

There were lots of reasons. His life had taken a terrible turn when his wife delivered twins prematurely and both babies died. In his grief, Farley started questioning his values, his goals, and his legacy. He kept turning to that spring afternoon in Detroit when he walked among the ruins of the Ford Model T plant where his grandfather worked. Was it his destiny to sell $60,000 Lexus sedans? Did he want to play it safe, climb the corporate ladder, and help the Japanese conquer the industry? Or should he take a chance, follow his heart, and be part of a comeback of the Ford Motor Company? Seventeen years at Toyota meant a lot to him—he had his friends, his reputation, his accomplishments. But he kept thinking back to those tiny infants he'd held in his hands, two beautiful little lives that never had an opportunity to do great things. What would they have wanted their daddy to do?

Farley pulled into the parking lot of the private hangar at LAX and realized he was sweating profusely. He took a long breath, held it a few seconds, and then walked into the building. And there was Mulally, waiting in the lobby. He bounded over and grabbed Farley's hand.

"Jim! It's so good to see you!" Mulally said. "Is everything okay? Hey, come with me. I've got a secret room back here. It's just for us."

Mulally had brought a book that was filled with drawings, charts, notes, and data. He showed Farley an intricate graphic of Ford—its brands, models, divisions, regional operations, lines of organization. "This is Ford," he said. "And it's a mess. There's like three hundred models here. Jim, it should be fifty. And here's my plan to fix it. We're going to transform our whole lineup. We're going to have global products in global segments. It's going to be one Ford. And we're going to unleash shareholder value in a way no one else ever has."

Their thirty-minute meeting went on for two hours. Farley was spellbound by how Mulally was as comfortable talking about engineering and technology as he was explaining his business strategy. His enthusiasm, as advertised, was remarkable. But more than anything else, Farley loved Mulally's plan. It was so simple and organic

and strategic, a lot like Toyota but with a visceral, emotional component. "We'd love to have you on the team," Mulally said. "What do
you think of it? Can we pull this off? I need you to come in and help
fix North America and globalize our lineup. How would you feel if
you were part of our team?"

Farley felt a little like a visitor from another galaxy. "I'm not
going to fit in," he said. "I'm a Toyota guy. I've been there so long."

Mulally wasn't buying that. He knew all about Farley. He could
tell how intrigued he was from his eye contact, his body language,
and the questions he asked. There was a kinship with Ford, a bond
already formed.

"Jim, it's me you're talking to," he said in a conspiratorial tone.
"I'm here. I'm from Boeing. I was in your shoes. It was a hard decision for me because I felt comfortable. I was in one place for such a
long time. But there's only one chance to do something like this. It
only takes a few of us. We can do it. And it's Ford, Jim! It's part of the
history of our country. It's Ford."

When Farley got home that night, he couldn't stop talking about
Mulally. "I have never met anyone like him," he told his wife, Lia.
"Oh my God, he's so approachable. He respects Toyota. He's down
to earth. And he knows what to get done."

But Farley couldn't walk away from Toyota right then and there.
He had invested so much of himself in the company and had worked
so hard to sell its Scions, Camrys, and Tundras. People relied on him
and believed in him. He wasn't ready to go until a few months later,
when he called Mulally again and reached him at a big Ford dealer
meeting in Dearborn.

"Jim!" Mulally said. "Jim, you can't imagine what just happened!
I'm meeting with all the dealers. It's unbelievable! They never had a
management team that loves them! I made all the Ford people turn
around and say 'We love you' to them. It was so cool!"

Farley was stunned. *He loves the dealers?* That sure didn't sound
like Ford. *Wow, this guy really gets it,* Farley said to himself. *Maybe we
can do this.*

And just like that, Farley was in. Mulally had the perfect job for him—head of Ford's global marketing plus U.S. sales, which would have him working closely with the product team. Ford was streamlining its structure, building teamwork, and developing a supersharp focus on the Blue Oval. But it needed consumers to care about the company again and, more important, trust it. That's where Farley came in. "The future of our industry is a meritocracy," Farley said. "We will win or lose on the merits—our products, the safety and the quality and the value. My approach is, you earn everything." He was officially hired in October and ready to start a month later.

Farley was so wound up on the day he left L.A. to move to Detroit that he threw up in the bathroom at the airport. He took the red-eye flight and landed at five in the morning. A Ford driver took him to the Glass House, a long, checkerboard monolith of windows and girders and 1950s-era architecture.

Wow, I'm in Detroit, Farley thought. *At Toyota, everything was brand-new and this was just so . . . old. I'm one of those people now, the ones that screwed everything up. I'm not one of the good guys anymore, the guys that make the Prius and Scion and Camry. I'm in Detroit now. I'm one of them.*

The building was very quiet, and he went up to his new office. It was big and empty and waiting for him. *This is what it's all about, Jim,* he said to himself. *Game time.*

He sat at his desk and started writing out a list for Mulally of everything he wanted to do in his first hundred days at Ford.

In his first year, Mulally had laid the foundation. A huge part of it was behavioral. His Thursday-morning business-plan reviews were now second nature. Each executive grew more comfortable playing his position. "Structure is best when it implements a strategy," Mulally preached. "Why are we organized the way we are? Because we are a team, and everyone is doing the best they can in tapping into the full global resources of our company."

Mulally was very sly. He had instilled a discipline that allowed executives to feel both empowered and secure. Better yet, the team policed itself. He didn't have to correct someone who spoke out of turn or started criticizing somebody else—the peer group took care of that. And Mulally was the role model. He worked so many hours and was so ebullient and gung-ho, people wanted to please him. His style was the opposite of the old, starchy, stiff-lipped Ford. If someone scored a breakthrough in purchasing or product development or sales, Mulally hugged him (or her) like a high school coach when a kid hit a home run. He was fun to be around, consistently stimulating, challenging, and motivating each and every Ford employee he came in contact with. When people tried to analyze or figure him out, he just laughed. "I want to be the best father," he said. "I want to be a great friend. I want to have one great, compelling plan. I want to be with people where the glass is half full, and I expect everybody to listen, help, and appreciate each other."

But changing behaviors was only half the battle. The buyouts in the plants and the bloodletting in the salaried ranks had slimmed down Ford considerably. Slowly but surely, its crushing overhead costs began shrinking. In the third quarter of 2007, the company narrowed its overall loss to $380 million. Revenues were inching up too, 10 percent for the period.

Yet there was still so much work to do. Ford had to break from one of its biggest strategic mistakes and put its European luxury brands up for sale. Jaguar and Aston Martin were already on the market, but Mulally wasn't stopping there. Land Rover and Volvo were also made available. A lot of executives in the company, including Bill Ford, had strong attachments to the brands, but this wasn't elective surgery. These were lifesaving operations. Every minute spent on building SUVs for Volvo or sedans for Jaguar was a minute not spent on fixing Ford. Dumping the luxury brands was not up for debate. It was a question of when, not if.

The real acid test was getting the best and the brightest in Dearborn to create a lineup where every vehicle was excellent, from a subcompact car all the way up to a heavy-duty pickup. Beyond that, was it possible to make cars that could be sold as profitably in Detroit as in Frankfurt, Rome, Shanghai, or São Paulo? This required a giant leap not only in integrating resources but in philosophy. A Ford is a Ford is a Ford the world over, Mulally believed, and that meant safe, reliable, stylish, enjoyable to drive, and efficient to own.

Mulally was relentless in his efforts to standardize parts and platforms and imbue each vehicle's design with a distinctive Ford look, feel, and character. Once the new products were into the engineering stages, the company had to pull off a massive shift in its factories. Truck plants quickly had to become car plants, and the beauty of the transformation was in the timing: every aspect of the organization was changing simultaneously. All these parallel initiatives needed to be constantly measured, graded, and improved upon. Even hardened veterans of the car business were swept up in the momentum.

The Ford team was rapidly adapting to this new leader and his expansive agenda. Mulally definitely moved to a different beat, where adrenaline was the fuel, and his vision was the destination. Sure, cars were complicated machines. But he'd spent years and worked with thousands of people to create one new airplane in his Boeing days. Just because the task was big didn't meant it had to be daunting. In fact, that just made the journey more thrilling.

He was the same all the time—blue blazer, white shirt, khaki pants, loafers, big smile. Mulally was like a corporate athlete; he loved tennis and golf and working and learning and interacting with people. But he stayed grounded. Every day he called his wife and five children in Seattle and his eighty-seven-year-old mother in Kansas. And he always took time in his hectic schedule to think by himself. Sometimes when he was alone he felt he could actually see the future, what Ford would be like when it all came together. The key was consistency of effort and attitude. Mulally spent hours perfecting a wallet-size, laminated card every employee in the world got: "One Ford . . . One Team . . . One Plan . . . One Goal." On the back, he listed his "Expected Behaviors," each one starting with one of the four letters in "Ford": "Foster functional and technical excellence . . . Own working together . . . Role-model Ford values . . . Deliver results." He didn't care if it seemed corny or old-fashioned to carry around a corporate mission statement. He believed in it. It was so important that everybody know there was a plan and how they fit into it. "You can't move forward," he said, "if everybody doesn't know all the pieces."

They knew the pieces, but he saw the whole. Getting Jim Farley into the mix was the last major personnel move. Mulally needed that creative force, that one guy whose life revolved around the wants, needs, and desires of consumers. He had inherited a fine product executive in Derrick Kuzak—a soft-spoken deep thinker who had a talent for making decent cars better. Mark Fields was excelling at running the North American operations. Even Don Leclair was getting along and applying his superior financial skills without browbeating people. All down the org chart, the talent was clicking.

And Bill Ford brought just the right dose of encouragement, support, and stability. Mulally appreciated what he had in Bill—a confidant, a partner, and a friend. "He's my private equity," Mulally liked to say, half jokingly. Bill and the Ford family and the board could keep the hounds of Wall Street at bay while he reinvented the business.

Every night, Mulally pondered the most important number in his head—thirty-five. At the end of the third quarter, Ford had $35 billion in cash to finance all the new products and all the improvements the plan called for. It should be enough, as long as the economy cooperated. But that was getting dicey. Ford had to be smart. If the market went bad or disaster struck, it had to react intelligently and forcefully. The plan was perfect—unless it had to be changed.

At Toyota, Farley's cars were at or near the top of every survey of consumer confidence and vehicle quality. He was pleasantly surprised to see Ford making some slow, steady progress in the all-important *Consumer Reports* and J. D. Power rankings. But Toyota's success always hinged on understanding the customers first and then building cars to meet their expectations. So he was excited when Derrick Kuzak pulled him aside during one of his first days at Ford. "Jim, there are a couple of interesting technologies that I think have potential, and I'd like to get your feedback on them," Kuzak said. "I'd like you to evaluate the DNA of our products—the steering, the brakes, the feel, the responsiveness."

Farley could hardly wait. He was spending his first weekend alone in the dreary Hyatt hotel near headquarters. Now he was pumped to get on the test track. Ever since he was a kid visiting family in Detroit, he'd wondered what went on behind the high brick walls at the top-secret Ford proving grounds. "That was a special moment for me when I drove in there for the first time," he said.

Kuzak and a small band of engineers were waiting for him. They wanted Farley to drive an early prototype of the next Focus small car. It had a special, European-style direct-injection turbocharged engine that Kuzak thought might do well in the United States. When Farley got behind the wheel, he tingled at the power of the engine and how the car handled in the curves and accelerated on the straightaways. After he pulled to a stop, he just about ran over to Kuzak. "Holy bananas!" he said. "I have never driven anything like this. It's really different. People are going to love this car. It's so different. This is the reason I left Toyota."

He wasn't as impressed by the marketing organization. After his first meeting with his top twenty managers, Farley was openly upset. "They just didn't get it," he said. "They thought they had all the answers. I'm like, 'This company has lost 1 percent of market share every year since 1994. They've had a new brand campaign every year for the past five years!'"

When one manager suggested that Ford advertise its latest gains in quality, Farley blew up. "You have to have the evidence before you open your mouth!" he snapped. "What should we say? We're getting close to Toyota? People don't believe that shit." He was going to give these people three months to get their act together—or else. "After ninety days," he told Mulally and Fields, "I'm going to have to make changes here."

For the first few weeks, Farley felt like he had to fit some abstract Detroit way of doing things. It was like wearing shoes that hurt. "I had to make a decision whether I was going to be a Ford guy or Jim Farley," he said. "And I decided it was probably time for me to be Jim Farley."

He called a town hall meeting for all his marketing and advertising people. After everybody took their seats, Farley opened with a gesture they wouldn't forget. "I'd like you to turn to the person next to you, I don't care if it's on the right or the left, and pat them on the back," he said. "You deserve it." Then he talked about his grandfather working for Henry Ford, owning his first Mustang, what he did at Toyota, and the day his baby twins died. The room got awful quiet then. He had their attention completely. "I hope you are ready to save this company," Farley said in a low voice, "because that's what I'm going to be doing every minute of every day." He was going to lead, and he expected them to follow. "We are at the precipice right now in North America," he said. "There's no more time. It's just us. We have to fix it, and we can do it."

They needed to get on board now, he said. "I'm going to push, and I'm going to challenge," he said. "I'm not here to be polite. I'm a change agent. This is what I do." Then he shocked them. Yes, he had worked for Toyota. He knew how much the customers loved their cars. He knew their reputation better than anybody. "But you know what?" Farley said. "You know what the problem is at Toyota? They are a fat and lazy competitor. And we are humble. We are hungry. And we will get this done!"

He felt good after the speech and asked for questions. Someone made the mistake of saying he'd had a lot of bosses over the years and that "outsiders don't last long" at Ford.

"That's pretty funny," Farley said, not smiling. "Have you told Alan that?"

While Farley was joining Mulally and the Ford team, Jim Press was wondering what he was doing at Chrysler. Press and Farley had never been close at Toyota, and their paths would diverge greatly once they both landed in Detroit.

While Mulally was creating cohesion and a sense of purpose at Ford, the opposite was happening at Chrysler. Cerberus had installed a management team that didn't know each other and blamed the Germans for everything that went wrong in Auburn Hills. It was like Chrysler needed to be disciplined and reprogrammed, even though LaSorda and most of its American executives were still in the building.

Nardelli was the taskmaster, sent from New York to show Chrysler the right way to do business. The conceit of private equity was the belief that distressed companies were obviously mismanaged and that with creative financing and some sharp new bosses, any corporation could be fixed. But car companies never turn around quickly, and Chrysler was no exception. "Once you got inside and saw what was there, it didn't add up," said Press. "It was like the aftermath of this huge battle."

The product lineup was woefully thin. Press followed Nardelli around the design dome as he ordered a blitz of cosmetic improvements to instrument panels, seats, and interior trim. But that wasn't going to lure new customers into the showrooms. Only fresh, new models could do that. And even the smartest minds in corporate America had not figured out how to develop a new automobile in a few months.

The only big new model coming was the restyled Dodge Ram pickup, Chrysler's single largest seller and one of its only profit producers. The hope was the Ram could carry the load while Auburn Hills got to work designing and engineering better cars.

But it was tough to stay focused when every expense and position in the company was being scrutinized. Nardelli and his new chief financial officer, Ron Kolka, were cutting budgets and jobs line by line, and preparing real estate and facilities to sell to "monetize assets." Chrysler's sales and revenue were falling because of inferior products, and Nardelli had to generate cash to keep the place running and to pay for the few product programs actually in progress.

He sold the corporate jets and leased them back. He wanted to sell the parts centers, but the union stopped him. Nardelli was becoming painfully aware that way more money was going out at Chrysler than coming in. He could not lose billions of dollars for Cerberus and last long. "Bob, you're the CEO," Feinberg told him. "We're going to back you. Do it your way. But you've got to be a winner on this one. You've got to make things work."

The top of the company was in complete flux. LaSorda was missing in action. Feinberg had assigned him to find international partners to defray costs and deliver small cars that Chrysler couldn't build profitably on its own. When Daimler was in charge, LaSorda had spent a ton of time cutting a deal to bring an inexpensive small car over from China. Now he had fallen into the arms of Carlos Ghosn. Chrysler was going to buy a subcompact made by Nissan in Mexico for sale in the United States. LaSorda was also pitching Ghosn on the idea of Chrysler using its excess factory space to manufacture trucks for Nissan. On paper, it seemed to make sense. Anything, it seemed, was worth trying at this point.

The holdover executives at Chrysler feared and misunderstood Nardelli. He worked long hours and came across as so buttoned-down and serious. But his underlings, like the marketing guru Peter Arnell, were off the wall, babbling about grandiose plans to reposition the brands and become a leader in electric vehicles, a technology in which Chrysler was way behind the competition. The designers, engineers, and purchasing execs knew all too well how little money had gone into new products in the past two years. Morale was sinking fast. Having just left Toyota, Press was appalled by what Chrysler had to offer. "The product line was decimated," he said. "Daimler knew they couldn't turn it around and they quit investing. Selling these cars was like pushing peanuts uphill."

Any feeling of trust and camaraderie had frayed to the breaking point. Nardelli's patriotic sermons fell on deaf ears. The staffs were suspicious, résumés were pouring out to other companies, and nobody knew whose head would roll if Chrysler crashed. Nothing was more divisive among senior management than compensation. If Cerberus sold Chrysler in the future, the top thirty or so executives could split a huge payout. LaSorda and Press could earn $10 million or more, and Nardelli would get a multiple of that. But below them, who would qualify, and how much would they get? It was a constant source of tense backroom conversation.

Everyone was wondering if they would be chopped off in the next downsizing. And they were starting to turn on each other. One of Nardelli's new hires, the marketing chief Deborah Meyer, was ordered to evaluate all the budgets in her department. She called in Jason Vines, the top communications exec who had worked side by side with Zetsche and LaSorda for years.

"We're spending three times what Toyota does at the auto show," Meyer said.

"Well," said Vines, "we have three press conferences at the Detroit show, and Toyota usually has one. So that's why we spend more."

"You're going to have to cut it," said Meyer.

Vines was already stressed to the max. The sale of the company, the secrecy of Cerberus, replacing Wolfgang Bernhard with Nardelli without telling anybody—it was all a train wreck from a PR standpoint. But Meyer pushed him over the edge. Chrysler's auto show events were always elaborate and newsworthy, and they never failed to attract enormous attention. It was the company's signature, its cachet, what set it apart from dowdy old GM and Ford. Who was this newbie telling him to cut budgets? Vines, a former stand-up comic, had a mouth on him anyway. But this time he outdid himself.

"You know what? Go fuck yourself," he said. "I'm going to quit. You and these lackeys like you are what's wrong with this industry."

Nardelli didn't care. So what if the senior public relations executive with twenty years of experience quit? He had bigger things to worry about, like making payroll and finding costs to cut. He wasn't going to worry about auto shows. That was fluff compared to the tough tasks on his plate. Besides, Chrysler already had a big press conference planned to introduce the new Ram at the 2008 Detroit show. He had plenty of PR people. Who needed Vines? He wasn't even going to replace him. Better to save the money.

Planning is everything in the car business. Maybe Nardelli should have looked a little closer at what Chrysler had in store for the auto show. If he did, he might have foreseen the debacle coming on January 14, 2008. Chrysler did, in fact, have a spectacular, showstopping press event ready for the Ram. One hundred and twenty longhorn steers and sixteen cowboys had been trucked in from Oklahoma for a cattle drive down Washington Boulevard in downtown Detroit. The idea must have sounded great on paper—TV crews from around the world would capture a herd of live cattle rumbling up the city streets to Cobo Center, where Nardelli and Press would be waiting outside with the new Ram pickup. It would be a supremely macho statement about a very rugged truck and make for great television.

People lined up four deep behind barricades to watch as the cowboys on horseback drove the feisty longhorns up the boulevard and toward the Ram. Press, in a western jacket, gamely played master of ceremonies. "If you think our truck is all hat and no cattle," he said into the microphone, "keep an eye on yonder horizon." But as he started describing the all-new pickup, he was drowned out by the crowd's laughter. Press couldn't figure out why—until he saw some of the cows were mounting each other in the middle of the road. The cowboys couldn't stop them. Nobody was paying attention to the truck or to Press, who tried his best to ad-lib. "Will you look at that?" he said. "The bulls want to see the trucks." But the amorous cattle were really getting into it now. "Well," Press said, "let's not look at that."

By the time Nardelli got to the stage in a heavy topcoat, the cattle were being herded off with the TV crews in hot pursuit. Hardly anyone was left to hear his speech about Chrysler's next comeback. He got a smattering of applause from the Chrysler employees left standing around, but he'd been upstaged by his own cows. Press was sort of in a daze. He had introduced dozens of Toyota vehicles at auto shows over the years, always with dignity and professionalism. Now it was pickup trucks and cowboy hats and humping cattle. "This is fucking unbelievable," he muttered. "Why in the hell did we do that?"

[Twenty-Four]

Ford had a billion-dollar truck to introduce too—the new F-series pickup, which had been the bestselling vehicle in America for many years running. An hour before the Chrysler cattle drive, the lights went down on the big stage at Cobo Center and Alan Mulally and Mark Fields brought out the F-150 with flashing strobe lights, fireworks, and an appearance by country music star Toby Keith. Ford had sold nearly seven hundred thousand pickups in the United States in 2007, a sharp skid after hitting almost a million just a few years before. Even so, this was Ford's most anticipated launch. Without the profits from the F-series, the formula for a North American turnaround could crumble. The company badly needed the money from pickup sales to buy time while it made the transition to cars.

But the more intriguing Ford press conference was the quieter, more sedate rollout of the Verve concept—a sporty little four-door sedan with a four-cylinder engine and interior controls designed to look like the keypad on a mobile phone. The car had a distinct European flair, a design ethic the company liked to call "kinetic." It was the working version of the next Ford Fiesta, which would be the smallest, least expensive, and most fuel-efficient global car in the Blue Oval lineup.

For years, Ford's finest engineers and hottest executives worked on trucks and SUVs. That was where the action was. But Derrick Kuzak was changing that. He was fifty-six years old and a native Detroiter, with swept-back, graying brown hair and a thick mustache. He was so quiet and laid-back, people underestimated his burning desire to prove that Ford could make competitive small cars. He had done it splendidly in Europe, and now Mulally had given him the resources to create global platforms for small sedans, coupes, hatchbacks, and wagons.

Pickups made big money, but demand for small cars was exploding around the world. Analysts projected that by 2012, thirty-eight million small cars would be sold annually—a 65 percent increase in less than a decade. Kuzak had done his stint working on sport-utilities and pickups in the 1990s. But he loved these crisp-handling, peppy little cars. He constantly tinkered to make them lighter in weight, and he worked to goose more horsepower from their small engines with the latest turbocharging technology. "We want a family of cars that are as exciting to drive as they are to look at," Kuzak said at the Verve event.

It was no surprise that Jim Farley joined him at the stand. Farley had lived and breathed small cars when he ran Scion at Toyota. He knew this baby was as good as anything the Japanese made, and it was critical to changing Ford's image to a progressive, green-minded automaker with a future. "Customers are smart," Farley said. "They value their vehicles, and the more efficient, the better."

He showed off the Verve to Michigan's governor, Jennifer Granholm, who came to the show with Ron Gettelfinger. Granholm was on the front lines of Detroit's depression; her state's economy and budget had been decimated by the Big Three's troubles. The petite blond governor gushed over the car but was disappointed to learn that Ford would not be making them in Michigan. It was the one vehicle the UAW had been unable to get a commitment for during the labor talks. Ford still could not make a profit building subcompacts with union workers. When the Verve came to production it would be manufactured in Mexico, not the United States.

The 2008 show captured an industry in transition. On one side were the trucks; on the other were small cars, gas-electric hybrids, and all-electric concept vehicles. With gas prices heading to $3.50 a gallon, a turning point was near. The Big Three had platoons of researchers to calculate when consumers would reach their breaking point on fuel. Was it when it cost a hundred bucks to fill the tank on the Suburban or the Jeep? Or was it when the fear took over that gas would just get more and more expensive, with no end in sight? If that happened, there would be a mass migration into more fuel-efficient and cost-effective cars.

At the same time, the sluggish economy had slowed consumer spending. Americans were squeezing their household budgets. A spike in gas prices would do serious damage to automakers accustomed to annual U.S. sales well above sixteen million vehicles. And any company without small cars to sell should expect to get slammed.

Farley smelled it coming. He was a maniac for data, and he was amazed at the reams of research generated by Ford's marketing staff. He pored over the numbers, zeroing in on which products sold well or lagged in the fifty biggest U.S. markets, paying special attention to the East and West Coasts, where Ford was weakest. He was struck by how rapidly the overall demand for pickups and SUVs was eroding. People who had bought trucks when they were trendy were trading them in for cars. And old-style sport-utilities had completely lost their appeal. Farley tried to think like the consumer. What was on the checklist for a new vehicle? Which attributes were really important? If it came down to a choice between two models, what drove the decision?

The data said people were fixating on their fuel gauges and calculating the cost every time a gallon of gas went up a dime. "One of the things Toyota does really, really well is put the voice of the customer right there at the table in front of the chairman of the company," he said. "When we're in Dearborn, where is the customer at the table? Who was at the table when all the profits for trucks and SUVs were rolling in? What happens if this doesn't continue forever?"

Farley was determined to be the customer's voice at Ford. And he knew the way to make it resonate was through the dealers. Farley bonded fast and hard with the Ford dealer body. In three months he had met hundreds of them, and he wouldn't stop until he met all four thousand. He flew dozens of them into Michigan, split them into groups of five, and then he and his staff watched behind one-way mirrors as they talked about the company's products, advertising, and management.

One big Texas dealer, Charlie Gilchrist, warned Farley he might not like what he would hear. "The reality in Detroit is not the reality we're dealing with," he said. But Farley was ecstatic when the dealers got brutally frank about the tired old ad campaigns. And it was during those sessions that he found his big message. He kept hearing that Ford had solid, fuel-efficient cars, especially the Fusion and the Focus. But the company's reputation was so lousy. Few people believed the cars were as good as Toyota's. If only Ford could get more potential buyers to try one.

Then it came to Farley. Not *try* one . . . *drive* one. That was how he'd start. It would be an open invitation to consumers to experience these cars and trust the company again. "The first thing we need to do is break this cycle of apathy," he said. "We need to show a Ford that people don't expect—a successful Ford."

It was buyout time again. After all the plant closings, job cuts, and labor negotiations, Detroit was still overproducing and needed to get smaller. Ford went first, offering each of its remaining fifty-four thousand American workers up to $140,000 in cash to leave the company and hoping at least eight thousand would take it. The automaker laid out a whole buffet of buyout deals, including one that paid college tuition for an entire family.

There were job fairs at all the plants, and Ford mailed to every worker a special DVD titled *Connecting with Your Future* that extolled the promise of new careers beyond the assembly line. It was strange to see recruiters for other companies inside Ford factories. Workers at the large Woodhaven stamping plant south of Detroit spent their lunch hour perusing pamphlets about starting pizza franchises or becoming electricians at the local power company.

It was a tough call—stick with Ford and hope for the best, or take the money and run. "I'm taking the money," said Stacy Haynes, a thirty-four-year-old mother of four children. "I've been here twelve years, and I can't believe I've lasted this long." Others weren't sure whether to roll the dice. "The only thing that would make me do it is the uncertainty," said Jerry Thomas, a millwright with a dozen years at the plant. "We just don't know what's going to happen with Ford."

GM matched everything Ford put on the table. It was a curious reversal of roles. All of a sudden, Ford looked healthier, quicker, and more focused. GM managed to keep its crown as number one in the world for 2007 by the slimmest of margins—9.369 million vehicles compared to Toyota's 9.366 million sold, a difference of three thousand (the number of pickup trucks GM sold in one day). But it couldn't shake its unique legacy woes. Delphi still didn't have a buyer in bankruptcy, which meant that GM would have to provide more financial support. To make matters worse, the UAW struck at one of its other corporate spin-offs, American Axle, which immediately forced GM to shut down three profitable truck plants when supplies ran out.

And nothing had been done to streamline its overlapping and costly bureaucracy. Downsizing production was one thing, but GM still supported eight separate brands in the United States and far too many models for its dwindling market share, which was now under 23 percent and falling. On March 3, the GM board made an important move and promoted Fritz Henderson to president and chief operating officer for the entire corporation. It was partly a reward for his yeoman work negotiating the union contract, selling off GMAC, minding the mess at Delphi, and finally fixing the accounting flaws and getting federal regulators off its back.

Becoming president of GM was a monumental step for Henderson. He had devoted his life to the company, as his father had before him. He was following in the footsteps of some of the most famous auto execs in Detroit history: Alfred Sloan, Ed Cole, Pete Estes, Jack

Smith—and Rick Wagoner. Henderson was a dedicated, hands-on executive, and he had been putting out major fires for two years as the CFO.

He relished the chance to run a real business again, as he had at GM Europe and in Asia and South America. His wife and two school-age daughters had stayed behind at their home in Miami ever since he moved to Singapore in 2002; it was the ultimate corporate sacrifice for a family man such as Fritz. Now he could get out of his rented condo, move his family to the Detroit suburb of Bloomfield Hills, and settle down to the round-the-clock job of getting GM to consistently deliver good products and sell them at a profit.

Henderson's promotion was also an admission by GM that Rick Wagoner needed help. Nothing was moving the needle in a positive direction for GM—not its new pickups and full-size SUVs, not the Chevy Malibu or Saturn Aura or Buick Enclave. The health care deal, the job cuts, the plants—it was all one step forward and two steps back. GM was losing a billion dollars a month. Its international operations were booming, but North America was hemorrhaging cash. And its biggest headache wasn't even the car business. The GMAC finance arm was getting pounded by the mortgage melt-down sweeping the country. The credit company had enormous exposure in home loans, and the losses were running in the hundreds of millions every few weeks. Fortunately for GM, it only owned 49 percent of GMAC. A little more than half of the red ink was being absorbed by its majority partner—none other than Steve Feinberg and Cerberus. Investors were taking a hard look at General Motors and concluding that it had one of the weakest balance sheets of any industrial company in the world. Henderson was an optimist and a true-blue believer by nature, but even he was floored by how fragile GM had become. "My God, we've got a big, fat negative net worth," he said. "We're just getting exposed here."

Not once during this period did Wagoner or the board of directors even suggest that bankruptcy was an option. Henderson wondered when, or if, that suggestion was coming. But it never did. "Rick didn't want people working on it," he said. "So we didn't work on it."

Still, there was no getting around the fact that the company had a limited amount of cash, even less than Ford. GM was going to need more money. The company could buy out workers and divest whatever assets it could, but Henderson figured that GM still had to go to Wall Street by the summer and borrow billions. It would not be easy. Even private equity deals had ground to a halt because of the tighter purse strings at banks crunched by the mortgage market. How would an old-economy goliath such as GM get loans when bankers were turning away even hotter business opportunities? Ford had timed its borrowing perfectly and had done so before the big money started drying up. Wall Street would not be so welcoming for GM.

Henderson's only recourse was to stop the bleeding. The big question was whether GM would kill brands such as Saab, Hummer, and Saturn that consumed billions in capital but were bit players in the market. GM had already hacked away at the blue-collar manufacturing base, and it had two very powerful American brands, Chevrolet and Cadillac. But it sustained whole divisions that could disappear and the ravenous car market wouldn't blink. The Pontiac division, one of the hallowed muscle-car nameplates of all time, sold 350,000 cars and SUVs a year in the United States and couldn't break even. Saturn was the biggest money pit in GM history. And Hummer, the gas-guzzling brute of the SUV world, seemed so out of step with consumer trends as to be laughable. These decisions were the toughest call in the business—give away volume by shutting or selling brands, but improve the core business as a result.

Wagoner still had a hangover from closing Oldsmobile, one of GM's other ancient divisions. It had cost the company a billion dollars to pay off all the Olds dealers protected by state franchise laws. He abhorred the idea of going through that again. And for someone who had been with General Motors for thirty years, Wagoner still kept most of the actual duties of building cars at arm's length. He deputized Bob Lutz to oversee everything.

Lutz and Wagoner didn't so much drift apart as go their separate ways. Lutz's domain was the GM tech center, the company's half-mile-square epicenter of design and engineering, where President Eisenhower had cut the ribbon at the opening in 1956. Fifteen thousand people worked on the pristine campus, an architectural landmark with twenty-five buildings, eleven miles of roads, and a twenty-two-acre lake in the middle. Lutz parked his personal helicopter right by the lake and ruled GM's global product development from a sleek lair of blond wood and polished metal on the second floor of the main offices. Close by were the studios where designers still fashioned car models out of clay, and the majestic design dome where Lutz and his lieutenants chose the next generation of GM vehicles.

If GM was to survive its trials and stay on top, it would be because the brainpower and experience assembled at the tech center produced excellent, attractive automobiles. That was Lutz's mission in life; there was no close second. But at the age of seventy-five, his patience had worn thin with the bureaucratic twilight zone at GM. Its counterpart to Mulally's weekly business reviews were the monthly meetings of the baronial Automotive Strategy Board, which had twice the number of participants as at Ford, and every agenda was meticulously vetted with pre-meeting questions and debate.

The scope of the meetings went way beyond Ford's compartmentalized appraisal of the company at that very moment. The ASB sessions covered a wide swath of topics, everything from a new-car program to an ad campaign to the endless internal discussions about personnel. Lutz could not abide the hours and hours spent on deciding whether promising young managers should be put on a functional track such as manufacturing or given a broader assignment. "Just put him on both lists!" Lutz griped at one meeting. "What the hell difference does it make?" And he hated the companywide obsession with the Performance Management Program, the dreaded PMP, which set micro-objectives for every member of management (numbering in the tens of thousands) and graded them on an intricate, ongoing matrix.

One day Lutz couldn't take it anymore. "Holy shit . . . these PMPs are not worth the fucking paper they are written on," he blurted out. "Two months into the year and the entire economy changes and we're asking these people what goals haven't they reached? What does it tell you about an executive team where guys have to consult a piece of paper to figure out what they're supposed to be doing?"

No way Lutz would last in one of Alan Mulally's no-distraction meetings. When the ASB sessions droned on, he amused himself by playing the *Brick Breaker* video game on his BlackBerry. He just could not stomach the "arcane, sequential, orderly bullshit" that Wagoner thrived on. Lutz liked Wagoner personally. And he appreciated the great confidence Wagoner showed in him. But he knew this was no way to make quick, decisive moves. And he was sick of the lists of corporate "priorities" and uplifting "values" every executive was supposed to follow. "One of our values was supposed to be a sense of urgency," he said. "Well that's not even a goal. It's an enabler." The actual product plans became almost abstract, just another topic equal in weight to all the bureaucratic paperwork. "Rick devoted his energy to too many different things that didn't matter in the final analysis," Lutz said. "If there was such a thing as being too intellectual for the automobile business, he was it."

Wagoner tolerated Lutz's criticism, but he wouldn't change GM for Lutz. "If we made Bob the dictator of product and didn't involve the regional presidents, would decisions have been made faster?" he said. "Yes. Would they have been made better? I'm not convinced of that." Still, he gave Lutz a lot of leeway. Product decisions were just not Wagoner's forte, his skill set, or even his interest. It was left to Lutz to motivate and ride herd on the engineers, designers, and planners in order to bring competitive vehicles to market. "For some reason our guys did not have a passion for greatness," Wagoner admitted. "Bob brought that out in them."

While he gave Lutz as much autonomy as possible, he had nearly as tricky a relationship with Fritz Henderson. He was never going to second-guess Lutz on a new car. But Wagoner had done most of the jobs Henderson was doing, and he had basically been the company's chief operating officer before the board promoted Henderson to the position.

No matter what Henderson did, he always felt Wagoner hovering over his shoulder. "Rick controlled a lot of things," Henderson said. "He liked to have things come to him. We had lots of meetings about roles and responsibilities, but he just didn't want to ever let go. Normally it would be, 'This is what you work on and this is what I work on.' That wasn't the way it was. It's always, 'Let's talk.' We'd talk about it before I did it."

Wagoner ran the corporate strategy and Lutz lorded over the product. But Henderson had the heavy lifting—the union, the plants, the cost cuts, Delphi, GMAC, and the responsibility to somehow reverse years of losses in North America. With gas prices going up and sales coming down, he would be facing some very tough calls very soon. "The biggest problem," he said, "was we had no idea where the bottom was."

Alan Mulally was so happy he could hug somebody. On March 26, Ford reached an agreement to sell its Land Rover and Jaguar brands for $2.3 billion to Tata Motors, one of India's largest conglomerates and a burgeoning power in the country's emerging auto industry. It marked the first time an established European or American brand had been acquired by an Asian manufacturer. The Japanese Three—Toyota, Honda, and Nissan—preferred to grow their own nameplates. But the new breed of automakers, such as Tata, was hungry, well-financed, and in a hurry to make its mark. And it was quite a coup for a company from a former British colony to acquire two of the great names in English automotive history.

Mulally couldn't have been more pleased. Not only was Ford getting a good price for Jaguar and Land Rover, it could stop subsidizing the losses at the two luxury brands. And he didn't care what the sale meant in terms of lost prestige for Dearborn. "It's a killer to keep all these brands and just think you're here to deliver market share," he said. "If it's not part of the core, it's gone."

The deal was a milestone for Mulally. He had done a remarkable job eliminating the sacred cows at Ford. Jaguar and Land Rover had been woven deep into the fabric of the company. And Volvo would be the next to go. He never forgot how many foreign brands he'd seen in the Glass House parking garage the day he arrived in Dearborn. If that's what the executives wanted to drive, how could he get them to really relate to what the Ford brand was putting on the road?

Now his executives and managers were channeling his point of view and marching to his beat. Unlike GM, the bureaucracy couldn't impede his transformation plan. It was now accepted and owned by the organization at all levels. At a town hall meeting at headquarters, Mulally pulled out his new "One Ford" card and called out, "Who's got theirs?" Right on cue, hundreds of Ford employees reached into their pockets and purses and wallets and held their cards high.

Mulally was surprising himself with how quickly the company was evolving. First and foremost was the progress made in simplifying Ford's hugely complex product portfolio. "Seventy percent of our total volume will be on eight platforms by 2012," he said. "You can only imagine what a tremendous improvement that will be." And he was finally seeing progress financially. While GM was losing billions in the first quarter of 2008, Ford might actually turn a small profit. That would be quite an achievement given the pressure on sales by rising gas prices and the shaky economy.

In early April, Mulally flew to Las Vegas for the end of a four-day summit between Farley and his sales team and fourteen hundred of Ford's top dealers. The meetings went extremely well. It was Farley's idea to bring sixty Ford engineers along to the event. He had them set up exhibits to show dealers all the latest innovations back in Dearborn, such as high-tech airbags, scratchproof paint, and recyclable interior parts. Several dealers crowded around a chemical engineer, Angela Harris, as she showed off soybean-based foam used in seats and other parts. A few dealers from farming communities asked for samples to take back home. Farley just beamed. "Do you know how happy it makes me to see a Ford engineer talking to Ford dealers about soybean foam so they can tell their customers who are farmers?" he said. "I mean, how freaking cool is that?"

At the final dinner, Farley captivated the gathering by recounting his personal journey from Toyota to Ford and his deep family connection to the Blue Oval. "I believe in many ways, the future of Ford is the future of our country," he said. "The work here is simply more important than the work I was doing at Toyota." When he finished, the dealers jumped to their feet and give him a rousing ovation. Then Mulally took the microphone, grinning as though he had just seen one of his players hit a game-winning shot. "What do you think of our latest new model, Mr. Jim Farley?" he said, prompting a roar of approval and a second standing ovation.

It was all going according to plan. And Ford's progress was starting to gain more and more attention, especially among investors. On the same day that Mulally addressed the dealers, Kirk Kerkorian secretly began buying blocks of Ford stock—lots of it. He was on his way to acquiring one hundred million shares over the next two weeks. Nobody at Ford knew about it. But when Mulally returned to Dearborn, there was a message that Don Leclair needed to see him. Leclair had recently had dinner with Jerry York, and York was very interested in meeting Mulally. Would it be okay if he came by Ford headquarters tomorrow?

Sure, Mulally said. Why not?

[Twenty-Five]

Tom LaSorda was getting his passport stamped more times than any other auto exec in the world. Every foreign operation Chrysler owned was essentially for sale, and he was constantly on the move, seeking buyers for factories and other assets to raise money. On the flip side, the company desperately needed new small cars to fix the gaping holes in its product lineup.

He spent weeks at a time traveling, trying to find partners to help Chrysler stabilize. He had been to Korea, China, and Japan multiple times and was close to a big deal—but not an alliance—with Carlos Ghosn and Nissan. In the spring of 2008, LaSorda had landed in Turin, Italy, hoping to sell an engine plant in Brazil to the Italian automaker Fiat. But he came away with a lot more.

He had just met with Alfredo Altavilla, the head of Fiat's global engine division. Fiat wanted to buy Chrysler's plant in southern Brazil, and it also had fuel-efficient engines and compact-car platforms that Chrysler could use. Just as they were wrapping up, Altavilla said, "Sergio would like to have lunch with you." LaSorda didn't need to be told who that was. Sergio Marchionne was the well-known chief executive of Fiat and an emerging star in the European auto industry. "Sure, sounds great," LaSorda said.

He was ushered into a private dining room, and a few minutes later Marchionne came in. Tall but stooped, with tousled, graying black hair, small rimless glasses, and his trademark black sweater over an open-collared shirt, Marchionne looked more like a car designer than the company's CEO. LaSorda popped up immediately when he walked in.

"Mr. Marchionne," he said, extending his hand. "I'm Tom La-Sorda."

"I know who the fuck you are," Marchionne said. "Sit down. Let's eat."

All through lunch, Marchionne questioned him: What was Chrysler's plan? Why had Cerberus bought the company? What did it need to succeed?

LaSorda was only too happy to break it all down. He didn't know Marchionne, but he respected his track record. Fiat had turned around quickly under his direction and was making money in the intensely competitive European market. Plus, Marchionne had negotiated the $2 billion windfall payment from GM for ending an unsuccessful joint venture with Fiat. That alone was a badge of honor.

So LaSorda felt comfortable opening up. "The one thing we need the most is a small-car platform," he said. "I'm really enjoying working with Alfredo, and maybe we can do something else with you."

Marchionne looked at him and got very serious. "Can you survive if sales in the U.S. go below ten million a year?" he said bluntly. "Because if you can't, then I think you've got an issue."

LaSorda wasn't sure he'd heard right. Annual sales hadn't dropped below ten million in the American car market for twenty-five years. For the past five, it had been well above sixteen million. Marchionne was talking about a 40 percent drop—not exactly possible.

"We're pretty sure we're going to be around fourteen, fifteen million," LaSorda said. "And we'll be fine at that."

Marchionne let it pass. Lunch was almost over. He liked the engine plant in Brazil and blessed that deal. And he liked LaSorda, who he figured must be capable if Dieter Zetsche had trusted him to run Chrysler. But Marchionne was pretty cynical about the company's chances. He knew Chrysler's feast-or-famine history. He saw it as a wounded animal that could perish in a harsh business climate.

"Tom, let me tell you something," he said. "I'm a lot more negative about future sales volumes than you are. In fact, the numbers you are talking about are outlandish. If you think your salvation is coming from the market numbers, you're wrong. You have to not be able to bleed to death at ten million to make it."

Marchionne's assessment was pretty raw. *This guy is a piece of work*, LaSorda thought, *a real prophet of doom*. But the rest of the lunch was all very pleasant. Marchionne invited him to come back to Italy with Bob Nardelli. Maybe then they could talk some more. "We might be able," he said, "to do some business together."

Jerry York felt like a teenager going on a first date. He didn't even try to contain his enthusiasm when he talked to Kirk Kerkorian about Ford. "It's pretty damn clear to me that Ford has a huge sense of urgency compared to GM," he said. "They are so fucking far ahead of them it's not funny." This was finally the right car company, he told Kerkorian. Forget Chrysler and General Motors. This guy Alan Mulally had what it takes. York loved everything Mulally did—borrowing money, stripping off the extraneous brands, fusing the global operations together, betting on smaller cars. And York found a kindred spirit during his conversations with Don Leclair; this was a tough-as-nails CFO after his own heart.

York's mission on April 4 was to break the news to Mulally and Leclair that Kerkorian was considering acquiring a major stake in Ford, while also not revealing that the buying had already begun. York figured that by the end of the month Kerkorian could own at least 5 percent of Ford's stock. Then they'd have to make a public disclosure. But the key now was to explain to Mulally that this was not a takeover or an assault on management. "It's very important that they know this is friendly," he told Kerkorian. "They shouldn't be anticipating anything even remotely hostile."

When York arrived at the Glass House, he was charming and laid the praise on thick. He told Mulally how much he admired his career at Boeing and what he'd accomplished so far at Ford. Oh, and did Mulally know that York had worked at Ford in the 1970s? York still had fond memories of those days. He tried to keep the conversation as casual and upbeat as possible, and then he sprang the news. "Kirk is interested in investing in the company," he said. "And if we do, we want to support you totally."

Mulally took it all in. He could tell York was extremely intelligent and had done a ton of homework before walking in the door. But he had to play this very carefully. Of course, he told York, Ford welcomed smart investors such as Kirk Kerkorian. The company was changing fast, hitting its milestones, and gaining momentum. He acted very interested in York and asked about his experience on the General Motors board. How had that been?

"It's really not a lot of fun when you're dealing with idiots like that," York said. "Life is too short."

The meeting concluded with a lot of smiles and handshakes, and a promise by York that he would stay in touch.

That afternoon Kerkorian's firm, Tracinda, bought another 6.5 million shares of Ford for $42 million.

When Mulally told Bill Ford that York had come to see him, Bill was shocked that he hadn't been informed of the meeting beforehand. Didn't Mulally realize who they were dealing with here? But what really set Bill off was when he learned that Leclair had been talking to York one-on-one for weeks. He could be fired for that offense. The chief financial officer was in no way authorized to hold private conversations with a representative of one of the most aggressive investors in America.

When Joe Laymon heard about it, he couldn't believe that Leclair had met with York and hadn't disclosed it to the chairman of the board. "He did it without Bill's knowledge?" Laymon said. "Shit, we might have to let Don go."

But Bill did not make moves in panic. Kerkorian hadn't done anything provocative yet. Ford was in for a tense waiting game now. And for the first time, Bill felt a twinge of doubt about Mulally's judgment. Meeting with York without first telling him and the board was a dangerous precedent. It could not happen again under any circumstances.

That was the effect Kerkorian had. He created an immediate distraction and concern to the management of any company he took an interest in. Kerkorian was never a passive investor. He had one goal when he bought a big stake in a business: "I just want to make money on my investment," he said.

York's motivation was slightly different. He wanted to be part of a successful auto company. He loved the industry; he always had and he always would. Ford was a fantastic opportunity. "Alan Mulally has the right stuff," he told a friend in Detroit. "He is going to do whatever it takes to fix Ford. I'm just blown away by this guy. He is forcing teamwork on these people. I couldn't stop thinking about it for twenty-four hours after I met him."

But even with Kerkorian moving in, the management team at Ford wasn't going to slow down. The company was determined to earn a profit in the first quarter. A profitable quarter would be a huge internal morale boost and would set Ford apart from the two other struggling Detroit automakers. It was, however, going to be very close.

On April 24, Ford surprised Wall Street and most of the auto world when it reported a slim $100 million profit on $39 billion in revenue in the first three months of the year. The company still wasn't earning money in North America, but the overall performance was what Mulally called a "proof point" that the plan was working. "More progress will be made in North America," he promised. "We are going to get to our $5 billion cost reduction goal by the end of this year." Then Mulally pledged that Ford would be solidly profitable in 2009. He didn't have to say that, and some company insiders wondered why he did. But Ford had the hot hand now. Why shouldn't he pump up the enthusiasm with a powerful promise of more success to come?

The next day, York contacted Leclair and told him that Kerkorian would go public with an offer for a significant amount of Ford stock in the very near future. And on April 28, the ninety-year-old billionaire announced in a federal filing that he had purchased one hundred million Ford shares for $691 million and was prepared to pay $8.50 a share in cash to buy an additional twenty million. That would give Kerkorian a total stake of about 5.5 percent in Ford and a prominent voice in the company's future.

After the federal filing, York started giving interviews about Mulally and the Ford comeback. Kerkorian, he said, was making a long-term investment in a great American car company. "We don't care what happens in the next two or three quarters," he said. "What we're looking for is a big, big hit five, six, seven years down the road."

He dismissed questions about whether Kerkorian wanted to take over the company. That was ridiculous, York said. "The reality is the Ford Motor Company has the best poison pill in the world against a hostile shareholder," he said. "And it's called 40 percent voting rights by the Ford family."

Was that where this was headed? Would Kerkorian try to buy out the Ford family? By coincidence, the extended family gathered in Dearborn a few days later for their regular spring meeting. A year earlier, the Fords had made a tough call to reject strategic advice from Wall Street bankers. But there was no dissent in the family now. They were united against Kerkorian. Bill Ford gave an impassioned speech to his relatives and assured them that nobody could bring down the family but themselves. The Ford Motor Company was their destiny, he said. Kerkorian could buy all the stock he wanted. But as long as the family held firm, they were in control. Mulally attended the meeting too, primarily to give a glowing update on the turnaround. He was not involved in the discussion about Kerkorian. That was a family matter.

While Ford's fortunes were rising, GM was running into a ditch. On April 30, it reported a stunning $3.2 billion loss in the first quarter. Red ink was everywhere. The strike at American Axle cost $800 million. Delphi sucked up another $700 million. Losses at GMAC were nearly $300 million. Crashing sales of pickups and sport-utilities put another big dent in its U.S. market share, which had now slipped below 23 percent.

"All the things we've done were necessary and important," said Fritz Henderson. "But we've got to do more." He cut truck production by almost 140,000 units in the second half of the year, which would force temporary layoffs and fewer shifts in the plants. And the financial vise was tightening. GM's cash reserves had fallen precipitously low; it now had about $25 billion. That figure alone kept Henderson and GM's new chief financial officer, Ray Young, awake at night. The company needed a bare minimum of $10 billion on hand just to stay in business and maintain its rolling schedule of paying suppliers for parts. But what happened if operations kept devouring money? The debt market on Wall Street was getting worse, not better. And there was no possible way GM could cut enough production or costs to balance out the losses.

The new sales environment was frightening. Once gas passed $3.50 a gallon, consumers stampeded into smaller cars as never before. One in five vehicles sold in the United States in April was a compact car. A decade before, the number of smaller vehicles was one in eight. Tiny models such as the Honda Fit and Toyota Yaris saw their sales soar 50 percent. For the first time in memory, vehicles with fuel-sipping four-cylinder engines outsold bigger V-6s and V-8s.

Meanwhile, truck sales were down 17 percent overall for the month. The sales specialists at the companies were awestruck. They had never seen this before. "It's easily the most dramatic segment shift I have witnessed in the market in my thirty-one years here," said George Pipas, the chief market analyst at Ford. Consumers weren't just rushing to get fuel-efficiency; they were bottom-feeding on price to weather the economic downturn as well. "We wanted to have good fuel economy, but we were equally concerned about the price of the car," said John Shelby of Phoenix, Arizona, the new owner of a $15,000 Honda Fit.

Rick Wagoner huddled with Henderson, Young, and GM's outside financial advisors, including his close friend Jay Alix, a Detroit restructuring guru who helped clean up the post-bankruptcy messes at corporate disasters Enron and WorldCom. Big decisions were mandatory. GM had decided to close four truck plants, two of which had been guaranteed future vehicles in the UAW contract. Product development had to be scaled back substantially, with the exception of small cars and the Chevy Volt plug-in hybrid. Hummer, the poster child for monster sport-utilities, needed to be sold, and other brands were in jeopardy. At a meeting of the Automotive Strategy Board, a monumental call was made to cancel the $2 billion CXX program to replace the flagships of the GM fleet—the supersized Escalade, Suburban, and Yukon SUVs. Even Bob Lutz didn't utter a word of protest. "It would be very difficult in today's environment to spend a couple of billion dollars to do a replacement," he said. "Reality had set in."

It sure had. All the financial machinations, turnaround initiatives, and labor agreements were no consolation. The hull of GM had cracked, and the company could not absorb these losses indefinitely. Internal calculations showed that without an infusion of new cash, General Motors would be insolvent by the fall. Not weak or unstable—insolvent, as in no money to pay the bills.

Inside the Renaissance Center, all eyes turned to Wagoner. The company was entering uncharted territory. Its values and history and size meant nothing now. GM was no different from any other corporation that had badly misjudged its market, spent way beyond its means, and lacked a blueprint for survival that might induce banks, oil-rich Middle Eastern investors, or sovereign wealth funds in Asia to take a flyer by lending it billions. Even Kirk Kerkorian, daring gambler that he was, would rather place a bet on Ford. In its time of need, GM was missing the one attribute that theoretically could save it: credibility.

Wagoner pressed on, and prepared to announce a gigantic corporate overhaul at the GM annual meeting in early June. In the meantime, his board of directors was getting more nervous. "Are we drowning here?" asked John Bryan at one meeting. "You really don't have time to find a solution when you're drowning." A couple of directors, Phil Laskawy and Erskine Bowles, hammered Wagoner with questions about cash flow and the possibility of Chapter 11 as a way out. But Wagoner refused to even discuss bankruptcy as an option. "He really didn't want to talk about it or prepare for it in any way," said Bryan. "It was not within his imagination to run scared or rally the troops with the threat of bankruptcy. It was anathema to him."

To Wagoner, this crisis was a test of will, brains, and stamina. The great teams don't throw in the towel when they're losing. They grit their teeth and step up to the challenge. In the midst of the war-room meetings and late-night strategy sessions, he would share his convictions in a way he never had before. On May 13, he stepped to the microphone in the middle of the football field at Wallace Wade Stadium in Durham, North Carolina, to give the commencement address at Duke University, his beloved alma mater. Duke was in Wagoner's blood; his father, his wife, his sister, and his oldest son were graduates, and another son was a junior at the school. He'd even named his dog Duke. This was where he learned a lifetime of lessons about hard work and achievement and contributing to society. And he wanted all of these promising young college graduates to know that even the chief executive of General Motors sometimes had to dig deep to triumph over adversity.

"A year and a half ago, some of the so-called experts were claiming General Motors was headed for bankruptcy, and I ought to be fired," he told the throng of graduates and parents, academic deans and professors. "Those were tough days for me." There would be difficult days ahead for all of them at some point, Wagoner said. That was when strength and character would rise to the top. "So my advice is simple," he said. "Go at life every day with passion and enthusiasm. And when challenges arrive, simply do not give up."

When the price of gas topped $3.80 a gallon in May, pickup sales dropped an astonishing 30 percent. SUVs were even worse. Jim Farley gaped at the numbers like a scientist studying the damage from an epic earthquake. "What we are looking at right now is an incredible, once-in-a-lifetime shift," he told his fellow Ford executives.

"We can't speculate where it will go. We just have to deal with it."

The euphoria that resulted from reporting a profit a few weeks earlier had evaporated entirely inside Ford. If this catastrophe wasn't met head-on, there wouldn't be any profits to celebrate for a long time to come. This was not a question of working harder or simply not giving up. This was save-the-company time.

On Sunday, May 18, Mulally summoned his senior executives for an emergency meeting in his office. Gas would hit $4 a gallon any day. There were two choices—ride it out and keep the plants working or drastically scale back truck production. "What can we do to deal with this, to move quickly?" Mulally asked.

They went around the room—Fields, Farley, Leclair, Kuzak—until everyone had weighed in. They all agreed to cut back big-time. A quarter of a million trucks and SUVs were slashed from future production schedules, and they would keep making adjustments if the situation got worse. "We are going to crank up the process," Mulally said. "Instead of meeting every week, we're going to meet every day."

On May 22, Ford humbly retreated from its pledge of delivering full-year profits in 2009. Instead, the Glass House braced for the worst. "We reached a tipping point," Mulally told Wall Street analysts in a conference call. "We needed to act now." Not only was pickup and SUV production radically reduced, but Ford was boosting its output of Focus and Fusion cars to appeal to fuel-conscious consumers. That sounded like a wise move to the legions of Ford dealers swamped with unsold trucks. "If you've got one [truck] on the lot," said Doug Erickson, a Ford dealer in Hastings, Minnesota, "you've probably got enough."

The atmosphere in Mulally's now-daily meetings was electric. Veteran execs such as Fields had never seen this level of effort among the leadership team. And Mulally seemed more energized than ever. "How do you handle adversity?" he asked. "You trust the process. Know everything, good and bad. If we know everything, we can collectively go to work on it."

Once again, his relative inexperience in the auto industry proved to be a competitive advantage. Traditionally, the Big Three reacted to a crisis by pulling back, cutting costs, and holding their breath until normal conditions returned. But why should they ever expect "normal" again? Mulally saw the data, trends, and growth charts from around the world. There was no going back. Ford had to change permanently. He wasn't satisfied just cutting truck production. Ford was going to dig into its cash reserves and retool three or more of its truck plants to build small cars. It would cost billions and take two years to complete. But if that was where the industry was headed, why not go for it? Mulally became so single-minded it was scary. He always bent over backward to be inclusive. But woe to the dissenting voice as the train picked up speed. "When he says we are going to resize this company," said Farley, "you better get on board now."

The GM board met in early June in Detroit to hear how management planned to stop the bleeding. It was an ugly picture. Since the UAW deal eight months earlier, the company's stock price had plunged 60 percent to $17—its lowest point in twenty-six years. GM's stock in total was worth less than $10 billion, compared to Toyota's market value of $150 billion. Another nineteen thousand union workers had taken the most recent buyout packages. And now four truck plants would shut their doors in Wisconsin, Ohio, Canada, and Mexico.

Wagoner, Henderson, and Lutz made presentations to the directors. They all hit the same point over and over: The time had come to put the SUV boom behind them for good, focus on new cars and crossovers in the United States, and accelerate expansion overseas. Wagoner proposed a "strategic review" of the flailing Hummer brand, though he did not recommend an outright sale. But what was there to review? Hummer sales had plunged 35 percent already in 2008, and there was no reason for that to change. It was hard to envision a good time ever again to buy a Hummer or anything else that got twelve miles to the gallon.

Lutz asked for the go-ahead on two new small-car programs and an improved four-cylinder engine, as well as final approval for the Chevrolet Volt, the greenest of all the GM vehicles in development. The directors approved it all. And George Fisher added a special coda to the package—another public vote of confidence for Wagoner and his troops. "GM has the best management team to get us through these difficult times," Fisher said.

GM was taking some big steps, but Ford kept taking even more. It announced a second round of production cuts, and astounded the industry by delaying the launch of the new F-series pickup by a full two months. This was highly unusual. All the suppliers were ready, the materials had been purchased, and the plants were prepared. Dealers were even taking orders from the few hardy pickup buyers anxious to get into the new model. But the Ford team was not about to risk flooding the market with new F-150s as long as gas prices kept climbing. It was a very tough call. The new pickups were a big potential source of revenue at a time when volume was falling off. Mulally, however, was determined to steer through the crisis first before flicking the switch on the F-series.

He was also working his way through the delicate situation with Kerkorian, who had formally commenced his tender offer for twenty million more Ford shares. The memory of that first meeting with Jerry York still stung Mulally. Ford felt it necessary to put out a statement denying that York had explicitly told him of Kerkorian's interest in taking a stake in the company. York's comments were considered "off the cuff" and had not been taken seriously, the statement said. Anyone who knew York would have found it hard to fathom that he would make casual remarks about investing Kerkorian's money.

But Kerkorian had become a nuclear issue inside the Glass House, particularly after he disclosed in a federal filing that he would be willing to lend Ford money to aid in its turnaround and to provide it with "business strategies." Bill Ford and some directors were extremely concerned that Kerkorian and York would try to sweet-talk Mulally into listening to their plans to improve Ford. Bill also knew that once that door was cracked open, Kerkorian's influence over the company could grow considerably.

Bill had to grab hold of the Kerkorian situation. This was out of Mulally's realm of expertise. He had more than enough to handle in keeping Ford afloat. A summit meeting was scheduled between the Ford side and the Kerkorian camp for June 17 at the Bellagio in Las Vegas. Bill hoped it wouldn't be a showdown. But he'd be ready if it was.

"What do you think it would cost to buy out the Ford family?" York asked a confidant in Detroit. "A billion dollars for all the class B stock? That's double what it's worth on the market. I'm not so sure these people wouldn't take it."

Technically, the class B shares were legally nontransferable beyond family members. So nobody could buy them and gain the same 40 percent voting power the Fords had. But the shares could be bought and taken out of the family's hands, which would open the playing field for an aggressive investor to grab control of the company with a big block of common shares.

But York wasn't making any decisions about taking over Ford; Kerkorian was. And Kerkorian wasn't going to make another move with Ford until he had personally met Mulally. If he was going to bet big on Mulally, he wanted to look into his eyes, feel the grip of his handshake, and hear him describe his vision. "I only knew Alan through Jerry's eyes," Kerkorian said. "I wanted to see for myself."

They met in one of the palatial high-roller suites at the Bellagio. Kerkorian, York, and Kerkorian's lawyer, Terry Christensen, sat on one side of the table, with Bill Ford, Mulally, and Leclair on the other. They were joined by a surprise guest—Richard Manoogian, a longtime Ford director. Bill had brought Manoogian along because of his long relationship with Kerkorian. They were both Armenian Americans and deeply involved in charitable activities related to their heritage. It was just a little extra insurance in case Kerkorian tried to muscle the Ford contingent.

But he wasn't like that at all. Kerkorian was soft-spoken, courteous, and generous in his praise of Ford. "I'm in this for the long haul," he said. "I want to be supportive of you all the way."

Bill asked what he thought of the Ford family and its stewardship of the company.

"I think it's great," Kerkorian said. "I think family ownership is a strength."

York and Christensen mostly kept quiet. This meeting was clearly for their boss's benefit.

And Mulally was very enthusiastic about meeting Kerkorian. His eyes lit up at the opulence of the Bellagio, and he clearly enjoyed taking Kerkorian through Ford's transformation plan. "We are saving an American icon," he gushed.

It was all over in an hour. Bill still wasn't sure what to expect next. But he had to hand it to Kerkorian. He was smooth. "He really sounded like he wants to be supportive," Bill said.

Kerkorian was pretty pleased with everything. After his disappointment with General Motors, these guys from Ford were like a breath of fresh air. "Boy, I really like Alan Mulally," he said. "And I think they like us."

[Twenty-Six]

Bob Nardelli wanted a small car so badly he flew to Italy in a body cast to see Sergio Marchionne. The Chrysler chief executive had been spending one of his rare weekends at his home in Atlanta, getting ready for his son's wedding. He was working out his frustrations after a long conference call with Auburn Hills and moving big cast-iron pots around his yard when he heard a *pop, pop, pop, pop* in his back and fell to his knees. Nardelli ended up in the emergency room with broken bones in his back and on the operating table a few days later.

Now he was in a removable cast and in extreme discomfort, and getting on the Chrysler corporate jet in Michigan to meet Tom LaSorda in Turin. Nardelli's staff was pretty amazed. He hadn't been able to walk after surgery on Wednesday, but he'd been working full-time by Monday morning. And the second he heard Fiat might have a little car ready to sell to Chrysler, he moved fast.

"I've got to come over there," he told Marchionne on the phone. "I need a small car."

LaSorda had been busy hunting for a foreign partner for Chrysler. He had been meeting nonstop with Carlos Ghosn's teams at Nissan in Tokyo and at Renault in Paris—basically the same executives who had discussed an alliance with GM. But so far Ghosn had been wary of entering into a full-scale partnership with Chrysler. Fiat, on the other hand, seemed like a hugely promising alternative to Nardelli. The Italians had exactly the type of cars he needed. But on the Gulfstream jet over the Atlantic en route to Italy, all Nardelli could focus on were the wretched sales numbers coming in for Chrysler and the entire U.S. industry. Even Toyota was getting hammered and was shutting down production at its plants for the first time ever. When oil hit $147 a barrel and gas climbed to $4 a gallon at the pump, Americans essentially stopped buying trucks and SUVs. That was it—the breaking point. Big vehicles were piling up at plants across the country. GM had a 174-day supply of GMC Yukons and Chevy Tahoes, which was some sort of record for unwanted inventory.

And Chrysler was starving on its meager diet of pickups and sport-utilities. Its sales were down more than 20 percent for the year so far, double the drop of the overall market. Nardelli had been cutting, selling, reducing, and redirecting the limited resources Cerberus had given him. But the Jeep, the Ram pickup, the big Dodge SUV—all of Chrysler's main revenue producers—were getting killed. Even the minivan was shunned because its gas mileage was poor. Nardelli was doing what he did best—making decisions. When he saw the June sales numbers, he immediately shut down the big minivan plant in Missouri. He and Jim Press were also deciding which subpar models to cut from the lineup. (Press was ready to get rid of half of Chrysler's cars on the spot.) And to cut costs even further, Nardelli had come up with a grand plan to open engineering centers in China and Mexico.

But Chrysler's balance sheet was just a wreck. It was losing hundreds of millions of dollars, and the only backstop was $10 billion in borrowed money. JPMorgan Chase and the rest of the banks were breathing down Cerberus's neck to get paid back. Feinberg had told his anxious private equity investors to be prepared for "significant risks" and "worst-case scenarios" for their prized automotive trophy.

The three-headed dog was already gagging on its huge losses with GMAC and its minority partner, General Motors. Cerberus may have pulled off the two worst deals in automotive history back to back. It bought GM's finance company right before its residential mortgage unit went up in flames, and then it acquired Chrysler and its weak product line just as auto sales were entering their worst period in decades.

Behind closed doors in his Park Avenue office, Steve Feinberg was kicking himself for taking on Chrysler. The one thing he prided himself on more than anything was timing. "And we really fucked that up," he said. "We thought we bought it cheap enough to absorb a lot of economic shit, but volume tanked so badly and so fast we were just fighting to keep our head above water."

Meanwhile, James Lee, the big mergers-and-acquisitions chief at JPMorgan Chase, was on Feinberg's back constantly about the loans that Chrysler owed the bank. The debt was a huge problem. If Chrysler ever did make money, Cerberus would have to give it to its lenders first. Chrysler needed new products fast if it was to have any chance to survive. Feinberg had to make a deal as soon as possible. He was spending a lot of time butting heads with Ghosn over his demand for 20 percent ownership of Chrysler in exchange for Nissan cars. "We're not willing to say, 'Here's a large piece of the company and all we want in return is product,'" Feinberg told him. But Ghosn was naturally wary after the charade with Kerkorian and GM. If the Renault-Nissan alliance was getting into bed with Chrysler, he sure wasn't going to get stuck on the short end of a deal.

But whether it was Nissan or Fiat or any foreign automaker, Feinberg needed to find a partner to prop up his not-so-excellent adventure in the car business.

When Nardelli landed in Turin, he went straight to see Marchionne at Fiat headquarters. The building was notable because it had a full-size test track built on the roof. Fiat was more than a hundred years old, a big force in Europe and very strong in South America. The company had established brands—Fiat, Lancia, Ferrari, Alfa Romeo—and unique, reliable small cars that were superior to anything that Chrysler produced.

Nardelli hobbled into the building with the stiff cast on under his suit, aching from the flight but pumped for the meeting. Marchionne was sort of shocked he showed up in this condition. "Bob, are you okay?" he asked worriedly. But Nardelli was excited to talk business. And when he saw the cars in the design center he swooned, especially over the adorable little Fiat 500, rounded like an egg and oozing automotive charisma.

"When could we bring that to Chrysler?" he asked.

That could be possible, Marchionne said, and proceeded to show Nardelli the four-cylinder engines and technology that could really put Chrysler in the small-car game.

But at lunch, they didn't talk much about Fiat. Marchionne was much more interested in discussing Chrysler. He had studied everything about it and knew all its weaknesses. And he had done a deep dive on Nardelli and his Home Depot and General Electric days. "This guy was supposed to be the crème de la crème," he said. He kept pressing Nardelli on the same question he had asked LaSorda. "How are you bastards going to survive," Marchionne said, "if sales go below ten million?"

Nardelli didn't have an answer. Marchionne wasn't surprised. This GE guy had no idea he was sitting on a ticking time bomb. In Marchionne's view, Chrysler was going down the tubes if something dramatic didn't change. Nardelli could look and touch his cars and engines all he wanted. But Fiat wasn't doing anything with Chrysler. Not just yet.

By midsummer of 2008, the nightmare scenario was coming to life—soaring fuel prices, a miserable economy, no credit for consumers. This was shaping up as the worst stretch in more than ten years for auto sales, and the market was deteriorating by the day. More than fifteen Big Three assembly plants were either idled or operating on reduced shifts. Twenty-five thousand UAW workers went on indefinite layoff, as Detroit frantically tried to cut production faster than sales fell. When GM's stock dropped under $10, it dragged down the entire Dow Jones average. The American auto industry was collapsing like a tent in a hurricane.

While Bob Nardelli was flying to Italy, Fritz Henderson was in Europe and Asia getting GM's foreign operations to crank out more small cars to ship to the United States. By July, General Motors had run out of wiggle room. Investors were fleeing the stock, and even the most conservative analysts estimated that GM needed another $10 billion to $15 billion in cash to make it. If this truly was the reckoning in Detroit that had been predicted for so long, Wagoner had to do something to buy GM more time. If he could come up with just one more big restructuring effort, maybe—just maybe—the banks would lend GM enough to stay alive.

On July 15, 2008, the top brass assembled for a major announcement at the Renaissance Center. Wagoner, Lutz, and Henderson were front and center. They were flanked by Ray Young, the new CFO, and Troy Clarke, the head of North American operations. At the start of the press conference, Wagoner immediately stated that GM was not going under—not yet. "We are highly confident that we have ample liquidity through 2009," he said. That admission alone was jarring. How could GM make it another eighteen months using up almost a billion in cash every three weeks?

According to Wagoner, the company was going to raise a $15 billion "cushion," primarily by cutting thousands of salaried jobs, suspending its dividend, freezing wages, canceling executive bonuses, and eliminating health care coverage for white-collar retirees over the age of sixty-five. On top of that, it would whack another three hundred thousand units of truck production, slash marketing costs (including dropping its giant NASCAR and pro golf sponsorships), cut spending on new products by 20 percent, and delay its first big payment into the UAW health care trust. The cuts, Wagoner said, would save GM about $10 billion. Then the company hoped to raise another $5 billion by selling anything and everything it could—the rest of GMAC, real estate, Hummer, and maybe other brands too. Last but not least, it would attempt to borrow whatever it could on Wall Street, using assets both in the United States and internationally as collateral.

It sounded like GM was burning the furniture so it wouldn't

freeze to death. Lutz swore the company would not compromise the quality of its new models, but that was hard to believe. These were survivalist tactics, the first time the company had cut capital spending this much since the recession of the early 1990s (something Alan Mulally and Bill Ford pledged never to do).

Wagoner looked grim. He wore a gray suit, a yellow striped tie, and a long face, the corners of his mouth frozen in a frown. As he sat with his hands folded in front of the bright blue GM logo, he appeared to be trying to convince reporters of something he had a hard time accepting himself. "Our plan is not a plan to survive," he said flatly. "It is a plan to win." The executives took questions but didn't really answer them. Henderson dodged every attempt to get clarity on this mysterious borrowing power GM claimed it had. Before the press conference even ended, the influential Moody's credit rating service downgraded GM's existing debt deeper into junk status.

And when Henderson made the first calls to the major banks in New York, it was like no one even wanted to answer the phone. Wall Street had shut down the debt market—period. The dominos were falling in an epic financial crisis. Bear Stearns had crashed a few months earlier and had been sold to JPMorgan Chase. Lehman Brothers was on life support. Merrill Lynch was up for sale.

Henderson found out quickly that going to the investment banks to raise a few billion dollars was a joke. "It was bad," he said. "The market was pretty much closed. . . . To raise any equity from your balance sheet, you needed an event. You needed something as a catalyst. And the only catalyst big enough would be a combination."

And it was with that realization that Henderson suggested to Wagoner that they approach Ford about a merger. To his surprise, Wagoner thought it was a great idea.

Bill Ford was told by his secretary that Rick Wagoner from GM was calling. He picked up in his office and heard Wagoner's familiar voice on the line.

"Hi, Bill, its Rick Wagoner. . . . I'd like to get together. You know, I think it's really time we put our companies together. We should talk."

What?

"We could come over there and talk," Wagoner said.

Bill wasn't sure he'd heard him right. Wagoner wanted to come to the Glass House to talk about a merger between Ford and General Motors?

Yes, said Wagoner. He'd bring Fritz Henderson, and Bill could get Mulally and Leclair to come. And then, he said, they could talk.

Bill was caught completely off guard. He'd had no clue this was coming. First Kerkorian, now GM? But he couldn't just turn Wagoner down. He had known him a long time, and they had worked together closely on the UAW, fuel economy regulations, the environment, and trade issues. They were as collegial as competitors could be.

So Bill said sure. Why don't you come on over, and bring Fritz.

The idea had been a subject of debate in Detroit for years. What if GM and Ford merged? What if the two biggest car companies in American history joined forces? Even in their shrunken state, they would have a combined 38 percent U.S. market share and an enormous international presence. All that purchasing power, manufacturing capacity, and technical skill would be under one roof. There would be thousands of overlapping jobs that could be eliminated to save money. A combination of Ford and GM would theoretically be a frightening prospect for competitors. Chrysler wouldn't even be included anymore in the discussion. Instead of the Big Three, there would just be a Big One.

But could it even be done? Could the Yankees merge with the Red Sox, or the Celtics with the Lakers? GM and Ford had competed head-on in every vehicle segment for the last fifty years. This was not just a rivalry; this was opposite sides of town, you-stay-on-yours-and-I'll-stay-on-mine. It had never seriously been considered by any senior executive at either company—until now.

Bill Ford didn't like the sound of this at all. GM must be in serious trouble if its execs were coming to Ford for help or answers. The whole concept of a merger made him nauseated, not to mention that this would be the ultimate hot button with the union. Gettelfinger would go nuts at the job cuts. It would make the health care talks look easy by comparison.

Bill met with Mulally, and they agreed they had to talk to GM, if for no other reason than to find out what was going on with Wagoner. This approach was very out of character. But maybe GM was in even worse shape than it was letting on.

It was a meeting that would profoundly affect the course of both automakers. Wagoner and Henderson arrived at the meeting with Ray Young, and they sat down with Bill Ford, Alan Mulally, and Don Leclair.

Wagoner led off the discussion. GM and Ford should merge, he said. The synergies would be phenomenal. There would be savings on administrative costs, R&D, and shipping and purchasing. The possibilities, he said, were endless.

Bill was shocked. GM seriously wanted to merge with Ford. Who, he asked, would be majority owner? As bad as Ford's stock price was, the company still had a higher market value than GM. And who would run the new company?

Wagoner pointed out that General Motors was a much larger company in terms of revenue than Ford. By all rights, GM probably should be in charge. But maybe they could share management, or talk about that later, he suggested.

Mulally mostly listened. He was dying to know more about the true state of GM. He sure didn't want any part of any merger. As far as he was concerned, General Motors was a roaring five-alarm fire that he didn't even want to get close to. But why, he asked, were they coming to Ford now?

Wagoner and Henderson took turns describing the liquidity crisis at GM and how they were running low on cash. By merging with Ford, they could go back to Wall Street and borrow more money.

So that's what this is about. GM is going broke, Bill realized. All he could think about was Ford's $30 billion in the bank. *That's what they really want.* This wasn't about Ford at all. It was about saving GM.

Bill didn't need to hear any more. "No thanks," he said. "This would never work out. You know what? We're too much alike. We're right on top of each other in every segment."

Now Henderson jumped in, trying to get this meeting focused on how good it could be. "Don and I did a lot of work on this earlier," he said. "I know GM inside and out, and Don knows Ford inside and out. Between the two of us we could figure it out pretty quickly."

But Leclair kept his mouth shut. Bill was doing the talking.

"No," Bill said. "No thanks."

Wagoner understood now. This wasn't happening. "Well, if you don't do it with us," he said, "we're going to look elsewhere." And then they left.

At first Bill was angry. "GM can be so arrogant," he said. "We were known as a culture of infighting. And they are a culture of arrogance."

But this whole approach was disturbing. If General Motors went bankrupt, a big part of the automotive supply chain in the United States could collapse within days. That would impact the entire industry, including Ford. Bill quickly became more worried than irritated. He respected GM's immense power and mass like no one else at Ford ever could. "I grew up in this town, and GM was the giant," he said. "We were a very tough competitor, but they were the giant. They set the tone in many ways for the whole industry. That was just the reality of life for me from childhood." And now GM was reeling. It just drove home to him how vulnerable Ford was too.

Mulally was slightly amazed at how desperate GM had become. He may have been an outsider, but he was as competitive an executive as had ever set foot in Detroit. From the day he came to Ford, he wanted to beat GM and beat them bad. If they were going belly-up or merging with someone, he wanted to know about it for sure. But Ford was on its own road. And he wasn't turning the wheel over to Rick Wagoner or anyone else.

. . . .

Henderson felt like someone had popped his balloon. So much for the event that would convince Wall Street to lend money to GM. "That would have been the catalyst," he groaned. "You could actually use it to raise capital because the amount of synergies would be massive. Massive!"

He felt a growing sense of dread. He had been counting on Ford to be a lifeline. At this point he knew GM's financial status better than anyone, even Wagoner. And as disappointed as he was, he couldn't blame Ford for slamming the door on his idea. "I thought we would find a way to make it work," he said glumly. "But sitting in their shoes, I could understand why they didn't want to do it. It wasn't a simple call for them."

Lutz was disappointed too when he heard how the meeting had gone. To him, a GM-Ford merger would prove once and for all that an American auto company could whip Toyota and anyone else in the world. "It could be one large, enormously powerful global automobile company," Lutz said. "You could shut one proving ground, one finance department, one tax department, a bunch of plants, get rid of a lot of engineering. We could get rid of the fixed costs even before the acquisition."

But Wagoner didn't even want to talk about it. They tried. It didn't work. Let's move on. It was another example of GM's dysfunction at the top. There was something missing between Wagoner, Lutz, and Henderson—chemistry or a cover-my-back mentality. They worked together, but not *together* like the Ford guys.

Nobody outside the two tight inner circles knew about the secret meeting between GM and Ford. To most of the outside world, the two companies were already joined at the hip as Detroit's version of *Dumb and Dumber*. The public, the media, and the talking heads on cable TV weren't distinguishing between any of the Big Three now; it was everybody's turn in the barrel.

That was driven home when the financial wreckage was released for the spring quarter: an $8.7 billion loss at Ford, the worst quarter in its 105-year history, and a $15.5 billion loss at GM, its third worst in a hundred years. The numbers were staggering. GM's revenue in

North America fell $10 billion—a breathtaking 33 percent decline—from the second quarter a year earlier. Ford took an $8 billion charge just to write down assets and offset the shrinking value of pickups and SUVs in its lease portfolios. The U.S. car market had imploded. GMAC and Ford Credit could barely loan money to consumers to buy cars anymore because no financial institution in America would securitize the loans. Auto leasing—for years a spectacularly effective way to move new models—was basically gone, over, nonexistent.

But the GM board was still in denial. In what had become a ritual every time the company took a big pratfall, lead director George Fisher couldn't wait to stand up and defend it. "I'm reading too much stuff in the papers these days that is wrong," he grumbled in an interview. "It's a distraction to the board and a distraction to management." Was GM in any danger of filing for bankruptcy? "The answer is no, absolutely not," he said. "It's our job to make sure that doesn't happen." How could it be avoided? "Rick and his team are taking some really significant actions," he said. "We've got some pretty astute people around here."

It was hard to understand Fisher's optimism. Wagoner and Henderson had just tried a Hail Mary pass to merge with Ford and it flopped. Sales were atrocious and getting worse. The cash reserves were dwindling by the day, and more expenses were coming in. Delphi was trying to find a private equity buyer to emerge from bankruptcy after three years, and it looked like GM would be on the hook for another $3 billion to $4 billion to cover its pension obligations.

There was no happy talk coming from Ford. In Mulally's daily sessions with his senior execs, the intensity level just kept rising. "What does a sustainable Ford look like, gentlemen?" Mulally asked them. "Why are we in business? We are in business to create value. And we can't create value if we go out of business." Excuses were unacceptable. Ford's survival was a matter of pride, determination, and conviction. "Why can't we make money on small cars?" he said. "Do you think Toyota can't make money on small cars?"

On the day Ford reported its huge loss, it rolled out the next phase of its transformation plan—converting three truck plants in

Michigan, Kentucky, and Mexico to small-car production, ramping up the output of four-cylinder engines, and introducing Derrick Kuzak's new wrinkle in engine technology branded "Ecoboost" that simultaneously increased power and fuel economy.

Industry analysts were floored that Dearborn was pouring so much money into capital improvements under such dire circumstances. But Mulally was so composed and seemingly impervious to the state of panic building in Detroit. "It's just so volatile now that we thought the best thing that we can do is really focus on what we're doing on the product side," he said.

Jerry York was ecstatic about Ford's determination to charge forward with its small-car plans despite its terrible financial results. "This is beautiful stuff, my friend," he told Leclair on the phone. "Pass our best regards on to Alan."

As long as Ford kept chugging, Kirk Kerkorian would keep buying. He owned 141 million shares now, almost 6.5 percent of its common stock. And he was convinced he had finally bet on a winner in Detroit.

In early August, Kerkorian walked into the Beverly Wilshire Hotel for lunch, his impressive-sized bodyguard at his side. Ninety-one years old, but as fit and trim as a man decades younger, he wore a white shirt, dark slacks, and a buttery soft white leather jacket. The maître d' at the hotel's posh restaurant, The Blvd, escorted him to his usual corner table, in the back near the kitchen. He ordered Evian water, a special vegetable soup the chef made just for him, a "small portion" of broiled chicken, and a little bowl of blueberries and strawberries for dessert. It was the daily repast of a billionaire who still drove himself around L.A. in an old-model Jeep and waited on line at the movie theater for tickets. Kerkorian wasn't at all like the caricature of the big-money mogul or tough takeover artist. He never felt comfortable talking a lot, never felt educated enough. "If I could talk like Trump, I would," he joked. "But I can't."

He was old-school. And that's what he liked about Ford. They talked the talk and walked the walk. "I really like them," he said over lunch. "Bill Ford is a really nice guy. Alan Mulally has been a success before. And we want success." The mention of Rick Wagoner's name caused Kerkorian to show a rare flash of anger. "He said he'd look at the Nissan deal honestly, and they never did," he said. "Now why would he say that when he didn't mean it?"

Kerkorian didn't want to meddle at Ford. If they needed money, he was there to help. He was already talking with his partners in Las Vegas—a group of oil-rich Saudi investors—about participating in a financial aid package for Ford Credit. And he saw no rush to do anything about the Ford family. "Why?" he asked innocently. "I prefer just buying the common shares." And how high was he willing to go? "I'd say that 9.9 percent sounds about right," he said. "Then we'll see."

One thing about Detroit always bugged him, and that was the notion that the Big Three's fates were intertwined, that failure was contagious in the American auto industry. Kerkorian didn't believe that for a second. "They say if one goes down, they'll all go down together," he said. "Now who would say that? Why?" If Ford had a better plan and better people, it could win. That, he said, was the way the game was played.

What about GM? Did he see a possibility that an investor might ride in and save General Motors? "Buy GM?" he said over a last bite of berries. "Well, now's the time for somebody to do it . . . before it really gets bad."

On August 4, 2008, while Mulally was strategizing with the Ford team in Dearborn, Bill Ford was on his way to the Michigan state capital, Lansing, to meet Senator Barack Obama.

The one-on-one with the frontrunner for the Democratic presidential nomination had been arranged by Governor Jennifer Granholm, who was a close personal friend and ally of Bill's. It was critical for him to get to know this young, environmentally minded candidate for president. The election was just three months away, and the Illinois senator was starting to look like a winner.

So much of what was happening to the domestic auto industry had political overtones. Ford was now aware that GM was planning to go to Washington soon to lobby for aid money. Specifically, Wagoner wanted to get his hands on some of the $25 billion in Department of Energy loans that had been authorized by Congress when it passed new fuel economy standards for cars and trucks. The loans were designed to be seed money for technology to meet the tougher standards.

But the $25 billion wasn't in the budget yet, and GM was taking no chances. It needed that money, and not just for greener cars. Bill had a growing sense that the federal government would be intimately involved with whatever went down in Detroit in the coming months. And he wanted to make a personal connection with Obama now and gain insight into how the industry would fit into his presidential agenda.

Obama had gotten a huge, enthusiastic crowd for his speech on energy at Michigan State University. And he had received a powerful introduction from Granholm, the second-term Democratic governor who was determined to deliver the state's electoral votes for Obama in the November election. The cheers came in waves when Obama promised to help Michigan out of its economic woes. "I know how much the auto industry and the autoworkers of this state have struggled over the last decade or so," Obama said. "But I also know where I want the fuel-efficient cars of tomorrow to be built—not in Japan, not in China, but right here in the United States of America. Right here in the state of Michigan!"

Afterward, the senator and Bill Ford met alone. Obama had been very forthright on the campaign trail about Detroit's past sins, such as its opposition to higher fuel economy rules, its dependence on gas-guzzling trucks, and its inability to change. He had echoed those points in his speech, which centered on his plans to end America's addiction to foreign oil.

"We desperately need a new energy policy in this country," Obama told Bill. "And I would like the domestic auto industry to be part of the solution, not part of the problem."

"I for one am really excited about that," Bill said. "We'd love to work with your administration. I passionately believe that Ford can and should be part of the solution. That's why I'm here. Frankly, we've been on this path now for some time, and I don't think we've told our story terribly well."

Then he went through Ford's transformation—smaller cars, cleaner engines, electric vehicles in development. "The vision I have is for us to be a global, green, high-tech company," Bill said. "And that's not just a vision. We have lots of concrete examples of what's here and what's coming."

The two men hit it off and then got technical—how to build batteries for electric cars, create an infrastructure of charging stations, target tax credits to shift consumers into superefficient vehicles. When it was over, they shook hands like new friends. Bill felt great. Everything Obama wanted, he wanted too. "I think he's exactly in line," Bill said, "with where society wants us to go."

Green cars were also very much on Rick Wagoner's mind. In late summer, Wagoner told Lutz that the single biggest product responsibility on his plate was to deliver a working version of the Chevrolet Volt plug-in hybrid by September 16—the day General Motors would celebrate its one hundredth birthday at a lavish ceremony at the Renaissance Center. "Bob, we need it then," he said.

Wagoner was gearing up for the ultimate sales job—to convince the federal government to help GM in its hour of need. The presidential campaign was about to kick into overdrive, with Obama, the liberal agent of change, matching up with the way more conservative Republican candidate, Senator John McCain of Arizona. The incumbent Bush administration was already swamped with the financial crisis on Wall Street, and Congress was in the midst of its own reelection frenzy. If GM was to get any kind of positive reception on Capitol Hill and in the White House, it needed a powerful message. It could not come limping in and begging for a bailout. GM had to represent progress, innovation, and a bright future. That's where the Volt came in. It was the one car that GM had that nobody else had, and the perfect blend of electric power and consumer convenience.

When the battery ran down, a little motor kicked in and kept it going. What could be smarter than that?

Lutz had already been riding the Volt team hard. He was just as psyched up about the car as Wagoner. For once, he could stick it to Toyota with a hybrid model that was better than theirs. But he wasn't sure about the September timetable. The Volt wouldn't even go on sale for another two years. Was it really necessary to have it ready for the GM birthday party?

Yes, said Wagoner. It wasn't an option. GM needed that car.

[Twenty-Seven]

How does a company celebrate its one hundredth anniversary? In GM's case, the planning had started three years early, with a special team, a multimillion-dollar budget, and a set of goals. Rick Wagoner was intimately involved from the start. "I want this to be 85 percent about the future and 15 percent history," he told his staff. Sometime along the way, he approved the theme: "GMnext." For all of its storied past, General Motors was looking ahead, secure in the belief that it would continue to lead the industry for years to come.

At 8:00 A.M. on September 16, hundreds of invited guests and employees took their seats and lined the balconies in the Renaissance Center's Wintergarden—a soaring, glass-roofed atrium of shops and restaurants overlooking the Detroit River. Outside, scores of people gathered to watch the proceedings on giant video screens. Fifty polished Corvettes gleamed in the autumn sun on the riverfront plaza, near a large map of the world inlaid in the walkway, with twinkling lights representing every GM factory on the planet.

But for all the pre-party buildup, GMnext Day was oddly static. For more than an hour, the assembled watched a stream of live videos beamed from around the world, as international executives made speeches into the camera about their GM business units in Mexico, Canada, Brazil, Germany, Italy, South Africa, Australia, Korea, China, India, and on and on and on. When that finally ended, Wagoner stepped to the podium.

General Motors has an "awesome" history and a "tremendous" heritage, Wagoner said. But its first century was only the beginning. GM had a responsibility to mankind, a duty to improve and perfect the machine that transformed people's lives. Then Wagoner told a story of how twenty months earlier, GM had set out to produce the most practical and fuel-efficient car ever made. "The Volt is symbolic of what GM stands for today," he said. "The Volt symbolizes GM's commitment to the future. General Motors' second century starts right . . . now." And then the Volt came onstage, with Bob Lutz behind the wheel—a small silver car powered by a four-hundred-pound battery pack, capable of going forty miles on electricity and another three hundred miles with the aid of a little four-cylinder engine. It was the answer, the statement, the proof that GM was still the king of the car world. The Wintergarden erupted in applause and cheers. The second the speech was over, the crowd swarmed around the car, drawn to it like a magnet. Lutz held court in the middle of the horde, like a proud father basking in the glow of his latest creation.

But Wagoner bolted right after the Volt arrived. A corporate jet was waiting at Detroit Metropolitan Airport to take him to Washington for meetings with House Democrats about the $25 billion in energy loans. That night, he addressed the Economic Club of Washington. In his speech, Wagoner emphasized that the energy loans were a key part of the 2007 legislation mandating a 40 percent increase in corporate average fuel economy (also known as CAFE). These loans were part of those regulations, not anything like the taxpayer dollars being spent to bail out Wall Street. "Nobody called it a bailout then, because it wasn't," he said. "And it still isn't."

The next day, Alan Mulally and Bob Nardelli joined Wagoner for a meeting with House Speaker Nancy Pelosi. The energy loans were available to any automaker that met the criteria for improved fuel economy, so it made sense for Ford and Chrysler to be there. Pelosi, a California Democrat and staunch believer in the highest fuel economy standards possible, was very reassuring. The loan money would be put in the federal budget, she told them. And a week later the House approved the $25 billion program, which was meant for projects exactly like the Volt. The Department of Energy had two months to write all the rules, and then it would accept applications. With any luck, the first loans would be available to the Big Three by the end of the year.

When Steve Feinberg found out about the unsuccessful GM-Ford merger talks, he dispatched Bob Nardelli to GM to offer Chrysler as an alternative.

Nardelli and Tom LaSorda had tried to pitch a GM-Chrysler deal in the early summer. But Wagoner hadn't been interested. "We've got too much else going on," he said. "Doing something with you guys would be too much of a distraction." A lot had changed since then. GM was now desperate for cash and had just moved to draw the last $3.5 billion in a long-existing credit line with JPMorgan Chase and Citigroup. As rickety as Chrysler was, it had about $10 billion in borrowed money on its balance sheet, which could stabilize GM in the short run.

Wagoner still wasn't keen on the idea, but this time Henderson and Lutz prevailed upon him. "Rick, we can pick up all their assets but not the fixed costs," Lutz said. "Shit, the first-year synergies alone are like $7 billion."

Nardelli went down to the Renaissance Center with LaSorda and Jim Press and enthusiastically made the case for a merger to Wagoner and Henderson. "Why shouldn't we put GM and Chrysler together?" Nardelli said. "There are billions and billions of dollars' worth of synergies—starting with me. I'm not trying to run it. I'll do everything I can to work through the transition and then leave."

It was a revealing comment. The walls were closing in on Nardelli at Chrysler. The losses were getting uglier and the company was scrambling for partners. In public, Nardelli remained confident, showing off electric concept cars and touting Chrysler's future plans. But in private, he complained about the constant uphill battle to make Chrysler relevant in the marketplace. "This is a million times harder than I thought it would be," he said. A GM merger was the perfect way out.

Nardelli had grown up in General Electric, where acquisitions were a way of life. He got goose bumps talking about the synergies (the code word for job cuts) between GM and Chrysler. "Why am I keeping Sterling Heights open with one shift when you've got plants open with one shift?" he told Wagoner. "I know you guys want our Jeep with your Hummer. We could rationalize everything!"

Feinberg and Jimmy Lee, the JPMorgan Chase executive, were agitating for the deal too. Chrysler had become such a burden that Feinberg was prepared to give it away for GM stock. Cerberus could then keep Chrysler Financial, marry it with GMAC, and hopefully salvage the credit side of the business. Feinberg's automotive nightmare kept getting worse. The Germans had come back to haunt him about Chrysler. Daimler was in a frenzy to dump its 19.9 percent interest in Chrysler and wanted Cerberus to buy it. Feinberg was sick of these people. Dieter Zetsche had sold him a shell of a car company with Chrysler, and now Daimler was demanding all sorts of payments for foreign taxes and distribution costs related to the deal. "The Germans are impossible on everything," Feinberg groaned. "I'm pretty sure they wanted us to fail from day one."

He worked hard to persuade the GM executives to take Chrysler. "We'll give our equity away," he told Fritz Henderson. "Bob will stay with it. We'll give you all of our guys, anything to make it a winner. If we put the two companies together, we can save $10 billion." Henderson didn't need any convincing. He was so stressed about GM's downward spiral, he'd try anything. But there were a lot of weird moving parts at Chrysler, especially with the banks that were lending it money.

Jimmy Lee was increasingly anxious to get JPMorgan Chase's

money back. But even as he pushed for a sale to GM, he wasn't willing to loosen the banks' stranglehold on Chrysler's assets.

Nevertheless, Henderson pushed back. "You need to release your collateral so we can actually close some of these plants," he said.

Lee said they were not going to do that.

"Well, then," said Henderson, "how do you expect to do this deal?"

It was hard to imagine how Henderson could even concentrate on Chrysler. U.S. auto sales fell below one million units in September, which hadn't happened in fifteen years. The entire market dropped 26 percent. GM actually did better than most of its competitors, but it was only because the company was pouring inventory into rental fleets. In early October, its stock price plunged below $7—the lowest since 1953. "I knew things were going to get really bad, so therefore I'm not surprised," Henderson said. "But these are the worst of times."

The strain was starting to show at Ford too. Mark Fields and Don Leclair were at each other's throats again. At one meeting, Fields was talking about how a new vehicle could help gain market share, but Leclair stopped him.

"What are you talking about?" Leclair snapped. "We haven't done that in fifteen years."

The situation was becoming toxic, the first fissure in the Mulally team. Leclair had alienated several senior executives with his abrasive comments and secretive ways. So far Mulally had tolerated it, though only because Leclair was valuable as a watchdog on costs. But in September, Fields and two other executives went to see Bill Ford and threatened to resign if Leclair stayed.

Fields had lost all patience with Leclair, and he let Bill know it. "You have got to talk to Alan, and you have got to take care of the situation," he said. "You're running the risk of losing key senior management, including myself." Then he stopped himself, realizing he shouldn't be telling the executive chairman of Ford what to do.

But Bill was ready to oust Leclair anyway. Joe Laymon had been whispering in his ear that Leclair had gotten way too close to Jerry York and couldn't be trusted. Bill had the same concerns.

Bill Ford sent Fields to see Mulally, who reluctantly agreed that Leclair had to go. Fortunately, the company had an able replacement ready in Lewis Booth, who was running Ford of Europe.

It all happened quickly. Leclair agreed to take his retirement package and leave quietly. Ford released an official explanation on October 10, saying that Leclair wanted to spend more time with his family. Mulally had kind words for the departed chief financial officer on his way out the door. "Don's expertise and business acumen have been invaluable," he said.

The praise was little consolation for Leclair, who had been with Ford for thirty-two years. His shining moment was the big borrowing in 2006 that was now saving the company. But Leclair was stuck in the old Ford, where internal warfare was the norm. He just couldn't adapt to the new culture.

"Don wasn't a team player," said Farley. "He didn't get along with the other executives. And he flat-out said several times that we couldn't stabilize market share . . . that we were dreaming."

Leclair turned down all interview requests and basically took a vow of silence about Ford. But his departure raised lots of questions from his biggest admirer. "What the fuck happened to Leclair?" Jerry York blurted out to a friend in Detroit. "I'm guessing the family pushed him out because of us. They must be scared shitless."

But it was actually Kirk Kerkorian who was getting worried. In ten days he would start selling off his Ford stock. The dismal economy had ravaged the market value of his casino empire. And as much as he liked Alan Mulally and Ford's long-term prospects, he couldn't afford to keep a big chunk of his fortune in a faltering auto company. In a brief statement, he said it was time to "reallocate" his resources.

The depths of Detroit's troubles were laid bare when the secret GM-Chrysler talks became public in the media on October 11, prompting both sides to characterize the discussions as "preliminary." The news rattled investors and analysts who failed to see how GM would be better off with broken-down Chrysler on board.

No one was more upset than Ron Gettelfinger, who immediately began hounding Fritz Henderson about the details. How many workers would be affected if GM bought Chrysler? When he learned that the estimates started at ten thousand job cuts—and escalated from there—he vowed to oppose the deal with all his might. Feinberg and Nardelli tried to convince Gettelfinger that GM and Chrysler would be stronger together than apart, that the banks would lend them money and Cerberus might even invest more. But he wasn't buying any of it. "Gettelfinger just doesn't like it," Feinberg said. "He's incredibly suspicious. He's afraid GM is just going to pound Chrysler."

Gettelfinger's opposition had major political repercussions. The union was working like mad to get Barack Obama elected president in November. The UAW was still one of most formidable constituent groups in the Democratic Party. At the same time, the union was a constant thorn for Republicans. Once it entered the picture, political stances hardened like cement. Few Democrats would support an issue the union didn't want. And conversely, anything that favored the UAW was like poison to many Republicans. The union was a lightning rod and added a volatile emotional element to any political debate about Detroit.

And that debate was drawing closer by the day. By mid-October, the market for new vehicles in the United States had completely unraveled. The annual selling rate had plummeted to ten million units. GM's sales were running 45 percent below those of the year before. Few businesses of any kind could cope with the loss of that kind of revenue. But the auto industry, with its enormous payrolls and fixed costs, was spectacularly ill-equipped to handle it. The banking crisis, the lack of available credit, the abysmal level of consumer confidence—it all added up to disaster.

Rick Wagoner was now convinced that GM was a victim of economic circumstances beyond its control and that it deserved the assistance of the federal government. The energy loans couldn't come quickly enough. The merger talks were a sideshow. The collapse was happening too fast for a deal to get done with Chrysler.

The GM board was shell-shocked. "These were unbelievable events taking place in the market," said John Bryan. "The board felt strongly that we needed to put our case before [the government]." Wagoner concurred. "If there hadn't been an explosion in the credit markets and the economy hadn't tanked in an unprecedented way, we wouldn't need any money," he said.

Wagoner was right. The economy and gas prices wrecked the environment to sell cars, and no one could have predicted that. But the car market had been tumbling for months. GM had made some tough decisions to cut costs and scale back production, but it hadn't made them soon enough and it sure hadn't prepared for a cash crunch like this.

The only source of immediate funding was the U.S. Treasury. Bob Lutz was skeptical that GM would get fair treatment in Washington. "Those people down there hate us," he moaned. But the government was doling out billions to financial institutions as part of the emergency Troubled Asset Relief Program (TARP). Henderson, however, shuddered at the thought of GM going down to Washington with its hand out. "Once you go to the government for financing, Pandora's box opens," Henderson wrote to Wagoner in an e-mail. "And it usually comes with a lot of different things you either expect or you don't expect—which could include, among other things, losing our jobs."

On October 13, Wagoner and two GM directors, John Bryan and Erskine Bowles, went to Washington for a meeting with Treasury Secretary Henry Paulson. Bryan was sent by the GM board specifically because he had a long relationship with Paulson, dating back to when Bryan was chief executive of the Sara Lee food company in Chicago and Paulson was his corporate banker with Goldman Sachs.

Before the meeting began, Paulson took Bryan into his office. Bryan could see that Paulson was totally consumed with the financial crisis and unable to focus on a sputtering car company from

Detroit. "He had bigger things going on," said Bryan. "He was just about to bring all the bankers in the world in to inject capital, and he really wasn't ready to sit down and help solve this problem." Paulson also had a philosophical bias against propping up GM. He told Bryan that big industrial companies can drag out their financial problems, as opposed to banks, which have to shut down the moment they can't cover their deposits.

"Hank, I don't think that's the case here," Bryan said. "We've got supplier payments on certain days. And we're running out of money."

Paulson recounted in his book *On the Brink* that he was reluctant to even entertain GM's request for aid. "I believed that TARP was not meant to bolster industrial companies but to prevent a collapse of the financial system," Paulson wrote. Still, he felt he owed GM an audience, and asked Commerce Secretary Carlos Gutierrez to attend the meeting as well.

Once the meeting started, Wagoner made a pitch for $10 billion in government funding—a $5 billion loan and a $5 billion line of credit. "We need a bridge loan, and we need it quickly," he told Paulson. "I don't believe we can make it past November 7."

But Paulson stopped him right there. "I have no authority to make a TARP loan to General Motors," he said bluntly. Though he understood the gravity of GM's situation, he was turning it over to Gutierrez. The Commerce chief, he said, would work with GM going forward.

The GM contingent was stunned. The Commerce Department had no funding or authority to save the company. But Wagoner could not have picked a worse time to appeal for help. He didn't know that President Bush was dead set against doing anything for GM before the November election. In his memoir, *Decision Points*, Bush wrote that he vowed not to make a politically charged decision about Detroit while the country was in the midst of choosing a new president. "I didn't think it was a coincidence that the warnings about bankruptcy came right before the upcoming elections," Bush wrote. "I refused to make a decision about the auto industry until after the vote."

. . . .

It was panic time. The talks between GM and Chrysler got more intense, with JPMorgan Chase applying additional pressure. The two sides were now discussing eliminating as many as forty thousand employees in a merger. At the same time, the banks in Chrysler's debt consortium were weighing in on which executive they would like to see manage the combined companies—Wagoner, Henderson, or Nardelli.

While the negotiations ground on, both automakers continued to cut costs. GM said it was preparing to lay off a large number of salaried workers. Chrysler planned to slash five thousand white-collar employees—a 25 percent reduction—by the end of the year. "These are truly unimaginable times for our industry," Nardelli said in a somber e-mail to employees. And in a move that underscored the dismal situation at Chrysler, Daimler said in a financial filing that it had written down the value of its 19.9 percent stake in its former partner to zero.

The rejection by the Treasury Department forced GM to go to plan B—Congress. The strategy was to lobby the House and Senate leadership to convert the $25 billion in energy loans into an emergency aid package and possibly to get additional money to fund the UAW health care trusts. The industry's point man was John Dingell, the eighty-two-year-old congressman from west of Detroit who chaired the House Energy and Commerce Committee. A group of governors from states with large automotive operations would also be involved. And hundreds of car dealers were being mobilized to support the effort, as well as GM employees and suppliers across the country.

The message was also crystallizing. This plea for help was not simply to save GM or Chrysler, but rather to prevent an economic catastrophe on the order of the Great Depression. A study by the industry-backed Center for Automotive Research began circulating to the media and lawmakers in Washington. The document calculated that more than three million jobs in the United States were related to auto manufacturing, from the plants to the supply chain to the dealers to the communities dependent on the Big Three. The numbers were not necessarily in dispute, but the thesis was frightening. If GM or Chrysler crashed, the entire industry would topple. Even the Japanese-owned factories in the United States would be impacted by a disruption in the supply network that made parts for all the companies. This was not just a question of using taxpayer dollars to fix Detroit. It was an investment in the national interest—and woe to the country if the money wasn't there.

By the end of October, Treasury officials were in contact with GM's finance executives on a daily basis about how much cash they had. The Commerce and Energy departments were also in constant discussions with the company, and the White House was monitoring the situation. Major media outlets around the world were covering Detroit as a fast-breaking story. The fate of the American auto industry had become a hot-button issue in the final days of the 2008 presidential election.

On November 5, 2008, Barack Obama was elected the forty-fourth president of the United States. The victory was greeted by cheers in Big Three auto plants, where union workers had turned out in large numbers for Obama. His election was a rare moment of triumph at Solidarity House in Detroit. For years Gettelfinger had been a vocal critic of the Bush administration's labor and trade policies, and he had invested tons of UAW resources into Obama's campaign. But the union chief was hardly in a mood to celebrate. He had reluctantly been drawn into the GM-Chrysler talks and was more worried than ever that the deal would devastate their workforces. The companies were leaning on Gettelfinger to support the deal or risk seeing two of the Big Three tumble into bankruptcy. He needed counsel and called Steve Girsky, the former GM advisor who was now working for a private equity firm.

"I need your help," Gettelfinger said. "GM and Chrysler want to get together, and they want us to make a decision quickly. Will you come on as an advisor for us?"

Girsky agreed and promptly reached out to Fritz Henderson, Tom LaSorda, and executives at Cerberus and JPMorgan Chase. Girsky thought he knew GM as well anyone on the outside. But he was shocked at how tenuous its financial condition had become. The company was headed for insolvency in a matter of weeks, and a merger wouldn't stop that from happening. Once he got a handle on it, he called Gettelfinger on Election Day from his home in West-chester County, north of New York.

"Ron, you don't need to worry about a GM-Chrysler merger," Girsky said. "You have to worry about something bigger. Your biggest constituency is going out of business."

Alan Mulally wasn't entirely sure why he was sitting next to Rick Wagoner, Bob Nardelli, and Ron Gettelfinger in Nancy Pelosi's office on November 6. But he knew he had to be there.

Wagoner had already been to Washington to ask for aid, and Mulally was aware that the energy loans could be a component of an assistance package for Detroit. But Mulally didn't have a clue about what would happen next. "I was generally aware that Rick was talking to the Bush administration," he said. "We were all in on the conversation now. But it was all being led by GM being clearer that they were moving toward a crisis."

The GM-Chrysler merger talks died in Pelosi's office when Gettelfinger started protesting the jobs at risk in such a deal. How could Washington give taxpayer dollars to two messed-up car companies that were cutting tens of thousands of American jobs?

The meeting also raised problems about the energy loans. Pelosi was not at all interested in redirecting that money away from fuel-efficient cars to pump up the balance sheet at GM. She would rather challenge the White House to give the industry money under the TARP legislation. The House Speaker also said if the government gave the industry any assistance, it would come with strings attached, such as limits on executive pay, strict oversight rules, and possibly a requirement to give stock to the government to secure the loans. A subsequent meeting with Senate majority leader Harry Reid, a Democrat from Nevada, underscored the message. If Detroit wanted help, it had better be prepared to have Washington intimately involved in its affairs going forward.

Mulally soaked it all in. His instincts had been right when Wagoner came to the Glass House. GM was on the edge, and that was dangerous. If General Motors collapsed, Ford could be in serious trouble very quickly. Mulally got queasy just thinking about it. Ford didn't need government money. But it could not afford to stand by while GM crashed. He had come too far to let its mistakes derail his plan.

The automakers' third-quarter results came out the day after the meeting with Pelosi. GM had lost $2.5 billion and consumed almost $7 billion in cash. Ford's numbers were just as bad, but it still had substantial cash reserves and a valuable line of credit to tap into. GM, on the other hand, was balancing on a tightrope over shark-infested waters. The merger talks had been suspended. "It's fair to say that liquidity is the top priority for the company," Wagoner said in a massive understatement. But GM would not under any circumstances file for bankruptcy, he said. That would scare off car buyers and make things worse. "We have no plans for anything other than running our business," he said.

Bankruptcy was Wagoner's blind spot. He always cited studies that said consumers would not purchase a new vehicle from a bankrupt carmaker. But the theory had never been tested. The same day that GM and Ford reported earnings, President-elect Obama held the first meeting of his economic transition team at the Hilton Hotel in Chicago. Jennifer Granholm had been chosen as one of its members. The Michigan governor's role was to promote manufacturing, as well as to safeguard the interests of midwestern autoworkers. There were some heavy-duty policy makers in the room: former Treasury secretary Robert Rubin, former Federal Reserve chairman Paul Volcker, and Lawrence Summers, who was in line to become the president's chief economic advisor. As the discussion about the auto industry went around the table, some members of the transition team uttered the phrase "quick-rinse bankruptcy" in reference to GM.

"Bankruptcy is not an option!" Granholm said loudly. "We cannot allow them to go bankrupt. No one will buy cars from a bankrupt company. There are studies that show this."

She noticed that no one else in the room backed her up.

On November 10, Obama met with George W. Bush in the White House. At one point, their historic conversation turned to the troubles in Detroit. The president-elect asked for some assurance from Bush that he would not allow the industry to collapse before Obama took office in January. "I told Barack Obama that I wouldn't let the automakers fail," Bush said in his memoir. "I won't dump this mess on him."

The next day, the House and Senate Democrats crafted a seven-page bill to make the Big Three eligible for $25 billion in TARP loans. But the bill immediately met resistance from the White House and Republicans in Congress. Some lawmakers suggested that the auto CEOs should resign in exchange for aid. All the attitudes and opinions about Detroit were seeping into the discussion: poor management, crummy cars, overpaid workers, too many gas-guzzling trucks. A *New York Times* columnist, Thomas Friedman, asked, "How could these companies be so bad for so long?" The *Wall Street Journal* weighed in with a banner headline: "Just Say No to Detroit."

In the Motor City, the entire community felt like it was being held up to ridicule and scorn. "I never knew," wrote *Detroit Free Press* columnist Susan Tompor, "that Detroit was a dirty word."

Meanwhile, GM was edging closer to disaster. It said in a federal filing that "its ability to continue as a going concern" was in doubt, and that it could run out of cash by January. In that event, the company would be unable to pay suppliers and employees, meet loan covenants, or cover its health care obligations. And without government assistance, there was no way to prevent it. "We do not have other traditional sources of liquidity available to fund these obligations," the company said.

Something had to give, and it would begin in the hearing rooms on Capitol Hill.

The sun was rising on November 18 as Rick Wagoner and Steve Harris walked across the tarmac at the Detroit airport to board a Gulfstream IV jet. Once they were on the plane, they settled into deep leather seats and within minutes were en route to Washington, D.C.

Harris had been at Wagoner's side for years as GM's vice president of communications. Now he would help his boss prepare for the biggest public appearance of his thirty-year career—testifying before the Senate Committee on Banking, Housing, and Urban Affairs. Alan Mulally, Bob Nardelli, and Ron Gettelfinger were on their way to the same hearing, but separately. The first time they would see each other that day was when they sat down side by side in Room 538 of the Dirksen Senate Office Building.

When the GM plane touched down, Wagoner and Harris were driven to the company's Washington offices. The plan was to hold a "mock hearing" over coffee and sandwiches, and to prepare Wagoner for questions from the Senate panel. His tutors were Ken Cole, GM's chief lobbyist, and Stuart Eizenstat, an attorney who had served as domestic policy advisor to President Carter when Chrysler received federal loan guarantees from Congress back in 1979.

Cole started off. The mood about bailouts was nasty, he said. Virtually every member of Congress had been skewered back home by constituents angry about the TARP loans for the banks and the insurance giant AIG. "This is not going to be a pleasant process, Rick," Cole warned. "It's going to be more like theater, a necessary pain you're going to have to get through. They're going to be taking free shots at you."

Then it was Eizenstat's turn. He didn't know Wagoner, but he knew that GM had lots of enemies—Republicans who were anti-union, southerners with Asian car plants in their states, liberals who despised SUVs. The list went on and on. He feared that Wagoner was going to be bombarded with animosity. Eizenstat wanted Wagoner to relax and show the human side of GM. "Rick, I think you've got to just speak from the heart," he said.

Harris had to jump in here. Wagoner never spoke extemporaneously. He followed scripts religiously. More important, Harris was sure there would be questions about money. Wagoner had to be prepared to tell the Senate panel how much cash GM would need to survive. "Rick, do you have a specific number?" he said. "I mean, how much do you need?"

Wagoner seemed hesitant. "Maybe a range," he said.

Another GM staffer, Greg Martin, knew this was a vital point. "They are going to want to know what the number is," he said.

Cole emphasized that the GM chief executive had to hold his own when the tough questions came. "Explain to us why you need this money," he said. "How you got into this mess . . . how you're going to get out of it . . . how you're going to pay us back."

The session went on for ninety minutes. At one point, Wagoner asked if a conference call had been set up with Mulally and Nardelli. When the three chief executives got on the phone, Wagoner asked them how long their statements were and whether they were bringing documents. Other than that, there wasn't much discussion and no coordination.

Harris had a sinking feeling. Cole wanted Wagoner to be ready for battle. Eizenstat thought he should be emotional. Nobody seemed to know exactly what GM was asking for. And Mulally and Nardelli had their own agendas. "This is a shitty game plan," Harris said to himself.

Just before 3:00 P.M. Wagoner walked into the Senate hearing room, which was jammed with reporters, legislative staffers, TV crews, and congressional aides. The room was set up like a courtroom, with the senators at one end and the witness table facing them. Wagoner sat beside Nardelli, who was next to Mulally, who was next to Gettelfinger. Then the gavel came down, and Senator Christopher Dodd, Democrat from Connecticut, brought the hearing to order. He looked out at the packed room and wondered aloud if a football stadium might have been a better venue. "If I had known the interest," he said, "I would have held this at RFK."

Each senator made an opening statement. Some were brief, some long. And after twenty minutes, Wagoner started feeling uncomfortable. The questioning hadn't even started yet, and he had to use the bathroom. *All that coffee was a big mistake,* he thought. *This is going to be rough.*

[Twenty-Eight]

W hy aren't you making money?"

Richard Shelby, a Republican senator from Alabama, was making Rick Wagoner squirm. Shelby had already painted Detroit with a broad, brutal brush—the Big Three were failures, they needed life support, they were begging for help after screwing up their businesses for years. Now he was breaking down the chief executive of General Motors with the bluntest questions possible.

"Because, well, I think two reasons," Wagoner said. "Our . . . our financial results reflected quite significant costs to restructure and . . . and that . . . that has cost . . . cost cash for sure. But hopefully the amount we have going forward, we won't have to decrease our capacity another 30 or 40 percent."

"What have you spent on restructuring, sir?" Shelby asked in a slow southern drawl.

"Sorry?" said Wagoner.

"What have you spent in the last five years on restructuring?" said Shelby. "You spent billions of dollars."

"We have," Wagoner said. "We've spent a lot. I can't give you the exact number, but I can—"

Shelby cut him off. "You can't give us a figure."

Wagoner tried to rally, but it wasn't working. When he lapsed into corporate-speak, he seemed evasive. And when he spoke plainly, it just sounded lame.

Shelby asked why the American people should expect success from Detroit after all its troubles, and Wagoner wasn't able to hit the pitch. "Well, I mean I would say, Senator Shelby, if you look at the actions we've taken this . . . this is hard stuff, and it's required a lot of . . . a lot of good cooperation with the unions," he said.

It got worse and worse. All three CEOs and Ron Gettelfinger tried to get the senators to understand that what was happening in the auto industry was a national calamity. Wagoner's opening statement had sounded scary. "This is all about a lot more than just Detroit," he said. "It's about saving the U.S. economy from a catastrophic collapse." Gettelfinger chimed in with his own grim prognosis. "Without question, in our mind, it is dire, it is critical, it is a crisis," he said. Bob Nardelli wasted no time casting blame elsewhere. "We're asking for assistance for one reason," he said. "To address the devastating automotive industry recession caused by our nation's financial meltdown." And Alan Mulally just seemed out of step, reciting facts about Ford's turnaround while making a formal speech about these trying times. "We believe we must join our competitors today in asking for your support," he said, "to gain access to an industry bridge loan that would help us navigate through this difficult economic crisis."

What the executives didn't appreciate was that the twenty-one senators on the panel—eleven Democrats and ten Republicans—were already well aware of how big the auto industry was, how many jobs it represented, and how vital it was to the nation's economy. That was not the issue. The senators were only interested in cause and effect: If the taxpayers loaned billions to these companies, what would they do with the money? How would the industry fix itself? Why should America trust Detroit now?

It was a bipartisan humbling, as senators from both parties took turns dressing down the four witnesses. Bob Corker, a Republican from Tennessee, bore in on which company would get what: "Of the $25 billion that you've asked for, how much of it have you guys decided is going to GM?"

"We felt that, given our proportionate market share of that—" Wagoner began.

"Well, just give me the number," Corker said.

Wagoner tried to answer. "Which would be in the $10 billion to $12 billion that, that we would have a—"

Corker cut him off. "And how much is Ford getting in this three-way pact?" he asked.

"Seven billion to $8 billion," Mulally said.

"Seven billion to $8 billion? So it's $7 billion to $8 billion, and $10 billion to $12 billion. Those are the numbers?" Corker said in an exasperated tone.

The lack of preparation and coordination among the four was obvious. But more startling was the absence of composure and confidence. Wagoner had led the industry to Washington without a coherent plan or a polished script. The hemming and hawing was bad enough, but the obtuse responses and seat-of-the-pants calculations just fed the stereotype of Detroit as a circus wagon of bumbling fools. Of course it wasn't true. These were extremely smart executives known for precision and decision making that affected hundreds of thousands of autoworkers. But that was hardly coming through.

When Wagoner said GM had spent $103 billion on health care and pensions over the past fifteen years, he got incredulous looks instead of sympathy. He was a titan of industry back home. But in the halls of Congress, he was just another corporate suit asking for a bailout. Nobody cared about the Volt—not when GM was burning through $2 billion in cash a month and asking for $12 billion from the U.S. Treasury.

"I'm inclined to be helpful," said Robert Menendez, a Democrat from New Jersey. "But I've got to have a fundamental understanding of why this number wasn't just picked out of the sky."

After three hours, Christopher Dodd, the panel's chairman, mercifully drew the hearing to a close. He knew this performance would not sway enough votes in the Senate to give Detroit anything. "I would love to tell you that in the next couple of days this is going to happen," Dodd said. "I don't think it is. You heard a lot of negative reaction to any ideas [about] providing help at this table."

As soon as the hearing ended, Wagoner jumped up and hustled toward the door. A GM security officer had been blocking the bathroom down the hall so Wagoner could get in there first. When he came out, Wagoner, Steve Harris, and the GM guys dashed into waiting cars and headed back to the company office.

On the way there, Harris tried to process how badly it had gone. "This was a Rick I had never seen before," he said later. "The stuttering, the stammering . . . he was so taken off guard." Wagoner seemed more himself when it was over. He did several TV interviews and went to dinner with Ken Cole and some members of Congress. At no point did he call Mulally or Nardelli to talk about the next day's House hearing.

The Senate treatment was gentle compared to the reception from the House Financial Services Committee on Wednesday morning, November 19.

Steve Harris braced for the worst when he learned that ABC News had filmed the GM, Ford, and Chrysler corporate jets on the ground in D.C. Flying private planes to Washington to ask for billions of taxpayer dollars would go down in the hall of fame of public relations disasters. Representative Gary Ackerman, a Democrat from New York, seized on the imagery. "There's a delicious irony in seeing private luxury jets flying into D.C. and people coming off of them with tin cups in their hands," Ackerman said. "It's almost like seeing guys show up at the soup kitchen in high hat and tuxedo. Couldn't you have downgraded to first class or something, or jet-pooled?"

It went downhill from there. Peter Roskam, a Republican from Illinois, homed in on executive compensation and asked each CEO if he would work for $1 a year in exchange for government loans.

"I don't have a position on that today," Wagoner said.

Mulally, who made $21 million in salary and bonuses in 2007, wasn't going there at all. "I understand the point of the symbol," he said. "But I think I'm okay where I am."

The hearing was tense, long, and oppressive for the four men at the witness table. Everything about Detroit was criticized—moving jobs to Mexico and China, paying union workers too much money, flying around in fancy jets, building big trucks that sucked up gas, acting as if autoworkers were somehow better than other people.

"The vast majority of my constituents are not making anywhere near what GM, Ford, and Chrysler are paying their employees," said Republican member Spencer Bachus of Alabama. The pent-up hostility was amazing. "My constituents do not trust you," declared Michael Capuano, a Massachusetts Democrat.

There was an alarming absence of goodwill or support, except from the midwestern members with auto plants in their districts. And the give-and-take was abysmal, all captured live on cable TV. Even on the second day, Wagoner still couldn't be specific about how much money GM needed. "It's going to depend," he said. "The amount is going to be significant."

By the end of the hearing, the legislation to loan TARP money to the Big Three was dead. The Democratic and Republican leaderships had both given up. "We have to face reality," said Senate majority leader Harry Reid. The votes simply weren't there. House Speaker Nancy Pelosi said the CEOs had failed badly to make their case. "Until they show us the plan, we cannot show them the money," she said. Congress was adjourning. The ball was back in the White House's court. If anyone was going to save Detroit now, it would have to be George W. Bush.

The Big Three were going home empty-handed, without a penny. Wagoner seemed drained and shaky afterward. "This is all part of what we signed up for when we made this request," he said. "I still remain hopeful."

Mulally was just relieved to get out of the hearing room. "My God," he said. "I never want to go through that again."

Gettelfinger, who had watched in amusement as the CEOs were

lambasted for corporate jets and fat paychecks, had the best line on his way out the door. "I have a plane to catch," he said.

The feeling in Detroit was like horrible indigestion, a combination of humiliation, anxiety, and anger. The American automakers were part whipping boy, part laughingstock. *Saturday Night Live* skewered the Big Three bosses in a skit about how their lousy cars broke down on the way to Washington. Editorial writers and conservative talk shows urged Congress to let the companies die a natural death. The *New York Post* illustrated its coverage of the hearings with a photo of the Three Stooges and a collapsed jalopy. A *Wall Street Journal* op-ed piece suggested the U.S. government broker a sale of Detroit's assets to healthy, foreign carmakers such as Toyota or Volkswagen.

Bob Lutz was so mad he could hardly see straight. How could Wagoner have let those politicians bully him like that? "The performance of the three CEOs led by Rick was disgraceful," he said. "It convinced the American public that these guys are idiots. They can't even come up with an argument." He was livid that he'd been instructed not to talk about it in public. "I've been muzzled," he moaned. "If I was testifying, I wouldn't take any of that shit. I'm going to tell my story. It can't possibly alienate them any more than they already are."

Fritz Henderson felt he had witnessed a grisly accident and was now in the wreckage. "It was a mess, it was a disaster," he said. "It was pretty much what I thought it would be."

Steve Feinberg watched the hearings by himself in his office in New York. None of the Cerberus executives wanted to be with him. "I watched it alone," he said, "in utter horror."

At Ford, the executives, engineers, and secretaries huddled around televisions for every minute of the proceedings, cursing and yelling at various members of Congress as they ran roughshod over Mulally and the rest of them. "We were all mad," said Mark Fields. "It was appalling. We're paying these people to represent us?"

At first, Jim Farley was shocked at the venom directed at Detroit.

"Why do these people hate us so much?" he said. Then it dawned on him that these emotions were important and were something that Ford could capitalize on. "The luckiest thing that can happen to us is if the country starts debating about our industry," he said. "It's cool, because we can say we're different than the other two."

Bill Ford got a frantic phone call right after the hearings from Jennifer Granholm, who was watching it in her hotel room in Tel Aviv while on a trade mission to Israel. "Bill, you have got to go down there and be the face of the industry!" she cried. "You have to get out there and tell Congress and the world that we are not afraid of being green, that we know what's important."

Bill had already been besieged with phone calls from Ford family members and suppliers and dealers, begging him to attend the second hearing in Mulally's place. He was as offended as anyone by the reception Ford had received in Washington. But he could not overstep Mulally. He was the CEO—for better or worse. "I couldn't do that to Alan," he said to Granholm. "It's his job, and I can't take it from him."

Nancy Pelosi held out a slim hope of financial aid for the Big Three the day after the hearings. If Detroit could come up with comprehensive plans to fix their businesses by early December, the Democrats would give the legislation one more shot. "We want them to get their act together," said Senator Reid. "The key here is accountability and viability."

Wagoner seized on the offer like a drowning man clutching a life preserver, even though if a new bill was passed, the money might not be there in time to save GM. "It's something that would be nerveracking for us," he said back in Detroit. "But it's the reality we face."

Meanwhile, the GM board finally decided it was willing to consider "all options"—including bankruptcy.

Wagoner still couldn't come to terms with that. "Why would you take that risk," he said, "when the economy is teetering on the brink?"

But at this point GM was pinning all of its hopes on Washington. Wagoner, Henderson, Ray Young, and the entire team would drive themselves to exhaustion to put together a top-notch reorganization plan for Pelosi and Reid. It was government assistance or nothing. There was no merger, bank loan, or mystery investor that could help General Motors—only Uncle Sam.

Chrysler already had its bankruptcy papers ready. Whether Cerberus would finance it if the company filed for Chapter 11 was unclear. Feinberg knew that, in the end, his firm would have to cut loose the car company if it accepted government money. He was just being realistic; there was little chance that Washington would approve a bailout that benefitted private equity.

If Chrysler ever made another comeback, it would be with another new owner. Carlos Ghosn didn't want any part of it; Renault-Nissan had broken off all talks. But Fiat was still hanging around as a potential partner. And despite Chrysler's dire prospects, Feinberg had made up his mind to let Nardelli continue working to save the company. "Bob is special," Feinberg said. "He's hard-nosed, he doesn't take any crap, and he gets the job done." Nardelli was already hunkered down in Auburn Hills, working nonstop to prepare the best possible restructuring plan to bring to Congress on December 2.

And Ford? The Washington hearings were another fork in the road for the guys in the Glass House. Ford did not need the money. Should it go back for another round of hearings just to support GM? Did it need to show Congress its plan?

Ford's first big executive meeting took place the day after the hearings. The conference room was totally silent as Mulally recounted his experience. "Nothing could prepare you for how mad and disappointed they were," Mulally said. "I felt like I was running guns or drugs." He understood the anti-bailout hostility, but it was incredibly revealing to hear how fed up people were with Detroit. "I mean, I came to help," he said. "I'm part of the answer, not the problem. I have a goddamned business plan. Stop yelling at me." He looked around the room at Bill Ford, Farley, Fields, Kuzak, and Lewis Booth, the new finance chief, and asked them the hard question. "So do we go back?" he said. "And do we submit a business plan?"

This was a juncture in history, the exact moment when the Big Three parted ways forever. For decades, these three auto companies had moved in lockstep, whether it was the cars they built or the wages they paid or the mistakes they made. They had always fought like brothers in the same house and played by their own unique, inbred set of rules. But not anymore. Ford was going in one direction, and GM and Chrysler were going in another.

Yes, Mulally thought Ford should go back to Washington when the time came. "If GM went into a free fall, it could turn the U.S. recession into a depression," he said. "So we had to go." But he would not ask for a loan or special treatment. He would be there to show the world that Ford had a plan and could stand on its own. Ford would do the right thing and support the industry. That was smart business. And in the process it would prove the doubters wrong and demonstrate that there was at least one car company from Detroit that had its act together.

The misery index kept climbing in the Motor City. On the day before Thanksgiving in 2008, five thousand salaried workers walked out of Chrysler, buyout checks in hand. People wept and hugged in the parking lots as they hauled out their personal belongings. Katrina Harris, a Detroit native who had started as a summer intern at Chrysler fourteen years before, said she wanted to get out with something before the company crumbled. Still, it was an emotional decision. "Chrysler is all I know," she said. "I'm giving myself a year to kind of tread water, and then I may have to move out of Michigan to find something." Jim Burns, a twenty-two-year Chrysler veteran, took the buyout too. "I've been through previous downturns, but there was always a light at the end of the tunnel," he said. "This time I'm not seeing any progress. I couldn't turn it down."

Other workers vowed to stick it out. "I'm better off collecting as many paychecks as I can and trying to hang on," said Diane Pierse, a forty-five-year-old mother of two. "There's a lot of hard work ahead of us, but I want to ride it out and be here when it turns around." But the empty cubicles were adding up at the Chrysler tech center. Whole floors in the headquarters tower were vacant. One of America's proudest industrial companies was being hollowed out in a last-ditch bid to cut costs and save itself.

It was time for big changes, both substantive and symbolic. GM shut down its corporate jet terminal at Metro Airport and said it was putting its seven planes up for sale. Ron Gettelfinger held a news conference at Solidarity House and offered two major concessions to help secure a bailout—suspending the jobs bank entirely and allowing the companies to delay their first huge payments into the retiree health care trusts. "We're willing to take an extra step here," he said.

On December 2, the new, improved business plans were submitted to Congress—with higher price tags. GM said it needed $4 billion in loans to stay afloat until the end of the year, and a grand total of $18 billion to survive. Chrysler requested $7 billion, while Ford asked for a $9 billion line of credit but no actual loans. All three companies vowed to further streamline their operations and accelerate production of their most fuel-efficient cars and hybrid models. GM also began negotiations with its bondholders to cut its debt in half to $30 billion.

To dramatize their newfound respect for frugality, the three chief executives drove from Detroit to Washington for the next round of hearings. Mulally conducted interviews on his cell phone while an aide drove a Ford Escape hybrid; Wagoner talked to Jennifer Granholm and others while he was cruising to D.C. in a hybrid version of the Chevy Malibu. "I know how politicians think, Rick," Granholm urged him. "Don't read from a script. Look them in the eye. Tell them that you are not going to resist change and that you are going to lead this industry to help the nation achieve its goals." Wagoner thanked her and promised that this time would be different.

And it was different. Wagoner seemed sharper and more direct, contrite rather than entitled. "We're here today because we made mistakes, which we are learning from, and because some forces beyond our control have pushed us to the brink," he told the Senate panel. "Most importantly, we're here because saving General Motors, and all this company represents, is a job worth doing."

Nardelli bore the brunt of criticism for—no surprise—Chrysler's links to Cerberus. Senator Corker provoked him with his brisk assessment that Chrysler was just a pawn in a private equity game.

"Chrysler doesn't really want to be a stand-alone business," Corker said. "You want to hang around long enough so you can date somebody and hope to get married soon before you run out of money."

The analogy riled Nardelli. "I can assure you, Senator, that I don't wake up every morning thinking of selling the company," he snapped.

Corker couldn't resist comparing Chrysler to a woman trying to make herself more attractive to a partner. "While this is happening you're going to be going to spas and getting facials and trying to get someone to marry you," he jibed.

That really set Nardelli off. "I've been married for thirty-eight years," he said.

Corker just shook his head. "I was talking about your company," he said.

But it was Mulally who seemed like a new man in the hearings. He had worked for hours and hours with his staff to craft a compact speech and mission statement that explained the One Ford plan and how Dearborn had already changed its ways. The operative wording was "used to be," as in how the old Ford behaved versus the new, improved Ford. "It used to be that we had too many brands," he said. "Now we have a laser focus on our most important brand: the Ford Blue Oval." He went through all the things Ford "used to be" and how it had evolved for the better.

Ford didn't want any government money, Mulally said. It would take a line of credit if it was offered but nothing more. Ford had nothing to apologize for and didn't need to beg. He promised that Ford was making a comeback on its own. "There is a lot more work to do," Mulally said. "But we are passionate about the future of Ford."

As the hearings dragged on, the Democratic leadership battled bailout fatigue to put together a new, palatable rescue plan for Detroit. A $15 billion short-term loan package was now in the works; Speaker Pelosi was even willing to use energy loan funds if they were replenished in the future. And there would be tough restrictions attached to the money—no executive bonuses, no private jets, no dividends, stock warrants equal to 20 percent of the loans, and a car czar appointed by the president to oversee operations and expenses.

But Republicans lined up to attack the package. They wanted wage and benefit cuts for the union workers too. President-elect Obama also shared his opinion, saying senior management "should go" if they couldn't make the hard choices to fix their companies. Senator Dodd went a step further and suggested Wagoner ought to resign to give GM a clean slate.

A showdown was looming on Capitol Hill, with the fate of GM and Chrysler in the balance. Would the economy collapse if General Motors closed its doors? Nobody wanted to test whether what Wagoner warned of would come true. But this was an edgy atmosphere— a lame duck Congress, a new president coming to the White House, growing resentment over TARP, and an old, battered industry on the brink. Washington would have to decide: Did America care enough about its automakers to rescue them?

In the streets and churches and taverns and community centers of Detroit, residents were worried sick about what might happen next. Every day, Bishop Charles Ellis III heard from his congregation at the enormous Greater Grace Temple on the city's northwest side. "They'd say to me, 'Bishop, please pray for us,'" he said. "You could feel the fears rising, the nerves unraveling."

Most of his people were union workers at Ford, GM, and Chrysler. They watched the hearings and saw the animosity directed toward their employers and their way of life. This was a threat and a challenge to rise up. "We finally realized this was not a slam dunk for the Big Three to get these loans," Bishop Ellis said. "So we came up with the idea to dedicate our Sunday service to the automotive industry."

On December 7, churches all over Detroit prayed for federal aid. At one, a sign out front beckoned worshipers to come in and hear about "God's bailout plan." Roman Catholic churches distributed a special letter from Cardinal Adam Maida, the archbishop, urging people to maintain their faith "at this darkest time of the year." And at Greater Grace Temple, the largest church in the city, four thousand people attended a special service called "A Hybrid Hope." Parked on the wide altar were three gas-electric hybrid sport-utility vehicles—a Chevrolet Tahoe, a Ford Escape, and a Chrysler Aspen. The service opened with a hymn, "I'm Looking for a Miracle," and a reading from the Book of Romans: "I consider that our present sufferings are not worth comparing with the glory that will be revealed to us."

Autoworkers and executives, union officials and car salesmen all crowded into the pews and around the altar to sing, pray, and join hands in a show of unity. One of the first speakers was General Holiefield, the head of the UAW's Chrysler division. "We have done all we can in this union, so I turn it over to the Lord," he said. In Bishop Ellis's sermon, he beseeched the United States Congress to help Detroit out of its desperate plight. "We have never seen as midnight an hour as we face this coming week," he said. "I don't know what's going to happen, but we need prayer."

On December 8, congressional Democrats sent a draft of a new auto rescue bill to the White House, but senior officials there raised specific concerns. The Bush administration insisted that any automaker asking for federal funds needed to come up with a long-term viability plan.

A key clause was inserted requiring extensive restructuring blueprints to be submitted to the government no later than March 2009. With that compromise written in, the House approved the $14 billion bailout for GM and Chrysler on December 10 by a vote of 237–170. The vote was largely split along party lines. The bill still faced huge hurdles in the Senate, where it needed sixty votes to pass.

That afternoon, President George W. Bush sent his chief of staff, Joshua Bolten, and Vice President Dick Cheney to pitch the legislation to Republican senators at their regular weekly caucus lunch. Cheney said the GOP ran the risk of being pilloried as "the party of Herbert Hoover" if they did nothing to prevent the auto industry's collapse.

But the Senate Republicans were in no mood to follow Bush's lead. They were upset that the UAW might benefit from taxpayer assistance without making any substantial concessions. And GM and Chrysler, they argued, would still be structurally unsound even after getting government money. Senator Richard Shelby dubbed the proposal "a travesty" and vowed to filibuster the bill if it made it to a vote.

The Senate minority leader, Mitch McConnell of Kentucky, deputized Bob Corker to negotiate tougher terms for both the automakers and the union. Early on the morning of December 11, Corker called Fritz Henderson, who was working at GM's offices in New York. The Republicans had three conditions, he said, to support an aid package: GM and Chrysler had to cut their debt by two-thirds, the union had to take stock instead of cash for half of their VEBA funding, and the UAW had to agree to reduce wages and benefits within a year to match the foreign transplant factories. Henderson readily agreed to everything. Then Corker called Ron Gettelfinger in Detroit.

Corker asked Gettelfinger if the union was willing to enter talks with him on the bailout bill. The union chief was very wary.

"Who are you representing here?" Gettelfinger asked.

Corker assured him he was speaking for the Republican caucus.

Okay, said Gettelfinger. He would send Alan Reuther, the union's legislative director and a nephew of UAW pioneer Walter Reuther, to negotiate on his behalf. That afternoon, Reuther arrived at the Capitol to meet with Corker and Democrat senators Christopher Dodd and Richard Durbin. They convened in the stately hearing room of the Senate Foreign Relations Committee for what would be a long, dramatic afternoon that wore on into the evening.

The sides came to an agreement fairly quickly on the VEBA funding, but the union balked at Corker's demands for parity in wages and benefits with workers at Japanese-owned factories. Reuther got the sense that Corker, a first-term senator and millionaire con-struction executive, wanted to rewrite decades of collective bargain-ing in a matter of hours.

When Reuther phoned Gettelfinger to update him, the union president felt the UAW had been drawn into an ambush. "The right wing of the Senate was trying to pierce the heart of organized labor," he said later. "It was like workers are expendable and wages mean nothing."

While the talks went on behind closed doors, the top lobbyists from GM and Ford gathered in an adjoining room. Steve Feinberg was there too. He was pulled into the negotiations briefly, but then was abruptly told to go wait with the others. "Dodd wouldn't let us leave," said Ken Cole of GM. Out in the cavernous hallway, groups of reporters and photographers staked out the scene, breathlessly waiting for some indication that the auto crisis was nearing a resolu-tion. The guys from the car companies felt trapped and finally ordered pizza. "When it came, we went at it like it was filet mignon," Cole said. "But there weren't any napkins. Then I saw that Feinberg had grabbed all the napkins!"

By nine o'clock that night the union and Corker had hit a brick wall. There was no way Reuther was authorized to agree to a blanket pay cut for workers. Who would decide what parity was? Would the UAW have to call a vote of tens of thousands of members to ratify the changes?

"We know there has to be more restructuring, but this is ludi-crous," Gettelfinger said. "It was like the Republican Party wanted to get even with us once and for all." It all boiled down to a target date—and the union would not agree to any major reduction in compensation before its contract expired in 2011.

Shortly after ten o'clock, Corker came out and faced the reporters and cameras. He didn't try to hide his disappointment. "We were about three words away from a deal," he groaned. The last-minute compromise efforts officially died on the floor of the Senate. There would be no bailout that day. "This is going to be a very bad Christ-mas for many people," said Senator Harry Reid.

The next day the White House held out the possibility of a financial lifeline. A spokeswoman for the Treasury Department said: "We will stand ready to prevent an imminent failure until Congress reconvenes and acts to address the long-term viability of the industry."

GM and Cerberus representatives began nonstop meetings with Treasury officials. General Motors had weeks—maybe days—before it defaulted on billions of dollars in payments to its suppliers. "The clock is ticking," said a worried Jennifer Granholm. "Automakers are drowning." To save money, Chrysler said it would close all of its plants for a month. GM announced emergency plans to idle twenty of its factories across North America. The company was tightening its belt in every way imaginable, including shutting off the lights and elevators in the Renaissance Center after 6:00 P.M. It was a chilling sight when GM's imposing headquarters complex suddenly went dark as night fell.

The frenetic discussions at Treasury revolved around how much money would go to GM and Chrysler, where it would come from, and what conditions would be attached. Henry Paulson was in the middle of the talks. Despite his reluctance to use TARP funds for the automakers, Bush told Paulson he would not let Detroit fail in the final days of his administration. "Although the president didn't explicitly say he would jump in to save the automakers, I knew he recognized the need for quick, decisive action," Paulson wrote in his book.

During his eight years in office, Bush had hardly been a fan of the Big Three. He had chided them for building substandard cars and for blaming their troubles on fuel economy rules and the trade advantages of foreign rivals. But Bush would keep his promise to Barack Obama. He would not allow Detroit's failures to cripple the economy before his successor took office. At 9:00 A.M. on December 19, Bush went on national television from the Roosevelt Room of the White House and said: "In the midst of a financial crisis and a recession, allowing the U.S. auto industry to collapse is not a responsible course of action."

He had approved emergency TARP loans with strict conditions attached: $13.4 billion for General Motors and $4 billion for Chrysler. Both companies had to submit in-depth restructuring plans by mid-February and prove their financial viability by March 31, or they would face bankruptcy. And there were very tough targets to meet along the way: cutting debt by two-thirds, funding half of retiree health care with stock, matching the wage rates of the Japanese-owned factories by the end of 2009. These were bridge loans that required considerable concessions not only by GM and Chrysler but by their lenders, workers, dealers, and retirees.

"We know we have a lot of work ahead of us," said a visibly relieved Rick Wagoner at a press conference. A grateful Bob Nardelli pledged that Chrysler would meet all of the government's conditions. "We intend to be accountable for this loan," he said.

That all sounded positive. But soon the automakers would have to reckon with Obama, who was signaling that Detroit had better change and change fast. GM and Chrysler, he said, "must not squander this chance to reform bad management practices and begin the long-term restructuring that is absolutely required." And the president-elect issued a warning. "The American people's patience," he said, "is running out."

[Twenty-Nine]

I can smell the fear in this town," said Sergio Marchionne. "I can feel it, the feeling of impending doom."

The Fiat chief executive had just wrapped up daylong negotiations with Bob Nardelli in Auburn Hills. Finally Chrysler had found its partner. Fiat was getting a 35 percent stake in Chrysler in exchange for providing it with badly needed new cars, engines, and vehicle platforms. The alliance was a critical component of the viability plan Nardelli needed to submit to the government by mid-February. For all its twists and turns, Chrysler was heading into a bizarre new phase.

Cerberus was on its way out, resigned to giving up ownership as part of the bailout. Steve Feinberg had tried unsuccessfully to sell Chrysler to the Treasury Department for $1 during the frantic last-minute loan discussions. Now the smallest of the Big Three was living from day to day on $4 billion in federal loans and appeared certain to seek more assistance when it returned to Washington. It was only a matter of time before Cerberus had to dole out chunks of its equity to fund the UAW health care trust and the banks that were still owed money. But was Chrysler even worth saving? Did it have a future? Marchionne wasn't sure. But he was willing to try.

He viewed the Chrysler deal as a way to bring Fiat back into the

American market. But the landscape was changing so fast. After spending several days in Detroit, Marchionne began to appreciate the constant, withering pressure coursing through the U.S. industry. GM and Chrysler were on government life support, Ford was crawling on its hands and knees, and suppliers, dealers, and employees seemed scared out of their wits.

He had warned Nardelli that Chrysler would crash if U.S. sales plunged to ten million, and he was right. Now he found a city in deep despair, doubting itself, fearing the worst. Marchionne was an intellectual, born in Italy, raised in Canada, held degrees in law and accounting. But he was also a supreme pragmatist and believed progress could be forged out of the chaos in Detroit. "You have to be brutally honest with yourself," he said in a husky Italian accent. "There's nothing worse than bullshitting yourself into oblivion. You have to snap out of it and fight your way back. You cannot live in fear forever."

General Motors got its first $4 billion TARP loan installment on the last day of 2008, and Chrysler received its check two days later. The government aid was a fitting climax to the worst year in the U.S. car market since 1992. Sales at GM and Ford fell more than 30 percent in December. Chrysler "led" the industry with a stunning 53 percent decline. Dealer showrooms were empty. The disposable income that created three-car families, go-anywhere SUVs, and weekend pickup trucks had dried up. There was no credit available, no leases, and no money to lure buyers in with rebates.

And the economy was getting worse. The Japanese automakers were tanking too. Even Toyota had reported its worst corporate loss in seventy years. A rabidly competitive and ambitious industry had overproduced for too long. Its customers couldn't keep pace because more and more were unemployed, losing their homes, and couldn't get a car loan if they tried. The industry was no longer looking at annual sales of sixteen million units or even the woeful thirteen million sold in 2008. The rate now was ten million—and falling.

The consequences of the bleak market were swift and cruel. During Christmas week, GM abruptly shuttered two of its biggest SUV plants for good in Wisconsin and Ohio, just as Chrysler was mothballing a major sport-utility factory in Delaware. All three of the plants had supposedly been guaranteed future products in the union contract. But those promises had disintegrated.

In Janesville, Wisconsin, where GM had churned out 3.7 million big sport-utilities since the 1990s, the last workers filed out of the ninety-year-old plant after building one final Chevrolet Tahoe. Dan Doubleday, a twenty-two-year employee, broke down in the snowy parking lot after the assembly line ground to a halt. "I used to be a forklift driver," he said as he glanced at his watch. "Until about seven minutes ago."

This was more than a reckoning. Economic justice was being meted out. GM's voracious consumption of capital had been cut off. Chrysler was comatose, its entire manufacturing network in suspended animation. Opinion polls showed the American people were increasingly angry and disgusted with dysfunctional companies that were sucking up taxpayer money. As the jobs disappeared, Detroit's freeways and ancient downtown got emptier and quieter. Michigan's unemployment rate passed 10 percent and kept rising. People were packing up and moving away in record numbers. The gathering gloom felt like mourning for a dying community.

Insults were heaped upon injury. Detroit's flamboyant mayor, Kwame Kilpatrick, had resigned in disgrace after pleading guilty to felony charges in a lewd political corruption scandal. And just after Christmas, the toothless Detroit Lions wrapped up the first winless sixteen-game season in National Football League history. No wonder Marchionne could smell the fear. This was the pits.

GM tried to put on a positive face. At the 2009 Detroit auto show, six hundred employees were rounded up at 7:00 A.M. to cheer on its first press conference, chanting "Let's go GM!" and waving blue-and-green placards saying CHARGED UP.

Jennifer Granholm led the pep rally, getting up onstage with Rick Wagoner and holding a HERE TO STAY sign. The company unveiled two new crossover vehicles and a Buick sedan, but the enthusiasm was forced and unconvincing. Wagoner told reporters that GM was talking with bondholders to reorganize its debt, negotiating with the union on health care and work rules, and making hard choices about which brands and models to keep. "Those are the major pieces, and they all add up to a business plan that meets the so-called viability test," he said.

One unexpected visitor to the flashy show stands was Bob Corker, the Tennessee senator who'd tried to put Detroit through the wringer in Washington. "I truly want to see these companies flourish," Corker said. "The solution I offered was tough love, but it was a solution."

On January 21, GM received another $5.4 billion in Treasury loans, the second installment of its ongoing federal bailout. The same day, the final tally for 2008 came in. Toyota had blown past GM as the world's number one carmaker, ending GM's seventy-seven-year reign atop the automotive world. The numbers weren't even close: the Japanese company sold nearly nine million vehicles for the year, six hundred thousand more than GM.

The title was worthless now anyway. The only way General Motors could keep the federal funds flowing was to slash brands—Hummer, Saab, and Saturn topped the list—and drastically curtail its overlapping and slow-selling models. It had to shrink to survive, including eliminating another ten thousand salaried jobs.

And the spiritual leader of GM's vast global product empire was calling it quits. Three days before his seventy-seventh birthday, Bob Lutz announced that he would retire at the end of the year. He couldn't take the disdain and outrage directed at GM any longer. His parting shots were beyond bitter. "We are a country that hates its own industry," he said. "The auto industry may be partly at fault for its situation, but not entirely." But Lutz would never concede defeat. GM, he said, would rise again. "I am convinced that when everyone is staring at the reality of the situation, and also staring at the alternatives," he said, "they will make the right decisions."

But who would make those decisions? GM was occupied territory in the days leading up to the loans, with government lawyers, accountants, and bureaucrats swarming over its financial statements, production schedules, and supplier invoices. Fritz Henderson and CFO Ray Young were totally at Treasury's command. Bankruptcy attorneys were now on the GM payroll, combing through its gargantuan organization for assets that might be sold quickly if and when the company descended into Chapter 11.

Rick Wagoner seemed depleted by his experience in Washington. Steve Harris fretted about his old friend and boss. "After the hearings," Harris said, "Rick just seemed to lose his confidence." When he reflected on the hearings, Wagoner sounded more hurt than anything. "For an industry that has contributed to the country in so many ways, it was astounding to get this treatment," he said. The politicians had forked over the money when Wall Street came to Washington. But Detroit got beat on like a piñata. "The financial guys got a little roughed up," Wagoner said. "But then we came in and it seemed that our industry was held to a radically different standard. The moral of the story is never put yourself in a position where you have to go down there."

It was too late for second-guessing. He'd made the call and GM had to live with it. Industry veterans wondered whether Wagoner was simply too proud or stubborn to have taken GM through bankruptcy two or three years earlier, when financing could have been raised for an orderly reorganization. It didn't matter. There was no semblance of order in the Renaissance Center anymore. Wagoner and his board had taken the first step toward abdicating control of General Motors.

The Obama administration was assembling a task force of investment bankers and economic advisors to judge the viability plans that GM and Chrysler were sweating to finish before the February 17 deadline. The plans were management's last shot to prove GM could reorganize and one day stand on its own again. Henderson at times felt overwhelmed by the pressure. But when he observed Wagoner, something didn't click. "It's hard to describe his frame of mind," Henderson said. "He was calm. I don't know why, because the business was just going to hell."

. . . .

"I think there is more awareness than ever," Alan Mulally said, "that Ford is on a different path." From a distance, it sure didn't look like that. Ford ended 2008 on a miserable note. It lost nearly $6 billion in the fourth quarter for a grand total of $14.6 billion for the year, its worst annual result ever. But Mulally was so gratified that Ford had been able to walk out of Washington without taking loans. Cash was extremely tight, and Ford had to draw down the last $10 billion from its credit lines to shore up its reserves. But Mulally was free to run the business as he and his team saw fit.

His days were consumed with keeping Ford on track and inching its way back to health. To save money, they turned the lights off early, cut the heat in the Glass House, and reined in white-collar health care insurance and merit pay. Executives took 30 percent pay cuts. All borderline expenses were eliminated.

But Mulally refused to sacrifice any product programs. While Ford's Detroit rivals virtually stopped work on vehicles in the development stage, Ford was gearing up to launch three new models: a forty-mile-per-gallon Fusion hybrid; a small, Euro-styled work van called the Transit Connect; and a shapely new version of the venerable Taurus sedan (the nameplate Mulally refused to give up on).

The One Ford plan hadn't changed a bit. If anything, the fervor to make it work ratcheted up. Every day the senior management team assessed its progress in its stuffy eleventh-floor conference room, the walls papered with charts and data tracking minute details of upcoming cars, factory changeovers, sales reports, and new technology such as hands-free entertainment systems and consumer-friendly software.

Bill Ford had watched the horror show in Washington and felt the resentment building toward his hometown industry. But like Jim Farley, he sensed that the backlash against floundering GM and Chrysler could be a phenomenal asset for Ford if it could deliver on its strategy. "People are frustrated and angry, and I completely understand that," Bill said. "But I'm really excited where we are. In times of great change, there's great opportunity." Ford had already taken advantage of the weakened state of GM and Chrysler. While they were dug in on viability plans, Ford quietly began talks with the union about funding half its retiree health care obligations with stock. The other guys had the government on their backs. Dearborn was calling its own shots.

Responsibility within the Obama administration for the loans to the auto industry was divided between Timothy Geithner, the new Treasury secretary, and Larry Summers, the president's chief economic advisor. Together, they selected the man who would lead the radical restructuring of Detroit's two fallen icons: Steve Rattner, a fifty-six-year-old New York financier and extremely well-connected Democratic Party fund-raiser.

A former *New York Times* reporter, Rattner had become a millionaire many times over as cofounder of the Quadrangle Group, a highly successful, media-focused private equity firm. Known for his keen intellect and aggressive deal-making skills, Rattner volunteered his talents to the new administration in some financial capacity. Short and slight in stature, with a high, broad forehead, tortoiseshell glasses, and longish sandy hair, Rattner didn't look like the caricature of the cutthroat private equity baron who sliced and diced wayward companies for a living. He was mild-spoken and extremely articulate, and he exuded a sort of boyish enthusiasm for big challenges.

When Geithner called him about taking the top position on the auto task force, Rattner was vacationing with his family in Spain. Initially he was taken aback; he admittedly knew little about the auto industry. But he accepted the post when he realized what a formidable and delicate task had been offered to him. "It was pretty clear that President Obama wanted to own this problem, not outsource the problem," Rattner said. "And this was not a management job. This was a financial restructuring, and that was something I had done a lot of."

Rattner's appointment drew protests from Michigan's congressional delegation because of his glaring lack of experience in the industry. Union leaders also weren't happy that the Obama administration had appointed a Manhattan tycoon who lived on Fifth Avenue and traveled in his own private jet to overhaul a gritty, tough-as-nails manufacturing industry. Rattner was more than sensitive to the prejudice and chose Ron Bloom, an investment banker with close ties to the national steelworkers union, as his chief deputy.

An easygoing Harvard Business School grad with a hangdog look and a crew cut, Bloom had been through some bruising restructuring battles in the steel industry. His experience would serve him well as the point man with the UAW. "You should know that my first goal is to preserve as many jobs as possible," Bloom told Rattner.

The rest of the task force came together from an ad hoc group eager to be part of the excitement and verve of the new presidential administration. Key members included another Wall Street banker, Harry Wilson; a top-notch bankruptcy attorney, Matt Feldman; and a thirty-one-year-old public policy expert, Brian Deese. Working out of bare-bones offices in the Treasury Department, the team started a feverish review of the balance sheets, organizational structures, and operations of GM and Chrysler.

Rattner's primary responsibility was first to dissect the problem, then recommend solutions. The president, of course, had the final say on whatever the government did. But Rattner had to have a reasonable expectation that dragging two giant auto companies through the bankruptcy process could turn them into viable, healthy competitors. It wasn't long before Rattner sized up the situation before him. "I thought bankruptcy was highly likely from the moment I started looking at this stuff," he said.

But he had to proceed cautiously. Wagoner & Co. had warned many times that consumers would flat-out shun cars made by a bankrupt company. Plus, the workers at GM and Chrysler were punch-drunk from plant closings and job losses. The cascade of cutbacks had created a culture of suspicion and constant worry. So many companies that went bankrupt never made it out (Delphi so far being one obvious example). How could General Motors, with all its image problems and shortcomings in the marketplace, recover from the dreaded stigma of bankruptcy?

But Rattner and his colleagues figured that Chapter 11 was the only legal tool sharp enough to extract the enormous concessions that GM and Chrysler had to get from the United Auto Workers, their lenders, their dealers, and their creditors. The thought of ushering GM into federal court kept Rattner awake nights in his rented Washington condo. "I couldn't see how you could restructure this company out of bankruptcy," he said. "And I was terrified about what would happen in bankruptcy."

GM and Chrysler limped into their negotiations with the union and their big lenders. General Motors had no leverage whatsoever with its bondholders and no way to get them to accept stock or warrants in return for cutting $27 billion in debt by two-thirds. Similarly, Chrysler could not convince its banks to budge off the nearly $7 billion still owed to them.

Gettelfinger was biding his time. He was negotiating a VEBA deal with Ford before he would give one to its two wounded competitors. Until they had deals on health care and debt, GM and Chrysler couldn't be in compliance with two critical conditions of their TARP loans. And when they filed their viability plans on February 17, the companies proved once and for all that their businesses had completely hit bottom.

The Bush administration had given GM $13.4 billion in loans. Now General Motors said in its reorganization plan that it needed an additional $16.6 billion. In return, the company promised to cut and cut and cut—eliminate forty-seven thousand more jobs, close five additional factories, sell or phase out three brands (Hummer, Saturn, Saab), downsize the Pontiac division, and slash its dealers by the thousands. These actions, it swore, would finally make it a competitive auto company.

But if it didn't get more federal aid, the only alternative for GM was bankruptcy. That, however, would be way more expensive. GM estimated it would need an astonishing $100 billion in debtor-in-possession financing to emerge from Chapter 11. And as far as the company was concerned, the only source of those funds was the U.S.

government. It was quite an ugly choice: pony up more bailout money or pay for the most costly bankruptcy in corporate history.

The numbers were staggering. But even more difficult to digest were GM's financial projections. According to the company's plan, it would swing from a huge cash shortfall to a surplus in just three years. How it would manage that was unclear. Skeptics wondered if the company could be trusted with another dollar of taxpayer money.

"Where does this end?" said Senator Corker. "A lot of tough questions need to be asked."

Fritz Henderson was confident the additional loan money would be enough to carry it through to prosperity—maybe. "There are no guarantees in life," he told analysts in a conference call. "But I do think we have sized the funding requirements correctly."

The Chrysler viability plan was strangely modest. The company wanted an additional $5 billion on top of the $4 billion it had already received. But its plan didn't involve more plant closings or job cuts. Only a handful of older models would be dropped. Its comeback seemed to hinge on selling assets, reducing fixed costs, and hooking up with Fiat. In fact, its whole product strategy seemed to rely on forging a vague alliance with Sergio Marchionne and the Italians.

But Chrysler was clear on one point: if the company didn't get additional federal loans, it would instantly file for Chapter 11. Financing a bankruptcy would cost an estimated $24 billion. And with no government money to pay for it, Chrysler would simply have to liquidate, putting forty thousand U.S. employees out of work overnight, shuttering more than three thousand dealerships, and wreaking havoc on its supply base. The government had been given two options: either prop up Chrysler with more loans or risk catastrophic job losses and a tide of misery rippling through the entire U.S. economy.

Steve Rattner's first reaction to the GM plan was disbelief. This was a professional restructuring job? Some of the calculations and projections that GM had submitted seemed off the wall. "These numbers are ridiculous," he said. "'If you give us this much money, we're going to be fine'? Oh no, you're not."

Without knowing it, both companies had crossed a critical line.

The Obama administration had to honor the loans and terms negotiated under President Bush. But once GM and Chrysler asked for more money, it changed everything. Any new funding would come with new conditions set by a new president. The U.S. Treasury wasn't an ATM machine for troubled corporations. Federal loans came with strings attached, and the Detroit Two would have to accept whatever Obama's team demanded if they wanted to get additional dollars. Rattner wasn't sure the government would ever recover the Bush loan money from the battered automakers. But he certainly would not recommend that GM and Chrysler receive more public funds without a reasonable possibility that the loans would be repaid.

The task force's bigger issue was deciding whether to give more aid at all. What if Obama decided to take a pass? Would uncontrolled bankruptcies at GM and Chrysler devastate the economy just a few short months into his presidency? The nation was already losing hundreds of thousands of jobs in February. A GM failure could double or triple that in an instant. "We were quite concerned about the downward spiral of a GM bankruptcy and the cascading effect," said Brian Deese of the task force. "This is a case of you don't know what you don't know."

The auto team took the viability plans for meetings with White House chief of staff Rahm Emanuel, Tim Geithner, Larry Summers, and other senior administration officials. In his book *Overhaul*, Rattner recounted with fascination Emanuel's salty language and devil's-advocate approach to the issue, questioning whether GM should even be saved. Polling data showed minimal public support for bailing out Detroit. But it wasn't time for a decision yet. The two automakers had made their best case for loans, and now "Team Auto" (as Rattner nicknamed his squad) had to do a huge amount of due diligence before formulating options for the president by the end of March.

Their job was roughly split in two. One half was like cramming for a massive test on how the automotive business worked. Day after day, the team interviewed industry analysts, academics, dealers, suppliers, officials from auto communities—anyone who could bring them up to speed fast on the complexities of the American auto industry. They also met with Marchionne and his Fiat executives, the committee representing GM's bondholders, and officials from competing carmakers.

The rest of their efforts were devoted to face-to-face meetings with management at Chrysler and GM. Bob Nardelli and his guys came first. Rattner was impressed with the Chrysler CEO's gung-ho attitude but not with his company's paper-thin blueprint for restructuring. The task force was extremely skeptical about the outlook for Auburn Hills. To them, Chrysler was looking like a lost cause already.

At the last minute, Marchionne had refused to let Chrysler include specific details of their alliance strategy, and the viability plan seemed way too speculative without the Fiat component. Nardelli was furious at Fiat's move. "What do you mean we can't use the numbers?" he barked at Marchionne. "We spent thousands of hours working on this thing!" Worse yet, Chrysler had been unable to extract any concessions from JPMorgan Chase and the other banks that had lent it money.

The six-hour meeting with GM was even worse. Rattner was instantly turned off by Wagoner's style and demeanor. The GM chief executive opened the session with introductory remarks, then handed off the entire presentation to Henderson and Ray Young. In the private equity world, Rattner was used to hyperaggressive management teams pitching their ideas and plans with vigor. By comparison, Wagoner seemed maddeningly detached and above it all. "He presided rather than rolled up his sleeves," Rattner said. "When you want to sell somebody on something, you've got to be a salesman."

The meeting was the beginning of a torturous, tempestuous relationship between GM and the task force. Over time, Rattner and the banker Harry Wilson developed great contempt for the General Motors executives—especially for Wagoner and Young. "It's a culture of losing," Wilson concluded. Rattner considered the company's finance department the worst he had ever seen and felt its management was insular, arrogant, and terribly resistant to change.

Rattner was especially irked by how GM acted as if it were entitled, too large and powerful to fail. With all the losses, mistakes, and humbling setbacks it had experienced, how could this organization go on believing it deserved the open-ended support of the federal government and American taxpayers? Rattner appreciated that GM had talent and skill, modern facilities, and a core of solid products. But he was offended by its self-important attitude. He didn't like Wagoner or his viability plan at all. "His homework assignment got a failing grade," Rattner said. "It wasn't a passing grade. So if you're the teacher, what do you do? You don't promote the kid." Ron Bloom was less judgmental but just as put off by what he heard. "No one at GM said, 'What we need to do is draw a clean sheet of paper and ask ourselves who we are and what we need to do,'" Bloom said. "It was like, 'Everything is going to be okay because the market is going to come back and we're going to tighten our belts.'"

The task force had uncovered what people in the auto industry had known for years: GM was all about muscle and scale and a righteous belief that it was the backbone of the American auto industry. It led, and Ford and Chrysler followed. In its view of the world, the only reason Toyota and the other Asian companies made more money was because "Generous Motors" had been too benevolent with its army of workers, retirees, and pensioners. Was it cursed by "friendly arrogance," as Rattner dubbed it, or a stubborn streak of misguided optimism? The men and women inside General Motors could privately admit when the company screwed up, but the corporation could not. There was always an explanation, never an admission that maybe, just possibly, GM had taken a false turn or made a bad move. How could the greatest car company on earth be wrong? Time and money were always the answer.

Bloom wanted a clean sheet of paper. General Motors brought an encyclopedia. This was an institution enthralled with its heritage, image, and mission. If the bigger fall harder, GM was crashing down with a force never before witnessed in American business. The sad part was that it didn't know how to be humble or admit that outsiders might actually have better solutions. It was an empire that accepted no limitations, always expanding, dedicated to replicating its U.S. footprint in China, India, Russia, and beyond. But its foundation, the ability to earn a profit in its home market, had been crumbling for years. Now its leaders had awoken to find that the dynasty had been overrun by the multitude of problems from within. The structure had given way. There was no tourniquet or prescription to save a company that had long ago run out of money and was living on borrowed time.

If Wagoner had a sliver of optimism left, it vanished later that day when GM reported a $30.9 billion loss for its final results for 2008. Revenues had plunged 17 percent. It had lost money in every region of the world in the fourth quarter. The company was burning through an average of $60 million every twenty-four hours. There was just enough of a cash cushion to keep paying the bills, but even that wouldn't last much longer.

The auto task force went to Detroit for a one-day visit on March 9. It was almost a perfunctory step. Rattner and his team were under extraordinary time pressures to draft recommendations for the president. Still, it was impossible to avoid seeing the plants, facilities, and people whose fate was in their hands. Rattner arrived in Detroit on an early-morning commercial flight. One of the first things he saw was the banner headline on the *Detroit Free Press*: "Hear Us Out. We're in Crisis."

While Team Auto was making snap judgments about the leadership at GM and Chrysler, the executives were doing the same with them. "This is a fiasco," Fritz Henderson said. "They want to come in and spend ten minutes looking at a plant and fifteen minutes driving the Volt? I mean, come on. I got the sense that this was check-the-box time: 'Okay, we visited Detroit.'" Bob Lutz thought Rattner and his crew were expecting decrepit factories and brain-dead engineers. "It was apparent in their attitudes," he said. "Everything was fucked up. Then the big surprise was how good our manufacturing, design, and engineering really was. Harry Wilson said to me, 'This is a nice plant, but how old is it? I'd like to go to the oldest plant possible.'"

The whole scene was surreal, with television news copters and a pack of media following the task force as they stopped at Solidarity House to meet with Ron Gettelfinger, then drove up to the GM tech center, and finally to Chrysler's Warren assembly plant. They didn't spend much time at the UAW, and that ticked off Gettelfinger. But at the GM tech center, they drove the Volt, had lunch with Wagoner and his executives, and got a full-court press on GM products.

The visit to Chrysler was not as smooth. Nardelli wanted the task force to come to Auburn Hills to see the best Chrysler had to offer. But the task force was crunched for time and wanted to at least step inside a real assembly plant. When they got to the Warren factory, Nardelli invited them into a conference room to talk before the tour. And it was then that Rattner decided to get very honest with him.

"Your plan is not viable," he said.

Nardelli was stunned. This was supposed to be an opportunity to show off Chrysler's cars, trucks, and state-of-the-art technology. Instead, Rattner was summarily dismissing the comeback plan Chrysler had spent five weeks slaving over. "I don't agree with you," Nardelli said. "This is not right. It's just not right."

But Rattner was in no mood for a debate. He had to catch a plane back to D.C.

Nardelli was steaming after they left. It was bad enough that Rattner had dumped all over his plan. But Nardelli had also learned that Fiat was holding its own meetings with the task force to talk about how the Italians could fix Chrysler! It all made sense now. His plan wasn't any good, so Fiat could just take over Chrysler and save the government the trouble of bailing out both Detroit clunkers. "Their mind was made up," Nardelli said. "Fiat wanted to take Chrysler off their hands. They couldn't sell two bailouts. So just give it to Fiat and be done with it."

Now he knew why Marchionne had refused to be part of the viability plan—the Italians had their own scheme to ride off with Chrysler cheap. From that point on, Nardelli gave Marchionne a new name: "Machiavelli"—like the Italian philosopher who wrote the book on cunning and deception.

The same day the task force was eyeballing GM and Chrysler, union workers at Ford approved an extraordinary round of concessions to let the company fund half the VEBA with stock, cap benefits, suspend cost-of-living raises, and cut holiday pay. This was exactly the deal GM needed—and Ford had set the pattern.

Alan Mulally and Lewis Booth, his new CFO, were also working on retiring $10 billion in debt by offering their bondholders cash and stock. GM needed the same type of arrangement, but its bondholders were holding out because they didn't want GM stock. The common stock would be the first pot of money to evaporate in a bankruptcy. But Ford's stock had promise. The Blue Oval wasn't going bankrupt—or taking government money. And that was becoming a more powerful message by the day. Jim Farley, his marketing guys, and especially the dealers were seeing it. Consumers were slowly but surely gravitating to Ford, the American car company that didn't want a bailout.

Sales numbers were down 41 percent for the entire industry in February. But at the Glass House, an internal momentum was building that was counter to the growing sense of panic at its crosstown competitors. "I don't think any of us were prepared for what was going to happen," Farley said. "But it became the best thing for Ford, all of the anger, the emotions, the hope, the pride. It was all coming out, and we changed as a team. We felt very special, all of us."

For Mulally, the resurgence was a thing of beauty. The hardship, the controversy, the competitive fire—this was what he lived for. Ford was winning. There was hope in Detroit. The market was terrible. But his people could not wait to get to work every day. "We believe in this plan . . . the dealers, the employees, the citizens of this country," he said. "Everybody is watching this unfold. In the first hearings we're all lumped together, we're all screwed up, 'you're horrible.' And now everything we're doing is why I came to Ford."

The task force was preparing for bankruptcies. Right after returning from Detroit, Rattner brought in Matt Feldman, whose legal specialty was the unique Section 363 bankruptcy, in which a company is split in two—the good, productive assets and the unwanted ones. Ron Bloom referred to it as creating a "shiny new GM"—without the redundant factories, dealerships, and brands that had been suffocating its margins for years.

Rattner was also in full-on deal mode. He was getting ready for a head-on collision with Jimmy Lee, the crafty JPMorgan Chase banker who held a third of Chrysler's almost $7 billion in bank debt. Lee was still pushing a merger between GM and Chrysler as a way for his bank to salvage its investment. But that wasn't happening. Instead Rattner was going to offer all the banks a billion or two at the most to walk away or else risk getting nothing in a bankruptcy. This was high-stakes hardball, the very reason Rattner had been brought in.

He also was preparing to fire Rick Wagoner. In mid-March, when Wagoner came to Washington for another round of talks with the task force, Rattner took the GM chief executive aside. "I sort of asked him about his plans," Rattner said. "You know, 'What are your plans? How do you think about life? What do you want to do?'"

This was Rattner's unsubtle way of letting Wagoner know he would be getting the axe and should start thinking about life after GM.

At first Wagoner seemed clueless. "I don't expect to be doing this until I'm sixty-five," he said. "But I think I have a few good years in me."

Rattner just looked at him, waiting for the real answer. Then Wagoner got the hint. He had once told Henry Paulson that he would resign if GM got Treasury loans. Was that what Rattner was getting at?

"Hey, I told the last administration that if it would be helpful in the effort that I would step aside," Wagoner said. "I'll give you the same message."

Good, thought Rattner. *Now he knows.*

March 26, 2009, was the day the president of the United States set aside time in the Oval Office to discuss what should be done with General Motors and Chrysler. The task force had been building its efforts methodically, and somewhat frantically, toward this moment. There was little debate among Rattner, Bloom, and the other six members about GM. Allowing GM to fail was not a serious option. But its plan had to be torn up and redone. And unless management could miraculously cut its debt and renegotiate its UAW contract, a controlled Section 363 bankruptcy was the best possible solution.

Chrysler was another matter. The task force was deadlocked on whether it was worth saving at all. Rattner voted to give Chrysler time to put together a lifesaving alliance with Fiat and turn its future over to Sergio Marchionne. Larry Summers broke the tie in support of that plan—mostly because an uncontrolled bankruptcy in Auburn Hills could destroy an estimated three hundred thousand U.S. jobs in a brief period of time.

The team also considered whether GM and Ford would be better off with Chrysler dead, so that they could capture some of its customers. That also might mean fewer federal dollars would be needed to pump up GM. But Chrysler would not go away quietly, without broader economic consequences. It would be up to President Obama to decide whether the country could live with that.

The morning meeting with Obama was just getting rolling when an aide interrupted and said another meeting was coming up fast. But the president wanted to keep the discussion going. "This is too important to decide in a rush," he said, according to Rattner's book. "We need to get together again later." They reconvened in the early evening in the Roosevelt Room in the West Wing. Geithner and Summers were there, as were Rahm Emanuel, David Axelrod, the president's senior political advisor, and Robert Gibbs, his press secretary. For forty-five minutes the task force detailed its findings to Obama, with Summers orchestrating the discussion.

Chrysler took the most time. There still wasn't consensus on whether to give it another chance. The president listened to all the arguments pro and con, then didn't waste much time deciding. "I'm prepared to give Chrysler thirty days to see if we can get the Fiat alliance done on terms that make sense to us," he said, according to Rattner. Then he accepted the task force's other recommendations.

Wagoner's firing was never even brought up, but it was already a done deal. Henderson had known it was coming when Wagoner told him about his earlier conversation with Rattner. Henderson had had his own discussion that same day with the task force chief about his future. "Steve wanted to know my views of the company, what I would do with it," Henderson said. "I thought to myself, this is not a social call."

On Friday morning, March 27, Wagoner, Henderson, and Ray Young arrived at Treasury to meet with the task force and review its findings before the all-important deadline on the loans four days later. Rattner asked to see Wagoner alone in his office. Henderson and Young waited together outside.

It didn't take more than a few minutes for Rattner to bring Rick Wagoner's GM career to an abrupt end.

"Look," Rattner said. "When we met a couple of weeks ago you very generously offered to step aside if it was in the best interests of the company, and unfortunately the conclusion of the administration is that it would be. I hope that's something you can live with."

Wagoner sat there a moment. "Okay," he said.

Then Rattner said that Henderson would be his interim replacement until a search for a permanent chief executive could begin.

"You shouldn't hire an outsider," Wagoner blurted out. "Alan Mulally called me with questions for two weeks after he got to Ford."

Rattner didn't get it. But he moved on. Henderson would be CEO, he said, and Kent Kresa, a longtime GM director, would take over Wagoner's other job as chairman. Would Wagoner please bring that up with Kresa at the board meeting being conducted by phone that afternoon? Wagoner said he would.

Then Wagoner made a comment that spoke volumes about how he perceived the fall of GM. "Are you going to fire Ron Gettelfinger too?" he asked.

That wasn't his job, Rattner said.

That was it. There was nothing more to say. The United States government had just changed the management of General Motors. Wagoner got up and left. A Treasury aide walked him back to where Henderson and Young were waiting. "Are you okay?" Young piped up. "Do we still have jobs?"

"No," said Wagoner. "They asked me to step aside. They want Fritz to be interim CEO."

The three of them just stared at one another. Then, as if nothing had happened, they went straight into the task force briefing on the president's upcoming auto speech. Wagoner sat stone-faced throughout it all, never saying a word.

After the meeting, Wagoner called Steve Harris in Detroit. "Here's the deal," he said. "I've been told I'm done. I've been asked to resign, and Fritz is going to replace me."

Harris listened in silence.

"This is going to be effective on Sunday," Wagoner said. "You need to think about what we need to say." Then he hung up.

At the same time, Henderson got a call on his cell phone from Rattner, asking him what he thought about being the new chief executive of GM.

"Thanks for your confidence in me," Henderson said. "But don't make me an interim. This company needs leadership. You can do whatever you want with me. But don't have an interim CEO—because if you do, we're never going to make it."

Rattner said he'd think about it. Then he fielded an angry phone call from George Fisher, GM's lead director. "I think you're doing most of the right things," Fisher said. "But there's one thing I disagree with, and that's taking Rick out." Later, Rattner had a tense conference call with the rest of the GM board. And after that unpleas-

antness, he went back to work, girding for a long weekend of preparations for the president's speech on Monday, March 30.

Wagoner, Henderson, and Young rode to the D.C. airport in silence
to catch their Northwest flight home. Henderson was glad nobody
spoke in the car. "It was better that way," he said. "It was better just
to stay quiet and be with him." But when they got to the terminal,
Henderson needed to do something to cut through the gloom. "I'll
tell you what, Rick," he said brightly. "I'll buy you a beer." So they sat
together in the airport bar, the three of them drinking beer, old colleagues comforting a friend who had just lost his job. They even
laughed a little. "They just had a different agenda," Henderson said
to Wagoner. "It was out of their playbook. It didn't matter how long
you had been there. You were going to get fired."

Wagoner just looked at him and nodded—tired, disappointed,
and sipping his beer.

When their flight arrived in Detroit, they got off the plane
together and began walking down the long airport concourse. Then
Wagoner picked up the pace and strode ahead, carrying his briefcase,
alone with his thoughts. About twenty yards behind him, Henderson
and Young were deep in animated conversation, trying to figure out
what was going to happen next.

Over the weekend, Wagoner talked to some GM directors and a
few of his closest friends in the company. The board formally accepted
his resignation and named Henderson the new chief executive, which
was how the government preferred it be handled. (The "interim" tag
was dropped.)

At one point Wagoner called Harris, very upset, saying he
wanted to get Rattner on the phone and tell him "to stuff it." Then
he calmed down and called again. "I'm going to come in on Monday," he said.

Harris was aghast at the idea of the just-fired CEO walking into
the Renaissance Center on Monday morning. "I can't imagine you
coming in," he said nervously. "I can't imagine you wanting to be

here." Finally Wagoner agreed. He wouldn't come in, even though he'd like to pack up and see everybody one last time.

But he did attend to one last duty. On Sunday, all the General Motors executives around the world, vice presidents and higher, dialed into a scheduled "senior leadership" call. Wagoner was patched in at the start. "I've appreciated all your support," he said. "And I know you'll do a great job for Fritz."

Then he hung up, and Henderson took over the meeting.

[Thirty]

President Obama called Jennifer Granholm on Sunday night, March 29, while she was in the governor's mansion in Lansing, Michigan. Obama was reaching out to her and to members of Congress on the night before his speech about GM and Chrysler. Granholm listened carefully, and then respectfully offered her perspective.

"People have to hear that you understand what this means to us," she said. "We need to hear that one way or another, you will not allow this auto industry to fail. Please, we need that."

"Believe me, I get it," Obama told her. "I've worked with the steel communities. I understand how devastating it's going to be."

At 11:07 A.M. on March 30, the president spoke live on national television from the White House. He talked about the pain of the recession and the failures of the American auto industry, which had lost four hundred thousand jobs in the past year alone. He singled out Michigan, where one in ten residents was out of work, the highest unemployment rate in the country. The problems of Detroit, he said, had been building for decades. Now was the time to solve them.

"We cannot, and must not, and we will not let our auto industry vanish," he said. "This industry, is like no other—it's an emblem of the American spirit, a once and future symbol of America's success.

It's what helped build the middle class and sustained it throughout the twentieth century. It's a source of deep pride for the generations of American workers whose hard work and imagination led to some of the finest cars the world has ever seen. It's a pillar of our economy that has held up the dreams of millions of our people. And we cannot continue to excuse poor decisions. We cannot make the survival of our auto industry dependent on an unending flow of taxpayer dollars. These companies, and this industry, must ultimately stand on their own, not as wards of the state."

The government would give General Motors and Chrysler one final opportunity to restructure and survive, he said. But their viability plans were not sufficient to warrant more aid now. They had to do much more. The president spelled out the terms. GM had sixty days to cut enough jobs, brands, dealers, and models to be profitable, and reduce its crushing debt and liabilities. He also said that Rick Wagoner was "stepping aside," and that a majority of the GM board would be replaced. These actions were necessary, he said, to infuse "fresh thinking and new vision" and to qualify the company for enough working capital to keep operating during its last-gasp overhaul. This was a lifeline, not a government takeover—at least not yet. "Let me be clear," the president said. "The United States government has no interest in running GM."

His conditions were much tougher for Chrysler, which was now arguably the weakest major car company in the world. Chrysler had thirty days to join up with Fiat, dump its debt, get union concessions, and, above all, form a plan to replace its truck-heavy lineup with more fuel-efficient cars. If Chrysler made it, another $6 billion loan would be extended. The terms revolved around a Fiat deal; Chrysler wasn't getting another dime from Washington without a partner.

Then the president broached the subject that sent shivers through all the auto towns in America—bankruptcy. If it was necessary to use the Chapter 11 process to speed these transformations, he would not hesitate to order it. Obama also unveiled broader rescue efforts for the entire industry, including using federal funds to help auto finance companies extend car loans, offering tax credits to consumers who traded in old models for new and more fuel-efficient ones, and speeding recovery funds to impacted communities. Putting the auto industry back together was now an integral part of the national economic agenda. This was the moment when the harsh reality of Detroit's precipitous decline was driven home to the entire nation. Two presidential administrations had stepped up now to keep these pillars of the domestic industry alive. The damage was widespread and substantial. But the question was whether these beaten-down, sputtering corporations had the heart and the strength to rebuild and march into the future.

Sergio Marchionne was watching the speech from a meeting room in Turin when he heard the president talking about Fiat. "What the fuck?" he said. "What the hell? The president of the United States is making reference to a bunch of schmucks like us?" It really hit him. He had wedged a good-and-getting-better Italian car company into the middle of the biggest industrial restructuring in U.S. history. Obama had said it: without Fiat, Chrysler had no hope.

It was a powerful negotiating tool. Marchionne was flying to Washington that night to start bargaining with Steve Rattner, Ron Bloom, and Bob Nardelli. Soon after, he would start talks with Ron Gettelfinger. However the deal was structured, he was not paying a penny of Fiat's money for control of Chrysler. And if he was going to run it, he would call the shots. His deputies were used to Marchionne's slightly manic, extremely demanding, and effective leadership. They didn't call him "the boss" for nothing. Marchionne had turned Fiat from an also-ran into one of the most solid carmakers in Europe. And he was ready, willing, and able to take over Chrysler. It was a blank canvas he could fill with well-built Fiat cars and engines. How could he not make it better? "I am a conduit," he said, "for change."

And it was the end of the line for Cerberus. Steve Feinberg had indicated to Treasury that his firm was willing to have its 80 percent stake in Chrysler divided up and given away to save Chrysler. Fiat would get a piece, and then another slice would go to the union for the health care trust. And if necessary, the government would own part of Chrysler to secure its interests after the company went into its seemingly inevitable bankruptcy.

Nardelli badly wanted to meet the nearly impossible conditions the task force had set for Chrysler to avoid Chapter 11. Feinberg tried to tell him the game was pretty much over. Fiat was taking charge. It was only a matter of time. "Bob, there are a lot bigger things going on here than us," he said. "We've got to line up and help the country. I think we could turn this thing around. But Fiat can do it faster." Nardelli couldn't help feeling he had failed in Detroit before ever getting a real chance to succeed. "I've got really mixed emotions here," he said. "I desperately want Chrysler to be successful. We haven't been sitting on our rear ends. We took out $5 billion in fixed costs. We had our heart and soul in this thing."

Fritz Henderson paced the stage in the Renaissance Center briefing room. This was his first press conference as chief executive, and his nerves were jumpy. He talked too fast and his mind raced from question to question, anxious to get back upstairs and into the endless work ahead of him. The roomful of reporters kept circling back to one issue: Was GM going bankrupt?

"Whatever it takes, we will get the job done," he said. "We will do it out of court, or we will do it in court."

GM had two months to achieve what it had been unable to do for twenty years—get into fighting shape. Some of the president's conditions were possible to meet. Others were not. Henderson had already accepted that he would go down in history as the CEO who led General Motors into bankruptcy. Wagoner wouldn't or couldn't do it. But Henderson was fully engaged.

The Obama administration did not really see Henderson as a long-term leader. Every executive in the company was considered tainted, part of the reviled GM "culture" that had gotten the government into this mess. But for now, he was entrusted to carry out Treasury's bidding. Rattner saw Henderson as a significant upgrade over Wagoner. "If we said to him, 'Faster and deeper,' he said, 'I get it,' "

Rattner noted. "He was willing to be more of a team player." The task force chief wondered why anyone even cared that Wagoner had been tossed. "To me it was a no-brainer," he said. "How do you keep a CEO who lost $45 billion in fifteen months and gives you a plan to turn around the company that doesn't make sense?"

Henderson had known for a long time that the numbers would never add up for GM. Who were they kidding? It was as if GM was playing with Monopoly money when it promised to put $24 billion into the union health care trust, or when it kept blowing billions every quarter buying out workers and paying Delphi's legacy costs. It was all about self-preservation now and keeping GM alive. Wagoner was right about one thing though: the very thought of General Motors liquidating into the weak economy like a massive oil spill brought swift action in Washington.

And once the president set the new sixty-day deadline, everything accelerated. A team of Treasury staff and task force personnel, led by the hardheaded banker Harry Wilson, parachuted into the Renaissance Center and would remain encamped there until GM had a new viability plan.

Henderson committed himself to complete cooperation with the federal fixers. He called together all of his senior executives—Gary Cowger with the plants, Troy Clarke in North America, Mark LaNeve in sales and marketing—and instructed them to do everything they could to help Wilson and his people carve up GM into a drastically smaller company. And it would be a bloody operation. Four brands would go away for sure: Pontiac, Saturn, Hummer, and Saab were history. At least one thousand dealers were slated for extinction. There would be more plant closings and considerably more job losses.

How management expected to run an auto company in the interim was never talked about. GM would spend several months in virtual hibernation, waiting for its financial freeze to thaw. So many plants were idled anyway, sales were pathetic, and the product pipeline had slowed to a trickle. By mid-April, Treasury officials directed GM to prepare for a "surgical" bankruptcy. Two weeks later, Henderson laid out the game plan. The company would produce 30 percent fewer models, cut twenty-three thousand more jobs by 2011, and close sixteen manufacturing plants within a year after that.

And the final price tag of the bailout was starting to come into focus.

GM had soaked up more than $15 billion in federal loans, and it required at least $11 billion more to jump-start its recovery. In exchange, Henderson and the lame duck board of directors proposed to give the government a 50 percent ownership stake, with the UAW and bondholders sharing the rest. All the shareholders' equity would be wiped out in Chapter 11. If the new transformation plan was accepted by Obama's watchdogs, GM would emerge from bankruptcy with the U.S. taxpayer as its majority owner.

Chrysler's banks tried to muscle the federal government but to no avail. Rattner had all the leverage. If JPMorgan Chase and the other lenders wanted to force Chrysler into liquidation and try to recover their money that way, good luck. By late April, the Treasury Department was offering $1.5 billion to the banks to retire almost $7 billion in loans. The banks were crying foul. But what recourse did they have? The government was not only a participant but also the referee and the promoter of the multilevel tug-of-war going on between Fiat, the union, Chrysler's lenders, and, to a lesser extent, Cerberus.

The most heated negotiations were the face-offs between Marchionne and Gettelfinger. The Fiat chief executive wanted megaconcessions from the union, including an unlimited number of $14-an-hour workers to replace the top-tier wage earners. At one ugly session, he lectured the union president about accepting a "culture of poverty" to shore up Chrysler's sick bottom line. Gettelfinger's response was to get up without a word and leave. He did that several times with Marchionne, letting the Fiat boss trade profanities and insults with General Holiefield. "Do you think I'm fucking stupid?" Marchionne yelled. "We need to come up with a competitive wage rate and structure here!"

Gettelfinger was not about to be bulldozed by yet another self-proclaimed Chrysler savior. "I believed the Germans when they came in," he told Marchionne. "Then I had no choice but to support Cerberus. You're the third guy saying you're going to save it. Why should I believe you?"

Marchionne understood completely. He knew he had a lot to prove. His tone changed abruptly. "I'm telling you that deep down, I know how to run a car company, not like that nonsense at Cerberus," he said. "I may be lousy at a lot of other things. But I know how to run a car company."

By late April, the two sides had reached a shaky truce. Gettelfinger would not back down on open-ended pay cuts, but he was resigned to taking potentially worthless Chrysler stock to fund the bulk of the health care trust. The VEBA would, incredibly, become the majority owner of the entire company, with a 55 percent stake. While it wouldn't have commensurate voting power on the new board, the symbolism was rich. Chrysler couldn't afford to pay the medical bills of its 170,000 retirees—so they got title to the business instead.

The banks howled in protest at what they branded favoritism toward the UAW. As secured lenders, they had expected to get top priority in these high-stakes settlement talks. But as Ron Bloom so succinctly put it, Chrysler needed workers to build cars, not banks. The four biggest banks, who together held 70 percent of the loans, capitulated to Rattner's terms and agreed to accept a $2 billion payment to retire all the secured debt. But some of the forty-six lenders—a group of hedge funds and private investment firms—were holding out for more. To appease them, Treasury sweetened the offer by $250 million. Then a tense ninety-minute deadline set on April 29 passed without agreement. The government held firm. No more bargaining. The last offer was yanked off the table.

On April 30, President Obama forced Chrysler into Chapter 11, making it the first major American auto company to seek bankruptcy protection since Studebaker in the 1930s. It was a stark, sobering moment for an industry that had been on the brink for so long. The filing in federal court in New York was the sixth-largest bankruptcy in

U.S. history—and another grim chapter in the saga of the nation's third-biggest automaker. Daimler hadn't wanted it. Cerberus had been unable to fix it. And now Chrysler was bust. The employees in Auburn Hills and at plants across the country had been holding their breaths, hoping that a last-minute rescue was at hand. But time had run out.

"It seems like an ugly word—'bankruptcy,'" said Chris Whiteman, an engineering supervisor at the Chrysler tech center. "It puts a lot of doubt in people's minds." Even so, there was a stubborn, seen-it-all streak in Chrysler's workers. They'd been counted out more than once before. And they would roll with this punch too. "You have to feel okay with it," said Frank Dusevic, a line worker at the Warren assembly plant, "because you have no control over it."

For Obama, bankruptcy was the most pragmatic, sensible option at hand. "This is not a sign of weakness, but rather one more step on a clearly charted path to Chrysler's revival," he said. There would, of course, be more pain—eight more plant closings, up to another ten thousand jobs vaporized, nearly eight hundred dealerships shut down. But Chrysler cruised into Chapter 11 with its exit strategy well mapped out. The UAW and Fiat negotiations had established the parameters of the reorganization. The union health care trust would get its 55 percent stake. The lenders had a framework of a deal in place to retire the debt (despite a vain legal fight by a few holdouts).

Fiat grabbed 20 percent ownership to start but could bump it to 35 percent and higher over time by hitting targets for American-made small cars and expanding exports of Chrysler products. And Marchionne was poised to take over as Chrysler's new CEO, putting him in a league with Carlos Ghosn as the only executive in the world to oversee two automakers at the same time. He couldn't wait to get under the hood of his latest reclamation project. "We're married to the damn thing now," he said about Chrysler. "And we are going to make it work."

Chrysler's attorneys and government advisors were, in fact, itching to get the Chapter 11 process rolling. The Section 363 bankruptcy was called a "quick rinse" for a reason. If all went well, the company could get out of court by the end of the summer, with $6 billion more in federal loans as its bankroll for a fresh start.

Chrysler would chart its new course without the help of the old guard. Tom LaSorda announced his retirement, and Bob Nardelli said he would leave Chrysler once it emerged from bankruptcy. He had rushed back to Auburn Hills after the grueling final days of negotiations in Washington. Nardelli wanted to be in the building, with his employees, when the president made his announcement. "This is really bittersweet for me," he said. "It's not the fate I would have chosen by any means. But it allowed us to save the company."

At the end of the first quarter, Ford said it had lost $1.4 billion, had seen its sales drop 43 percent, and was spending more than a billion dollars in cash every thirty days. And in the woefully weak auto environment of 2009, this qualified as very good news. So good that investors bid Ford's stock up 11 percent to $5 a share—triple the value it had had two months earlier.

The Ford Motor Company was the one bright light in Detroit's darkest hours. It had enough money to keep the new products coming. The company had convinced its lenders to accept cash and stock to lower its debt by nearly 30 percent, saving $500 million in annual interest payments. And the big research firm Auto Pacific had found in a study that 72 percent of consumers were more likely to buy a Ford product because the company didn't take government loans.

While Chrysler and General Motors were spinning their wheels under government oversight, Ford was gaining traction. "I don't take any joy in watching GM and Chrysler struggle," said Bill Ford. "I wish them well, but I wish us better. I want us to win."

And when Alan Mulally was invited down to D.C. to share his insights about the industry with the task force, he saw the One Ford plan up on the wall. "They were using the Ford plan in the restructuring of GM!" he said. "Can you believe it? They were implementing the Ford plan at GM!"

. . . .

GM's first-quarter loss was $6 billion, and its cash burn was now an inferno, about a billion dollars a week. Steve Rattner and the task force were sweating bullets about the federal money that was going up in smoke. Still, the president had given GM sixty days to get deals with the union and its bondholders, and Henderson and Treasury were racing to make it happen. Gettelfinger was under excruciating pressure to do a deal.

In mid-May, Ron Bloom put a final offer on the table. The union would get a 17 percent stake in GM and additional preferred stock and warrants instead of the huge cash infusion specified in its contract for the health care trust. Gettelfinger resisted mightily. Over the past three years, the UAW had negotiated for thousands of hours with GM on health care. And now he had to cut a new deal under the gun and accept stock in a company in intensive care to cover the medical bills of hundreds of thousands of retired workers and their widows and loved ones? It wasn't fair. But he would not stand in the way of anything Obama was doing to save Detroit. Gettelfinger made his decision to accept the Treasury offer after a solitary walk through the streets of Washington. Afterward, he called Bloom and agreed to the terms. "Would we have liked to have gotten more? Probably," he said later. "But everyone is sacrificing here. We did the best we could."

The negotiations with GM's bondholders were just as tricky. The $27 billion in debt was held by a broad cross section of big and small investors. What was once considered a relatively safe investment had become a travesty because of GM's death spiral. The company was supposed to make a $1 billion payment on one set of bonds by the end of the month, but it couldn't even afford that. The president's terms required General Motors to get 90 percent of all the bondholders to agree to swap their debt for stock, an extraordinarily tall order. As the sixty-day deadline approached, a large contingent did agree to a deal that would give them up to 20 percent of GM's stock.

The matrix of negotiations had grown exponentially. The Canadian government was also kicking in billions in loans for GM. What would it get out of a deal? And Henderson was desperately trying to sell off GM's European operations (a monster deal under normal conditions) to prevent that part of the business from tumbling into bankruptcy as well.

The deadline was drawing near as GM stakeholders around the world tried to protect their financial interests. Every day brought new headlines about labor talks, worried investors, dealers on the firing line, political fallout . . . and the one overriding question that simply could not be answered: Would bankruptcy work? Though Chrysler was speeding through the process, GM was a different animal. The costs were numbing. The U.S. government was prepared to pump in another $30 billion (on top of more than $19 billion already loaned) and the Canadians an additional $9 billion. Would it be enough? It was impossible to know. Beyond that, could General Motors emerge from Chapter 11 as a government-owned corporation and have a reasonable chance to succeed as an automaker?

By May 29, Henderson and his executives were ensconced at the GM Building on Fifth Avenue in New York, the company's financial nerve center for decades. The board was locked down there too. The U.S. government was shepherding GM into bankruptcy. But legally only GM's board of directors could approve a filing. A battalion of lawyers was on hand for meetings that went on around the clock. Thousands and thousands of documents were reviewed and re-reviewed. There wasn't much time left.

Early the next evening, Henderson officially informed the board that the company's only path to salvation was Chapter 11. By now, the vote was a formality. General Motors was a basket case, about to be led into federal court by a U.S. president who refused to let it die. It once had represented the pinnacle of industrial power and prestige, its very name conjuring up images of stability and strength. Now it was a penniless burden to the people it once had towered over. So much wealth created over so many years, all gone now. If there was to be a comeback, it would have to start at the bottom, in bankruptcy, where failures go to get a second chance.

GM filed for protection from its creditors under Chapter 11 of the U.S. bankruptcy code at 7:57 A.M. on June 1. The main filing listed assets of $82 billion and liabilities of $172 billion. Its stock, once handed down by generations as the bluest of blue-chip invest- ments, became instantly worthless. The voluminous court papers detailed the myriad reasons for the bankruptcy, but one sentence summed it up: "The transaction is the only realistic alternative for the company to avoid liquidation that would severely undermine the automotive industry."

Just before noon, President Obama addressed the nation from the White House. The United States government, he said, was invest- ing another $30 billion in GM in bankruptcy and would come out owning 60 percent of the company. "Understand we're making these investments not because I want to spend the American people's tax dollars, but because I want to protect them," he said. He realized this was hard for many taxpayers to accept while they were already beset by their own economic problems. "But I want you to know," he said, "that what you're doing is making a sacrifice for the next genera- tion—a sacrifice that you may not have chosen to make, but a sacri- fice you were nevertheless called to make so that your children and all of our children can grow up in an America that still makes things, that still builds cars, that still strives for a better future."

When Obama was finished, Fritz Henderson started walking from the boardroom high above Fifth Avenue to the press conference he had never wanted to attend. On his way he passed a portrait of Alfred Sloan, the visionary CEO who had created the modern GM more than a half century before. If Sloan were there that day, Hen- derson thought, he'd have encouraged him to make the most of this opportunity to repair and rebuild their fallen company. And when he went on live television, the first thing Henderson did was apologize. "Give us another chance," he said into the cameras. "The GM that many of you knew, the GM that in fact has let too many of you down, is history."

[Thirty-One]

Chrysler emerged from bankruptcy in mid-June, and GM came out a month later. These were remarkably rapid transformations. Two new companies were created. Then the shells of the original corporations "sold" the best brands and plants and assets to the new entities.

The court proceedings had trial-like intervals. Bob Nardelli and Fritz Henderson were called to the witness stand to testify how the automakers had ended up in bankruptcy and why it had been their only recourse for survival. But that was the legal process. What mattered was scraping off the decades of dysfunction and the legal obligations. The "new" companies came out clean and pristine, with sharply lower debt and loaded with taxpayer dollars. The "old GM" and the "old Chrysler" were junkyards laden with the rusted parts and pieces of an industry that had fallen on very hard times. There wouldn't be much demand for any of it. The nation was littered with shuttered auto plants. Since 2004, the Big Three had closed twenty-two major factories in the United States; only eight had found buyers. Most were just abandoned industrial hulks sprawled over hundreds of acres, left vacant while they awaited demolition, environmental cleanups, and willing developers. Now another sixteen plants would be added to the roster of the used up and discarded.

The new GM was hardly recognizable (which was the main point of Chapter 11). Pontiac, the legendary maker of muscle cars, was closed down. So were Saturn and Hummer. Saab, the little Swedish niche brand, was flung into the deep end of the pool to drown, only to be fished out by a European investor group. It wasn't just cars and trucks and brands that were disappearing. More than four hundred of GM's thirteen hundred U.S. executives were asked to resign or retire. The company got seven new board members, most of whom were handpicked by the government. They constituted a majority on the board (five holdovers remained) and would be the driving force for change at the top of the company.

The new chairman was Ed Whitacre, the retired chief executive of the communications giant AT&T. He was recruited intensely by Steve Rattner, who had scoured corporate America for a no-nonsense leader to ride herd on GM management and drive a stake in the heart of its insular culture.

"I told you no twice already," Whitacre said when Rattner kept pestering him to take the job. "Hell, I haven't had a suit on in six months." A tall, grizzled Texan with white hair and a steely glare, Whitacre had retired to his ranch in San Antonio to hunt, fish, and play with his grandkids. And at age sixty-seven, he wasn't interested in any job, anywhere. But Rattner was desperate. He didn't think Henderson could reform GM without a powerful authority figure holding him accountable. And the Obama administration had vowed to stay far away from the actual management of what its critics were already calling "Government Motors."

Finally Rattner wore down Whitacre by appealing to his sense of patriotic duty. "If helping with this company is important to the country," Whitacre said with a sigh, "I'll come do it." He didn't pretend to have any expertise in autos whatsoever. But "Big Ed" was one tough hombre of a manager, as Henderson would soon learn.

GM was dumping executives left and right. But Henderson needed to keep Bob Lutz, who postponed his retirement and segued into a new role as chief of marketing and communications. Who better to pitch GM's products than Lutz, Detroit's ultimate car guy?

Otherwise, Henderson was working nonstop to streamline the monolithic GM organization chart. He scrapped the glacially slow automotive strategy board in favor of weekly meetings of a small executive committee. And he dipped deep into the GM talent pool for younger, hungrier executives such as forty-five-year-old Mark Reuss, who received a huge promotion from running GM's Australian division to become its head of global engineering. The company's crash landing in bankruptcy had sickened Reuss and countless other dedicated engineers and designers. "We lost our damn edge," Reuss said bluntly. "I'm in the never-again business. We can never let this happen again."

When Reuss started his new job, he brought all of the top GM engineers from around the world to the Milford proving grounds for a two-day meeting. Their mission was to drive, critique, and systematically upgrade every GM car and truck. They met before dawn, ready to test-drive the newest products. Reuss, clad in a black-and-red leather racing jacket, addressed the group before they hit the road. "There has been fear in this organization, and people are afraid for their jobs," Reuss said. "But what we need to do now is trust each other, and be honest about our strengths and weaknesses."

Whitacre and the new board gave Henderson one hundred days to kick the cultural revolution into overdrive. But the CEO was under attack from the start. Two new directors, private equity honchos Dan Akerson and David Bonderman, were particularly caustic in their assessment of management's competence and strategies. Another persistent critic was, of all people, Steve Girsky, who was selected for the board by Gettelfinger to represent the union's health care stake. But no one fanned the fire under Henderson the way Whitacre did. "This business isn't that complicated, Fritz," Whitacre lectured. "You get good leaders, you set objectives, and then you get the hell out of the way. If someone doesn't have the ability, then you get rid of them and get somebody else."

The board second-guessed Henderson's every move. "My biggest strength is I've been here twenty-five years," he said. "And my biggest weakness is I've been here twenty-five years." He took the blame for lousy cars in the past, poor sales in the present, trying to sell off the European business instead of fixing it, and on and on and on. Whitacre demanded speed, change, new faces, and one-page memos on topics that used to fill binders. "If it can't fit on one page," he grumbled, "I don't want it."

The new directors didn't choose Henderson; they inherited him. And he was torn apart beginning at their very first meeting, when he plunged into the day's agenda instead of articulating some brave, new corporate vision. Akerson, an executive with the big Carlyle Group private equity firm and a former U.S. naval officer, repeatedly chewed him out for lax discipline and shoddy quality. "You know, in the navy we used to X-ray every valve and seal on a nuclear submarine," Akerson told him. Henderson wondered what that had to do with building cars. ("Maybe this guy would listen," Henderson said, "if he ever stopped talking.") Bonderman was a brutal inquisitor, railing at management for overspending on engines instead of just buying them from competitors. Girsky bore in on the holes in the product plan. And Whitacre just hammered his mantra: sell more vehicles. "Our business is to sell cars and make money," he said. "This company should be growing, not shrinking."

For years, the General Motors board had bent to Rick Wagoner's will. This group challenged Henderson on everything. The constant attacks on GM's products and reputation pushed Lutz over the edge. "According to our new board, everything we did was stupid," he said. "Bonderman used the word 'incompetent.' He'd say, 'If you have good people, how come you went Chapter 11?'" At one dinner meeting with the directors, Lutz stood up, threw his napkin down, and vented. "I have never felt so disrespected in my entire career by people who don't know anything about this industry!" he said, and then stormed out of the room. Whitacre calmed him down, but most of the directors couldn't have cared less. They were brought in to exorcise the old GM, which had fouled its own nest and left the taxpayers to pay the cleanup bill.

Whitacre wanted management to pick up the pace, get energized, and break free from the past. But he had never seen morale so low in any organization. "Everybody has a long face around here," he said in his slow Texas drawl. "People are afraid. I want them to get mad enough to show the world that GM really is a great company." He started roaming around the corporation, popping into offices unannounced, going to the plants, wandering the food court at lunch, getting to know people, pumping them up with little pep talks. "I want people to feel good," he said. "But I also want them to do their damn job."

The most oppressive element in creating a new GM was the same thing that saved it—the government bailout. Henderson was determined to start the wheels turning for a public stock sale by 2010. The scrutiny and shame that came with being a ward of the state was demoralizing and was handicapping GM with consumers. "I'm optimistic that we can pay back the loans faster than people think," he said. It was possible. GM now had a superclean balance sheet, much lower costs, and a revved-up product team eager to put better vehicles in the showroom. The bankruptcy cleansing could make it an attractive buy for investors when the car market recovered.

But Henderson would never see the day when General Motors became a normal, publicly traded automaker again.

Steve Rattner wouldn't be around for that either. The task force chief abruptly quit his post days after GM came out of Chapter 11. The architect of the Detroit bankruptcies was ensnared in an investigation by federal and New York officials in an influence-peddling probe of the state's public pension fund. He had been on the job in Washington for all of six months. Now Ron Bloom, the unsung hero of the bailout negotiations, was driving the president's auto agenda.

Sergio Marchionne swept through Chrysler like an avenging angel. "I need to get this place detoxed," he proclaimed. Bankruptcy cleansed Chrysler's balance sheet; now Marchionne would purify its organization. He flushed out several veteran executives with ties to the Cerberus regime. One of the first to go was Jim Press, the old Toyota hand. "You're out," Marchionne told him. "You don't fit in. I've got to break eggs around here." Press protested. He had financial problems, he said, and needed a job. He asked for a chance to distribute Chrysler vehicles in international markets. Marchionne said maybe, and then fired him again. Press had nearly forty years of experience in the auto industry. But in Marchionne's new order in Auburn Hills, he was just dead weight to be thrown overboard. "Sergio is truly from hell," Press said. "He'll look at you and smile, then turn around and stick a knife in your balls."

Marchionne systematically went through the ranks, slicing off managers who didn't fit his plans and promoting ambitious young talent. "These are kids who sat there and watched the intelligentsia of this house destroy their future," he said. "Now they can make a bloody difference." They all reported directly to him—no intermediaries, no bureaucracy, and no traditional chain of command. He alone ran the show in Auburn Hills, just as he did in Turin, juggling multiple cell phones to keep track of the torrent of information and decisions at two auto companies on separate sides of the world.

He had stark plans for Chrysler, cutting back sharply on incentive spending and allowing its worst vehicles to wither in the marketplace. He would let sales sink until Chrysler settled to its natural, competitive level—all the way down to a miserably low 6 percent of the U.S. market. "I had to go find out how deep this damn trough was," he said. "Let it go. Sink the thing."

GM pulled out all the stops to rebuild its reputation, including offering sixty-day money-back guarantees on its cars. Chrysler's product line was stripped, while Marchionne crafted a plan to build it back up with more fuel-efficient, Fiat-based models.

But Ford didn't need sales gimmicks or extended rehab. In the third quarter of 2009, the Glass House stunned the industry by reporting an unexpected billion-dollar profit. Dearborn was gaining market share by the day. Some of the improvements were due to the consumer backlash against its bailed-out Detroit rivals. But the engine driving its comeback was a lineup of better, more attractive models. U.S. auto sales in 2009 crashed to 10.4 million vehicles, the lowest level in more than twenty-five years. GM fell 30 percent; Chrysler dropped 36 percent. But Ford's decline bucked the trend, falling just 15 percent. And the trend line grew more positive with each new vehicle introduction.

The "Drive One" advertising campaign had taken root. Customers testified in TV spots why they had traded in their Toyota for a Ford. While GM and Chrysler were undergoing emergency surgery, Ford was pumping iron, getting healthier and more confident with each monthly sales report. "This isn't a turning point," Alan Mulally declared. "This is a proof point of the strategy we've been following for three years."

And Mulally was on the road spreading Ford's wings, announcing plans for a new plant in China and an expansion of its fledging Indian operations. The One Ford strategy was more than an idea and a goal. The company was blending its geographic operations and products, accelerating development of cars with the Blue Oval that could be built and sold the world over.

The U-turn at Ford was so startling that its union workers rejected another round of concessions that had been granted to GM and Chrysler on their way to bankruptcy. Rank-and-file UAW members voted down the givebacks in part because of Ford's sunny financial results. Some union locals even protested Mulally's executive pay by printing up fake dollar bills with his picture on them. But a little backlash from the factory floor was a small price to pay for Ford's burgeoning success.

"You better send someone else to L.A.," Henderson said to one of his communications executives. "The next board meeting is coming up, and I've got a bad feeling about it." He was scheduled to make a major speech at the Los Angeles auto show, but GM's chief executive sensed that his time was running out. The new directors just had no use for him. Henderson had been CEO for all of eight months. He had stepped into the breach when Wagoner was fired, piloted GM into and out of bankruptcy, and presided over the nascent stages of its resurrection as a government-owned automaker. It was not enough to save his job.

On Tuesday, December 1, the GM directors told Henderson to resign. They reached their decision by a unanimous vote in executive session after another contentious board meeting. Whitacre broke the news to him afterward. The company wasn't changing fast enough, he said. Henderson's effort and commitment were admirable, but GM needed a clean break from the past. "It's not your fault, Fritz," he said.

Henderson agreed. "I never really had a chance, did I?" he said.

Whitacre became the new chief executive and chairman, chosen by the new board picked by the U.S. government to shepherd GM into a new era. "It was never in my game plan," he said. "But the board asked me if I would step up and do this and I volunteered." His first press conference that evening lasted about five minutes. "I look forward to working with the entire GM team as we now begin the next chapter of this great company," Whitacre said. He did not take questions.

Bob Lutz packed his bags in a rush to take Henderson's place at the L.A. show. When he took the stage at the Los Angeles Convention Center, he tried to keep his emotions in check. But he couldn't help himself. Henderson was a friend and a teammate. Somehow all GM had ever accomplished meant nothing. It had become the pariah of the automotive industry, and now Henderson had taken the fall. Usually when the chief executive is canned, the topic is off-limits for his colleagues to even reference in public. But this one hurt too much to let it pass.

"Fritz was and is an outstanding executive, and I'm very sorry to see him go," Lutz said to the standing-room-only crowd. "He guided General Motors through perhaps the most difficult period in its history. I think all of us were surprised, and the whole GM team is genuinely saddened over what transpired."

Back in Detroit, Henderson gathered together his senior executives and office staff. Some were crying, others red with anger. It wasn't fair, they told him. Henderson choked up. "Don't feel bad for me," he said. "I'm deeply disappointed that I won't be here to see it turn around, and it will. It's okay. You guys need to give Ed and the company all you've got." Then he broke down and let the tears come. "What I'm going to miss most," he said, "are the people."

The following day, Whitacre convened a group session of executives. He started assigning new jobs, essentially reconfiguring the top management of the company in four hours. Mark Reuss was bumped from head of engineering to chief of all North American operations. New leaders were named in marketing and international operations. Girsky became a special advisor to Whitacre. And Lutz lost all his operational responsibilities. The last link to GM's storied and troubled past was now a roving advisor to designers and the new product boss, Tom Stephens. No one in the company reported to Lutz anymore.

[Thirty-Two]

The car zoomed around the Ford test track in Lommel, Belgium, taking the curves at high speed, accelerating like a bullet down the straightaways, stopping on a dime. It was sleekly aerodynamic, very fuel-efficient, loaded with the latest technology, and destined to be sold in every market around the world. The new Ford Focus would be the company's first truly global car, built to the exact same specifications in America as in Europe and Asia. The new vehicle platform was designed to yield two million small vehicles a year, saving billions of dollars in costs.

But what Derrick Kuzak cared about was how it drove. And when the new Focus finished its workout on the track, Ford's product chief allowed himself a small, satisfied smile. "When I drive the vehicle, I am the customer," he said. "And we have exceeded our own expectations."

The formula was no different now from when it was Henry Ford cranking out Model Ts in Detroit in the early 1900s. A hundred years later, Ford had been headed down the same ugly path as GM and Chrysler. Their rivals crashed in a heap and had to beg the

American people for help. But Ford didn't need a rescue. Its road to recovery was painful but simple: Listen to the customer. Start fresh. And stick to the plan. The Blue Oval rose out of the maelstrom of an industry that collapsed under its own weight. And its comeback echoed the advice once uttered by its legendary founder. "Failure is only the opportunity," Henry Ford once said, "to begin again more intelligently."

Fifteen hundred Chrysler workers roared when President Obama walked out onto the floor of the Jefferson North assembly plant on Detroit's east side. More than a year had passed since the company had come out of Chapter 11, and Chrysler's outlook had changed dramatically. New products were on the way, including the Jeep Grand Cherokee, which was rolling off the line at Jeff North. GM and Chrysler had turned the corner. Ford was making big money. And the president was taking a victory lap. "The fact that we're standing in this magnificent factory today is a testament to the decisions we made and the sacrifices that you and countless stakeholders across this country were willing to make," Obama said. "So today this industry is growing stronger. . . . You are proving the naysayers wrong, all of you!"

The president had hit a sweet spot—an economic success in the manufacturing hub of the industrial Midwest, Downtrodden old Detroit had risen. The workers beamed at the sight of him, shaking their heads, giddy at the idea that the president had come to Chrysler to praise them. Robert Shoulders, a second-generation autoworker with sixteen years on the job, reveled in the excitement. This was blue-collar, hardworking, get-your-hands-dirty Detroit. Those people who blasted the auto industry bailout? They weren't welcome here. "This is no tea party," he said. "It's hot chocolate in here!"

Sergio Marchionne watched from the side of the stage. He had made sure the plant was spit-shined for the president. And when Obama extolled Chrysler, its products, and its comeback, even this tough Italian taskmaster got a little emotional. "Fourteen months later, and the heart is beating," he said. "I can only tell you as a CEO, when you see this sort of thing, it's the best feeling on the face of the earth."

Ed Whitacre sat across the breakfast table from Ron Gettelfinger. The sun hadn't even come up in downtown Detroit when the chairman and chief executive officer of General Motors met the president of the United Auto Workers in the humble Motown Coney & Grille, just up the road from Solidarity House. The restaurant was a favorite of the guys coming off their shift at the Chrysler plant. Gettelfinger had been a regular since he was elected to lead the union seven years before. But he had never had a meal quite like this—not at the Motown or anywhere else. "I cannot believe that the chairman of GM would come have breakfast with me in this diner," he said. Whitacre just laughed. He didn't care how GM's top dogs had dealt with the UAW in the past. He wanted to get to know Gettelfinger better, break down some barriers, and work together on saving this thing called GM.

Whitacre wasn't a complicated man. He had been born in the small Texas town of Ennis, the son of a railroad worker, and his first job had been climbing telephone poles and running wire for Southwestern Bell. After a slew of promotions and corporate mergers, he'd ended up running mighty AT&T. But Whitacre never forgot the value of serving the customer, which he'd learned on the dusty streets of Dallas, fixing phones, providing service, getting a job done. He saw no reason to change now that he was in charge of America's biggest car company. "It's a people business first and foremost, and it comes before everything else," he said. "If people are not satisfied with their job and don't have a desire to excel, well, you just can't make them."

Whitacre hit it off with Gettelfinger, who was so tickled by their meeting that he had Steve Girsky take Whitacre's picture with

Gettelfinger and the diner's owner, and then had it framed and hung on the wall. Girsky had been around GM a long time—as a Wall Street analyst, an advisor to Rick Wagoner, a UAW strategist, and now a board member and Whitacre's right-hand man. He was more than happy to take this photograph. "Ron was devastated by everything that's happened in the industry," Girsky said. "Then all of a sudden the chairman of GM shows up, just to talk things over? I mean, how unbelievable is that?"

Whitacre had two goals for GM. First, management needed to restore the pride and accountability in the company. Then it had to get the government out of its affairs as soon as possible.

The first task was straightforward. Whitacre was a big believer in managing by walking around, whether it was donning jeans and a sweatshirt to work a few hours on an assembly line in Flint, nosing through the GM tech center unannounced, or prowling the offices of the Renaissance Center and asking employees what they were doing right at that minute. When he convened his senior executives for their Monday-morning meeting, the agendas were one page and no more. "Are you executing the plan?" he said. "The success of this company depends on the things you do. So go do it. Nobody is going to be fired for trying something around here. Nobody is going to get run off. Just go out and do it."

Freeing GM from the stigma of government ownership was much harder. Whitacre ran out of patience and energy before it happened. He ended up serving as CEO just about as long as Fritz Henderson did. He left in August 2010, tired of living in a condo in Detroit and dragging himself back and forth to see his family in Texas on the weekends. By then, GM was profitable again. The bankruptcy, the federal money, and the pent-up power of its engineers and designers and blue-collar workers had made GM a leaner, far more effective competitor. The company got a break when Toyota became ensnared in a series of disastrous recalls tied to the unintended acceleration of its vehicles. When Toyota's sales plunged, GM benefitted. And the better the company performed, the closer it got to an initial public stock offering that would allow the Treasury Department to begin selling off its 60 percent ownership stake.

Whitacre badly wanted to stay through the stock offering. But the GM board and the company's lawyers were adamant that the CEO who took the company public needed to steer its course afterward. How could investors come back to GM without feeling confident about its long-term leadership? So Whitacre left reluctantly and turned the reins over to Dan Akerson, one of the directors picked by the government in the waning days of bankruptcy. "I wish I were five years younger," Whitacre said. "I think this company is going to sell a lot of cars and make a lot of money."

On November 18, 2010, Akerson rang the bell to open trading on the New York Stock Exchange and kick off the largest initial public stock offering in American history. After months of planning and management road shows for investors, 457 million shares in the new GM sold for $33 a share. The U.S. government cashed in nearly half its stake, reaping $13 billion of the $50 billion it had invested in General Motors. By the end of the year, taxpayers owned just 26 percent of GM and were poised to sell off another big chunk in the summer of 2011.

Two weeks later, Akerson stood in front of hundreds of cheering workers at GM's Hamtramck assembly plant smack in the middle of Detroit. Most of them had never seen him before. After all, he was their fourth CEO in less than two years. But it wasn't the man they were applauding. It was the car—the Chevrolet Volt, built right there in the heart of "the D" and ready to go on sale. In the end, it was all about the car—designing, engineering, assembling, and selling a product that consumers wanted to own and drive. And when the Volt came out onstage, the applause was deafening. It was the most technologically advanced, fuel-efficient plug-in hybrid car ever made. And it was their baby.

"It's the beginning," Akerson said, "of a whole new auto industry."

. . . .

What Jim Farley really wanted to do was kick the daylights out of General Motors. "I'm going to beat Chevrolet on the head with a bat," he said with a slightly wicked smile. "And I'm going to enjoy it."

There was a saying going around Ford: GM was like the kid who was born on third base and yells out, "Hey, Ma, I hit a triple!" Farley and his fellow Ford executives and workers were ready to rumble. They were on a hot streak and didn't care if Dan Akerson had a million Volts to sell. GM had gotten a bailout, but Ford had much more. In 2010, the company reported its best year in more than a decade—$6.6 billion in profits. The Blue Oval was shining brighter by the day. The only way the company's success could be better was to have some old-fashioned competition with the guys on the other side of town.

This was like the glory days again—Ford versus GM, let the better car company win. "We're going to beat on them, and it's going to be fun," said Farley. "Fuck GM. I hate them and their company and what they stand for. And I hate the way they're succeeding. Ford is back because people trust us. And that is a powerful message. I'm a car guy. I wake up each morning thinking about cars. Watch out. We're only going to get better."

In his corner office on the top of the Glass House, Alan Mulally had a new favorite picture on the wall. It was an advertisement for the Ford Motor Company that had appeared in the *Saturday Evening Post* in 1925. He liked to read the script, written by Henry Ford himself, and contemplate the headline: "Opening the highways to all mankind."

It was the first thing Mulally saw when he came into the office every day at 5:15 A.M. and turned on the lights. "Opening the highways to all mankind," he said, cherishing the words. "Isn't that something? We are standing on the shoulders of Henry Ford. It was his original vision. We're relevant again. We're making things people really care about. It's a whole different feeling to be wanted."

He walked to the window and looked out at the city of Detroit in the distance. Sometimes he thought about that summer day in 2006 when he'd hugged Bill Ford in his driveway, talked about the Blue Oval in his living room, and dreamed out loud about the future. He had never doubted it would come true. It was all in the plan.

[EPILOGUE]

It would become one of the most memorable car commercials of all time. The idea came to Olivier Francois as he drove the streets of Detroit. Born and raised in Paris, Francois had been plucked from Fiat's Italian operations by Sergio Marchionne and installed as the new chief marketing officer at Chrysler. For months, the urbane Frenchman had grappled with how to convey the company's unlikely comeback in words and images, to cut through the controversy of bailouts and bankruptcies and show the dignity, the strength, and the never-say-die attitude that fueled the resurrection of Chrysler and the American auto industry. "I saw that Detroit was no place for wimps," Francois said. "Detroit had a story to tell, an American story."

A devotee of French cinema, Francois envisioned a documentary-style commercial shot with a hand-held camera that showcased Detroit in all its tattered glory—the burned-out buildings, the enormous factories, the grand architecture of a faded era when the city put the world on wheels, juxtaposed with the people, young and old, black and white, who lived and worked and believed in the Motor City. The visuals inspired a script, an almost poetic ode to the spirit of Detroit that Francois called "Born of Fire." And in his head he always heard the song "Lose Yourself," a pulsing, rhythmic mega-hit by hometown rapper Eminem, whose rags-to-riches life story personified the tenacity of a town that refused to be beaten.

On a gray December day in 2010, Francois and an aide, Saad Chehab, made their pitch to Marchionne in his cluttered office in the heart of the sprawling Chrysler Technical Center. Armed with storyboards and a working narrative, they asked him for permission—and millions of dollars—to film a commercial with Eminem to be aired at halftime of Super Bowl XLV. The plan carried significant risks. Polls showed that many Americans despised the taxpayer-funded bailouts of the auto companies. And despite its steadily growing sales, Chrysler was still losing money and owed the federal government billions in loans. How could this battered car company stir an emotional connection without seeming wounded or, even worse, desperate? Marchionne and his people were working back-breaking hours trying to turn the business around. The last thing he wanted was sympathy. "I have no problem with us being honest and straight because that's what we are," he told Francois. "But don't take me down the route of, you know, I'm in the shithole now, and therefore I need your fucking help."

On February 6, 2011, more than a hundred million Super Bowl viewers around the world saw a two-minute ad that redefined the debate about Detroit. Instead of frazzled executives testifying before Congress or plants shutting down or acres of unsold cars, the "Born of Fire" spot captured the soul of a proud and determined city, scars and all. From the belching smokestacks and husks of abandoned structures, to the four-ton sculpture of a massive fist on the riverfront and the epic murals of auto workers in the Detroit Institute of Art, to the hard stare of a businessman crossing a snowy street and the grace of a young figure skater on an outdoor rink, the mood was solemn, intense, almost reverent. "I've got a question for you," a voice intoned at the start. "What does this city know about luxury? What does a town that's been to hell and back know about the finer things in life?" The question hung for a beat, like a challenge. "Well I'll tell you, more than most," said the unseen narrator. "You see, it's the hottest fires that make the hardest steel."

As the camera panned through downtown and the neighborhoods and the assembly plants, the chunky guitar chords of "Lose Yourself" swelled up, the soundtrack of a tough, righteous place. "Now we're from America," the narrator continued. "But this isn't New York City or the Windy City or Sin City. And we're certainly no one's Emerald City." A heavenly chorus of a gospel choir began to rise in the background, as a black Chrysler 200 sedan cruised down Woodward in the dark, stopping under the neon lights of the elegant Fox Theater. And out came Eminem, in a gray T-shirt and hooded sweatshirt, the spokesman of an in-your-face generation, looking like he just stepped out of his own 2002 autobiographical film, *8 Mile*. He walked through the empty theater, joined the choir onstage, their heads bowed, and glared at the camera. "This is the Motor City," he said, pointing his finger right into the lens. "And this is what we do." The screen faded to black, and a message emerged in white letters: "Imported," it said, "from Detroit."

The response was off the charts. The number of consumers considering Chrysler products nearly tripled overnight, and the spot generated more than ten million hits on YouTube. Suddenly, improbably, Detroit was hot again. It was like a jolt of adrenaline for a city that just a couple of years earlier had been left for dead. As a marketer, Francois craved that visceral sensation when the audience not only identified with the car, but admired where it came from. "A good product is not enough," he said. "It has to come from a company that stands for something." Marchionne just marveled at the ability of his people to pull it off. He knew when he acquired Chrysler there were no shortcuts to success. Some industry experts and rival executives branded him as an opportunist who took a crippled company off the hands of the U.S. government. But Marchionne was way craftier than that. After its failures with Daimler and Cerberus, hitting bottom was the best thing that could happen to Chrysler. Because then Marchionne could rebuild it his way. He replaced squads of older managers with hungry upstarts, and required the top two dozen officers to report directly to him, every day. He became famous for juggling multiple cell phones and computers to simultaneously control Fiat and Chrysler, and commuting back and forth from Europe on the Italian automaker's corporate jet. No detail was too small for his attention. The first time he visited Chrysler's aged Jefferson North plant he made a point to stop in one of the restrooms. He walked out with a look of disgust on his face. "I wouldn't let my dog shit in there," he snapped at the stunned executives and managers trailing him around the factory. After that, every restroom in the plant got very clean very fast.

And slowly but surely, the cars and trucks and SUVs and minivans that Chrysler produced got better, from the stitching on the seats to the fit of the dashboards to the reliability of the engines and transmissions. It was hardly brain surgery. So many corners had been cut for so long that every engineer and designer in Auburn Hills was dying to make improvements. But it took Marchionne's force of personality—rough, profane, sentimental, cerebral, and, at times, wickedly funny—to inspire them like no Chrysler chief executive had since the legendary days of Lee Iacocca. "He is the boss," said Gualberto Ranieri, his long-time communications exec. "And we all know it." Like Alan Mulally at Ford, people wanted to perform well to please him, which is the rarest of all loyalties. Marchionne returned their dedication in kind, working late into the night in the Tech Center, and rarely setting foot in the isolated corporate offices on the fifteenth floor of the headquarters tower next door. "The reason why Chrysler is working is because the team is working," he said. "I mean, they feel a moral obligation to get this job done." But woe to the employee who committed the cardinal sin of overconfidence. "I see a guy who either gets too comfortable or gets arrogant in the chair," he said, "I'm going to yank that fucking chair right out from under his ass."

His ultimate goal was an audacious one—to merge Fiat and Chrysler into one profitable, trans-Atlantic automotive goliath. But to accomplish that, he needed to put the Chapter 11 mess behind Chrysler forever. And the only way to do that was by retiring its bailout loans: $5.9 billion to the U.S. Treasury Department and another $1.7 billion to the Canadian government. In the spring of 2011, Marchionne embarked on a three-week mission to convince investors to buy into a package of bonds and debt offerings arranged by the biggest banks on Wall Street.

By borrowing money the old-fashioned way, Chrysler could not only pay back its government loans, saving hundreds of millions of dollars in interest payments, but also rebrand itself as a noble survivor of the economic recession. It was the last hurdle to Chrysler's independence from the stigma of bankruptcy, and Marchionne was getting close to making it happen. On April 28, Treasury Secretary Timothy Geithner came to the city to address the Detroit Economic Club. Before his speech, he toured the Jefferson North plant with Marchionne. As the two men peered through safety goggles at Jeep Grand Cherokees on the assembly line, the Chrysler C.E.O. pulled the cabinet secretary close for a private word.

"We're looking for ways to refinance the loans," Marchionne said.

"Perfect," said Geithner. "You know if we can help you in any way . . ."

Marchionne cut him off right there.

"Just be the happy recipient of the check or the wire transfer when you get it," he said.

A month later, all the pieces were in place. Two years after going bankrupt, Chrysler had just posted its first quarterly profit—$116 million in the first three months of the year. Revenues were up 35 percent from the same period in 2010. Its new financing had been locked up, and Fiat was investing $1.3 billion in a deal that would increase its overall ownership of Chrysler to 46 percent. All that was left was to pay off the government loans that saved America's third biggest automaker from the scrap heap.

On the morning of May 24, Marchionne took a call in his office from Vice President Joe Biden. The sense of relief from Washington was almost audible. The bailouts of General Motors and Chrysler had been among the most controversial policy decisions made by the Obama administration. If either company crashed and burned, the political fallout would have been brutal. Instead, the smallest of Detroit's Big Three was ready to settle its debts.

"We could have looked like goats here," Biden told Marchionne. "This could have been incredibly messy. And it isn't. So thank you."

The call was a welcome distraction for the Chrysler boss. His gut was already churning in anticipation of the moment he would address all the professionals in the Tech Center, and thank them for their loyalty and dedication and hard work. He stepped into the building's grand rotunda, and saw them packed tight on the floor and all the way up on the circular balconies. Eight thousand men and women lined up, looking at him, totally silent as Marchionne moved to the microphone. He swallowed hard, and thought of a quotation from the author Primo Levi, an Italian survivor of a Nazi concentration camp. The words came out different, but the sentiment was the same. "Survivors are different people," he said. "They are special people. You and I, together with all our other colleagues at Chrysler, are survivors."

A few hours later, Marchionne walked into the Sterling Heights assembly plant, one of the factories that barely survived the deep cuts of bankruptcy. He was joined on stage by Ron Bloom and Brian Deese, the two senior members of President Obama's auto task force still working in Washington.

The government loans, Marchionne told hundreds of cheering auto workers, were officially retired. And to drive the point home, a giant red, white, and blue banner hung from the ceiling with the simplest of messages: "PAID."

Russell Bell, an electrician with thirty-eight years at Chrysler, watched from the crowd with a sense of awe. He had been there when the company needed government help way back in 1979. But this was more emotional. After being sold three times in the past thirteen years, Chrysler finally had a future. "There's just a whole different feeling to it," Bell said with a grin. "It's history being made. We got the lifeline that we needed."

. . . .

The month of May produced remarkable results for the Big Three. For the first time in five years, GM, Ford and Chrysler finished first, second, and third in sales of new vehicles in the U.S. The earthquake and tsunami two months earlier in Japan had devastated the supply chains of Toyota, Honda, and Nissan, and Detroit had taken full advantage. Its biggest gains were in gas-sipping small cars like the Ford Fiesta and Chevrolet Cruze. And the surge in sales was producing big profits at GM and Ford. It was an amazing transformation. Since 2006, General Motors had shed more than 50,000 jobs, closed nearly half its U.S. plants, and dropped four major brands—and still maintained about the same market share as before. Ford had just announced its biggest first-quarter profit in thirteen years. Not only had the industry weathered the storm, but the American automakers had come out of it as shockingly efficient competitors. The entire economic landscape had changed, thanks in large part to the $80 billion that U.S. taxpayers contributed to the rescues of GM, Chrysler, their finance companies, and a large number of suppliers. The question was no longer could Detroit keep up with the Koreans and the Japanese and the Germans, but would it reclaim the leadership role that seemed lost for good just a few years earlier.

So much was dependent on the next round of labor talks. The United Auto Workers had a new president, Bob King, and a provocative agenda for negotiations on a new contract. After all the buyouts and plant closings, the combined blue-collar workforce at the Big Three had shrunk to 111,000 people in the summer of 2011. A small but growing minority were new, "entry-level" employees who earned half of the traditional union wage of $28 an hour. The two-tier pay system was an extraordinary break from past practices, and presented a huge opportunity to further close the gap on labor costs with the foreign-owned auto factories in the U.S. GM, for example, was gearing up to build inexpensive, subcompact cars at a Michigan plant where 40 percent of the employees earned the cut-rate, lower wage. But King and his negotiators were committed to getting more money for Detroit's rank-and-file workers, not less. They wanted better wages for the new hires, and a larger share of the profits for the veteran employees who had hung on to their jobs during the drastic downsizing of Detroit.

The wiry, bespectacled King was a former Ford plant worker with a law degree, and a seasoned bargainer who had worked closely for years with Ron Gettelfinger. He faced a delicate balancing act. King appreciated that Detroit's recovery was fragile, and an onerous contract could derail its comeback. What's more, the union was still a lightning rod for criticism from Republicans and conservatives who believed that Obama had favored it over the interests of private investors in the government bailout negotiations. Both GM and Chrysler had won no-strike clauses from the UAW as part of the Chapter 11 restructurings. King had to extract what he could for his members, yet not push too hard and risk a messy arbitration process or a possible strike at Ford, the healthiest of the three companies. "You know, we're not out of the woods yet," the union president said. "If we end up with a strike or arbitration, I'd feel like I failed."

The current contract was set to expire on September 14, and the question gripping Detroit was whether the no-strike clauses at GM and Chrysler would penalize Ford, the only American auto company to make it on its own. Inside the Glass House, Mulally and his labor execs constantly war-gamed the negotiations. They worried that either GM would hurt them by cutting a deal that they couldn't match, or that the UAW would threaten a strike to leverage extra-large bonuses and job guarantees from Ford. Either way, the executives in Dearborn felt handicapped by the no-strike protection enjoyed by their bitter rivals at General Motors. It was up to King to pick the target company, get a deal, and then try to overlay the basic terms on the other two. Talks started first at Chrysler on July 25. The lead negotiators on both sides shook hands in the company auditorium in Auburn Hills, and laid out their positions. King vowed that the union would bargain fairly to justify the money and trust that Washington had extended to keep Chrysler in business. "We have a larger responsibility here to the American public," he said. But Chrysler's chief negotiator, Al Iacobelli, made it clear that the company was dead-set on controlling labor costs so it never had to beg for government help again. "We have a responsibility to ensure we don't go back to our old formula," he said. "Unfortunately we have a rich history of not getting it right."

The ceremonial handshake at GM showed how much the relationship between union and management had changed since the industry's near-death experience. GM's chief executive, Dan Akerson, wanted to make a statement by having the event at the Volt assembly plant in the gritty Detroit enclave of Hamtramck. What usually was a stiff, scripted affair turned into a pep rally. GM's senior executives showed up wearing blue polo shirts, and cheered the introduction of the UAW bargaining team. The union leadership returned the favor by applauding for Akerson and his people. The steely stares and posturing of past negotiations were noticeably absent. Bankruptcy had humbled both sides, and the usual atmosphere of confrontation seemed to have evaporated. "For us to be successful," said Joe Ashton, the lead UAW negotiator, "GM has to be successful." But the new spirit of cooperation only went so far. During the post-ceremony press conference, Bob King was asked how the union could leverage more money for its members without upsetting GM's comeback. King related a saying that German auto workers used to describe their relationship with corporations like Volkswagen and BMW. "You don't kill the cow that gives the milk," King said. The metaphor got laughs from the reporters in the room. But it did not sit well with Akerson. "I'm not a cow," he said with a grimace. "And I don't want to get milked."

Akerson was the big unknown in GM's turnaround. A stocky, bald former U.S. Navy officer in his early sixties, he emerged from GM's post-bankruptcy board as its consensus choice to replace Ed Whitacre as chairman and CEO. A veteran executive in the telecommunications industry, Akerson had made a fortune as a partner in the Carlyle Group investment firm. He was probably the richest man to ever run GM, and certainly the least experienced from an automotive perspective. Blunt, opinionated and intensely competitive, Akerson was determined to change GM's corporate culture in a hurry. He broke tradition by bad-mouthing rival carmakers, dubbing Toyota's top-selling Prius hybrid a "geekmobile" and telling a *Detroit News* reporter that Ford should "sprinkle holy water" on its struggling Lincoln brand. But he reserved his toughest comments for his own company.

"This place lacked a lot of vision," he said. "They were all over the map. Where was the vision?" At a town-hall meeting of GM engineers and product planners, he startled the group by suggesting that they weren't working hard enough. In his first meeting with the Volt team, he challenged them to take an unheard-of $10,000 in costs out of the car within a year.

His management team was a constantly evolving mix of outside hires and younger execs getting big promotions. And Akerson had zero patience for the old way of doing business at the Renaissance Center. "I want the gene pool of this company to always be in flux and changing and mutating," he said. "Sometimes we'll make mistakes. If they are smart and aggressive they will adapt." But while General Motors was mutating, its competitors were shifting into a higher gear. And once Chrysler paid off its government loans, GM was stuck as the sole poster child of Detroit's federal bailout. No matter how well its cars sold or how much money it made, GM could not shake its distasteful distinction as Government Motors. One reason the board picked Akerson as CEO was to shepherd the company through its all-important initial public stock offering in the fall of 2010. The offering was successful by all measures except one: American taxpayers still owned 26 percent of the stock after GM went public. The Obama administration decided to hold on to its remaining shares until the stock price increased. But that could take months or even years. Until it happened, GM would have to carry the baggage of the bailout.

GM needed to reestablish itself as an industry leader, and the labor talks offered an opportunity to craft a fresh, progressive image. Akerson gained King's trust quickly by freezing salaries and bonuses for GM managers as a prelude to keeping a lid on blue-collar wages. Unlike previous CEOs, he participated in face-to-face negotiations. King was shocked one day to enter a low-level meeting on local factory issues and find the GM boss sitting across the table. "I'm not looking for concessions," Akerson was saying. "I just want a fair agreement." Over the course of the summer, GM gradually took the lead role in the talks. The UAW negotiated simultaneously with Ford and Chrysler. But GM was in the midst of a stellar year; the company would ultimately earn more than $7 billion in profits. And Akerson was willing to give raises to the entry-level employees and sizable bonuses to the older workers, as well as guarantee thousands of new jobs. He even agreed to reopen an idled assembly plant in Tennessee. The GM and union bargainers worked around the clock right up to the September 14 deadline—then kept right on going despite the expiration of the contract.

King's decision to pursue an agreement first with GM created the only real drama in the negotiations. By doing so, the union president personally offended Sergio Marchionne, who cut short a business trip to Europe to attend what he thought would be final negotiations between Chrysler and the UAW. When King skipped their meeting to continue bargaining at GM, the Chrysler chief blew up. "We fucked around for two months," he said. "And then we get to D-day and he isn't here." Chrysler grudgingly agreed to wait until GM and Ford settled. But Marchionne gave King an earful when they finally cut their deal. Because Chrysler was earning far less money than the other two companies, he refused to match the worker bonuses promised by GM and Ford. What's more, Marchionne let King know—in the plainest possible language—that he would never follow the pattern of any contract negotiated for the benefit of his larger rivals in Detroit. "You think I'm the same as GM or Ford," he told King. "I'm not. I hate to tell you this but they're my competitors. You say we're all the same? We're not fucking the same."

The union president just let the emotional Italian vent. He understood the pressure Chrysler was under. Given the upheaval just a couple of years earlier, the UAW was fortunate that Chrysler was even around to negotiate a contract with. In the end, the union won sweet deals across the board that boosted entry-level wages to $19 an hour by the end of the four-year agreement, and added more than 13,000 new jobs at the Big Three. "This is a good contract in very bad times, and that's an unusual achievement," said Harley Shaiken, a labor professor at the University of California-Berkeley. On the other side, this would go down as one of the cheapest set of contracts ever achieved by the Detroit companies. Labor costs were projected to rise only about one percent annually, compared to an average of five percent in previous contracts. "I think the union and the company came to a good place, common ground," said Dan Akerson. "Both of us can say we did well for our constituencies."

It was a much-needed victory for GM and its new leader, and looked like a turning point. U.S. auto sales hit an eight-month high in October, and a month later the company reported its seventh consecutive profitable quarter. But the good feelings would not last. A time bomb had been ticking inside GM for several months, ever since the lithium-ion battery in a Chevrolet Volt had caught fire in Wisconsin after a crash test by federal regulators. No one outside of General Motors or the government's safety agency even knew about the incident.

But in mid-November, a second series of tests resulted in another fire. And on November 25, the National Highway Traffic Safety Administration announced it had opened a "formal defect investigation" into GM's pride and joy, the Volt plug-in hybrid. It was Akerson's first major crisis in fifteen months as GM's chief executive. On the weekend after Thanksgiving, the company's top brass convened for an emergency conference call to plan their reaction to the federal probe. Akerson led the discussion from his home in Virginia. "This could be a defining moment for us," he warned his team. After a lengthy debate, the executives decided to publicly defend the Volt's safety, and take the unusual step of offering free loaner cars to its owners during the government's inquiry.

What followed was GM's worst nightmare. Not only was its highest-profile, most environmentally efficient car caught under the cloud of a federal safety investigation. But all the pent-up frustration in the country about the government bailout came pouring out. This was the flash point that GM feared. Conservative talk-show hosts and Republican presidential candidates seized on the Volt's problems to attack President Obama and his rescue of Detroit. Within weeks, the automaker and federal regulators agreed on a series of repairs to protect the Volt's battery from potential fires. But the damage had been done. Once again, a GM chief executive was called to appear before Congress, this time to assure lawmakers that one of its finest automobiles was safe for people to drive. Akerson could barely contain his anger when he testified. "We didn't engineer the Chevrolet Volt," he said, "to be a political punching bag." Yet that was the price GM had to pay for its $50 billion bailout. The American taxpayers had saved General Motors from oblivion. In return, every misstep it made was scrutinized and critiqued.

In March 2012, GM temporarily closed the Volt plant for several weeks. The shutdown had nothing to do with the fires. The government had long since cleared the car of any defects. It was the market that decided. Consumers simply weren't buying enough Volts, and inventory was beginning to pile up. It was hardly a failure. In truth, the decision was the sign of a healthy car company making a rational assessment of demand for one of its products. In the old days, General Motors would have tried every kind of incentive and sales promotion to move a model that wasn't selling. That was how the game was played—and it nearly killed Detroit. Overproduction filled parking lots with unwanted vehicles and wasted billions of dollars. Workers were paid even when they weren't making cars. An entire industry lived beyond its means, and crept closer to the edge each day. And when the economy tanked and Wall Street got in trouble and consumers shut their wallets, the reckoning came. Ford barely survived on its own. GM and Chrysler weren't so fortunate. Without federal disaster relief, they would have crumbled under the weight of their debts and obligations.

Car companies make mistakes. Manufacturing automobiles is hardly an exact science. Successful automakers are fueled by passion and drive and curiosity and commitment. Sometimes the humble clay model in the design studio becomes an elegant machine that consumers are proud to pay their hard-earned money for. Yet almost as often, a promising concept falls flat by the time it reaches the showroom. That's the beauty and the risk of the business. Billion-dollar bets on new cars can generate huge profits and provide liveli-hoods for thousands of working men and women and their families. But if the public doesn't want that particular vehicle in their garages, it doesn't matter how much money and brainpower went into creat-ing it. The auto industry works when it serves the customer, period. Anything less is a recipe for failure.

Just a few miles from the Volt plant, Derrick Chatman punches the time clock on the second shift at Chrysler's Jefferson North assembly plant. Forty-four years old and a native of Detroit, Chat-man was laid off from Home Depot and working construction when he heard that Chrysler was hiring new workers. The entry-level pay wasn't great, just over $14 an hour. But he had never wanted a job as badly as this one. "It's Chrysler," he said. "It's one of the Big Three. You're talking about an opportunity to build cars. This is one of the jobs I've been trying to get all my life."

Chrysler received more than ten thousand applications in 2010 for nine hundred new jobs at Jefferson North. The plant was expand-ing production because its product, the Jeep Grand Cherokee, was one of the hottest vehicles on the market. The company could hardly keep any in stock. That's how the business works at its best. Success in the marketplace means more work for more people. New employ-ees like Chatman hope that, in time, they will move up the ladder to full-wage positions. But for now, he is simply grateful. Every day, he works in the "tire room," one of the final stops on the assembly line. It is hard, rugged labor. Yet Chatman considers himself to be a lucky man. It wasn't long ago, when Detroit was on its deathbed, that he wondered if he'd ever get this chance. "I just couldn't see Ford or Chrysler or General Motors going away and never coming back," he said. "I just couldn't see looking out the window and that new Chrys-ler or new Ford wasn't going down the street. I couldn't believe that would ever happen. Just in the nick of time, someone will come along and save the day. And it happened." He paused for a moment to reflect on his own words. It all could have come to an end, this way of life. "Now I see a car going down the street and I say, I did that," he said. "I put that fender on. I put that wheel on. And that's a beautiful thing."

There's a third shift starting up at Jefferson North in 2013, bringing on another thousand new workers. They are coming because this is a good factory building solid vehicles on the east side of the city of Detroit. Because it's the Motor City—and this is what they do.

[Author's Note]

The idea for this book arose from my coverage of the American auto industry as a reporter for the *Detroit News* and, since January 2008, as the Detroit bureau chief for the *New York Times*. The primary source materials were compiled from more than one hundred interviews done specifically for this book. I also drew on interviews and research conducted during the course of my reporting for the *Detroit News* and the *New York Times*. Among the other sources of information used extensively were corporate documents, federal court records, SEC filings, and transcripts of hearings, speeches, and press conferences.

The bulk of the interviews were conducted on a background basis, with the understanding that the information would be used but not attributed to a specific source. Also, every interview was done with the agreement that the material compiled was specifically for this book and not for publication elsewhere. Conversations were reconstructed based on the recollections of at least one participant; others involved were asked about the accuracy. The author assumes sole responsibility for the versions of events as portrayed in the book. If a quote was used from another publication, the source is credited as such.

Reporting for the book was done primarily in Detroit, New York, Chicago, Los Angeles, and Washington, D.C., as well as in several cities and towns with automotive plants in the United States.

I am very grateful to all those people who generously gave their time and trust to me during the reporting process. The list of individuals who cooperated is quite long. But I would like to specifically thank the following people: Bill Ford Jr., Alan Mulally, Mark Fields, Jim Farley, Rick Wagoner, Fritz Henderson, Bob Lutz, Ed Whitacre, Steve Girsky, George Fisher, John Bryan, Carlos Ghosn, Dieter Zetsche, Tom LaSorda, Bob Nardelli, Steve Feinberg, Jim Press, Sergio Marchionne, Steve Rattner, Ron Bloom, John Casesa, Jennifer Granholm, and Kirk Kerkorian. And I owe a special thanks to Jerry York, a good friend and trusted source, who died in March 2010.

This book could not have been done without the aid and encouragement of many friends and colleagues. I want to thank Larry Ingrassia and other editors of the *New York Times* for allowing me to take two unpaid leaves of absence during the reporting and writing process. I also owe a great deal of thanks to Adam Bryant, my editor during my first two years at the newspaper, and to my reporting partners in Detroit, Nick Bunkley and Micheline Maynard. At the *Detroit News*, the following people were instrumental in my understanding of the auto industry and the events chronicled in this book: Mark Truby, Sue Carney, Brett Clanton, Christine Tierney, Sharon Terlep, Bryce Hoffman, and Charlie Tines. Words cannot express how grateful I am for the advice and help provided by my literary agent, Jane Dystel. And thanks to Henry Ferris, my editor at William Morrow, for his extraordinary patience and understanding in seeing this book through to completion.

Most of all, I want to thank the people who were so supportive during this long, arduous process: my dear friend Molly Feely; my wonderful children, John, Dan, and Katie; and my loving parents, Robert and Nancy Vlasic. I could not have done this without you.

[Index]